Lecture Notes in Computer Science   10662

Commenced Publication in 1973
Founding and Former Series Editors:
Gerhard Goos, Juris Hartmanis, and Jan van Leeuwen

More information about this series at http://www.springer.com/series/7410

Sk Subidh Ali · Jean-Luc Danger
Thomas Eisenbarth (Eds.)

Security, Privacy, and Applied Cryptography Engineering

7th International Conference, SPACE 2017
Goa, India, December 13–17, 2017
Proceedings

 Springer

Editors
Sk Subidh Ali
Indian Institute of Technology
Tirupati, Andhra Pradesh
India

Thomas Eisenbarth
University of Lübeck
Lübeck
Germany

Jean-Luc Danger
Institut Mines-Télécom
Paris
France

ISSN 0302-9743   ISSN 1611-3349 (electronic)
Lecture Notes in Computer Science
ISBN 978-3-319-71500-1   ISBN 978-3-319-71501-8 (eBook)
https://doi.org/10.1007/978-3-319-71501-8

Library of Congress Control Number: 2017959611

LNCS Sublibrary: SL4 – Security and Cryptology

Printed on acid-free paper

This Springer imprint is published by Springer Nature
The registered company is Springer International Publishing AG
The registered company address is: Gewerbestrasse 11, 6330 Cham, Switzerland

Preface

This volume contains the papers accepted for presentation at the 7th International Conference on Security, Privacy, and Applied Cryptography Engineering 2017 (SPACE 2017), held during December 13–17, 2017, at the Don Bosco College of Engineering, Goa, India. This annual event is devoted to various aspects of security, privacy, applied cryptography, and cryptographic engineering. This is indeed a very challenging field, requiring expertise from diverse domains, ranging from mathematics to solid-state circuit design.

This year we received 49 submissions from about eight different countries, out of which, after an extensive review process, 13 papers were accepted for presentation at the conference, and one shorter paper was accepted for short presentation. The submissions were evaluated based on their significance, novelty, technical quality, and relevance to the SPACE conference. The submissions were reviewed in a double-blind mode by at least three members of the 36-member Program Committee (one more if at least one of the authors was member of the Program Committee). The Program Committee was aided by 50 additional reviewers. The Program Committee meetings were held electronically, with intensive discussions.

The program also included seven invited talks and four tutorials on several aspects of applied cryptology, delivered by world-renowned researchers: Asaf Ashkenazi, Shivam Bhasin, Jean-Luc Danger, Thomas Eisenbarth, Harry Halpin, Mike Hamburg, Gary Kenworthy, Victor Lomne, Axel Poschmann, Karim Tobich, Ingrid Verbauwhede, and Yuval Yaron. We sincerely thank the invited speakers for accepting our invitations in spite of their busy schedules. Like its previous editions, SPACE 2017 was organized in co-operation with the International Association for Cryptologic Research (IACR). We are thankful to Don Bosco College of Engineering for being the gracious host of SPACE 2017.

There is a long list of volunteers who invested their time and energy to put together the conference, and who deserve accolades for their efforts. We are grateful to all the members of the Program Committee and the additional reviewers for all their hard work in the evaluation of the submitted papers. We thank Cool Press Ltd., owner of the EasyChair conference management system, for allowing us to use it for SPACE 2017, which was a great help. We thank our publisher Springer for agreeing to continue to publish the SPACE proceedings as a volume in *the Lecture Notes in Computer Science* (LNCS) series. We are grateful to the local Organizing Committee, especially to the organizing chair, Roseline Fernandes, who invested a lot effort for the conference to run smoothly. We are further very grateful to Vishal Saraswat, program chair of SPACE 2016, for his guidance and active support toward organizing SPACE 2017. Special thanks to our general chairs, Rev. Fr. Kinley D'Cruz, Neena Panandikar, and Sandeep Shukla, for their support and encouragement. Our sincere gratitude to Debdeep Mukhopadhyay, Veezhinathan Kamakoti, and Sanjay Burman for being constantly involved in SPACE since its very inception and responsible for SPACE reaching its current status.

Last, but certainly not least, our sincere thanks go to all the authors who submitted papers to SPACE 2017, and to all the attendees. The conference is made possible by you, and it is dedicated to you. We sincerely hope you find the proceedings stimulating and inspiring.

October 2017   Sk Subidh Ali
                                                              Jean-Luc Danger
                                                            Thomas Eisenbarth

Organization

Honorary General Chair

Rev. Fr. Kinley D'Cruz   DBCE, India

General Co-chairs

Neena Panandikar   DBCE, India
Sandeep Shukla   IIT Kanpur, India

Program Co-chairs

Sk Subidh Ali   IIT Tirupati, India
Jean-Luc Danger   Institut Mines-Telecom, France
Thomas Eisenbarth   Worcester Polytechnic Institute, USA

Organizing Chair

Roseline Fernandes   DBCE, India

Steering Committee

Sanjay Burman   CAIR-DRDO, India
Veezhinathan Kamakoti   IIT Madras, India
Debdeep Mukhopadhyay   IIT Kharagpur, India

Program Committee

Sk Subidh Ali (Co-chair)   IIT Tirupati, India
Reza Azarderakhsh   Florida Atlantic University, USA
Lejla Batina   Radboud University Nijmegen, The Netherlands
Guido Marco Bertoni   STMicroelectronics, Italy
Shivam Bhasin   NTU, Singapore
Swarup Bhunia   University of Florida, USA
Lilian Bossuet   University St. Etienne, France
Claude Carlet   University of Paris, France
Rajat Subhra Chakraborty   IIT Kharagpur, India
Pandu Rangan   Indian Institute of Technology Chennai, India
   Chandrasekaran
Anupam Chattopadhyay   NTU, Singapore
Dipanwita Roy Chowdhury   IIT Kharagpur, India
Jean-Luc Danger (Co-chair)   Institut Mines-Telecom, France

Thomas Eisenbarth (Co-chair)	Worcester Polytechnic Institute, USA
Junfeng Fan	Open Security Research, China
Sylvain Guilley	GET/ENST, CNRS/LTCI, France
Tim Guneysu	Universität Bremen, Germany
Indivar Gupta	DRDO, Delhi, India
Naofumi Homma	Tohoku University, Japan
Subhamoy Maitra	Indian Statistical Institute, India
Bodhi Satwa Majumdar	IIT Indore, India
Stefan Mangard	TU Graz, Austria
Mitsuru Matsui	Mitsubishi, Japan
Philippe Maurine	LIRMM Montpellier, France
Debdeep Mukhopadhyay	IIT Kharagpur, India
Svetla Nikova	KU Leuven, Belgium
Thomas Poeppelmann	Infineon Technologies, Germany
Emmanuel Prouff	ANSSI, France
Bimal Roy	Indian Statistical Institute, India
Kazuo Sakiyama	UEC Tokyo, Japan
Somitra Sanadhya	IIT Ropar, India
Vishal Saraswat	Indian Statistical Institute, India
Francois-Xavier Standaert	UCL Crypto Group, Belgium
Mostafa Taha	Western University, Canada
Ming Tang	Wuhan University, China
Carolyn Whitnall	Bristol, UK
Yuval Yarom	University of Adelaide, Australia
Amr Youssuf	Concordia University, Canada
Yongbin Zhou	CAS Beijing, China

Additional Reviewers

Alexandre Berzati	Bernhard Jungk
Sarani Bhattacharya	Brian Koziel
Urbi Chatterjee	Manoj Kumar
Wei Cheng	Yogesh Kumar
Guillaume Dabosville	Hui Ma
Joan Daemen	Marco Martinoli
Nilanjan Datta	Pedro Maat Massolino
Dhananjoy Dey	Sihem Mesnager
S.V. Dilip Kumar	Yasin Muhammad
Lorenzo Grassi	Zakaria Najm
Daniel Gruss	Sikhar Patranabis
Nupur Gupta	Shuang Qiu
Amir Jalali	Francesco Regazzoni
Dirmanto Jap	Guenael Renault

Aniket Roy
Debapriya Basu Roy
Rajat Sadhukhan
Peter Schwabe
Michael Schwarz

Raphael Spreitzer
Diangarti Bhalang Tariang
Srinivas Vivek
Tim Wood
Yan Yan

Organizing Institute

Don Bosco College of Engineering, Goa, India

Invited Talks/Tutorials

On the (in)Security of ChaCha20 Against Physical Attacks

Shivam Bhasin

Temasek Labortaries, Nanyang Technological University Singapore
sbhasin@ntu.edu.sg

The stream cipher ChaCha20 and the Poly1305 authentication are adopted in several products including Google Chrome [1], or OpenSSL [2] etc. For instance, Google Chome often uses ChaCha20 for secure communication when the underlying platform lacks hardware support for AES. The two algorithms have potential to be adopted across multiple domains in the future. The ChaCha20-Poly1305 cipher suite is advertised as being easier to implement in a side-channel resistant way [3], especially compared to ciphers based on substitution permutation networks. However, the side-channel security claim is only limited to timing based leakage. In this talk, we investigate the security of ChaCha20 against two commonly known physical attacks: *side-channel attacks* and *fault attacks*.

The first part focuses on power [4] or electromagnetic [5] based side-channels. The development of the omnipresent Internet of Things (IoT), or the connected car increases the amount of embedded appliances, which can be attacked using these side-channels. Hence, it is important to understand the security of deployed cryptographic algorithms not only against attacks on the timing side-channels but a wider attack suite. We analyze the stream cipher ChaCha20 [3, 6] and show how the secret key can be completely extracted. While first attack recovers the key from initial round of ChaCha20, another attack demonstrates key retrieval exploiting the final addition.

The second part will look into active attacks realised using fault injection [7]. Often stream ciphers are believed to be harder to attack against fault injection attacks owing to the complexity of the required offline analysis. We propose four differential fault analysis (DFA) attacks on ChaCha20 running on a low cost microcontroller, using the instruction skip and instruction replacement fault models. The attacks target the keystream generation module at the decryption site, and entirely avoid nonce misuse. We practically demonstrate our proposed attacks using a laser fault injection setup.

The talk is based on recent joint works. The part on side-channel attack is based on recent work with Bernhard Jungk from NTU, Singapore [8]. Fault attacks was investigated with co-authors from IIT Kharagpur, India and NTU, Singapore [9].

References

1. Bursztein, E.: Speeding up and strengthening HTTPS connections for Chrome on Android (2014). https://security.googleblog.com/2014/04/speeding-up-and-strengthening-https.html
2. Staruch, M.: Support for ChaCha20-Poly1305 (2015). https://github.com/openssl/openssl/issues/304
3. Nir, Y., Langley, A.: ChaCha20 and Poly1305 for IETF Protocols. IETF RFC 7539 (2015)
4. Kocher P., Jaffe J., Jun B.: Differential power analysis. In: Wiener, M. (eds.) CRYPTO 1999. LNCS, vol. 1666, pp. 388–397. Springer, Heidelberg (1999). https://doi.org/10.1007/3-540-48405-1_25
5. Agrawal, D., Archambeault, B., Rao, J.R., Rohatgi, P.: The EM side—channel(s). In: Kaliski, B.S., Koç, K., Paar, C. (eds.) CHES 2002. LNCS, vol. 2523, pp. 29–45. Springer, Heidelberg (2003). https://doi.org/10.1007/3-540-36400-5_4
6. Bernstein, D.J.: ChaCha, a variant of Salsa20. In: Workshop Record of SASC - The State of the Art of Stream Ciphers (2008)
7. Barenghi, A., Breveglieri, L., Koren, I., Naccache, D.: Fault injection attacks on cryptographic devices: theory, practice, and countermeasures. Proc. IEEE **100**, 3056–3076 (2012)
8. Jungk, B., Bhasin, S.: Don't fall into a trap: physical side-channel analysis of chacha20-poly1305. In: 2017 Design, Automation and Test in Europe Conference and Exhibition (DATE). IEEE, pp. 1110–1115 (2017)
9. Kumar, S.D., Patranabis, S., Breier, J., Mukhopadhyay, D., Bhasin, S., Chattopadhyay, A., Baksi, A.: A practical fault attack on arx-like ciphers with a case study on chacha20. In: 2017 Workshop on Fault Diagnosis and Tolerance in Cryptography (FDTC). IEEE (2017)

How to Digitally Construct and Validate TRNG and PUF Primitives Which Are Based on Physical Phenomenon? (Tutorial)

Jean-Luc Danger

Telecom ParisTech, University Paris-Saclay, Scientific Advisor at Secure-IC
September 23, 2017

Abstract. In digital devices, the cryptographic functions are dependant on peripheral primitives, like the True Random Number Generation (TRNG) and Physically Unclonable Function (PUF) which generates a random number and an identifier respectively. The source of these primitives is not defined by a digital algorithm but comes from physical phenomenon, notably the noise. Consequently a conversion is necessary to output a digital random number or identifier. Indeed, these two types of primitives exploit the noise, but at different stage. At the manufacturing stage, the variance of the manufacturing process creates mismatches between transistors. These slight differences are fixed once the chip is fabricated, they should be transformed by the PUF to a digital variable when an identifer is called by the application. When the chip is in used, the environmental noise is extracted by the TRNG to generate a digital random number. In case of PUF, we can say that the entropy is "static", whereas the entropy for the TRNG is "dynamic". The dynamic entropy is a major problem for the PUF which is natively not steady because of the environmental noise. The TRNG is very sensitive to an external noise, which can be malevolently generated by an attacker, and can bias the TRNG output. Consequently, it is necessary to add to the primitives an evaluation or correction block to detect or enhance their behavior. This means that some tests and metrics have to be be specified to define what is a good identifier and a good random number.

We will see in this tutorial, the different constructions of PUF and TRNG, but also the methods to validate their quality to ensure a minimum level of trust.

Cache Attacks: From Cloud to Mobile

Thomas Eisenbarth

University of Lübeck and Worcester Polytechnic Institute
thomas.eisenbarth@uni-luebeck.de

Abstract. The microarchitecture of modern CPUs features many optimizations that result in data-dependent runtime behavior. Data-dependent execution behavior can result in information leakage, enabling malicious co-located processes to overcome logical isolation boundaries of hypervisors and operating systems. For instance, cache attacks that exploit access time variations when retrieving data from the cache or the memory are a powerful tool to extract critical information such as cryptographic keys from co-located processes.

This tutorial introduces several methods of how to exploit cache-based side channels. Modern attacks and their behavior in various application scenarios, from cloud to mobile and embedded processors will be discussed. It will be shown of the introduced techniques can be applied to extract sensitive information from a co-located processes or VMs across cores and even across processor boundaries and how such attacks can be prevented.

May the Fourth Be With You:
A Microarchitectural Side Channel Attack
on Several Real-World Applications
of Curve25519

Daniel Genkin[1,2] Luke Valenta[1], and Yuval Yarom[3,4]

[1] University of Pennsylvania
{danielg3,lukevg}@cis.upenn.edu
[2] University of Maryland
[3] University of Adelaide
yval@cs.adelaide.edu.au
[4] Data 61, CSIRO

In recent years, applications increasingly adopt security primitives designed with better countermeasures against side channel attacks. A concrete example is Libgcrypt's implementation of ECDH encryption with Curve25519. The implementation employs the Montgomery ladder scalar-by-point multiplication, uses the unified, branchless Montgomery double-and-add formula and implements a constant-time argument swap within the ladder. However, Libgcrypt's field arithmetic operations are not implemented in a constant-time side-channel-resistant fashion.

Based on the secure design of Curve25519, users of the curve are advised that there is no need to perform validation of input points. In this work we demonstrate that when this recommendation is followed, the mathematical structure of Curve25519 facilitates the exploitation of side-channel weaknesses.

We demonstrate the effect of this vulnerability on three software applications—encrypted git, email and messaging—that use Libgcrypt. In each case, we show how to craft malicious OpenPGP files that use the Curve25519 point of order 4 as a chosen ciphertext to the ECDH encryption scheme. We find that the resulting interactions of the point at infinity, order-2, and order-4 elements in the Montgomery ladder scalar-by-point multiplication routine create side channel leakage that allows us to recover the private key in as few as 11 attempts to access such malicious files.

Parameter Choices for LWE

Mike Hamburg

Rambus, USA

Abstract. All widely-deployed public-key encryption algorithms are threatened by the possibility of a quantum computer that can run Shor's algorithm. The most popular approach for future, "post-quantum" encryption is the "learning with errors" (LWE) problem, and its variants Ring-LWE, Module-LWE, Integer-Module-LWE, etc. Compared to elliptic curves, LWE systems are tricky to parameterize. The relationship between the parameters and the security they provide is complex, and there is also the threat of attacks based on decryption failures.

In this talk, I will cover how to choose parameters for LWE systems. I will focus especially on how to estimate failure probabilities, and the difficulty of attacks based on decryption failure.

IoT Insecurity – Innovation and Incentives in Industry

Axel Y. Poschmann

DarkMatter, Abu Dhabi, United Arab Emirates

Abstract. Why is the Internet of Things going to be a security and privacy nightmare (it is already, but we have only seen the beginning)? What does it have to do with disruptive innovation, incentives in industry, time-to-market trade-offs, and quantifiability? This talk—a collection of thoughts and observations, really—walks along these questions to conclude with a set of promising research directions.

Hardware Enabled Cryptography: Physically Unclonable Functions and Random Numbers as Roots of Trust

Ingrid Verbauwhede

KU Leuven – COSIC
Ingrid.verbauwhede@esat.kuleuven.be

Abstract. Intelligent things, medical devices, vehicles and factories, are all part of so-called cyber-physical systems. These systems will only be secure if we can build devices that can perform the mathematically demanding cryptographic protocols and algorithms in an efficient way in an embedded context. Unfortunately, many of devices operate under extremely limited power, energy and area constraints. At the same time, we request that the implementations are also secure against a wide range of physical attacks and that keys or other sensitive material are stored securely. Often forgotten but of utmost important are the sources of randomness to support the cryptographic protocols and algorithms. This will be the focus of this presentation. We will therefore focus on two roots of trust: Physically Unclonable Functions and True Random Number generators. We will discuss design principles and how to make them suit embedded devices. We will explain how they can fit in FPGA or ASIC. We will also discuss possible attacks and test strategies. We will include myths and realities and discuss future trends for PUF and TRNGs.

Acknowledgements. This research summarizes the work of several PhD students, who are gratefully acknowledged. The research is funded in part by the Research Council KU Leuven: C16/15/058, and the Horizon 2020 research and innovation programs under grant agreement No 644052 HECTOR and Cathedral ERC Advanced Grant 695305.

Efficient Side Channel Testing
of Cryptographic Devices Using TVLA
(Tutorial)

Gary Kenworthy

Rambus Cryptography Research
gkenworthy@rambus.com

Abstract. Power and EM side channels are very powerful attack vectors for cryptographic devices. Protecting against these attacks is an important design consideration for any cryptographic implementation, and validating the effectiveness of countermeasures is critical to verify their effectiveness. Whereas an attacker has potentially unlimited time and resources to mount an attack, the validation against such attacks must be done in an efficient and cost effective way. Test Vector Leakage Assessment (TVLA) is a methodology that can "level the field" and provide an objective, quantified assessment of leakage and the protection afforded by the design. In this tutorial, we will first review the risks of simple power analysis (SPA) and differential power analysis (DPA) and their EM counterparts (SEMA and DEMA). The concepts behind TVLA will be presented, with case studies and demonstrations correlating the TVLA measurements with actual attacks. TVLA measurements will be demonstrated on protected and unprotected hardware cores. Limitations and cautions of using TVLA will also be discussed.

Contents

An Industrial Outlook on Challenges of Hardware Security in Digital Economy —Extended Abstract—

Shivam Bhasin[1]([✉]), Victor Lomné[2], and Karim Tobich[3]

[1] Temasek Laboratories, Nanyang Technological University,
Singapore, Singapore
sbhasin@ntu.edu.sg
[2] NinjaLab, Montpellier, France
victor@ninjalab.fr
[3] UL Transaction Security, Basingstoke, UK
karim.tobich@ul.com

Thanks to the seminal works of Kocher on side-channel attacks [1,2] and Boneh et al. on fault injection attacks [3] in the 1990s, the domain of physical attacks has emerged as an active research domain as well as a potential threat on commercial devices. Practical hacks using physical attacks have been demonstrated on commercial products like NXP MiFare [4], KEELOQ [5], Sony PlayStation, etc. The threat becomes even bigger with the emergence of the Internet of Things (IoT), digital economy and identity. Digital economy is a push towards cashless society, encouraging digital banking with use of modern payment methods based on smartcards and now smartphones. Digital identity now uses biometric data, like fingerprints, to authenticate people. Several governments are giving a push for digital economy and identity. This has led to rapid adoption of mobile payments, cashless solutions, biometric identities. Often biometrics are linked to payment solution.

However, the deployed systems must be secure and trusted to avoid frauds and malicious exploitation. This is even more relevant now as the attackers have cyber as well as physical access to the devices (credit cards, passports, smartphones, etc.) and almost unlimited attack time (as the lifetime of banking cards and passports are of several years). The objective of this work is to give a high-level overview on how manufacturers, evaluation laboratories and certification schemes are assessing the security of such products. The overview is divided in two distinct parts: *payment solution* and *biometric passport*.

The first part will present the certification process of a Secure Element (SE) in banking evaluation context. It will start with a review of the banking transaction flow, based on a contact protocol. Then a practical banking evaluation process will be described from an evaluation lab, by giving concrete examples of assessment on some EMVCo [6,7], VISA [8] or MasterCard applications [9]. The concept of successful evaluation will be discussed as well.

The second part will present the certification process of a Common Criteria evaluation of a biometric passport. First some basics about Common Criteria certification will be given, explaining how it works, and how the different

© Springer International Publishing AG 2017
S.S. Ali et al. (Eds.): SPACE 2017, LNCS 10662, pp. 1–9, 2017.
https://doi.org/10.1007/978-3-319-71501-8_1

stakeholders interact with each other (manufacturer, evaluation laboratory, certification scheme). Then a concrete example of a biometric passport certification will be described, explaining the different tasks performed to assess its security.

1   A *Successful* Evaluation of a Banking Transaction

1.1   Three Parties' Process

To reduce the risk of bribery or corruption and keep independence between certification body and client, the industry pushed to have a three party process with the creation of evaluation labs. These labs are paid by customers to assess their products but they are under the authority and agreement of the certification body. This means that without agreement there is no work for them and without customers there is no revenue. A service based on a trust and a business to business model (B2B) became a reference, since quite a while now at least in the security domain. As a main role, the certification bodies are leading the industry by setting consortium and creating specifications and reference documents. They are assessing labs to give them the accreditation, or getting it back. They are reviewing the evaluation labs reports and guiding them about any new attack techniques that need to be used within these evaluations. The evaluation labs need to please to customers to get revenue but are watched by the certification body to do a proper assessment. They have to innovate by following the scheme recommendation but as well based on their own expertise and their own proper R&D and innovation strategy.

1.2   Banking Transaction Flow

As any industrial process, a strong flow was implemented and has been updated over the time to meet the market demand. The security was the main concern and is still the case over all these updates. A global view of this transaction flow is given in Fig. 1(a).

Based on the Application Data Protocol Unit (APDU) the transaction is initiated by the terminal using a set of library command (see Fig. 1(b)). This step is used to SELECT the right payment application as the card may have different ones (credit, debit ...) followed by a GET PROCESSING OPTIONS to initiate the application by incrementing the *Application Transaction Counter* (ATC). This is updated for each new transaction which make it unique and secure against any replay attack. A read application data is performed by using a READ RECORD command to get all these data related to the card capabilities such as the *Primary Account Number* (PAN), the *Card Risk Management* (CRM) and other details as the *Application Interchange Profile* (AIP) that might be needed for the transaction. The INTERNAL AUTHENTICATE command initiates the computation of the Signed Dynamic Application Data to perform an Offline Data Authentication. Depending on the capabilities of the card and the terminal, a *Static Data Authentication* (SDA) or a *Dynamic Data Authentication* (DDA) or

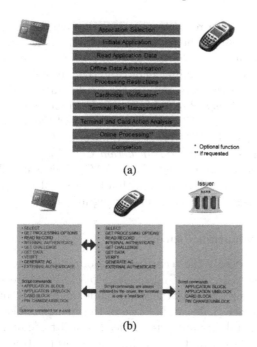

Fig. 1. (a) Transaction flow, (b) command library

a *Combined Dynamic Data Authentication/Application Cryptogram Generation* (CDA) will be performed to authenticate the application.

Next, a processing restrictions function is performed to determine the degree of compatibility of the application in the terminal with the application in the Integrated Circuit Card (ICC) and to make any necessary adjustments, including possible rejection of the transaction. The Cardholder verification is then performed to ensure that the person presenting the ICC is the person to whom the application in the card was issued. Based on the *Cardholder Verification Methods* (CVM) the terminal will ask for a paper signature or a PIN verification by using a VERIFY command. This one can be processed offline or online. A terminal risk management is then performed to ensure that transactions initiated from the ICC go online periodically to protect against threats. It consists of: A floor limits checking, a random transaction selection and usually a velocity checking. These checks will be performed by using GET DATA command.

Further, the terminal and card action analysis is performed. This starts with the terminal, which will make the first decision as to whether the transaction should be approved offline, declined offline, or transmitted online. Followed by the ICC that may decide to complete a transaction online with an *Authorisation ReQuest Cryptogram* (ARQC) or offline with a *Transaction Certificate* (TC) or reject it with an *Application Authentication Cryptogram* (AAC). This will be done by using a GENERATE AC (Application Cryptogram) command, commonly known as 1st GAC. Online processing is performed to ensure the issuer can review and authorise or reject transactions that are outside acceptable limits of risk defined by the issuer, the payment system, or the acquirer. As a response the issuer may generate an *Authorisation ResPonse Cryptogram* (ARPC) to validate the transaction. The terminal shall issue then an EXTERNAL AUTHENTICATE command to the card only if the card indicates in byte 1 bit 3 of the *Application Interchange Profile* (AIP) that it supports issuer authentication using the EXTERNAL AUTHENTICATE command. Followed by the generation of an AC using a GENERATE AC (Application Cryptogram) to complete and accept the transaction with a *Transaction Certificate* (TC) or reject it with an *Application Authentication Cryptogram* (AAC). This is usually called the 2nd GAC. A completion step will be done with a last variables update. It closes the processing of a transaction. A script processing may then be performed.

1.3 Banking Evaluation Process

To be able to assess deeply the security of a product, a white box evaluation is considered since few years now. Under a Non-Disclosure Agreement (NDA), an evaluation lab can have access to the source code, analyses it and highlights the finding to the customer. This can be done in the client premise or in the evaluation lab. This vulnerability analysis will lead to a list of findings and different phases of attacks. These could be classified as software attack using malwares and *Application Protocol Data Unit* (APDU) command, or more hardware and firmware attacks using side-channel attack and fault injection techniques. A combined attack regrouping software and hardware attacks could be used as well to assess the security of a product. Each command may contain different assets and each asset is associated with a level:

- A primary level is: a successful attack on the asset breaks the core security level expected from the application and may lead to harmful consequences for the payment process. Compromising a primary asset leads to a security evaluation failure.
- A secondary level is: a successful attack on the asset may expose a primary asset. Compromising a secondary asset usually leads to a specific notice in the evaluation report.

The level of these assets varies from one application to another and from one scheme to another due to their specific implementation.

To maintain a high level of security, security architects and developers need to follow different guidelines. Some are more related to the core of the security, whereas some are more related to a performance issues, pushing security architects and developers to balance between security and performance.

As an example of recommendation the following could be considered as generic guidance to protect assets against software attacks, side-channel attacks and fault injection attacks:

- Every time the platform or the application is run, raise security errors upon detection of a configuration not compliant with the functional specifications.

- Every time an APDU command is received by the platform or by the application, raise security errors upon detection of parameter combinations not compliant with the functional specifications.
- When possible, implement checks to any functions that have assumptions on parameters and execution context.
- Make all operations on sensitive data independent of the sensitive data value from the attacker's perspective: timing, power consumption level/electromagnetic emanation level.
- Avoid implementing two consecutive operations on sensitive data that provide exactly the same electrical or electromagnetic behavior, such as
  - Adding random masking
  - Involving changing parameters in calculations (such as in counters)
- Reduce freedom on chosen input format on sensitive data with values known or unknown to the attacker.
- Make time synchronization with the targeted operation difficult for the attacker.
- Cross-check every sensitive operation, such as:
  - Redundancy
  - Complementary checks (such as RSA verification after signature)
- Cross-check every sensitive data value (such as integrity checking).
- Cross-check program execution, such as: sequence of instructions, function calls.
- Add hidden dummy operations with random timing.
- Add global random execution time of operations.

The evaluation laboratories will have the mission to assess the conformity of the implementation with these security guidelines and mainly the one related to the core security. This will be done using tools and techniques which are at the state of the art. Nowadays a laboratory who hasn't got these tools or equipments can be under surveillance process and can loose its accreditation. As well as the expertise of the evaluators and their skills sets need to be considered to keep an accreditation. In fact, to keep a consensus between evaluation labs, certification labs and schemes started setting skills matrix and jobs descriptions to differentiate proficient form expert and senior expert in their accredited labs. Skills matrix and job specification to define a real expert in their accredited labs. From tools perspective, the major needed ones are listed by the scheme or the certification lab, the following ones can be considered as a generic example. The pattern recognition tool used to detect and find targeted timing area and avoid any random jitter, the tearing card mechanism tools to interrupt the saving process of the any fault detection counters and extend the sample live time, the bandwidth frequency analyser tool to reduce the noise and distinguish operations such cryptographic operations . . . these tools are common for side-channel and fault injection attacks.

Specific benches might be used to assess a product these could be based on Electromagnetic fault injections [10], glitching using the FBBI or RBBI technique [11], some recent research highlighted the use of X-ray tools to reprogram a circuit [12], some labs may use Infrared laser or blue laser instead, but the most common goal is to fire with 3 or 4 spots as the circuits are more and more based

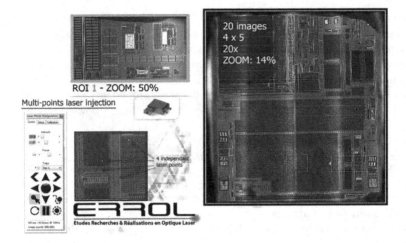

Fig. 2. Multi-spot laser system

on multi-core architecture or on hardware redundancy security mechanism. The first 2 spots will be on the targeted area and its redundancy, while the 3rd one on the cross-check operation (See Fig. 2 [13,14]). Side-channel technique are as well used to assess the code execution leakage different attack technique are used DPA, DEMA, HO, and recently the deep learning.

1.4   Concept of *Successful* Evaluation

Concept of *successful* evaluation is a complex notion. In fact, as the evaluation is a three parties process, each of them will have its own goal and criteria of success. For sure the main goal will be to ensure that the product will not be hacked during its lifetime in the market. But this is an absolute goal shared by the three entities. In day to day work, the manufacturer will push to spend less time on evaluation as the market is not going to wait for them. A successful evaluation will be a quick one with minor findings which will keep or set them as pioneer in the market with this product. From an evaluation lab, a successful evaluation will be based on different findings which will induce proper break during the attack phase. These could be on primary assets or secondary assets. From a certification lab or scheme, a successful evaluation will be based on good report highlighting the findings and the patches that have been applied, along with the techniques and tools that has been used and deployed for that assessment.

2   Common Criteria Certification of a Smartcard - Application to Biometric Passport

Common Criteria is an international standard (ISO/IEC 15408) for IT products security certification. It is especially used for assessing the security of embedded devices like smartcards and similar products, e.g. biometric passport. More precisely, Common Criteria works as a framework in which:

1. Users specify their security requirements
2. Vendors implement the security requirements in their products
3. Evaluation laboratories evaluate the security of the products
4. Certification bodies certify the products security by checking the correctness of all steps.

Among the key concepts, the *Target Of Evaluation* (TOE) is (a part of) the product that is the subject of the evaluation, e.g. the biometric passport and its environnment. The *Security Target* (ST) is a document that identifies the security properties of the TOE, and may refer to a *Protection Profile* (PP).

A PP is a document, typically created by a user or users community, which identifies security requirements for a class of security devices. For instance PP for biometric passport can be found at [15].

Common Criteria provides key documents defining an evaluation methodology where six different classes must be verified, each one being linked to a step of the product development or to its features. Whereas five classes check TOE conformity, one class checks the TOE security (AVA_VAN), in regards to the ST. Furthermore, for every Common Criteria certification, an *Evaluation Assurance Level* (EAL) is defined. EAL can be seen as a global rating of the classes, where each class has to reach a certain value.

For the certification of smartcards and similar devices like biometric passport, the final product usually follows several certification steps. First the security *Integrated Circuit* (IC) developed by an IC manufacturer is evaluated, in regards of the security of its hardware functionalities (e.g. CPU, RAM, non volatile memory, cryptographic co-processors, ...).

Once the security IC is certified, a smartcard vendor develops an *Operating System* (OS) and a dedicated application (in our case a biometric passport application) on top of the IC. The full product follows then a second evaluation procedure. This concept is called a composite evaluation, where an evaluation of a product relies on the certification of a part of the product.

When assessing the security of smartcards and similar products, a specific methodology has to be used [16], where several attack paths have to be considered. More precisely, physical attacks (microprobing, FIB attack, memory reading attack, ...), perturbation attacks (glitch, laser, electromagnetic injection), fault based cryptanalysis, side-channel attacks and software attacks are applied to the TOE.

When an attack is successful, its rating is computed by considering two steps:

1. Identification: effort required to imagine, develop and apply the attack to the TOE for the first time.
2. Exploitation: effort required to apply the attack to the TOE by knowing the methodology developed in the identification step.

An attack is divided in attack factors, allowing to evaluate the difficulty of the different attack aspects. The more an attack factor is difficult to apply, the more its rating is high. The full rating of an attack is obtained by summing the rating of all attack factors of both steps.

If one successful attack has a rating higher than the one defined by the EAL the TOE has to reach, then the evaluation is not successful. In this case, the developer can patch its product, and the evaluation laboratory has to perform once again the attack to check that the patch corrects the vulnerability previously discovered.

Finally, when no attack is successful, or has a rating higher than the one defined by the EAL, then the TOE can be certified.

3   Conclusion

A brief overview of process followed by industry and challenges faced to evaluate a secure product. In particular, the overview covers two key components of a digital economy, payment and identity. The first part discusses aspects of certifying a SE in context of banking and payment evaluation. Next, the role of Common Criteria is discussed in evaluation of a smart card oriented for biometric passport. Owing to these certification and trusted processes, the foundation of a safe and secure digital economy can be realised.

References

1. Kocher, P., Jaffe, J., Jun, B.: Differential power analysis. In: Wiener, M. (ed.) CRYPTO 1999. LNCS, vol. 1666, pp. 388–397. Springer, Heidelberg (1999). https://doi.org/10.1007/3-540-48405-1_25
2. Kocher, P.C.: Timing attacks on implementations of Diffie-Hellman, RSA, DSS, and other systems. In: Koblitz, N. (ed.) CRYPTO 1996. LNCS, vol. 1109, pp. 104–113. Springer, Heidelberg (1996). https://doi.org/10.1007/3-540-68697-5_9
3. Boneh, D., DeMillo, R.A., Lipton, R.J.: On the importance of checking cryptographic protocols for faults. In: Fumy, W. (ed.) EUROCRYPT 1997. LNCS, vol. 1233, pp. 37–51. Springer, Heidelberg (1997). https://doi.org/10.1007/3-540-69053-0_4
4. de Koning Gans, G., Hoepman, J.-H., Garcia, F.D.: A practical attack on the MIFARE classic. In: Grimaud, G., Standaert, F.-X. (eds.) CARDIS 2008. LNCS, vol. 5189, pp. 267–282. Springer, Heidelberg (2008). https://doi.org/10.1007/978-3-540-85893-5_20
5. Indesteege, S., Keller, N., Dunkelman, O., Biham, E., Preneel, B.: A practical attack on KeeLoq. In: Smart, N. (ed.) EUROCRYPT 2008. LNCS, vol. 4965, pp. 1–18. Springer, Heidelberg (2008). https://doi.org/10.1007/978-3-540-78967-3_1
6. EMV Book 2 - Integrated Circuit Card Specifications for Payment Systems - Security and Key Management v4.2 (2011). https://www.emvco.com/
7. EMV Book 3 - Integrated Circuit Card Specifications for Payment Systems - Application Specification v4.3 (2011). https://www.emvco.com/
8. VISA. https://technologypartner.visa.com/Library/
9. PayPass-M/Chip Requirements. https://www.paypass.com/PP_Imp_Guides/PayPass-MChip-Requirements-2013.pdf

10. Poucheret, F., Tobich, K., Lisarty, M., Chusseauz, L., Robissonx, B., Maurine, P.: Local and direct EM injection of power into CMOS integrated circuits. In: FDTC, pp. 100–104. IEEE, Nara (2011). http://ieeexplore.ieee.org/document/6076472/
11. Tobich, K., Maurine, P., Liardet, P.-Y., Lisart, M., Ordas, T.: Voltage spikes on the substrate to obtain timing faults. In: 2013 Euromicro Conference on Digital System Design, DSD 2013, Los Alamitos, CA, USA, pp. 483–486, 4–6 September 2013. http://ieeexplore.ieee.org/document/6628318/
12. Anceau, S., Bleuet, P., Clédière, J., Maingault, L., Rainard, J., Tucoulou, R.: Nanofocused X-ray beam to reprogram secure circuits. In: Fischer, W., Homma, N. (eds.) CHES 2017. LNCS, vol. 10529, pp. 175–188. Springer, Cham (2017). https://doi.org/10.1007/978-3-319-66787-4_9
13. https://www.errol-laser.com/
14. http://www.alphanov.com/
15. Biometric passport Protection Profile. https://www.sogis.org/uk/pp_en.html
16. Application of Attack Potential to Smartcards. https://www.sogis.org/documents/cc/domains/sc/JIL-Application-of-Attack-Potential-to-Smartcards-v2-9.pdf

The Crisis of Standardizing DRM: The Case of W3C Encrypted Media Extensions

Harry Halpin[⊠]

Inria, 2 rue Simone Iff, 75012 Paris, France
harry.halpin@inria.fr

Abstract. The process of standardizing DRM via the W3C Encrypted Media Extensions (EME) Recommendation has caused a crisis for W3C and potentially other open standards organizations. While open standards bodies are considered by definition to be open to input from the wider security research community, EME led civil society and security researchers asking for greater protections to be positioned actively against the W3C. This analysis covers both the procedural issues in open standards at the W3C that both allowed EME to be standardized as well as for vigorous opposition by civil society. The claims of both sides are tested via technical analysis and quantitative analysis of participation in the Working Group. We include recommendations for future standards that touch upon some of the same issues as EME.

Keywords: Digital Rights Management · W3C · Security · Privacy · Standardization

1 Introduction

Encrypted Media Extensions (EME) has been recommended by Tim Berners-Lee in his role as director of the World Wide Web Consortium (W3C) as the first official Web standard for Digital Rights Management (DRM).[1] This has been a controversial decision: A large number of security researchers, ranging from Ron Rivest to Bruce Schneier, have signed a petition demanding the W3C not recommend Encrypted Media Extensions until protections for security researchers could be put into place, as suggested by a "covenant" put forward by the Electronic Frontier Foundation [8].

Encrypted Media Extensions (EME) is the only standard to enable DRM across all major web browsers (including Google, Microsoft, Apple, and Mozilla), deploying an open standards body to enable spread of DRM, a technology traditionally associated with preventing open access to information. It is also the only Web standard to lead to street protests outside of the office of W3C/MIT,[2] statements from civil society and academics against standardizing EME, and massive

---

[1] https://lists.w3.org/Archives/Public/public-html-media/2017Jul/0000.html.
[2] On a personal aside, including my resignation from W3C staff.

© Springer International Publishing AG 2017
S.S. Ali et al. (Eds.): SPACE 2017, LNCS 10662, pp. 10–29, 2017.
https://doi.org/10.1007/978-3-319-71501-8_2

negative feedback on social media. Although EME was eventually in 2017 eventually approved by Tim Berners-Lee as a W3C Recommendation, overriding the objections, the repercussions of this decision could threaten the continued existence of W3C itself in the future.

The crisis brought about by standardizing DRM at the W3C goes beyond the particulars of the W3C and EME, as the entire episode shows the benefits and difficulties of an open standards process where civil society, security researchers, and the private sector all can directly participate. Open standards are defined as "open" in terms of participation, in contrast to "closed" standards bodies such as the ITU or ISO where participation requires government status. While open standards are typically required by commercial actors for anti-trust reasons, open processes also tend to be good practice from a security perspective, as the review of multiple experts typically discovers security flaws. However, when an open standards body like the W3C decides to standardize DRM at the bequest of a few actors in private industry, despite many security researchers protesting that EME will lead to increased security vulnerabilities, what can and should be done in terms of standardization?

Judging the harm to users caused by enabling a new capability that also introduces a new attack surface in a browser is not a straightforward trade-off, but requires serious analysis of both technical and social claims in the process of security standardization. After first exploring the often labyrinthine process of standardization at the W3C in Sect. 2, we'll explore the Encrypted Media Extension standard itself, including its relationship to HTML5 in Sect. 4. This lets us analyze each of the arguments made both for and against standardizing EME in Sect. 5. Section 6 presents a data analysis of the mailing-lists to validate claims around the composition and participation of the W3C Working Group that standardized EME. Lastly, we'll suggest ways forward to avoid the problems inherent in standardizing DRM in security standards in general in Sect. 7 before summarizing our findings in Sect. 8.

2   The World Wide Web Consortium

The World Wide Web Consortium is one of the pre-eminent standards bodies of the Internet, founded by Tim Berners-Lee in 1994 as a "break away" standards organization from the IETF (Internet Engineering Task Force) [4]. The W3C would specialize in web standards focused on the application layer in the browser, in contrast to standards focused on the networking layer as done in the IETF. The W3C is a "virtual organization" that maintains no official incorporated (non-profit or otherwise) status, and does not even have its own bank account, instead relying on its hosts and offices. This is unusual among standards bodies, as the IETF has its bank accounts ran through the Internet Society (ISOC), an officially registered non-profit. Unlike ISOC's relationship to the IETF, the W3C is a sponsored research activity within MIT (similar to a DARPA or NSF contract). As global headquarters of W3C, MIT maintains three host agreements with Keio, Beihang, and ERCIM (France) for regional hosts. The costs of running the consortium are paid by annual re-occurring membership dues from their (as of July 2017) 475 members, where the dues range from 77,000 USD for a large enterprise to 7,900 USD for non-profits and government agencies (although costs are lower developing countries).[3] The revenue from membership dues primarily goes to pay W3C employees and the corresponding overhead costs from their host. The W3C staff are paid to be neutral technical and administrative arbiters, which the W3C states justifies the cost of membership.

3   W3C Patent Policy

A crucial advantage to W3C membership is that the W3C is in effect a patent pool for the World Wide Web.[4] W3C standards are explicitly licensed by W3C members under a royalty-free license.[5] In contrast, the IETF "Note Well" policy simply requires disclosure of known patents by individuals.[6] The much stronger W3C policy essentially creates a kind of "patent war-chest" composed of all W3C standards, from XML to HTML5. This patent war-chest is then enforced by a 'balance of terror' so that any member that makes a patent claim on a W3C standard triggers their loss of royalty-free licensing for *all* W3C standards.

This patent policy is purported to defend W3C members against patent trolls, and as most large Silicon Valley companies (with the noticeable absence of Amazon, but including Google, Microsoft, Oracle, IBM, Apple, and the like) are members of the W3C, one likely result of the Royalty-Free licensing policy is to prevent lawsuits between W3C members as well. It can even be hypothesized that this is one explanation for the success of Javascript as a common cross-platform programming language, a role originally envisioned to be that of Java.

One of the victories of the W3C is the preservation and extension of the Web as one of the world's largest and continually evolving programming platform that is not under the control of a single vendor. Given the history of patents stifling innovation and deployment in cryptography, ranging from the RSA to Schnorr to Certicom patents, there has been moves to even add work such as Curve 25519 to the W3C Web Cryptography API solely in order to provide patent protection.[7]

3.1   W3C Process

Another benefit of open standards bodies such as the W3C and IETF is governance. For the W3C, this is defined by the W3C Process Document, an elaborate document that is updated nearly yearly, although most of the process of standardization has remained nearly the same since the W3C was founded [15].

---

[3] https://www.w3.org/Consortium/membership.

[4] Note that a patent holder can still claim patent infringement even if an idea is embodied in a standard (such as an IETF RFC) and in open source code.

[5] https://www.w3.org/Consortium/Patent-Policy-20040205/.

[6] http://www.rfc-editor.org/rfc/rfc3979.txt.

[7] https://www.w3.org/2014/08/18-crypto-minutes.html.

In contrast to the IETF's slogan of "We reject kings, presidents, and voting ... we believe in rough consensus and running code," the W3C is ran as a sort of parliamentary monarchy, with all decisions ultimately resting on the authority of the Director, who has always been Tim Berners-Lee. There is no way to nominate another Director or transition plan if he departs from the role. Although the Director ultimately makes all decisions, his decisions are ratified and voted on by the W3C Advisory Committee, where each W3C member gets a single vote regardless of the type or size of the member. For example, in the Advisory Committee, both Google and the EFF have a single vote. The goal of the W3C is to make decisions by consensus, with the Director being able to override any lack of consensus, although members can launch a "formal objection" that requires the Director and W3C staff to provide an official written comment on why the objection has been overridden in their decision-making.

In order to create a new standard, the W3C runs workshops with open invitations (as the "open invitation" is needed to recruit new dues-paying members) in order to determine if there is enough momentum for standardization. If successful, the W3C staff and Director create a charter for a new W3C Working Group, with the charter going out to the Advisory Committee for approval via voting. If the vote garners a substantial amount of approval, the Working Group is launched and W3C members may join, as long as they commit their patents to the charter of the Working Group (as the standard itself does not yet exist yet). Eventually, a draft of the standard is matured by the Working Group to be a Candidate Recommendation after the text of the standard is considered complete in terms of features by the Working Group and interoperability has been shown for each feature by at least two implementations.

If the membership agrees with continuing the standardization process, the standard becomes a Proposed Recommendation, which is expected to be stable (as textual stability is needed for the royalty-free patent licensing) and presented for an Advisory Committee vote. During this stage, it is expected that each W3C member that votes on the standard is prepared to commit its patents to the Proposed Recommendation. If the vote is successful, the finalized standard is published as an official W3C Recommendation.[8] In order to update a standard, the Working Group must be rechartered and the another vote must go on, although the Working Group may begin again directly at the Candidate Recommendation phase [15].

3.2   HTML and EME at the W3C

While having democratic features, the power of determining what precisely to standardize in the traditional W3C process lies entirely with the W3C staff and the Director, as there is no ability for members to vote to create a new Working

---

[8] Note that patent protections are not given by all W3C member companies, but only those that commit to the final vote. Therefore, this considerably weakens the patent protections, as they are effectively "opt-in.".

Group Charter.[9] After the success of W3C XML, the W3C decided to stop development of HTML in 2000 and replace HTML with XHTML. Although the XHTML 1.0 W3C Recommendation was finished in 2002 with modest deployment, the work started at W3C on a XHTML 2.0 standard had no backing or implementation from browsers. As the W3C HTML standards increasingly diverged from the reality of browser implementations, all browser vendors except Microsoft started the informal WHATWG (Web Hypertext Application Technology Working Group), an informal "standards" body to curate the future of the HTML in 2004.[10] Rather than follow the cumbersome W3C process, HTML was considered to be a "living standard" that reflected consensus amongst browser implementations. Berners-Lee and the W3C focused primarily on standardizing Semantic Web technologies, which are considered irrelevant by the browser vendors to the future of the Web. Yet when Berners-Lee saw the rapid uptake of WHATWG's version of HTML, the W3C decided to formally "fork" the WHATWG HTML standard into HTML5 by putting the text of the WHATWG HTML specification through W3C Process in 2007 and ending work on XHTML 2.0 in 2009. As there was concern from browser vendors that the W3C was too slow-moving and the rechartering process would limit the ability of HTML to be extended, two new processes were made. The first was a fully automated system for creating W3C Community Groups meant for pre-standardization work.[11] The second process, unique to the W3C HTML Working Group, was to allow HTML Extensions to be defined without rechartering in order to speed up the W3C HTML Working Group and counter criticisms from WHATWG that W3C Process made it impossible for the W3C HTML Working Group to evolve HTML in an agile manner.[12]

Although there had been workshops on standardizing DRM at the W3C since 2001,[13] the W3C had never managed to create a DRM Working Group until 2012. Technically, the reason had been due to the W3C's desire to build on work such as MPEG-4 IPMP but add a more flexible (and likely in RDF or XML) language for expressing "intellectual property rights." Legally, standardizing DRM in HTML was mired in the vast number of patents on the DRM systems themselves.[14] With the rising popularity of streaming video in 2012, new W3C member Netflix

---

[9] Instead, W3C members may submit "Member Submissions" of potential standard, but the only requirement is that the W3C staff provide textual feedback on the maturity and suitability of the work as a W3C standard, and historically very few eventual W3C Recommendations have been Team submissions.

[10] https://whatwg.org.

[11] https://www.w3.org/community/.

[12] https://www.w3.org/html/wg/wiki/ExtensionSpecifications.

[13] In particular, the highly attended "Workshop on Digital Rights Management for the Web" hosted by W3C Staff Rigo Wenning in January, see https://www.w3.org/2000/12/drm-ws/.

[14] Personal communication with Daniel Weitzner in 2016, W3C Staff Counsel in 2000.

proposed "Encrypted Media Extensions" in 2012 as an HTML Extension. This was approved as an extension by the chair of the HTML Working Group, Paul Cotton (Microsoft), and work proceeded on EME in a unofficial "task force" of the W3C HTML Working Group, unnoticed by the outside world.

Yet when EME was brought up to be part of the official W3C HTML Recommendation as an extension, a number of members issued concerns over EME and the Electronic Frontier Foundation joined W3C in order to organize against what they considered the dangerous addition of DRM to Web standards; this first took the place of an argument over the extension of the HTML Working Group's charter to include the use-case of "content protection."[15] After objections from the HTML Working Group that the controversial and (at the time) unimplemented EME standard would slow the development of HTML5, EME and MSE (Media Source Extensions[16]), were spun off from the HTML Working Group into the separate HTML Media Extensions Working Group in 2013. This new Working Group was joined by all major browser vendors, including Mozilla. The Electronic Frontier Foundation (EFF) and others filed formal objections to the creation of the Working Group after I wrote, as a W3C employee at the time, that it was "now or never to save the open web." [13]. However, the work continued and EME was soon deployed later in 2013 by Netflix. The standard soon reached the point where it was a Candidate Recommendation in 2016, with all major browser vendors (Google Chrome, Microsoft Edge, Mozilla Firefox, and Apple Safari) demonstrating interoperable support of EME.

As it became clear that EME would move from Candidate Recommendation to Proposed Recommendation, the EFF circulated a petition in January 2016 stating that all work on EME should be halted until a "covenant" could be put in place to defend users and security researchers from prosecution under Chap. 12 of the DMCA [8]. At the Advisory Committee meeting in April 2016 at Cambridge, the W3C decided not to go forward with an official vote on the adoption of the covenant and to progress Encrypted Media Extensions to a Candidate Recommendation regardless. This led to the first-ever street protest against the W3C organized by the Free Software Foundation (FSF). I threatened to quit if W3C continued to approve EME, and at the time I was the staff contact for both the Web Cryptography and Web Authentication Working Groups.[17] A number of objections were filed by W3C members, W3C employees (including both myself and staff legal counsel Wendy Seltzer[18]), and ordinary programmers (with no official W3C affiliation) to the continuation of EME. Despite the protest and even staff resignation from the W3C, the W3C approved the transition to a Proposed Recommendation in July 2016. The issue finally started to gain attention

---

[15] https://www.eff.org/deeplinks/2013/10/lowering-your-standards.

[16] MSE is standard needed to select the source of streaming media.

[17] https://motherboard.vice.com/en_us/article/jpgpjx/we-marched-with-richard-stall man-at-a-drm-protest-last-night-w3-consortium-MIT-joi-ito.

[18] https://lists.w3.org/Archives/Public/public-html-media/2016Aug/0007.html.

from outside the W3C, with civil society organizations ranging from UNESCO to the JustNet Coalition (NGOs from the Global South) filing statements asking Berners-Lee not to approve EME. After a nearly tied W3C vote on whether or not to approve W3C EME as a Recommendation (and thus, quite far from consensus), Tim Berners-Lee in his role of W3C Director finally approved EME as a Recommendation in July 2017. Given that more than 5% of W3C members were against W3C, the EFF triggered the never before used option to repeal a Director's decision.[19] The recall vote was divided, but the majority (108) of W3C members approved of the progress towards Recommendation while a substantial minority (57) objected and (20) abstained.[20] Therefore, EME is now an official W3C Recommendation.

4   Encrypted Media Extensions

EME is a Javascript API that provides access to a Content Decryption Module (CDM) in order to restrict the playback of video to only those who possess an authorized cryptographic secret key on their own client device. Without this key, the encrypted media stream cannot be decrypted and so can not be displayed on the video output of the user's client device. EME does not mandate a single CDM to decrypt encrypted video media. This allows the various patent pools around CDM itself to be avoided while applying the W3C patent royalty-free licensing to the API itself, allowing interoperability between "plug and play" CDMs. In terms of EME support, Microsoft Edge supports the PlayReady DRM system, Google supports the Widevine CDM, and Mozilla has removed Adobe Primetime for Windows and switched to Google's Widevine CDM.[21]

EME is an extension to the standard `HTMLMediaElement` element. In brief, this element unifies both popular `video` and `audio` elements into a single framework, as well as defining text tracks for subtitles via `track` attribute. EME extends `HTMLMediaElement` (and thus both audio and video) to include a new `MediaEncryptEvent`, so that there can be encrypted blocks waiting for decryption or playback but blocked due to waiting for a key. EME defines the framework for the use of these decryption keys for DRM systems, and consists of the following components, whose relationship is given in Fig. 1.

- **Content Decryption Module:** The component in the platform or browser that provides decryption for a Key System.
- **Key System:** A uniquely identified CDM that is bound to the server that served the request for a key.
- **License:** Licenses are an array of one or more `MediaKeys` IDs that can be used to decrypt the media.

---

[19] https://boingboing.net/2017/07/12/save-the-web.html.

[20] https://lists.w3.org/Archives/Member/chairs/2017JulSep/0154.html.

[21] https://www.ghacks.net/2017/01/10/firefox-52-adobe-primetime-cdm-removal/.

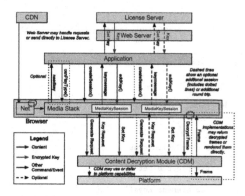

Fig. 1. Encrypted Media Extensions (from W3C Recommendation [9])

- **MediaKeys:** One or more uniquely identified decryption keys needed to decrypt encrypted media data and bound to a session. These can be manually loaded into a CDM via an explicit `update` call.
- **MediaKeySession:** An ID for a series of uses of a `MediaKeys` object to decrypt media. License information and associated `MediaKeys` are cleared from the browser after the end of a session, but may be re-used across sessions.

Simplified code of an example usage of EME using a single key (and license requested from a server and data to discover the key) is given below in Fig. 4. The typical flow of EME is as follows to decrypt media from an `MediaEncryptEvent` is as follows:

1. Call the `requestMediaKeySystemAccess` with a `licenseUrl` variable that designates the URL where the license with the needed `MediaKey` IDs is. The license is retrieved using the `licenseRequestReady` function either from the URL (which the Web Server redirects to a License Server) or from a licenses stored locally on the Web Server.
2. This license request is passed via the browser to the CDM. If the key IDs requested by the license are returned to the browser from the CDM, new `MediaKeys` are created via the `createMediaKeys`, where the keys are bound with a Web Server using a server certificate.
3. After a `MediaKeySession` is created, these `MediaKeys` are sent to the CDM where, if they fulfill the license, they can be used. If needed, the license is updated and provided to the CDM in order to request more keys and thus a new `MediaKeySession`. This step may repeat one or more time in the form of multiple `MediaKeySessions`.
4. Once all `MediaKeySessions` have been created that fulfill the license, the media is decrypted by calling the originating `HTMLMediaElement` with a `MediaKey` as well as any needed initialization data.

```
<script>
  var licenseUrl;
  var serverCertificate;

  function createSupportedKeySystem() {
    someSystemOptions = [
     { initDataTypes: ['keyids','webm'],
       videoCapabilities: [
         { contentType:'video/webm; codecs="vp8"' }
       ]
     }
    ];
    return navigator.requestMediaKeySystemAccess('com.example.keysystem',x-options).then(
      function(keySystemAccess) {
        licenseUrl = 'https://example.com/getkey';
        serverCertificate = new Uint8Array([ 0x01111fef010 ]);
        return keySystemAccess.createMediaKeys();
      }
    ).catch(
      console.error.bind(console, 'Needed DRM system not present or license not supported')
    );
    promise.then(
        function(createdMediaKeys) {
          return video.setMediaKeys(createdMediaKeys);
        }
      ).catch(
        console.error.bind(console, 'Unable to set MediaKeys')
      );
    promise.then(
        function(createdMediaKeys) {
          var initData = new Uint8Array([...]);
          var keySession = createdMediaKeys.createSession();
          keySession.addEventListener('message', handleMessage,
              false);
          return keySession.generateRequest('webm', initData);
        }
      ).catch(
        console.error.bind(console,
          'Unable to create or initialize key session')
      );
    }
  );
}


  function handleInitData(event) {
    var video = event.target;
      createSupportedKeySystem().then(
        function(createdMediaKeys) {
          video.mediaKeysObject = createdMediaKeys;
          if (serverCertificate)
            createdMediaKeys.setServerCertificate(serverCertificate);
          for (var i = 0; i < video.pendingSessionData.length; i++) {
            var data = video.pendingSessionData[i];
            makeNewRequest(video.mediaKeysObject, data.initDataType, data.initData);
          }
          return video.setMediaKeys(createdMediaKeys);
        }
      ).catch(
        console.error.bind(console, 'Failed to create and initialize a MediaKeys object')
      );
    }
  }
</script>
<video autoplay onencrypted='handleInitData(event)'></video>
}
```

5   Objections to W3C EME

The arguments for EME is that the Web itself needs to be extensible to include "access to protected content" without the use of a plug-in.[22] As many content producers require DMCA-compliance, platform providers such as Netflix believe that enabling DRM in the browser is necessary for streaming video in order to "say goodbye to third-party plugins, making for a safer and more reliable web"[23]. The W3C holds the position that EME is necessary for a Web without plug-ins for DRM: "Developers who use HTML5 for video can create play back video directly without external dependency on third party apps (like Adobe Flash or Microsoft Silverlight) and without inheriting security vulnerabilities from those third party apps."[24] The W3C maintains that EME improves security and privacy without impacting accessibility negatively.

The general argument against the standardization of Encrypted Media Extensions at W3C is that DRM contradicts the W3C's official mission to lead to "Web to its full potential", in particular to the make benefits of the Web "available to all people, whatever their hardware, software, network infrastructure, native language, culture, geographical location, or physical or mental ability" via open standards.[25] Objectors like EFF and FSF believe that DRM by design is meant to prevent users from accessing content that is encrypted via DRM in a manner that by definition discriminates against both security researchers and users, including those lawfully exercising their rights. A more broad objection to adding DRM is that by making DRM a W3C standard, the amount of DRM on the Web will increase, as DRM will now work seamlessly in a cross-platform manner across all major browsers, which previously led DRM systems to be too cumbersome to use by many video content providers. The lack of cross-platform compatibility was one of the major reasons why DRM systems were ultimately not adopted by the music industry [17]. As EME makes it much easier for content providers to add DRM, there is concern that the Web itself may eventually become a "pay-to-play" closed space similar to pre-Web services [13].

Although Encrypted Media Extensions only covers media, the proposed W3C Digital Publishing Working Group includes general purpose DRM for text in HTML in its use-cases for future W3C standardization.[26] Although the W3C has stated that "EME is not DRM for HTML" as EME "defines a common API that may be used to discover, select and interact with such systems as well as with simpler content encryption systems," it is unclear what other purpose EME could possibly serve except to enable DRM-based systems inside of HTML. The concerns therefore are with DRM on the Web. The concerns can be given in terms of (1) user control and fair-use (2) accessibility (3) privacy and (4) security. For each of these arguments, first we will first state the W3C argument for standardizing EME and then summarize the arguments against standardizing EME.

---

[22] https://www.w3.org/2013/09/html-charter.html.

[23] https://www.w3.org/2017/09/pressrelease-eme-recommendation.html.en.

[24] https://www.w3.org/2016/03/EME-factsheet.html.

[25] https://www.w3.org/Consortium/mission.

[26] https://www.w3.org/dpub/IG/wiki/DRM_UC#DRM-1.

5.1   User Control and Fair Use

The W3C has stated that users demand protected content, and any attempt to halt the standardization of DRM on the Web is effectively limiting their rights to watch DRM-protected content [3]. In contrast, EFF holds the position that DRM systems seek to take away control from users of what Doctorow calls "general purpose computing" in order to enforce copyright restrictions.[27] This is the same concern brought up by free software advocates, namely that DRM restricts user control over their own computer and thus violates user freedom. Even under laws like the DMCA that DRM systems are meant to enforce, a user often has "fair use" rights to copy even copyrighted material, such as for educational purposes, parody, or sharing the same media across multiple devices [19]. However, the "fair use" doctrine cannot be implemented via the strictly technically enforced key-based decryption enabled by DRM systems, as "fair use" depends on knowledge of social context that cannot be accessed by the purely technical capabilities of DRM systems. There are a wide variety of limitations and exceptions to copyright law across various nation-states, and any purely technical system such as EME is unlikely to be able to justice to all of these heterogeneous legal regimes. As W3C is a global standards body, it is surprising that various national legal regimes are ignored. For example, there are even heterogeneous limitations and exceptions between European nations as shown by the fact that re-streaming certain content may be legal in Greece but not in the United Kingdom [2]. Due to this reason, EME has caused a motion in the European Parliament to determine if EME violates limitations and exceptions to European copyright law.[28] Some countries like India had for years copyright protection that did not clearly "criminalise the manufacture and distribution of circumvention tools" and still today give courts more leeway than in the DMCA [18].

5.2   Accessibility

DRM has been thought to damage accessibility, but accessibility experts at W3C have claimed that EME is compatible with accessibility goals,[29] as EME only encrypts the media content and `HTMLMediaElement` has a separate `track` for textual descriptions (such as subtitles) that is not encrypted by EME. Therefore, EME does not present any obstacles for the playing of subtitles, although it also offers no improvement per se over HTML5 without EME. However, this feature shows a potential weakness in EME as a DRM system, as EME may not fully satisfy the needs for copyright control if the copyright claims include the text given by subtitle tracks. More importantly, EME cannot support access to audio and video media for accessibility reasons, because the media itself can still only be decrypted only by EME. This prevents accessibility tools that can automatically create accessible subtitles from the media content directly using

---

[27] https://www.youtube.com/watch?v=gbYXBJOFgeI.

[28] https://juliareda.eu/2017/04/open-letter-to-the-european-commission-on-encrypted-media-extensions/.

[29] https://www.w3.org/2017/03/eme-accessibility.html.

automatic speech detection and other machine-learning techniques that require access to video and audio before it is played. These tools for the automatic creation of accessible media are likely to become more widespread in the future.[30]

5.3   Privacy

Tim Berners-Lee wrote that "the EME system can sandbox the DRM code to limit the damage it can do to the users privacy" [3]. As given in Sect. 4, EME functions in virtue of the request and retrieval of uniquely identified keys (MediaKeys). In this way, EME could violate privacy for a single origin. The EME specification states that "key IDs may contain any value" and thus "these data items could be abused to store user-identifying information" [9]. Furthermore, EME key systems "may access or create persistent or semi-persistent identifier(s) for a device or user of a device" and thus as "identifiers are present in Key System messages, then devices and/or users may be tracked" [9]. Although care is taken to note that CDM instances should abide by the same origin policy by associating only one MediaKey for a CDM per origin and usage identifiers "must ensure that... session data is not shared between MediaKeys objects or CDM instances," these goals are nowhere enforced in EME, as the naming control and duration of MediaKey objects are entirely left to the control of the content provider. EME even admits that MediaKey objects are likely to be used for tracking, as "within a single origin, a site can continue to track the user during a session, and can then pass all this information to a third party" [9].[31]

Despite these vague recommendations not to use personally identifiable information to attach a user to key material, these gestures towards privacy are not technically enforced in the specification. For example, EME states that "user agents must take responsibility for providing users with adequate control over their own privacy" although the W3C rejected a formal objection that would disable the CDM without user consent.[32] Although the EME specification clearly outlines the privacy dangers of the technique of associating a user with a uniquely identified key, given the functioning of DRM requires uniquely identified keys to be associated with a uniquely identified CDM in order to see if a user has fulfilled the licensing conditions, there is no testing to see if the various guidelines given by EME to enforce user privacy will be respected in EME implementations.[33] Even if they were respected, these privacy properties are not tested for conformance in the W3C test suite, possibly due to fears of violating the anti-circumvention provisions of the DMCA, which may apply not just to the CDM but to handling of key material by EME. In this way, the statements in the specification about EME respecting user privacy appear to be red herrings that are contradicted by the real-world functioning of DRM.

---

[30] https://www.technologyreview.com/s/603899/machine-learning-opens-up-new-ways-to-help-disabled-people/.

[31] Although if they are used, they "must be encrypted, together with a timestamp or nonce, such that the Key System messages are always different" [9].

[32] https://github.com/w3c/encrypted-media/issues/386.

[33] https://w3c.github.io/test-results/encrypted-media/all.html.

5.4 Security

The EFF and other opponents clam that the DMCA makes it illegal to discuss the security of the underlying CDM. While the DMCA's 1201 clause does state that "no person shall circumvent a technological measure that effectively controls access to a work protected under this title" and EME enables such a technological measure across web browsers, there are explicit exemptions for security research in the DMCA [7]. However, these exemptions are difficult to enforce in practice, because while it is legal under the DMCA to reveal "information derived used solely to promote the security of the owner or operator of the tested computer system" as long as that "information obtained is shared directly with the developer of the system," this information becomes illegal as soon as "information obtained distributed in a way that might enable copyright infringement or other legal violations" [7]. This final restriction essentially forces the vulnerability to only be disclosed to the DRM system manufacturer, even if the DRM system manufacturer does not fix the flaw. This law was used against security researchers first in the threats to Snosoft by Hewlett-Packard in 2002,[34] and over fifty court-cases have been launched against security research as of 2016.[35] Unfortunately, legal precedent also shows academic publications on vulnerabilities in DRM systems violate the DMCA and so result in the censorship of the academic work, as shown by the Felten case over Sony DRM [12]. Although no known DRM case has involved EME and browser-based DRM, it is reasonable to hypothesize that security audits by researchers on browser-based DRM systems will suffer a "chilling effect" due to the DMCA and that there will be increased DRM circumvention cases if DRM on the Web grows.

The W3C recognizes the possible security threats of CDMs in the EME specification as well, noting that "user agent implementers must ensure CDM implementations can and will be quickly and proactively updated in the event of security vulnerabilities" [9]. However, the W3C also claims that, unlike browser plug-ins that have privileges for every origin in an entire browser, EME is restricted per origin and that the CDMs may be sandboxed, providing "security and privacy superior to native platform alternatives."[36] In particular, the W3C continues to note that sandboxing may at least limit the damage as "DRMs under EME can be sandboxed" to enforce the requirement of the EME specification that "the CDM must not make direct out-of band network requests" [9].

Unfortunately, there is more sand than box in 'sandboxing' on the Web. Although a browser may be sandboxed from the rest of the computer in the same way any other computer program, origins are not defended adequately from each other inside the browser. Javascript is constrained per origin, but security flaws are not constrained per origin in browser memory. In modern web browsers, there are a limited number of content processes (Firefox recently went up to 4 or 5, while mobile browsers often have one). Normally, each origin does not have its

---

[34] https://www.cnet.com/news/security-warning-draws-dmca-threat/.

[35] https://www.eff.org/files/2016/03/17/1201_reported_case_list_revised.xls.

[36] https://lists.w3.org/Archives/Public/public-html-media/2017Jul/0000.html.

own content process, as that would cause a performance slowdown and so each content process shares memory. Therefore, if there is a flaw in the underlying CDM that has access to the browser via EME, it's access will not be limited to the origin, but to the entire shared memory space of the content process. As security flaws are simply more likely in a CDM that can't be inspected to see if it has flaws or follows EME security's guidelines and by default this CDM will be sharing a content process, thus the CDM is not sandboxed in any actual sense of the word if there is a security vulnerability.

Another concern is the scope of the DMCA and whether or not it can be implemented in open source. EME provides a technique to keep the key material unencrypted in the browser, called "clear key" that can be implemented without a CDM in order to keep compliance possible for open-source browsers and browsers without CDMs, as the keys are generated locally and stored in cleartext in the browser take the place of the license server. However, one danger is that the "clear key" technique is subject to DMCA, and thus the EME specification inflicts an inherently insecure yet DMCA-compliant system on all browsers due to the "clear key" option.

In order to protect security researchers, the EFF created a "covenant" modelled on the W3C Royalty-Free Licensing Policy that would allow W3C members to make a legally binding commitment not to prosecute security researchers investigating EME-related DRM systems. In a petition, over 100 security researchers as well as many W3C staff members [8]. The EFF covenant stated that: "Each participant irrevocably covenants that it will not bring or join suit against any person under 17 U.S.C 1203, or under any other law of any jurisdiction that regulates the circumvention of technological measures that effectively control access to a work protected by copyright, where the act complained of relates to (a) the circumvention of any implementation of the specification; (b) the publication of any non-compliant implementation of the specification; or (c) the publication or disclosure of any vulnerability in the specification or in any implementation of the specification"[10]. The issue of security also caused interventions from civil society, with UNESCO pointed out that the same infrastructure used by DRM to control content could also be used for censorship and surveillance.[37] However, the W3C stated that "despite much work those efforts were not successful and consensus among the W3C Membership was not achieved" on the covenant. Yet the EFF covenant was never formally put forward to an actual vote by W3C, so the EFF called for a revocation of the W3C Director's decision to make EME a W3C Recommendation through a repeal process that requires 5% of the Advisory Committee to uphold. As of July 2017, the process of appeal is underway. However, as it has historically never happened at W3C, it is unclear if the result will be the removal of EME as a Recommendation and its patent status.

---

[37] http://en.unesco.org/news/be-careful-about-proposed-technical-change-web-says-u nesco-s-rue.

6   Quantitative Analysis

Two claims have been made by opponents of EME standardization at W3C that touch upon actual involvement in "open standards." The Free Software Foundation has claimed that the W3C is controlled by content providers and browser vendors without suitable representation from wider civil society and security researchers: "It looks like a select few organizations are pushing and influencing their power unduly."[38] The JustNet Coalition (JNC) has called EME a form of "digital colonialism," as JNC claimed that EME excludes those in the Global South who are struggling for access to information at the expense of a few North American and European corporations.[39]

In terms of participation, the total number of members in the group is 273, with 70 invited experts. Using the origin country of the member to determine a rough estimate of the geographical breakdown of the Working Group (and thus excluding Invited Experts), there was a majority participation from the United States (66%) and less from Asia (33%). Asian representation did not include anyone from India. There were a few representatives from South America (1%), one member from Australia, and none from Africa. In terms of the types of participation (excluding Invited Experts), the majority of the Working Group consisted of browsers and DRM manufacturers (53%) with smaller representation from civil society (4%) and accessibility experts (4%), and these being roughly balanced by pro-DRM trade associations (4%), as given in Fig. 2. The amount of email sent on the list is 3,427, with clear spikes of activity that correspond to debates where civil society tried to stop progress on EME advancing in the formal W3C process, as given by Fig. 3. There was indeed little participation from the Global South outside large companies like Baidu from China, Samsung from Korea, and

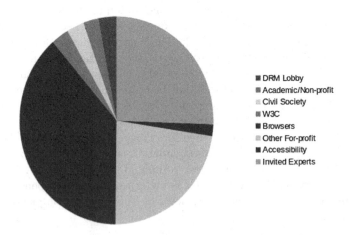

Fig. 2. Categories of members of the EME Working Group

---

[38] https://www.youtube.com/watch?v=SPfdOOiuOHI.
[39] https://justnetcoalition.org/2017/W3C_EME_objection.pdf.

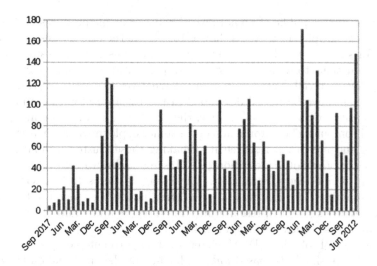

Fig. 3. Email frequency to EME mailing list

Sony from Japan. There was domination by browsers and for-profit corporations in the Working Group, but there was significant if much smaller representation from civil society and accessibility experts, with civil society (in particular EFF) being active in bursts. This analysis of the HTML Media Extensions Group is in line with similar analysis done of participation in the HTML Working Group that also noticed a lack of participation from the Global South [11].[40]

7   Is Harm Reduction for DRM Possible?

Is there a solution towards standardizing DRM that can avoid the problems of the EME specification that the W3C has encountered? As explored in Sect. 5, standards bodies should recognize that there are legitimate concerns with privacy and security with DRM systems for end-users. Both legal and technical approaches can be applied to reduce the harm of EME, but to the generic problem of the need for DRM standards. While it is too late to pursue these approaches for EME at W3C, applying these approaches should be best practices for future standards.

Technically, DRM has the potential to be privacy-invasive and possible security issues, but this is true of all software. However, modern DRM implementations in the consumer market essentially work by violating Kerckhoffs' principle, namely that the security of cryptosystem should rely only on the protection of key material, so that the cryptosystem must be secure even if everything else

---

[40] Note these numbers are preliminary, and a more detailed and careful analysis is under preparation that also takes into account the origins and roles of Invited Experts and git repo of EME is underway.

about the system is public. To ignore Kerckhoffs' principle produces broken systems, as cryptographic history has shown [16]. It is in the best interest in terms of security for standards bodies, content providers, and users to base standards on security reductions to well-studied cryptographic primitives and securing cryptographic key material. There exist many alternatives to classical DRM, such as traitor tracing, have been well developed in the research literature and do not require security by obscurity [6]. Lastly, there has been a corresponding growth of "trusted computing" environments in consumer deployment, such as the ARM Trustzone, and increasing research into making these trusted computing platforms capable of remote attestation [1]. This research into attestable "trusted computing" is not ready for market: The ill-fated Microsoft Next-Generation Secure Computing Base that was canceled after having been found to have security vulnerabilities [5]. Still, research into more secure and auditable computing systems for access control is ongoing [14].

Access control, of which DRM systems attempt to enforce by obscurity on the client device should be based *only* on having any key material on the client under user control. This key material can be stored in a trusted and attestable way, including the usage of hardware tokens or "trusted computing" with secure enclaves. In terms of usability, users can correctly handle private user-centric key material and this key material can respect the same origin policy, as shown by a new generation of standards like the W3C Web Authentication API.[41] Future standards may avoid the controversy of DRM systems as long as (1) the key is under user control and (2) the security of the DRM system is reducible to the security of the key and the publicly known cryptographic primitives.

As current DRM systems are not deployed following Kerckhoffs' principle and thus there are possible security bugs that cannot be detected by an audit of the CDM, DRM systems should simply be installed only when officially requested by a user, and should be not installed by default. A user can be empowered to take the risk of installing and activating a CDM, but a DRM system should be disabled by default. At least with plug-ins, a user had the chance to refuse to install the plug-in, so standards should not remove that user choice. A modification enforcing "opt-in" of DRM could be easily added to W3C EME by forcing a dialogue with the user warning them that they are installing or activating a CDM, similar to the user interaction needed to install Adobe Flash-based DRM systems pre-EME as well as the use of a user-prompt to access the potentially privacy-invasive microphone and video as needed by WebRTC.[42] Although the W3C Working Group claimed that a one-time user-centric privacy prompt would defeat usability (as "being able to visit a site and watch video without annoying and confusing consent prompts is a user experience benefit"), but no evidence of prompts causing retention issues was provided.[43] A "one time" prompt at first use of EME-encrypted video seems unlikely to reduce usage, and is less restrictive than WebRTC's usage of getUserMedia). This standpoint risks being

---

[41] https://www.w3.org/TR/webauthn/.

[42] https://www.w3.org/TR/webrtc/.

[43] https://lists.w3.org/Archives/Public/public-html-media/2017Apr/0013.html.

hypocritical, as the W3C has argued that controversial privacy-invasive features to web browsers should require user interaction, and this would logically include EME. At least with a DRM plug-in, a user could refuse to install the plug-in if they had security concerns.

On the legal framework, there is a long-term gain for security to made by supporting reform of the DMCA. The primary reason for the controversy around EME is not due to the technical details of the specification itself, but the legal framework that prevents reasonable security audits. The EFF has claimed to W3C that DMCA ends up handing too much power to the companies in terms of their control of the disclosure of vulnerabilities.[44] On a larger note, the EFF has also started a court-case arguing that the DMCA should be overturned as it violates the free-speech of researchers, stifles innovation, and damages cybersecurity.[45] The Copyright Office of the United States has recently issued a statement agreeing that the provisions of the DMCA restrictions requiring the need for security researchers to require authorization from vendors, stating that "the exemption for encryption research under section 1201(g) may benefit from similar revision, including removal of the requirement to seek authorization and clarification or removal of the multifactor test."[46]

Times have changed since the DMCA has been passed: Today, security should be more important than copyright enforcement. As it the best of interest of any security standard to have open review, security standards bodies should provide legally binding guarantees that there can be open and legal audits of the standard (as well as of the implementations of a standard) that do not require permission in order to check conformance to specified normative security and privacy properties. More concretely, although the W3C created a "W3C Security Disclosures Best Practices" document, it failed to have any support (much less adoption), as most companies already have security disclosure policies.[47] While it is possible the DMCA will be revised to allow open security audits, the EFF covenant was likely unacceptable to many vendors as it would override their existing commitments to enforce the DMCA without clear benefits, such as that provided by W3C Patent Policy. However, if each member changed their existing security disclosure policy to agree to not prosecute with both security researchers engaged in audits of implementations and users who are not violating copyright law, as well as co-operate with security disclosures, then concrete harm reduction could be done around the possible security vulnerabilities introduced by DRM systems.

In terms of the W3C EME standard, this would require not signing a single covenant, but to engage with each member of the Working Group to ensure that their security disclosure document included suitable language that prioritized

---

[44] https://www.eff.org/deeplinks/2017/02/indefensible-w3c-says-companies-should-get-decide-when-and-how-security.

[45] https://www.eff.org/press/releases/eff-lawsuit-takes-dmca-section-1201-research-and-technology-restrictions-violate.

[46] https://www.copyright.gov/policy/1201/section-1201-full-report.pdf.

[47] https://w3c.github.io/security-disclosure/.

the security of the Web in terms of CDM implementations for EME, where the decision over whether a particular security policy complied was left to a neutral third party, such as the independent policy council of the W3C. As there are only three major EME systems supported by the four major browser vendors (Microsoft, Google, and Apple, as Mozilla has dropped support for Adobe's CDM in favor of simply using Google's Widevine CDM) and one non-browser system (Netflix), there are only four major security disclosure policies to be taken into account.

8   Conclusion

In conclusion, the W3C EME standard has garnered unheard of controversy, but the security standardization community should learn from their example in order to determine how to successfully deal with the standardization of DRM systems that present possible security and privacy threats. We have shown that the controversy is founded due to the privacy concerns inherent in uniquely identifying keys and CDMs, and that there are also real dangers posed in terms of security and the prevention of open security audits by the DMCA. Otherwise, no actual technical guarantees can be given about the security and privacy properties of a system. Quantitative analysis shows that the critiques of the large amount of influence by vendors and content providers from Europe and North America is indeed correct. We have suggested two ways forward that have not been considered by the W3C but that are easily considered by future standards. Security standards should indeed by open to inspection and depend only on the security of the key material, which should remain under the control of the user. If there is any reason to believe a system may introduce privacy and security issues, explicit user consent should be required. Lastly, companies should expand their security disclosure policies to include co-operation and explicit non-prosecution of security researchers. By taking these steps, security standards can regain the trust of the general public, and have that trust validated by scientific research.

References

1. Bai, G., Hao, J., Wu, J., Liu, Y., Liang, Z., Martin, A.: TRUSTFOUND: towards a formal foundation for model checking trusted computing platforms. In: Jones, C., Pihlajasaari, P., Sun, J. (eds.) FM 2014. LNCS, vol. 8442, pp. 110–126. Springer, Cham (2014). https://doi.org/10.1007/978-3-319-06410-9_8
2. Batchelor, B., Jenkins, T.: FA premier league: the broader implications for copyright licensing. Eur. Compet. Law Rev. **33**(4), 157–164 (2012)
3. Berners-Lee, T.: On EME in HTML5 (2016). https://www.w3.org/blog/2017/02/on-eme-in-html5
4. Berners-Lee, T., Fischetti, M.: Weaving the Web: The Original Design and Ultimate Destiny of the World Wide Web by its Inventor. Harpers Information, New York (2000)
5. Brumley, D., Boneh, D.: Remote timing attacks are practical. Comput. Netw. **48**(5), 701–716 (2005)

6. Chor, B., Fiat, A., Naor, M.: Tracing traitors. In: Desmedt, Y.G. (ed.) CRYPTO 1994. LNCS, vol. 839, pp. 257–270. Springer, Heidelberg (1994). https://doi.org/10.1007/3-540-48658-5_25

7. US Congress: Digital millennium copyright act. Pub. Law **105**(304), 112 (1998)

8. Doctorow, C.: Security researchers: tell the W3C to protect researchers who investigate browsers (2016). https://www.eff.org/deeplinks/2016/03/security-researchers-tell-w3c-protect-researchers-who-investigate-browsers

9. Dorwin, D., Smith, J., Bateman, A., Watson, M.: Encrypted Media Extensions (2017). https://www.w3.org/TR/encrypted-media/

10. EFF: Objection to the rechartering of the W3C EME group: Covenant (2016). https://www.eff.org/pages/objection-rechartering-w3c-eme-group

11. Gupta, H.: (Lack of) representation of non-western world in process of creation of web standards (2016). https://arxiv.org/pdf/1609.01996.pdf

12. Halderman, J.A., Felten, E.W.: Lessons from the Sony CD DRM episode. In: USENIX Security Symposium, pp. 77–92 (2006)

13. Halpin, H.: DRM and HTML5: it's now or never for the Open Web. Guardian (2013). https://www.theguardian.com/technology/2013/jun/06/html5-drm-w3c-open-web

14. LaMacchia, B.A.: Key challenges in DRM: an industry perspective. In: Feigenbaum, J. (ed.) DRM 2002. LNCS, vol. 2696, pp. 51–60. Springer, Heidelberg (2003). https://doi.org/10.1007/978-3-540-44993-5_4

15. McCathie-Neville, C.: W3C process document (2016). https://www.eff.org/deeplinks/2016/03/security-researchers-tell-w3c-protect-researchers-who-investigate-browsers

16. Mercuri, R.T., Neumann, P.G.: Security by obscurity. Commun. ACM **46**(11), 160 (2003)

17. Petrick, P.: Why DRM should be cause for concern: an economic and legal analysis of the effect of digital technology on the music industry. Berkman Center for Internet and Society at Harvard Law School Research Publication (2004)

18. Prakash, P.: Technological protection measures in the Copyright (Amendment) Bill 2010 (2016). http://cis-india.org/a2k/blogs/tpm-copyright-amendment

19. Rosenblatt, B.: DRM, law and technology: an American perspective. Online Inf. Rev. **31**(1), 73–84 (2007)

Tackling the Time-Defence: An Instruction Count Based Micro-architectural Side-Channel Attack on Block Ciphers

Manaar Alam$^{(\boxtimes)}$, Sarani Bhattacharya, and Debdeep Mukhopadhyay

Indian Institute of Technology, Kharagpur, Kharagpur, India
alam.manaar@iitkgp.ac.in,
{sarani.bhattacharya,debdeep}@cse.iitkgp.ernet.in

Abstract. Hardware Performance Counters (HPCs) are present in most modern processors and provide an interface to user-level processes to monitor their processor performance in terms of the number of micro architectural events, executed during a process execution. In this paper, we analyze the leakage from these HPC events and present a new micro-architectural side-channel attack which observes number of instruction counts during the execution of an encryption algorithm as side-channel information to recover the secret key. This paperfirst demonstrates the fact that the *instruction* counts can act as a side-channel and then describes the *Instruction Profiling Attack* (IPA) methodology with the help of two block ciphers, namely AES and Clefia, on Intel and AMD processors. We follow the principles of profiled instruction attacks and show that the proposed attack is more potent than the well-known cache timing attacks in literature. We also perform experiments on ciphers implemented with popular time fuzzing schemes to subvert timing attacks. Our results show that while the countermeasure successfully stops leakages through the timing channels, it is vulnerable to the Instruction Profiling Attack. We validate our claims by detailed experiments on contemporary Intel and AMD platforms to demonstrate that seemingly benign instruction counts can serve as side-channels even for block cipher implementations which are hardened against timing attacks.

Keywords: Micro-architectural side-channel attack · Hardware performance counters · Cache-timing attack · Block-cipher

1 Introduction

The state of a computing environment gets affected by the processes executing on it. Modern cryptosystems are vulnerable against growing threats in the form of information leakages about the secret key through side-channels like power, radiation, timing, etc. One category of such threats uses the information leakages created because of the variations (in say timing) caused due to the presence of a cache memory in processors. The cause of the variation is that the access time for

© Springer International Publishing AG 2017
S.S. Ali et al. (Eds.): SPACE 2017, LNCS 10662, pp. 30–52, 2017.
https://doi.org/10.1007/978-3-319-71501-8_3

a data present in the cache is much lower than the data not present in it, as the processor first looks into the cache memory before processing with a data. This disparity in the access time is the fundamental notion of all cache-attacks. Block ciphers like Data Encryption Standard (DES), Advanced Encryption Standard (AES), Clefia, Blowfish, etc. are vulnerable to cache-attacks as they require key dependent table lookup for their encryption operations.

Two important classes of cache-attacks are - cache trace attacks and cache timing attacks. For a cache trace attack, an adversary needs to profile the cache access patterns, in terms of cache-hits and cache-misses during the encryption operation. Cache timing attacks, on the other hand, only require the information regarding overall execution time of the encryption process, thus making it more threatening than the other form of cache-attacks. An adversary can easily capture the timing information over a network, without the need of any sophisticated measuring instrumentation, thereby, creating a chance of possible remote attacks. It can be pointed here that these threats have been shown to be pertinent even in a remote server running an encryption algorithm [2,4].

There have been some seminal works of cache timing attack on block ciphers, both with large tables like AES and small tables like Clefia. Bernstein [4] demonstrated that statistical correlation between the profiles of the execution time of AES for a known key and an unknown key could be used to extract the secret key bytes. In the same way Rebeiro et al. [20,21] described that the timing profiles for the Clefia encryption for both the known and unknown key could be used to obtain the round keys and thereby trivially determine the secret key.

Numerous works have been done to counter the risks of cache timing attacks [8,11,16,19]. A notable work to prevent these attacks is described in [11] by Martin et al. They presented a general mitigation strategy to limit the fidelity of fine-grained time-keeping, thereby making it difficult for the adversary to distinguish between different time-stamps. The authors mainly focused on the RDTSC (Read Time Stamp Counter) instructions, which returns the current value of TSC (Time Stamp Counter) register, to design their countermeasures and eliminated the possibility of information leakages through other micro-architectural events. But, on the contrary to their claim, the advent of *perf_event* system call and performance monitoring tool PAPI [18] allows an adversary to monitor any micro-architectural event of a system with user privilege and with higher granularity. Also, the work reported in [6] has shown the possibility of timing attack in spite of the presence of time obfuscation. Most modern processors contain hardware performance counters which count the total occurrences of different micro-architectural events. The PAPI tool gives an upper hand to an adversary to mount an attack in the presence of the defense by time fuzzing technique.

A micro-architectural attack has been proposed based on Instruction cache (I-cache) [1] for public key cryptographic implementation, however, the hardware event *instruction* count has not been quite explored in the case of block ciphers. A possible reason could be as block ciphers do not have key-dependent conditional branches like public key ciphers, the number of instructions does not intuitively leak the secret key. In this paper, we look into this issue of exploring whether the micro-architectural event, instruction-count, can be utilized to reveal secret keys of block ciphers. We propose an Instruction Profiling Attack (IPA), which thus exploits this not-so-researched side-channel, i.e., instruction counts, and determines secret keys from block cipher executions faster than traditional cache timing attacks. A related fall-out of this attack is that, block cipher implementations which are time-resistant by fuzzing time stamp counters are still vulnerable against the proposed IPA.

The attack methodology is validated on two different types of block ciphers, namely AES and Clefia on two separate processors, Intel Core i5 and AMD A10.

Main Idea and Motivation

The cache timing attacks work on the intuition of non-uniform cache memory accesses due to cache hits and cache misses. These memory operations are nothing but simple load- store instructions spawned by the CPU. In the presence of timing obfuscation defense mechanism, an adversary is unable to analyze the timing differences and gain secret information but can monitor the number of instructions executed in the system. The total number of load-store instructions executed during the encryption process will vary based on the secret key, as the cache access pattern will be different for different secret keys. A cache-miss operation will result in an extra load instruction and this disparity in the executed instructions is the main idea behind this work. The motivation is to use the instruction count event as an information leakage source and mount an attack.

Most of the modern encryption implementations use time obfuscation technique, which can be implemented easily with little performance overhead, to mitigate the threats of cache-timing attacks. Distributions, like OSX, Ubuntu use deliberate time delay after entering the wrong password to invalidate the timing analysis done by an adversary [24]. The present paper strives to evaluate the security of such apparently secured systems against timing attacks in the face of the newly proposed threat.

Our Contribution

We have investigated the presence of information leakage of an encryption process using the hardware event *instruction* count. The prime contributions that we made through this work are:

- We have proposed a new side-channel attack, namely Instruction Profiling Attack (IPA), tailored for block ciphers using HPC event: *instruction*. We have also demonstrated the effectiveness of IPA by successfully retrieving the secret key bits.
- We have evaluated our proposed attack method on both Intel and AMD platforms. The time complexity of a successful IPA is shown to be much lesser than a successful cache-timing attack.

– Additionally, in this paper, we show that the success rate of IPA is not affected by time-obfuscation countermeasures like timewarp, which can successfully thwart attacks based on timing channels.

The rest of the paper is organized as follows: the next section presents an overview of the necessary preliminaries related to this work. Section 3 analyzes a new form of side-channel leakage by analyzing the security of block ciphers. Section 4 discusses our attack methodology with the help of a case study on AES block cipher. Section 5 demonstrates all the experimental results, and Sect. 6 discusses the practicality of the proposed attack methodology in different environments. Finally, Sect. 7 presents the conclusion of this work.

2 Preliminaries

In this section, we first discuss the basic operations of two block ciphers, namely AES and Clefia. Next, we describe a time obfuscating countermeasure to thwart cache-timing attacks. Then we present a brief overview of hardware performance counters which are instrumental to the proposed attack. We follow for evaluating the proposed attack methodology.

2.1 AES Block Cipher

AES [7] is a 10 round cipher which takes a 16 byte secret key $K = (k_0, k_1, \cdots, k_{15})$ and an input of 16 byte plain text $P = (p_0, p_1, \cdots, p_{15})$. Its implementation in software, based on Barreto's code, is widely recognized [3]. The first 9 rounds of the algorithm uses four 1 KB lookup tables T_0, T_1, T_2, and T_3 and then an additional look up table T_4 for the final round. Though the use of lookup tables optimizes the performance of the algorithm, the size of the lookup table is large. The following equation shows the structure of the cipher in each round, encapsulating the four basic operations of AES, namely the *SubBytes, ShiftRows, MixColumns* and *AddRoundKey*: For each round r, $(1 \leq r \leq 9)$ the input is the state S^r comprising of 16 bytes $(s_0^r, s_1^r, \cdots, s_{15}^r)$ and the key K^r to the round is split into 16 bytes $(k_0^r, k_1^r, \cdots, k_{15}^r)$. The next state S^{r+1} is the output of the rth round. The input and round key to the first round S^1 is $(P \oplus K)$ and K^1 respectively.

$$
\begin{aligned}
S^{r+1} = \ & \{T_0[s_0^r] \oplus T_1[s_5^r] \oplus T_2[s_{10}^r] \oplus T_3[s_{15}^r] \oplus \{k_0^r, k_1^r, k_2^r, k_3^r\} \\
& T_0[s_4^r] \oplus T_1[s_9^r] \oplus T_2[s_{14}^r] \oplus T_3[s_3^r] \oplus \{k_4^r, k_5^r, k_6^r, k_7^r\} \\
& T_0[s_8^r] \oplus T_1[s_{13}^r] \oplus T_2[s_2^r] \oplus T_3[s_7^r] \oplus \{k_8^r, k_9^r, k_{10}^r, k_{11}^r\} \\
& T_0[s_{12}^r] \oplus T_1[s_1^r] \oplus T_2[s_6^r] \oplus T_3[s_{11}^r] \oplus \{k_{12}^r, k_{13}^r, k_{14}^r, k_{11}^r\}\}
\end{aligned}
$$

2.2 Clefia Block Cipher

Clefia is a small lookup table based 128-bit block cipher [21]. It has a generalized Feistel structure. There are three key lengths of 128, 192 and 256 bits defined in the specification [22]. For the 128-bit key based specification the input is of 16 bytes, P_0 to P_{15}, grouped into 4 byte words. For each of the 18 rounds in the cipher, the first and third words are fed into functions F_0 and F_1 respectively. These functions are non-linear in nature. The collective outputs of F_0 and F_1, is known as F functions. These outputs are ex-ored with second and fourth words. In addition to this, at the beginning and end of the encryption the second and the fourth words are whitened.

To create the non-linearity in the F functions two sboxes S_0 and S_1 are used. These sboxes are in the form of 256 byte lookup tables, from each F function they are invoked twice. This makes a total of eight table lookups per round. Thus, for the entire encryption 144 such lookups are needed. Following are the equations of the functions F_0 and F_1:

$$F_0 : \{y_0, y_1, y_2, y_3\} = (S_0[x_0 \oplus k_0], S_1[x_1 \oplus k_1], S_0[x_2 \oplus k_2], S_1[x_3 \oplus k_3]) \cdot M_0$$
$$F_1 : \{y_0, y_1, y_2, y_3\} = (S_1[x_0 \oplus k_0], S_0[x_1 \oplus k_1], S_1[x_2 \oplus k_2], S_0[x_3 \oplus k_3]) \cdot M_1$$

Along with four round keys, k_0, k_1, k_2, k_3 the F functions take four input bytes x_0, x_1, x_2 and x_3. After the sbox lookups, the bytes are diffused by multiplying them with (4×4) matrices M_0 and M_1. Following are the structure of the matrices M_0 and M_1:

$$M_0 = \begin{pmatrix} 1 & 2 & 4 & 6 \\ 2 & 1 & 6 & 4 \\ 4 & 6 & 1 & 2 \\ 6 & 4 & 2 & 1 \end{pmatrix} \quad M_1 = \begin{pmatrix} 1 & 8 & 2 & A \\ 8 & 1 & A & 2 \\ 2 & A & 1 & 8 \\ A & 2 & 8 & 1 \end{pmatrix}$$

The whitening requires four whitening keys WK_0, WK_1, WK_2 and WK_3 along with thirty six round keys $RK_0, \cdots, RK_{35}$. A two step key expansion process is used. Firstly, from the secret key a 128 bit intermediate key L is generated, using a GFN function [14]. Then, the round keys and the whitening keys are generated from this. The structure of Clefia is such that the knowledge of any set of 4 round keys $(RK_{4m}, RK_{4m+1}, RK_{4m+2}, RK_{4m+3})$, where $m \bmod 2 = 0$, is sufficient to revert the key expansion process to obtain the secret key.

2.3   Time Obfuscating Countermeasures

The main principle for cache-timing attacks is the profiling and analysis of timing information returned by the Time-Stamp Counter (TSC). An adversary uses RDTSC instructions to access these TSC for granular timing information. A very common countermeasure to thwart attacks using timing channel is to provide the adversary a modified timing information instead of the real one. The obfuscation of RDTSC [11] can be done in two ways, first by introducing the concept of the real offset, which is the insertion of a real-time delay that stalls RDTSC execution, and then using the apparent offset that is by modification of the return value of the instruction by a small amount. The time is conceptually divided into *epochs* (denoted by E) to calculate these offsets. Epochs vary in length randomly from 2^{e-1} to $2^e - 1$ cycles, where e is denoted as the current level of obfuscation.

The real offset delays the execution of each RDTSC until a random time in the subsequent epoch, and this requires that the TSC register is always read on an epoch boundary. The current execution will be stalled until the end of the current epoch, Whenever an RDTSC instruction is encountered. TSC register will be read, on the epoch boundary. The instruction will be stalled continuously for a random number of cycles in the range $[0, E)$ of the subsequent epoch. The real offset denoted by D_R, is defined by the sum of these two stalls. These modifications result in hindering the malicious processes in user-space from making fine grain timing measurements to a granularity smaller than 2^{e-1}. This makes micro-architectural events undetectable as long as the largest difference between on-chip micro-architectural latencies is less than 2^{e-1}.

2.4   Hardware Performance Counters

Hardware Performance Counters (HPCs) are a set of special purpose registers, which are present in most of the modern microprocessor's Performance Monitoring Unit (PMU). These registers can be programmed to store the number of occurrences of different types of hardware and software events related to the execution of a program, such as cache misses, retired instructions, retired branch instructions, and so on. HPCs were primarily designed to debug the performance of complex software systems, but currently, they are widely used for collecting the run-time behavioral information of software execution. HPCs work along with the event selectors, which specify the hardware events to be monitored and a digital logic which increments a counter based on the occurrence of the specified hardware events. These performance counters can be accessed very fast without affecting or slowing down any software execution. Some of the recent literature [25–27] have used HPCs to dynamically profile a system.

The most useful mode of operation of PMUs is the interrupt-based mode. The main working principle behind this mode of operation is, a system interrupt is generated when a specified event occurs more than or equal to a predefined threshold value or a preset amount of time has elapsed. This mode of operation makes both event-based and time-based sampling possible. High-level libraries like PAPI [18], OProfile [15] provide interfaces to HPCs. Linux perf [17] among them is a widely used new implementation of performance counters support for all Linux 2.6+ based systems, which we can access from user-space. This tool is capable of providing per-process, per-CPU, and system-wide statistical profile. We used this tool for our experimentation purpose. Perf tool is based on Linux perf_event_open() system call, which can be used to profile system in very low granularity. Almost every popular operating systems have HPC-based profilers, though the type and number of hardware events may vary across different Instruction Set Architectures [9].

2.5 Metrics of Evaluation

Several formal security metrics [12] have been proposed in the literature to evaluate various attack methods and compare different cryptographic design with side channel perspective.

Success Rate. A side channel attack is defined as an experiment $Exp_{A_{E_K},L}$, where $A_{E_K,L}$ is an adversary with time complexity τ, memory complexity m and making q queries to the target implementation of the cryptographic algorithm, where K denotes the key space and a leakage model for the key is denoted by L. In the experiment, for any k chosen randomly from K, when the adversary, $A_{E_k,L}$ outputs the guessing vector g, the attack is considered as a success if the corresponding key class denoted as $s = f(k)$ is such that $s \in g$. The success or failure of the attack is indicated by '0' or '1', returned by the experiment. The oth order *success rate* of the side channel attack $A_{E_K,L}$ against the key classes is defined as [12]:

$$Succ^o_{A_{E_K},L}(\tau, m, k) = Pr[Exp_{A_{E_K},L} = 1]$$

Guessing Entropy. The above-mentioned metric for an oth order attack implies the success rate for an attack where the remaining workload is o-key classes. Thus the attacker has a maximum of o-key classes to which the required k may belong. While the success rate for a given order is fixed with respect to the remaining work load, the *guessing entropy* provides a more flexible definition for the remaining work load. It actually measures the average number of key candidates to test after the attack. The Guessing Entropy of the adversary $A_{E_k,L}$ is defined as [12]:

$$GE_{A_{E_K},L}(\tau, m, k) = E[Exp_{A_{E_K},L}]$$

In the next section we analyze a new source of side-channel in the form of `instruction` count using AES as a case study.

3 Information Leakage Due the Event Instruction Count

In this section, we describe the basics of performance monitoring tools which we used to observe the total number of retired instructions during the execution of the encryption process. In this context, we have explored the types of instructions using a more detailed analysis. The tools that we used are *perf* and *PAPI*, which we discuss next.

Perf is a performance analyzing tool in Linux which is available to all user level processes and has been included in the Linux kernel source tree for version 2.6.31 onwards. This user-space tool can be accessed from command line providing many sub-commands. It is capable of statistical profiling of the entire system by instrumenting the hardware performance counters. *perf* supports a list of hardware events to monitor, like cache-misses, branch-misses, cpu-cycles, etc.

For our proposed attack we observe the event *instruction* to analyze the source of side-channel. The total number of instructions executed for a single iteration of an encryption algorithm (say AES) is measured using the following command in perf:

```
perf stat − e instructions ./aes <plaintext>
```

The executable ./aes has a specific secret key and provides an output ciphertext value for a given <plaintext>.

PAPI. One limitation of the perf tool is that we can observe the total number of instruction executed but can not further distinguish between types of instructions. **P**erformance **A**pplication **P**rogramming **I**nterface (PAPI) provides a user with a consistent interface and methodology for monitoring performance counters and can even show counts of finer hardware events like number of control instructions, number of data transfer instructions, etc.

PAPI is more sophisticated than perf tool since it provides a larger number of hardware events for monitoring. The total monitored instruction count, as measured by perf tool, is further divided into specialized hardware events in PAPI interface such as:

– PAPI_BR_INS: This event can be used to measure the total branch instructions executed for an encryption algorithm.
– PAPI_LST_INS: This event can be used to measure the total load/store instructions executed for an encryption algorithm.

The above two events provide us with the handle to analyze and investigate the source of information leakage.

3.1 Correlation of Cache Events to Instruction Counts

Efficient implementations of block ciphers use lookup tables to perform the computations involved in encryption and decryption operations. As described in Sect. 2.1, the look up table accesses during the encryption process are dependent on both the input plaintext and the secret key. The respective memory addresses of these lookup table accesses vary depending on the input plaintext as well as the secret key. The cache timing attacks reported in literature exploit the non-uniformity in access times of these table lookup requests to retrieve the secret information. The non-uniformity of timing observations are typically attributed to cache memory events such as cache hit and miss.

A cache-miss occurs whenever the requested data is not present in the cache. On a cache-miss event, the memory controller needs to fetch the requested data from the main memory and loads it into the cache. Thus on a cache miss, a memory element from the cache memory (which is being replaced by the newly requested data block) is written back in the main memory, followed by loading of a new data element in the particular location of the cache. The decision of which block to be replaced for a new request is partially determined by the virtual to physical address mapping of the data block and partially governed by the cache replacement strategies implemented by the memory controller. Thus the number of instructions executed by the processor has a direct correspondence to the event encountered by the cache memory. Since on a cache miss, the processor requests the memory element to be brought from main memory to the cache; this event is inherently performed with a higher number of instructions. However, in the case of a cache-hit event, the processor will not issue any additional instructions to load the data from the memory as the required data is already present in the cache. This brings us to the conclusion that the cache events will have an alternative effect on the instruction count event.

3.2   Profiling the Instruction Counts

In the previous subsection, we have elaborated that individual cache events have a direct correspondence to the instruction counts. In this subsection, we demonstrate that the average deviation for instruction counts have a similar profile as that of the timing profile constructed for cache timing attacks. We conduct an experiment on the OpenSSL [23] AES encryption. The plaintext byte p_0 is varied randomly from 0 to 255, keeping all other bytes unchanged. Initially, we obtained a timing profile using RDTSC instructions as shown in Fig. 1a for the key byte k_0. Keeping the experimental setup unchanged, next, we observed the instruction profile as in Fig. 1b which plots the deviation from the mean of the total instruction count. The deviation from the average value of the monitored event for each byte of p_0 is shown in Fig. 1. This graph is known to be the characteristics curves for the monitored events. A significant deviation from the average for a particular key byte shows the existence of information leakage. We can easily see that both the characteristics curves for timing and instructions are similar and hence supports our claim that instruction can be used as an alternative to the timing profile.

However, the event cache-misses can also be observed from the HPCs, and thus we had replicated the same experiment replacing instruction count with cache misses, and the cache miss profile is illustrated in Fig. 1c. The event

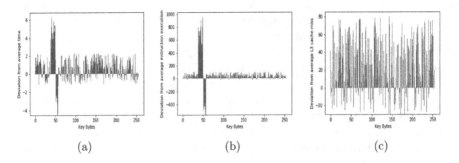

(a)   (b)   (c)

Fig. 1. Deviation of total execution time (a), total instruction counts (b), and total L3 cache-misses (c) during an AES encryption operation from average for different plaintext byte p_0 generated randomly keeping the other bytes unchanged

monitored through PAPI observes the cache misses from all the three levels of cache. This information is highly noisy as in the figure and bears no resemblance to the timing observation. The reason for this behavior is mainly because the cache misses plotted in the figure are for the L3 cache, while we assume the lookup accesses for encryptions are mostly happening from L1 and L2 caches. Liu et al. presented the practicality of a cross-core, cross-VM LLC-cache based *Prime+Probe* attack [10] and showed that a proper eviction algorithm is needed to mount a successful attack, which is difficult in the real noisy environment.

We can conclude from the figures presented in Fig. 1 that instruction count bears a direct correspondence to the timing side channel rather than the event cache misses. In the next section, we will move a step deeper to validate the claims that we have made in this section.

3.3 Analyzing Load/Store Instruction Counts

In the previous subsection, we have observed that the total instruction count generates similar profiles as that of timing attacks. In this section, we further explore the different types of instructions using the tool PAPI to investigate the type of instructions responsible for generating similar profile as timing. The hardware events which are related to the total instructions are given as follows:

1. Data Manipulation Instructions
   - Consists of arithmetic instructions, logical instructions, shift instructions, etc. Provides computational capabilities to the computer by performing different operations on data.
   - The hardware events for monitoring these instructions are PAPI_INT_INS, PAPI_FP_INS, etc., which measure the total integer instructions, total floating point instructions respectively, spawned by the processor. However, the PAPI tool does not provide the handle to observe these hardware events.
2. Data Transfer Instructions
   - Transfer data between memory and registers, register & input or output, and between processes register without changing the data content.
   - PAPI tool gives the handle to monitor these instructions using the hardware event PAPI_LST_INS.
3. Program Control Instructions
   - Direct or change the flow of a program. Mainly consists of all the branch instructions.
   - We can observe these instructions with PAPI tool by using the hardware event PAPI_BR_INS.

We demonstrate another experiment as the previous one to find and validate the actual type of instructions which are mainly responsible for generating the profile same as timing. Here, we observe the events PAPI_BR_INS (type 3) and PAPI_LST_INS (type 2) using the PAPI tool to get the characteristics curve for each event. The cache-miss and cache-hits are related to data transfer instructions as a cache miss will result in loading data into a particular cache line.

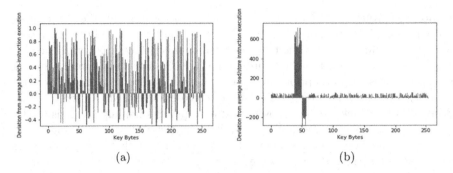

Fig. 2. Deviation of total branch instructions (a) executed and total load/store instructions (b) executed during an AES encryption operation from average for different plaintext byte p_0 generated randomly keeping the other bytes unchanged

We can validate this from Fig. 2b, where we can observe, the profile generated by the event `PAPI_LST_INS` has the same resemblance to the profile of the total instructions. However, Fig. 2a, shows that the profile generated by the branch instructions are not at all similar to that of the total instructions, and hence works as noise in the observations. Figure 2 shows both the characteristic curves for branch instructions and load/store instructions respectively and the behavior of the characteristics plots validates that load and store instructions bear a direct resemblance to the timing characteristics and thus are a potential source of leakages.

In the next section, we present a formal description of the proposed attack methodology, IPA, with a case study on AES block cipher.

4   Instruction Profiling Attack Description

The previous section describes the hardware event `instruction` as a potential side-channel threat because of the resemblance of its profile to that of time. In this section, we give a formal description of our attack methodology that we have used in this paper.

4.1   Instruction Count Analysis for AES

For an AES encryption each table T_0, T_1, T_2, and T_3 is accessed four times in every round for the first nine rounds, while table T_4 is accessed 16 times in the final round. In all, there are 160 table accesses. Following the analysis presented in [19], if n_h is the number of cache hits and n_m is the number of misses, then the total instructions executed during the encryption process can be written as:

$$I = n_h * I_h + n_m * I_m$$
$$= n_h * I_h + (160 - n_h) * I_m$$

Here, I_h is the number of instructions executed when a cache-hit occurs and I_m is the same when a cache-miss occurs. Note, we are focussing on data transfer instructions, as they are the suspected contributors to the leakage. Furthermore, it may be emphasized here that when we perform the actual attacks, we consider the variation of the total instruction count, and not exclusively instructions of any specific type. This improves the practicality of the attack. The difference of instruction counts between two encryption processes can be written as:

$$\Delta I = \Delta n_h * \Delta I_h + \Delta n_m * \Delta I_m$$
$$= \Delta n_h * (\Delta I_h - \Delta I_m)$$

Now, the parameters $\Delta n_h, \Delta I_h$, and ΔI_m depend on the cache-access patterns. The difference in number of hits, Δn_h, occurs because of the differences in accessing the Tables T_0 to T_3 during the encryption for AES. The difference $(\Delta I_h - \Delta I_m)$ depends on both plaintexts and the key, which are inputs to the cipher. So, by monitoring and statistically analyzing the instruction count we can obtain a profile which is dependent on the secret key, and thus potentially determine it by comparing with templates for known keys.

4.2   Description of IPA

In this subsection, we describe the proposed attack methodology taking Bernstein's attack on AES as a case study [13]. The proposed attack consists of three different phases: offline profiling, online attack, and correlation, which are discussed below.

Offline Profiling. In the profiling phase, we generate a set of random plaintext $P = \{p_0, p_1, \cdots, p_l\}$ and submit each of them to the encryption server with a known secret key k. We observe the total instruction count for each encryption, which can be written as $ins(E_{AES}(p_i, k))$. We store the average instruction count for each byte and for each value of that byte in a matrix $I[16][256]$. This can be formally stated as, for each plaintext p_i ($0 \leq i \leq l$) and for each byte ($0 \leq j \leq 15$) we successively compute the elements of the matrix $I[16][256]$ as below:

$$I[j][p_{j,i}] = I[j][p_{j,i}] + ins(E_{AES}(p_i, k))$$

where, $p_{j,i}$ is the jth byte of the ith plaintext. Eventually, we have for $0 \leq j \leq 16$ and $x \in \{0, 1, \cdots, 255\}$

$$I[j][x] = \sum_{\{i | p_{j,i} = x\}} ins(E_{AES}(p_i, k))$$

We then calculate the average number of instructions taken by each byte for each value of that byte using

$$v[j][y] = \frac{I[j][y]}{num[j][y]} - \frac{\sum_j \sum_x I[j][x]}{\sum_j \sum_x num[j][x]}$$

where, $num[16][256]$ stores the total number of measurements per value of a byte value. This phase profiles the encryption server for randomly chosen but known plaintexts and a known key.

Online Attack. In this phase, we again generate a random set of plaintexts $P' = \{p'_0, p'_1, \cdots, p'_l\}$. We follow the same approach as discussed in profiling phase and calculate two matrices I' and num' for the unknown key k'. We then calculate the matrix v' as defined before.

Correlation. In this phase, we correlate the two matrices v and v' obtained from the previous steps. A matrix $c[16][256]$ is created using the following definition for $0 \leq j \leq 15$ and $0 \leq u \leq 255$.

$$c[j][u] = \sum_{w=0}^{255} v[j][w] \cdot v'[j][u \oplus w]$$

The elements of the matrix c are then sorted in decreasing order for each row. The highest correlated key value for a particular byte is the candidate key for that key byte.

The results of the correlation phase will provide us with partial secret key recovery based on the quality of instruction profile for the known key. The full secret key can be recovered by *Brute Force* search for the remaining secret key bytes with very narrow search space.

In the following section, we discuss and validate our claims using experimental results in two different environments, and for two different block ciphers.

5   Results and Discussion

In this section, we focus on the performance and qualitative evaluation of the proposed attack scheme. We demonstrate the instruction profiling attack on two very well-known block ciphers such as AES and Clefia, implementation provided by OpenSSL library. To illustrate the performance of this attack we follow the same principle demonstrated in the work by Bernstein on AES [4] and Rebeiro et al. on Clefia [21]. The attack has been performed in following steps:

- `Instruction Profiling for Known key`: In this phase of the attack, the adversary observes the total instruction counts from the HPCs for an execution of AES/Clefia. Following the steps discussed in the previous section, we construct an instruction profiling table consisting of the cumulative values of the instruction counts suffered by the executable under the assumption of a known key.
- `Instruction Profiling for Unknown key`: In this phase, similar profile for instruction counts are constructed for the same executable, but with the assumption that the key is unknown.

Table 1. Description of experimental setups

1	Setup 1	Intel Core i5-4570 CPU with 3.20 GHz clock frequency, 256 KB of L1 Data Cache, 1 MB L2 Data Cache, 6 MB L3 Data Cache
2	Setup 2	AMD A10-8700P CPU with 1.8 GHz clock frequency, 320 KB of L1 Data Cache, 2 MB of L2 Data Cache

- **Correlating known and unknown key profiles**: In this phase, we chose very popular **Pearson's** correlation metric to determine the shift between the instruction profiles observed over the known and the unknown keys.

It has to be noted that the entire analysis is performed based on a particular byte of the input. So to retrieve the entire key, this analysis has been carried out for each byte of the input. The effect of each byte being independent of each other, this analysis is usually performed concurrently on each byte using a divide and conquer approach which adds to the elegance of the attack and does not add up to the time complexity. In this paper, without loss of generality, we have demonstrated all our experiments on the first secret byte of the key. Also, we have validated all the experiments in two different environments like Intel and AMD systems to get a generalized performance measure of the proposed technique. Table 1 briefly states different setups used in our experiment.

5.1 Performance Evaluation of IPA in Comparision to Classical Timing Attack

In this subsection, we evaluate the efficiency of the proposed attack methodology to the timing attack proposed in [4] using the formalism for Guessing Entropy as discussed in Sect. 2.5. The convergence of the plot to a lower rank for a particular key byte signifies the successful retrieval of that byte. Figure 3a illustrates the

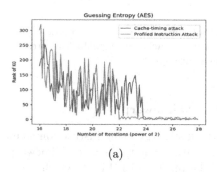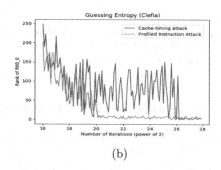

(a)   (b)

Fig. 3. Guessing Entropy plots of proposed attack in comparison to cache-timing attack for setup 1 to predict secret key-byte k_0 of AES (a) and round key-byte $RK0\_0$ of Clefia (b) respectively (Color figure online)

guessing entropy plots of cache-timing attack and profiled instruction attack to predict the secret key byte k_0 of AES on setup 1 (as in Table 1).

We illustrate in Fig. 3a that cache-timing attack needs 2^{24} iterations, whereas, IPA requires 2^{22} iterations of the AES encryption algorithm to correctly predict the secret key byte k_0. Thus IPA needs to profile instruction counts from perf for orders of magnitude lesser than cache-timing attack to correctly retrieve the secret key bytes. Similarly, Fig. 3b shows that, the proposed attack methodology is much faster to predict the round key byte $RK0\_0$ of Clefia encryption by profiling 2^{20} iterations in comparison to 2^{26} iterations of cache-timing attack.

5.2 Performance of Timing Attack in Presence of Time Obfuscation

A popular countermeasure to obfuscate timing channel is to randomize the timing observation from the RDTSC instruction. One such implementation is proposed in [11] named Timewarp. In this paper, we show that the classical timing attack fails to retrieve the correct key bits when timewarp has been implemented. The *blue* lines in Fig. 4 displays the ineffectiveness of the cache-timing attack in the presence of timewarp defense mechanism. The *blue* lines plotted in Fig. 4a and b shows that even after 2^{28} iterations of both the AES and Clefia algorithms, the cache timing attack fails to predict the correct secret key bytes.

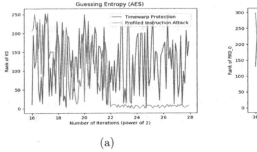 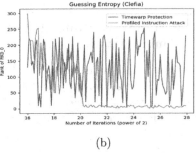

(a)   (b)

Fig. 4. Guessing Entropy plot of proposed attack to predict key-byte k_0 of AES (a) and round key-byte $RK0\_0$ of Clefia (b) in comparison to cache-timing attack in presence of timewarp implementation on setup 1 (Color figure online)

5.3 Performance of IPA in Presence of Timewarp

In this subsection, we perform the same attack strategy using instruction count from HPCs in the presence of the time obfuscation countermeasure: Timewarp, implemented in the system. We elaborate the results with Fig. 4, which shows the competency of our proposed attack method to retrieve the secret key bytes of the encryption algorithm even in the presence of timewarp defense mechanism. The figure demonstrates the results for both AES and Clefia algorithms.

The *yellow* lines in Fig. 4a and b show that the proposed profiled instruction attack can retrieve the secret key bytes even in the presence of timewarp implementation with 2^{20} and 2^{22} iterations of AES and Clefia algorithms respectively. The line plotted with *yellow* in Fig. 4 establishes the superiority of the proposed IPA to cache-timing attack as shown in *blue* plotted line, since it fails to retrieve the secret key-byte k_0 of AES and round key-byte $RK0\_0$ of Clefia respectively in the presence of the defense mechanism.

Retrieving the Secret Keys. Here, we discuss the effectiveness of our proposed attack methodology regarding the extraction of the secret key. We conducted each of the experiments in the presence of timewarp implementation. Here, we present the results for both AES and Clefia and for both the setups.

AES. In this section, we demonstrate the full-key recovery of the AES-128 implementation. As explained in the earlier sections, the entire key recovery can be done in a divide and conquer approach such that, all the key bits can be retrieved simultaneously since there is no mutual dependence. We have performed our experiments over several random key sequences of 128 bits.

Without loss of generality, we illustrate all of our results on a randomly chosen bit sequence. The **bold** bytes in the following results represent the correctly predicted secret key bytes.

Table 2 presents the final retrieved key bytes of AES using the proposed IPA in the presence of timewarp implementation. We can clearly see from Table 2 that the proposed IPA is able to retrieve the correct secret key bytes apart from k_2, k_8 and k_{11} in Setup 1 and k_5 and k_{11} in Setup 2 respectively, which we could later recover with brute-force search with lesser search space. This result shows the high effectiveness of the proposed attack methodology in recovering the secret keys of AES even in the presence of time obfuscation defense.

Table 3 shows the retrieved key bytes (having highest correlation value) of AES for both the setups using the cache-timing attack. We can clearly observe

Table 2. Correctly retrieving secret key of AES using IPA with Timewarp countermeasure

		k_0	k_1	k_2	k_3	k_4	k_5	k_6	k_7	k_8	k_9	k_{10}	k_{11}	k_{12}	k_{13}	k_{14}	k_{15}
	Actual Key	e2	6d	b3	f5	64	42	c6	92	3e	0f	96	b6	a1	52	9d	86
Predicted	Setup 1	**e2**	**6d**	a4	**f5**	**64**	**42**	**c6**	**92**	3a	**0f**	**96**	ae	**a1**	**52**	**9d**	**86**
Key	Setup 2	**e2**	**6d**	**b3**	**f5**	**64**	b8	**c6**	**92**	**3e**	**0f**	**96**	34	**a1**	**52**	**9d**	**86**

Table 3. Fail to retrieve secret key of AES using timing channel with Timewarp countermeasure

		k_0	k_1	k_2	k_3	k_4	k_5	k_6	k_7	k_8	k_9	k_{10}	k_{11}	k_{12}	k_{13}	k_{14}	k_{15}
	Actual Key	e2	6d	b3	f5	64	42	c6	92	3e	0f	96	b6	a1	52	9d	86
Predicted	Setup 1	d9	ea	b3	24	4d	08	6d	64	4f	fc	c2	6d	af	dc	64	88
Key	Setup 2	72	8a	3b	6e	7f	4c	dc	1c	7f	42	af	a6	76	20	7c	b2

Table 4. Fail to retrieve secret key of AES using branch instructions with Timewarp countermeasure

		k_0	k_1	k_2	k_3	k_4	k_5	k_6	k_7	k_8	k_9	k_{10}	k_{11}	k_{12}	k_{13}	k_{14}	k_{15}
	Actual Key	e2	6d	b3	f5	64	42	c6	92	3e	0f	96	b6	a1	52	9d	86
Predicted	Setup 1	57	48	2f	6e	66	d2	16	73	23	82	bc	02	04	01	4f	96
Key	Setup 2	4f	96	64	82	c4	56	a5	8c	16	96	3c	d3	b0	10	cb	dc

from the table that, the cache-timing attack fails to retrieve any of the secret key bytes of AES for both the setups (as expected). Table 4 shows the final retrieved values of the AES secret keys considering branch instructions for profiling. We can easily verify from the table that, for profiling using branch instructions the attack method can not retrieve any of the secret key bytes correctly, which validates our claim that branch instructions do not play any role for the secret information leakage for these class of ciphers. This is also intuitive as block cipher implementations do not have conditional branches, which could leak information about the key. But the interesting part is that there the overall instruction count can still be exploited, because of the reasons as mentioned above to determine the secret key.

Clefia. In this subsection, we demonstrate the full-key recovery of Clefia implementation. We have experimented using different secret keys for Clefia to validate our proposed attack methodology, though for the demonstration purpose the 128-bit secret Clefia key that we considered is 6a 1a 58 e2 12 30 35 e7 fd aa 3b 6e f4 8e d4 5f. The Round Keys corresponding to the given secret key are given in Table 5. Without loss of generality, we show the recovery of round key RK0_0. We perform the experimentation with the assumption of clean cache at the start of every encryption. The correct value of the round keys depend on the previous round keys for Clefia; thus we considered at least 2^{20} iterations so that the correlation value of the predicted key is at least twice the higher than all other probable keys. Like previous results, the bytes written in **bold** face represent the correct key bytes.

Tables 6 and 7 presents the final retrieved values for the $RK0$ round key in Setup 1 and Setup 2 respectively using proposed IPA. Both the table shows the top four candidate for the probable round key bytes. The values in the

Table 5. Round keys for Clefia

RK0	0xbe	0xf8	0xe7	0xae
RK1	0x75	0x61	0xb8	0x30
RK2WK0	0x91	0xe1	0x3e	0x46
RK3WK1	0x34	0x1f	0x5f	0x6f
RK4	0x70	0xc7	0xcc	0xd8
RK5	0xb8	0x90	0xb3	0xec

Table 6. Retrieving round keys RK0 for Clefia in Setup 1 using total instruction count with Timewarp countermeasure

	Top-4 probable RK0 round keys (correlation value)			
RK0_0	**0xbe (250.167)**	0x6b (30.158)	0x7e (31.148)	0xee (23.137)
RK0_1	**0xf8 (260.326)**	0xd1 (34.242)	0xfc (33.682)	0xe8 (31.024)
RK0_2	**0xe7 (255.388)**	0x9f (57.648)	0x31 (56.957)	0x7a (54.515)
RK0_3	**0xae (255.851)**	0x87 (33.130)	0xbe (32.455)	0x41 (30.312)

Table 7. Retrieving round keys RK0 for Clefia in Setup 2 using total instruction count with Timewarp countermeasure

	Top-4 probable RK0 round keys (correlation value)			
RK0_0	**0xbe (260.166)**	0x6b (34.153)	0x7e (31.147)	0xee (30.130)
RK0_1	**0xf8 (265.456)**	0xd1 (33.478)	0xfc (32.147)	0xe8 (31.200)
RK0_2	**0xe7 (247.457)**	0xae (57.124)	0x43 (57.008)	0x95 (54.214)
RK0_3	**0xae (259.567)**	0x87 (47.247)	0xbe (46.211)	0x41 (40.589)

Table 8. Retrieving round keys RK0 for Clefia in Setup 1 using timing attack with Timewarp countermeasure

	Top-4 probable RK0 round keys (correlation value)			
RK0_0	0xce (314.699)	0x65 (289.491)	0x20 (276.232)	0xae (213.873)
RK0_1	0xac (775.449)	0x68 (761.411)	0xbb (603.751)	0xb2 (577.428)
RK0_2	0x56 (453.751)	0xd7 (417.697)	0xc8 (347.645)	0xfe (249.147)
RK0_3	0x37 (598.248)	0xac (548.479)	0x6b (497.268)	0xd5 (457.314)

Table 9. Retrieving round keys RK0 for Clefia in Setup 2 using timing attack with Timewarp countermeasure

	Top-4 probable RK0 round keys (correlation value)			
RK0_0	0xd7 (478.324)	0xba (421.984)	0x2e (394.157)	0xcf (350.496)
RK0_1	0x1e (367.459)	0xf9 (314.496)	0xa1 (296.549)	0xd9 (247.693)
RK0_2	0x8a (724.967)	0x4d (695.349)	0xa0 (645.945)	0x09 (634.235)
RK0_3	0xe4 (676.935)	0x45 (645.453)	0x00 (601.239)	0xda (509.486)

braces are the correlation value of the probable keys. We can easily observe from the tables that the proposed IPA is able to recover all the bytes of the round key $RK0$ for both the setups in the presence of timewarp defense mechanism. The correlation values for the correctly predicted key bytes are much greater than the subsequent candidate keys.

Tables 8 and 9 presents the final retrieved values for the $RK0$ round key in Setup 1 and Setup 2 respectively using cache-timing attack like the previous

Table 10. Retrieving round keys RK0 for Clefia in Setup 1 using branch instructions with Timewarp countermeasure

	Top-4 probable RK0 round keys (correlation value)			
RK0_0	0x2f (869.143)	0xda (649.786)	0x38 (575.880)	0x62 (561.020)
RK0_1	0xde (668.557)	0x3e (615.218)	0xdd (587.463)	0xab (499.769)
RK0_2	0xdd (584.990)	0x6d (512.642)	0xd3 (456.590)	0xaa (448.524)
RK0_3	0xd (703.281)	0x90 (619.583)	0x3f (577.043)	0x3e (552.067)

Table 11. Retrieving round keys RK0 for Clefia in Setup 2 using branch instructions with Timewarp countermeasure

	Top-4 probable RK0 round keys (correlation value)			
RK0_0	0x2f (749.457)	0xda (657.457)	0x38 (602.983)	0x62 (597.237)
RK0_1	0xde (457.698)	0x3e (421.697)	0xdd (403.743)	0xab (347.573)
RK0_2	0xdd (726.147)	0x6d (689.478)	0xd3 (623.951)	0xaa (599.974)
RK0_3	0xd (714.649)	0x90 (687.967)	0x3f (567.697)	0x3e (547.546)

Table 12. Top-2 predicted round keys of Clefia

Round key bytes	Correct key	Predicted key (Setup 1)	Predicted key (Setup 2)
RK0_0	be	**be** (250.548) 6b (33.518)	**be** (331.478) 72 (30.347)
RK0_1	f8	**f8** (236.478) d1 (34.398)	**f8** (347.149) 0e (32.478)
RK0_2	e7	**e7** (259.496) 9f (31.759)	**e7** (312.479) e9 (35.478)
RK0_3	ae	**ae** (249.247) 87 (30.974)	**ae** (299.647) 5e (31.479)
RK1_0	75	**75** (239.479) 6e (29.647)	**75** (357.457) 14 (29.475)
RK1_1	61	**61** (213.795) 0a (37.198)	**61** (378.147) 2d (47.149)
RK1_2	b8	**b8** (297.347) 54 (30.789)	**b8** (249.647) 64 (36.759)
RK1_3	30	**30** (267.126) 7c (31.496)	**30** (432.148) 1f (26.478)
RK2_0 + WK0_0	91	**91** (257.214) d3 (34.189)	**91** (496.487) 77 (31.478)
RK2_1 + WK0_1	e1	**e1** (269.147) b6 (33.698)	**e1** (249.657) 36 (32.768)
RK2_2 + WK0_2	3e	**3e** (259.347) fb (31.478)	**3e** (387.162) 32 (26.479)
RK2_3 + WK0_3	46	**46** (249.347) df (29.678)	**46** (321.338) 3c (47.147)
RK3_0 + WK1_0	34	**34** (298.147) 87 (35.148)	**34** (410.814) cc (43.549)
RK3_1 + WK1_1	1f	**1f** (267.348) 8d (31.987)	**1f** (490.703) c6 (29.647)
RK3_2 + WK1_2	5f	**5f** (249.347) ff (34.158)	**5f** (228.757) f9 (33.679)
RK3_3 + WK1_3	6f	**6f** (219.347) 38 (36.489)	**6f** (353.479) f2 (29.624)
RK4_0	70	**70** (278.498) 1a (32.489)	**70** (228.749) 7e (45.697)
RK4_1	c7	**c7** (264.369) b0 (29.634)	**c7** (249.647) 53 (49.547)
RK4_2	cc	**cc** (249.149) 66 (34.214)	**cc** (349.248) 04 (23.452)
RK4_3	d8	**d8** (278.694) 24 (28.365)	**d8** (324.479) 2e (32.479)
RK5_0	b8	**b8** (324.496) 68 (49.324)	**b8** (367.457) 33 (36.139)
RK5_1	90	**90** (257.354) 83 (31.647)	**90** (246.479) e6 (29.498)
RK5_2	b3	**b3** (264.236) 2c (26.498)	**b3** (226.714) bf (36.249)
RK5_3	ec	**ec** (321.698) 43 (45.268)	**ec** (314.789) f2 (33.149)

results. We can observe from the tables that cache-timing attack fails to recover the round key $RK0$ for both the setups in the presence of timewarp defense mechanism. The correlation values for the top four candidate keys are very close to each other, in both the setups, thereby creating the difficulty in predicting the actual secret key correctly. Similarly, Tables 10 and 11 presents the final retrieved values for the $RK0$ round key in Setup 1 and Setup 2 respectively by profiling through branch instructions, which shows the expected inefficiency in retrieving the secret keys using branch instructions.

Table 12 shows the retrieval of all the Clefia round keys using IPA in the presence of timewarp defense mechanism to show the efficiency of the proposed attack. The table shows the `top two candidate key` with respective correlation in the braces for both the setups. We observe that full recovery of the secret key is possible with the proposed IPA for Clefia encryption.

5.4   Success Rate of the Proposed IPA

The success rate for a side-channel attack is represented as the fraction of the secret key bytes recovered. For any successful side-channel attack, success rate increases with the number of iterations of the monitored encryption algorithm. Here, we present the success rate of the proposed IPA with the cache timing attack in the absence of timewarp defense mechanism to show the effectiveness of the IPA in retrieving the secret key bytes with lesser time. Figure 5 shows the success rate of both IPA and cache-timing attack in Setup 1. The figures represent the part of the secret keys retrieved successfully with the increase in the number of iterations. Figure 5a and b show the success rate in retrieving the secret key bytes of AES and Clefia. The lines plotted with *blue* color represent the success rate of the proposed IPA, and the success rate of classical cache-timing attacks is represented by *yellow* colored lines. It is to be noted that the *yellow* line is always below the *blue* line for both AES and Clefia, signifying the better success rate of IPA than the classical timing attacks for both the ciphers.

In the next section, we discuss the practicality of the proposed attack methodology in different environments along with a possible countermeasure.

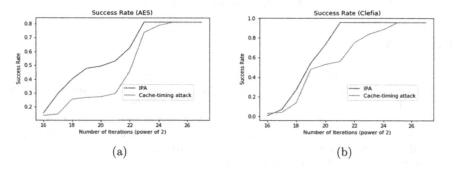

Fig. 5. Comparison of Success rate of IPA with cache-timing attack in Setup 1 in predicting secret key-bytes of AES (a) and Clefia (b) respectively (Color figure online)

6   Practicality of the Proposed Attack

The proposed attack methodology discussed in this paper is a primitive implementation, which does not require the assumption of shared cache memory between different users. This gives the attack an advantage over other types of attacks like Prime + Probe attacks. There are inherent protections in most of the modern processor architectures, like Intel SGX, which guard against cache trace based attacks using secure enclaves. However, the event instruction count reflects the effect of cache access patterns in spite of this security. We aim to explore these architectures in our future study.

A possible countermeasure for this attack is the implementation of block ciphers without requiring any table lookups. There are some modern cryptographic libraries like NaCl [5], which provide us the block cipher implementations having no table accesses. This provides an interesting approach to mitigate the proposed attack methodology.

7   Conclusion

In this paper, we have investigated a new side-channel leakage through the HPC event *instructions* and successfully designed an attack methodology, namely Instruction Profiling Attack (IPA). We demonstrate that surprisingly even total instruction counts can be utilized to perform side channel analysis on block ciphers, which because of the absence of conditional branch instructions were not targeted previously for instruction based attacks. In fact, we demonstrate that the proposed IPA has better performance than classical cache- timing attacks, and are better side channels than the customary timing information. We also attempt to bring out an implication of the attack, that defenses against timing attacks which are based on time fuzzing, will not be able to prevent the proposed IPA. We validate our claims with results for two different environments, namely Intel and AMD. The paper proves once again that the cache memory is an important artifact for side channel leakage; rather than trying to obfuscate channels like timing it is more important to design micro- architectures with security-awareness in the early phase of the design cycle.

References

1. Aciiçmez, O.: Yet another microarchitectural attack: : exploiting I-cache. In: Proceedings of the 2007 ACM Workshop on Computer Security Architecture, CSAW 2007, Fairfax, VA, USA, 2 November 2007, pp. 11–18 (2007)
2. Aciiçmez, O., Schindler, W., Koç, Ç.K.: Cache based remote timing attack on the AES. In: Abe, M. (ed.) CT-RSA 2007. LNCS, vol. 4377, pp. 271–286. Springer, Heidelberg (2006). https://doi.org/10.1007/11967668_18
3. Barreto, P.S.L.M.: The AES block cipher in C++
4. Bernstein, D.J.: Cache-timing attacks on AES. Techical report (2005)

5. Bernstein, D.J., Lange, T., Schwabe, P.: The security impact of a new cryptographic library. In: Hevia, A., Neven, G. (eds.) LATINCRYPT 2012. LNCS, vol. 7533, pp. 159–176. Springer, Heidelberg (2012). https://doi.org/10.1007/978-3-642-33481-8_9

6. Bhattacharya, S., Rebeiro, C., Mukhopadhyay, D.: Unraveling timewarp: what all the fuzz is about? In: HASP 2013, The Second Workshop on Hardware and Architectural Support for Security and Privacy, Tel-Aviv, Israel, 23–24 June 2013, p. 8 (2013)

7. Federal Information Processing Standards Publication 197. Announcing the Advanced Encryption Standard (AES)

8. Granger, R., Page, D., Stam, M.: Hardware and software normal basis arithmetic for pairing-based cryptography in characteristic three. IEEE Trans. Comput. **54**(7), 852–860 (2005)

9. Intel 64 and IA-32 Architectures Software Developer's Manual Volume 3 (3A, 3B, 3C & 3D): System Programming Guide (2010)

10. Liu, F., Yarom, Y., Ge, Q., Heiser, G., Lee, R.B.: Last-level cache side-channel attacks are practical. In: 2015 IEEE Symposium on Security and Privacy, SP 2015, San Jose, CA, USA, 17–21 May 2015, pp. 605–622 (2015)

11. Martin, R., Demme, J., Sethumadhavan, S.: Timewarp: rethinking timekeeping and performance monitoring mechanisms to mitigate side-channel attacks. In: 39th International Symposium on Computer Architecture (ISCA 2012), Portland, OR, USA, 9–13 June 2012, pp. 118–129 (2012)

12. Mukhopadhyay, D., Chakraborty, R.S.: Hardware Security: Design, Threats, and Safeguards, 1st edn. Chapman & Hall/CRC, Boca Raton (2014)

13. Neve, M., Seifert, J., Wang, Z.: A refined look at Bernstein's AES side-channel analysis. In: Proceedings of the 2006 ACM Symposium on Information, Computer and Communications Security, ASIACCS 2006, Taipei, Taiwan, 21–24 March 2006, p. 369 (2006)

14. Nyberg, K.: Generalized Feistel networks. In: Kim, K., Matsumoto, T. (eds.) ASIACRYPT 1996. LNCS, vol. 1163, pp. 91–104. Springer, Heidelberg (1996). https://doi.org/10.1007/BFb0034838

15. OProfile (2015). http://oprofile.sourceforge.net/news/

16. Osvik, D.A., Shamir, A., Tromer, E.: Cache attacks and countermeasures: the case of AES. In: Pointcheval, D. (ed.) CT-RSA 2006. LNCS, vol. 3860, pp. 1–20. Springer, Heidelberg (2006). https://doi.org/10.1007/11605805_1

17. perf: Linux profiling with performance counters (2015)

18. Performance Application Programming Interface (2016)

19. Rebeiro, C., Mondal, M., Mukhopadhyay, D.: Pinpointing cache timing attacks on AES. In: VLSI Design 2010: 23rd International Conference on VLSI Design, 9th International Conference on Embedded Systems, Bangalore, India, 3–7 January 2010, pp. 306–311 (2010)

20. Rebeiro, C., Mukhopadhyay, D., Bhattacharya, S.: Timing Channels in Cryptography: A Micro-Architectural Perspective. Springer Publishing Company, Incorporated, Cham (2014). https://doi.org/10.1007/978-3-319-12370-7

21. Rebeiro, C., Mukhopadhyay, D., Takahashi, J., Fukunaga, T.: Cache timing attacks on clefia. In: Roy, B., Sendrier, N. (eds.) INDOCRYPT 2009. LNCS, vol. 5922, pp. 104–118. Springer, Heidelberg (2009). https://doi.org/10.1007/978-3-642-10628-6_7

22. Sony Corporation: The 128-bit blockcipher Clefia: Algorithm specification (2007)

23. The OpenSSL Project. http://www.openssl.org

24. Unix Stack Exchange. https://unix.stackexchange.com/questions/2126/why-is-the re-a-big-delay-after-entering-a-wrong-password
25. Wang, X., Karri, R.: Numchecker: detecting kernel control-flow modifying rootkits by using hardware performance counters. In: The 50th Annual Design Automation Conference 2013, DAC 2013, Austin, TX, USA, 29 May–07 June 2013, pp. 79:1–79:7 (2013)
26. Wang, X., Karri, R.: Reusing hardware performance counters to detect and identify kernel control-flow modifying rootkits. IEEE Trans. CAD Integr. Circuits Syst. **35**(3), 485–498 (2016)
27. Wang, X., Konstantinou, C., Maniatakos, M., Karri, R.: Confirm: detecting firmware modifications in embedded systems using hardware performance counters. In: Proceedings of the IEEE/ACM International Conference on Computer-Aided Design, ICCAD 2015, Austin, TX, USA, 2–6 November 2015, pp. 544–551 (2015)

Hey Doc, Is This Normal?: Exploring Android Permissions in the Post Marshmallow Era

Efthimios Alepis and Constantinos Patsakis$^{(\boxtimes)}$

Department of Informatics, University of Piraeus,
80, Karaoli & Dimitriou, 18534 Piraeus, Greece
kpatsak@unipi.gr

Abstract. Billions of hand-held devices are used globally in daily basis. The main reasons for their wide adoption can be considered the introduction of various sensors that have completely reshaped user interaction standards as well as the development of myriads of applications that provide various services to the users. Due to the daily usage of these applications and the wide information that can be deduced from the sensors, a lot of private and sensitive information can be leaked unless access control is applied to the installed applications. In Android, this control was applied upon installation of each application, when the user would be asked to grant the requested permissions. However, this policy has changed in the last versions, allowing users to revoke permissions and grant "dangerous" permissions on demand. In this work we illustrate several flaws in the new permission architecture that can be exploited to gain more access to sensitive user data than what the user considers to have granted.

Keywords: Android · Security · Permissions · Privacy

1 Introduction

Android is the most widely used platform for hand-held devices having a huge user base of the scale of millions. While the core of Android is Linux, the platform has been radically redefined by Google to meet the specific needs of the users in devices with constrained resources. Android as well as iOS are less than a decade old and entered the market when other operating systems were monopolizing. Nonetheless, they quickly conquered the market, currently owning more than 90% of the market share. This quick shift in the market can be attributed to a big transformation in the functionality that both operating systems allowed: the installation of third party applications. Companies and independent developers quickly started developing mobile applications for both these platforms exploiting the new capabilities that these devices are equipped with, creating a new ecosystem.

Evidently, over the last years of smartphone development, modern mobile devices needed more fine-grained security models for their users since very sensitive data were handled, other can be extracted from the embedded sensors

© Springer International Publishing AG 2017
S.S. Ali et al. (Eds.): SPACE 2017, LNCS 10662, pp. 53–73, 2017.
https://doi.org/10.1007/978-3-319-71501-8_4

and most importantly, because these devices are being constantly used in most peoples' everyday life. As a result, users who were inexperienced with computers, as well as children and elderly are nowadays smartphone users. Therefore, users are nowadays more prone to experience security and privacy threats. To address these issues, a security model that would inform users about permission settings only once during application installation has been considered as insufficient. Unfortunately, the main reason for this was the fact that many users did not take these permission settings into consideration and this has often resulted in them being misled or even deceived. An improved model that would handle security and privacy threats during runtime was first introduced in iOS 7 from Apple, and in Android Marshmallow from Google. The intention of these models is to provide the required information and request permissions during applications' runtime once the application needs to access them. Therefore, an application must not only declare which permissions are necessary for its incorporated functions, but users would also have a broader view of how their sensitive data are handled whenever and even each time these data were handled by the application. Hence, access to the respective resources and sensors has the explicit permissions granted by the user.

Having used the new security model of Android, developers have significantly changed their programming logic, since a large amount of smartphone applications dependends on the granted permissions to interact with the operating system's environment. As a next step after the incorporation of the new permission "logic", an evaluation of the first results of the new model must follow to determine whether the applications' behavior has been improved compared with the older model. In this sense, the authors of this paper have developed some smartphone applications that would be used as testbeds for the new security model.

Main Contributions: Recently, Android has received a lot of criticism due to the revelation of severe security issues e.g. breaking full disk encryption[1] or even exploiting vulnerabilities on Android devices built on Qualcomm to gain root privileges[2]. Our goal in this work is to go a step before the implementation, and discuss the actual permission model of Android, which essentially describes how sensitive information is handled by applications. In this regard, the contributions of this work are twofold. First we provide a detailed description of Android's permission model, analysing the needs that led to its introduction. Further to just stating the new features of the model, we proceed to an in depth analysis of problems we have identified and others that are augmented. To validate our claims we have developed a number of test applications some of which are used for comparison, while others expose serious security and privacy issues.

Road Map: The rest of this work is structured as follows. We first provide a brief overview of Android platform and related work in Sect. 2. Then, in Sect. 3 we detail the new permission model in Android and how it is applied. Section 4

---

[1] http://bits-please.blogspot.gr/2016/06/extracting-qualcomms-keymaster-keys.html.
[2] http://blog.checkpoint.com/2016/08/07/quadrooter/.

highlighs several fallacies of the model and the risks that users are exposed to. Section 5 discusses remedies for the security issues that are presented in this work. Finally, the article concludes with some remarks and ideas for future work.

2 Related Work

Each application in Android is installed through an APK file which is a compressed package that contains everything that the application needs to be executed, such as the bytecode, icons and metadata. This APK is installed by invoking the Package Manager. The official and most widely used method is through *Google Play*, an application which connects to Google's application market and downloads the requested applications enabling also the indexing and a reputation system. Users may also invoke the Package Installer by downloading or copying an application to the phone storage and asking Android to open it. Finally, advanced users may use Android Debug Bridge (ADB) a tool, provided by Google which provides additional functionalities. If a user selects to install an application using the first scenarios, he will be presented with a screen which notifies him which permissions have to be granted in order to run in his device. Up to Marshmallow, the user was forced to either accept the proposed permissions and install the application, or to reject them, thus canceling the installation process. Therefore, permissions were given once to application and they could not be revoked, unless the user decided to uninstall the application.

This "take-it-or-leave-it" policy was also present in iOS, nevertheless, modding communities introduced fine grained policies in rooted devices[3,4]. In this case, users were allowed to explicitly revoke access on installed applications, nonetheless, this quite often affected the stability of these apps. Therefore, while users gained more control of their devices and data, it reduced the quality of user experience.

When Android and iOS first introduced their application markets, developers were not requesting a lot of permissions. However, they soon realised that the capabilities of these devices, such as location awareness, access to contact lists, usage patterns etc. could provide them a great wealth of information that could be exploited and therefore monetized, and became greedy. In many occasions, simple applications require absurd permissions only to harvest user data [32]. While in some instances this can lead to malicious acts, unfortunately it has paralyzed user reflexes towards such requests. As shown by Felt et al. [22], the continuous increase of application permission requests for access to sensitive permissions or unrelated to their core functionality, made users to ignore Android warnings and install them without understanding to what risks they expose themselves, a result which was also verified in other cases [7,27].

While Android permission model is considered secure, from time to time, several issues have appeared. For instance, Davi et al. [13] showed that they could escalate the access privileges of applications by performing calls to other

---

[3] http://repo.xposed.info/module/biz.bokhorst.xprivacy.

[4] http://www.cyanogenmod.org/.

applications which had already granted the respective privileges. Since Android does not perform checks on transitive calls, they managed to create a chain of calls between applications, so that the combination of the applications gains the necessary privileges. In the scenario of Davi et al. a malicious application exploits the vulnerabilities of a legitimate application to execute the malicious code. Since the malicious application was not initially granted the privileges to perform an action, it is most likely to evade the respective checks and continue its nefarious acts. Orthacker et al. [29] extended the aforementioned scenario to show that an adversary could use *permission spreading*, that is split the necessary privileges to different applications, and through intercommunication launch the attack. Similar approaches regarding app collusion and spread of permissions have been reported by Dimitriadis et al. [15] as well as Blasco and Chen [10].

On top of the aforementioned issues, Grace et al. [25] found that many applications would use plain HTTP to download code and execute it on client's device. While insecure, this method is often seen in Android applications [31], allowing an adversary to alter the downloaded file during its transfer. This is amplified by an inherent threat to all Android applications: The access level to a resource is granted *per application* and *not per component*. Theoretically, this does not raise any important issue, since all the components are handled by the same entity, the developer who created the app. However, as discussed in the following paragraphs, this is not always the case.

In general, ads have started becoming more and more greedy about users' information. In fact, the more installations an app has, the more privacy invasive it tends to be [12]. Apart from requests to get user's location, ad libraries, may perform WiFi scans to determine users' location, scan whether the user has accounts in social networks or even scan the device to find which applications have been installed [11]. Recently, more advanced ad libraries manage to link devices by playing inaudible sounds from one device and collecting them from the microphone of mobile devices that use applications where such an ad library has been embedded [24].

Yang et al. [35] attempted to crowdsource users' permissions preferences in a semi-automatic way. Their application, Droidganger, executed an application monitoring its behavior, and gradually revoked permissions to determine problems with its execution. When issues appeared, the user would be prompted to comment them, and the results were aggregated in a central server. This approach could potentially remove unnecessary permissions from applications which requested far more permissions than they actually needed, which accounts for a huge market share and whose acts could be characterised as malicious [11,34]. To decrease user interaction, automated approaches have been introduced such as the work of Bartel et al. [9] and Tsiakos' and Patsakis' [33], with the latter aiming towards advertisement networks.

Marshmallow, introduced many changes in Android, many of which are focused on the security and privacy of the platform. The new version has drastically decreased the number of dangerous permissions, which had reached more than 260 in API level 22. Some of these permissions are illustrated in Table 1.

Contrary to the line of previous versions where, as highlighted by Wei et al. [34], the permissions were made to satisfy vendors, the new permission model is focused towards developers. Nonetheless, as it is going to be discussed, by no means the new model has become more fine grained, and more importantly, it cannot be considered transparent. Nonetheless, starting from Marshmallow, the user can revoke permissions or grant them upon request to further refine access rights.

Table 1. Some of the Android permissions in API level 22.

Permissions		
ACCESS_ALL_EXTERNAL_STORAGE	ACCESS_LOCATION_EXTRA_COMMANDS	ACCOUNT_MANAGER
ACCESS_CACHE_FILESYSTEM	ACCESS_MOCK_LOCATION	ALLOW_ANY_CODEC_FOR_PLAYBACK
ACCESS_CHECKIN_PROPERTIES	ACCESS_MTP	ASEC_ACCESS
ACCESS_COARSE_LOCATION	ACCESS_NETWORK_CONDITIONS	ASEC_CREATE
ACCESS_CONTENT_PROVIDERS_EXTERNALLY	ACCESS_NETWORK_STATE	ASEC_DESTROY
ACCESS_DRM_CERTIFICATES	ACCESS_NOTIFICATIONS	ASEC_MOUNT_UNMOUNT
ACCESS_FINE_LOCATION	ACCESS_PDB_STATE	ASEC_RENAME
ACCESS_FM_RADIO	ACCESS_SURFACE_FLINGER	AUTHENTICATE_ACCOUNTS
ACCESS_INPUT_FLINGER	ACCESS_WIFI_STATE	BACKUP
ACCESS_KEYGUARD_SECURE_STORAGE	ACCESS_WIMAX_STATE	BATTERY_STATS

Prior to Android Marshmallow, when a user decided to install an application, the first check that would be performed was about its permissions. Should the user accept the requested permissions, the application is installed. However, since Marshmallow, the installation of the application is made regardless of the required permissions. Then, whenever the user opens an application which requires dangerous permissions, pop up windows are going to request them, allowing the user to select which ones should be granted. Therefore, the user has more control over his phone, as he can selectively grant permissions. Moreover, the user is able to revoke permissions after the installation.

To provide more fine-grained permissions, Jeon et al. [26] developed some tools which can be used to detail which permissions are granted to an application and which are not, in order to make them comply with the principle of least "permissions". For more on Android the old permission model and security, the interested reader may refer to [19,20]

3   The New Permission Model

From the very beginning of Android, in 2007, until version 6 (all API levels until 23), application permissions were accepted by users in the first steps of their installation. With this move, Google wanted to achieve two goals: firstly to inform the user which operations an application may perform and secondly to mitigate possible attacks by limiting the application access. The permission model provided a "take-it-or-leave-it" approach as users would either accept the requested permissions and install the application, or the application would not be installed. After many years of using this approach, the Android team brought a new model in October 5, 2015, with the code name Marshmallow. As Google states, Android 6.0 (API level 23) includes a variety of system changes and API behavior changes, improving resource allocation, stability and performance. Nevertheless, probably the most notable change, is the complete redesign of its permission model, which is listed on the top of Google's list of changes as "Runtime Permissions". According to Google's developer site[5], Android 6.0 introduces a new permission model, where users can directly manage app permissions at runtime. It is also noted that this model gives users improved visibility and control over application permissions.

The new permission model allows users to selectively revoke dangerous permissions, Fig. 1a, and facilitates users' privacy control by grouping applications according to granted permissions, Fig. 1b. Moreover, the applications are not granted dangerous permissions during installation, but on runtime, even if they are included in the system image. The new model mandates all apps to check for and request permissions at runtime.

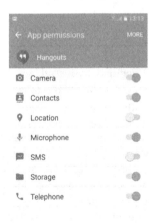

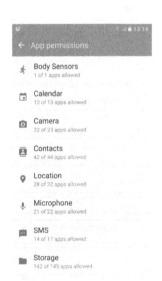

(a) Changing permissions after installation.

(b) An overview of the granted permissions.

Fig. 1. Managing permissions in Marshmallow.

Permissions in Android are characterized according to the risk implied when granting them into the following four categories:

---

[5] https://developer.Android.com/about/versions/marshmallow/Android-6.0-changes.html.

- Normal: These permissions can be regarded as the ones that expose the user or the system to the least possible risk when granted. Therefore, the system automatically grants them at installation, without asking for the user's explicit approval.
- Dangerous: In this category the risk is higher as granting these permissions can expose private user data or allow control of the device. Since these permissions imply a potential high risk, explicit user approval is required to be granted. Typical such permissions include access to the microphone, contacts, camera etc.
- To allow interoperability, Android application may exchange information through inter component communication (ICC). Nonetheless, to guarantee that specific applications are granted some permissions, Google has introduced the *signature* permission. Therefore, Android grants access to an application only if the requesting application is signed with the same certificate as the application that declared the permission without user notification.
- In order to cater for the needs of applications that are supplied by the manufacturers, Google has introduced the *signatureOrSystem* permission. This permission is granted only to apps that reside in the Android system image or that are signed with the same certificate as the application that declared the permission. Such privileges allow apps to reboot a device or to allow an application to clear the caches of all installed applications on the device. Essentially, this permission is designed for manufacturers.

Apart from the above four main categories, several additional flags can be used to further characterise the protection level of a permission such as *privileged*, also known as *system*, used when multiple vendors have applications built in to a system image to determine who can use what, *installer*, *verifier* for applications which install and verify packages respectively etc. For a detailed list of these permissions and where they apply, the interested reader may refer to [6]. Moreover, since many unprotected APIs were found in previous versions [28], additional protection mechanisms have been integrated for many intents.

According to Google[6], the categorization of permissions to normal and dangerous implies the existence of a *direct* privacy risk. It is worth noticing that prior to Marshmallow, Android had numerous permissions, part of them shown in Table 1, flooding the user with information. This fact was often exploited by developers who for instance would request many permissions which would not actually be used, so that the user would not be able see in the landing screen the dangerous ones on top. The normal permissions since API 23 are illustrated in Table 2.

To counter such issues, Android further grouped "dangerous" permissions according to their access level in terms of functionality, as it is illustrated in Fig. 2. These groups facilitate users, as they group permissions according to a specific functionality, e.g. "Manage SMS", instead of granting permissions to each functionality independently e.g. receive, read, send SMS, the user grants permissions per application to a group of permissions, enabling full access to the

---

[6] https://developer.Android.com/training/permissions/requesting.html.

Table 2. Normal permissions in Marshmallow.

Permissions	
ACCESS_LOCATION_EXTRA_COMMANDS	NFC
ACCESS_NETWORK_STATE	READ_SYNC_SETTINGS
ACCESS_NOTIFICATION_POLICY	READ_SYNC_STATS
ACCESS_WIFI_STATE	RECEIVE_BOOT_COMPLETED
BLUETOOTH	REORDER_TASKS
BLUETOOTH_ADMIN	REQUEST_IGNORE_BATTERY_OPTIMIZATIONS
BROADCAST_STICKY	REQUEST_INSTALL_PACKAGES
CHANGE_NETWORK_STATE	SET_ALARM
CHANGE_WIFI_MULTICAST_STATE	SET_TIME_ZONE
CHANGE_WIFI_STATE	SET_WALLPAPER
DISABLE_KEYGUARD	SET_WALLPAPER_HINTS
EXPAND_STATUS_BAR	TRANSMIT_IR
GET_PACKAGE_SIZE	UNINSTALL_SHORTCUT
INSTALL_SHORTCUT	USE_FINGERPRINT
INTERNET	VIBRATE
KILL_BACKGROUND_PROCESSES	WAKE_LOCK
MODIFY_AUDIO_SETTINGS	WRITE_SYNC_SETTINGS

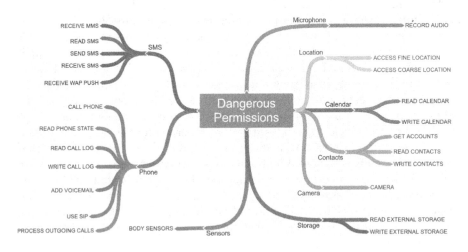

Fig. 2. Dangerous permissions groups.

rest of the permissions in the same group. Certainly, this approach significantly improves user interaction and experience as users have to respond to significantly less notifications.

Prominently, Google introduced several features in the permission model which are not apparent from the description above in order to further protect users' privacy. For instance, since Marshmallow, developers are expected to request ACCESS_FINE_LOCATION or ACCESS_COARSE_LOCATION permissions to access hardware identifiers of nearby external devices via Bluetooth and Wi-Fi scans. This change was introduced to prevent location disclosure, as many applications were trying to exploit this knowledge to correlate this information with the location of already known devices. However, hardware identifiers can still be still be extracted to locate users, e.g. as shown in [3] unique hardware identifiers can be extracted by the use of WiFi-P2P.

Moreover, to protect users from phishing and ransomware attacks, since Marshmallow, an app has to explicitly request the permission to overlay itself over others. In fact, to indicate the criticality of granting such a permission, Android breaks the usual user interface redirecting the user to another settings menu to grant this permission, with indicative screens. Nonetheless, this protection mechanism is rather flawed as it will be discussed later on.

The enforcement of the permission model is a multi-step process, but before we describe this process we have to highlight that each application in Android is considered as a different user, hence it is granted a different UID. The reason for this choice is in order to prevent applications from accessing the data and private resources of the other installed apps. Once an app performs a call to the framework API, this is accompanied by the UID of the app. The framework then checks whether it has been assigned upon installation in the AndroidManifest.xml file. Should this be the case, Android checks the permission level of this call (normal, dangerous etc.). If it is a normal permission it is granted and access to the API is provided. However, if it is a dangerous permission, the system will query whether access to this resource has been granted by the user and accordingly allow or deny the access. Finally, if the permission is signature or signatureOrSystem, then the system will have to check the signature of the app with the requesting UID before granting the corresponding access.

4   Drawbacks of the New Model

The aforementioned permission categorization may seem quite secure, improving the previous model, as sensitive information seems to be protected and selectively disclosed. Nonetheless, the implementation of the new model introduces several drawbacks which are going to be discussed in the following paragraphs.

4.1   Privilege Escalation via Intents

As already discussed, Kywe et al. [28] identified plenty of unsecured APIs that could be taken advantage of allowing applications without permissions to exploit them therefore, the new versions of Android have introduced security mechanisms to address these issues. However, the authors have identified and responsibly disclosed to Google, that there are even more issues which rise from intents. For instance, in order to access the microphone, the dangerous permission "RECORD_AUDIO" needs to be granted, nonetheless, an adversary can use an intent to launch the Speech-to-Text API and automatically convert all microphone input to text without requesting any permission. The latter can be used in combination with the Text-to-Speech API or simple audio to execute arbitrary commands on the device via intents to Voice Assistants [2], extending and automating the attacks of [14].

4.2   Transparency and Lack of Control

Inarguably, both user interaction and user experience are improved due to the introduction of the new permission model. Nonetheless, we argue that the current implementation lacks in terms of transparency and fails to provide fine grained control to its full potential. Additionally, we argue that the process of granting permissions on runtime does not necessarily improve the previous state where permissions were granted prior installation.

To validate our claims we experimented by developing PoC applications which enable us to compare the previous approaches to the current one. First, we start the comparison with the previous model trying to indicate the actual changes during the installation and execution of some applications. To this end, we developed an application which requests a small number of security permissions, more precisely, permissions to receive, read and send SMSs, and also the permissions to access the location of the device through fine and coarse location permissions. For the evaluation, we created two versions of the application, one that is targeted to API level 22 (Android 5.1) and one that is targeted to API level 23 (Android 6).

In API level 22, during the installation process, the user is prompted to accept all the permissions in order to proceed with the installation, Fig. 3a.

(a) Application installation.   (b) Application running.   (c) Application info.

Fig. 3. API level 22.

Having successfully acquired the device's location, the application runs smoothly, Fig. 3b, and the user can later review the permissions that are granted to the application, Fig. 3c, without of course being able to revoke them.

Similarly, we perform the same actions using API level 23, which incorporates the new permission model. Notably, Fig. 3a shows that there is no permission required to proceed with the application's installation. Even more interestingly, a user facing this screen is informed that "This application does not require any special access". This information is already misleading since the application really requires some "dangerous" permissions, however they are going to be requested after the installation, to be discussed afterwards. Figures 4b and c illustrate the first launch of the application where two groups of permissions are deliberately requested. Perhaps the most important thing to notice in this process is the fact that these two permissions have not been requested by the application when they were really needed during runtime, but surprisingly during an unrelated to them event, namely the application's first launch. Apparently, granting permissions is not performed on usage request, but when the application is executed. As illustrated in screenshot of Fig. 3b, the mobile application uses both location and SMS features in the corresponding events of two buttons. The application successfully acquires the devices exact location, nevertheless, no popup window or alert message informs the user that location service is being used by the application. Finally, Fig. 4d illustrates the application's settings, in the application manager.

(a) Application in- (b) Granting loca- (c) Granting access (d) Application info.
stallation.   tion pemission.   to SMS.

Fig. 4. API level 23.

Having carefully examined the above two use cases where the same application is running targeted to API level 22 and 23 respectively, some important issues arise. Firstly, newer applications, targeted to APIs equal to or greater than

23 do not inform users properly about permissions during installation. Clearly, the information that users receive during installation that all applications do not require any special access can be considered as either unnecessary or misleading. Moreover, the timing of appearance of the alert requesting a specific permission is also misleading. One would expect that a permission notification would appear once an application tries to access a resource related to that permission. However, applications may ask access to dangerous permission groups on unrelated occasions, when there is no actual need for using them. In our case, this was made during the first launch of the application. Afterwards, the application was able to access these dangerous resources, namely SMSs and Location services, at any time, even if the application was restarted.

This behaviour is rather important for the user. More precisely, the user is constantly being "nagged" to accept a permission, but when it is accepted he will not be prompted again. The naive user for example would therefore accept the permission permanently, whereas, if he was prompted again, even if he had accepted once, he would occasionally revoke this permission. A typical example can be considered in location-aware applications where users would like to selectively disclose their location to the service provider and not to perform a long sequence of actions to revoke such a permission.

Going a step further, one can claim that the permission model can become even more misleading in the cases of the dangerous permission groups. For instance, we discuss the use case where a user installs an application that requires some access to the phone's capabilities. When the app requests to read the phone state (permission READ_PHONE_STATE); a widely used permission, the user will be asked to grant access for this request. Nonetheless, after accepting the permission, the user has granted, indirectly, more access to the application, as the application is actually granted full access to the dangerous "phone" permission group. Therefore, the application may read and change the call history (READ_CALL_LOG, WRITE_CALL_LOG), or even make phone calls (CALL_PHONE) without any user notification. Actually the permission request is stated as "*Allow* **ApplicationName** *to make and manage phone calls?*". The statement is quite vague, so it may frighten the user, nevertheless, as users are accustomed to such requests most likely they will accept. Nonetheless, the user cannot determine which of the actual permissions has been granted to the application and cannot revoke the permission to a single member of the category.

The confusion of the user may even be greater than the aforementioned notification, as the new permission categorization does not improve transparency. During installation users are not allowed to see what actual permissions are going to be requested by an application. More interestingly, since many permissions of Table 1 have not been categorized as dangerous, the user is not prompted about them and they are automatically granted on installation. More on these issues are discussed in a following section.

An important factor that was overseen in this radical shift is that users would be accustomed to use the new permission model. Therefore, a user is expected to always have the control of dangerous permissions during runtime, regardless of what he has done in the installation procedure. Exploiting this false concept, malware authors have specifically targeted Marshmallow, using the backwards compatibility which allows it to install and execute applications developed for previous API versions. However, in this case, things are not as users would expect. If an application has been developed for `target_sdk` 22, then once a victim installs the application to Marshmallow, it will be granted the permissions upon installation. Definitely, the victim will be shown the "dangerous" permissions upon installation, but since the user is not accustomed to following this procedure during installation (as a result of being used to the new runtime permission model), it is highly likely that he will accept it, hoping that when he launches the application, he will be able to apply his permission policies. This user experience gap has already been exploited by malware such as Android.Bankosy and Android.Cepsohord. Although apps do not launch automatically, such apps would exploit this gap to collect as much personal information as possible before the user revokes his permissions.

A final consideration concerning the lack of transparency that has been introduced since the Android Marshmallow is introduced by another experiment conducted by the authors of this paper. More specifically, we have showcased that by requesting only normal permissions, Android apps obscure these permission from their users. In the cases where a dangerous permission is included in a set of requested permissions, users are able to navigate to the app's settings and reveal both the dangerous and also the normal permissions that are required by the app. However, after installing an app that has no dangerous permission included in its "Manifest" file, users have no access to the underlying permissions through the app's settings menu, since this capability is surprisingly disabled. This can be considered as a very important security issue, not only because of its "lack of transparency" dimension, but also since its exploitation can lead to obvious app metamorphoses attacks. In this case, apps could be initially installed without any permission requirements and would subsequently acquire an arbitrary number of normal permissions in automatic updates, leaving users with complete lack of control over them. One could argue that since these permission are not marked as dangerous, the impact could be rather small. However, this is not the case since both normal permissions have been proven to conceal security threats [3,4,28], and also because our research has also revealed that even "System" permissions are mistakenly handled by the system behaving as normal. The `SYSTEM_ALERT_WINDOW` permission, is considered by Google, as a "System" permission that: "*Very few apps should use this permission; these windows are intended for system-level interaction with the user*" [5]. Nonetheless, our research has revealed that not only it is automatically granted for all apps that come from the Google Play store, without user interaction, but also, in the case of being include in the "normal permission set", described above, it is also hidden by the users.

4.3 Access to External Resources

Clearly, the `INTERNET` permission, as its name suggests, allows an application to connect to the Internet. Up to API 22, Google considered `INTERNET` permission a dangerous one, however, since Marshmallow this is not the case. It is considered a normal one so the user is not notified about it during installation nor afterwards. Notably, due to the Android security model, the user cannot block an application from accessing a domain or the Internet, and additionally, he will not be notified of such actions. One of the core ideas behind this change is the fact that many applications were requesting this permission. As highlighted in [17,21], while the INTERNET permission is widely used and in many cases it is used only to fetch advertisements [8], yet it is often used to leak private user information, such as location. Google considers that since in Marshmallow there is an inherent mechanism to control access to sensitive pieces of information, an application cannot leak important data about the user without his consent, that is grant access to dangerous permissions.

In order to illustrate the changes in this particular permission, since the run-time permission model we have used Tacyt[7]. More specifically, we have noticed that there is a significant change in the usage of the Internet permission. Since Tacyt reports the results according to app versions and not per app, in what follows the reported figures refer to versions. Up to the release of Marshmallow, 89.24% of the uploaded versions were using the Internet permission. With the introduction of Marshmallow, this percentage has been increased by more than 7%, reaching 96.26%, indicating that many apps took advantage of this change to allow themselves to have access to the Internet.

Nonetheless, the very existence of a channel that enables an application to connect to the outer world through the Internet, without the user's consent or control essentially augments many security and privacy issues. The reason is that several "benign" actions do not imply any risk for the user, however, if someone can control them remotely or get a result out of them, can greatly expose the user. A typical example of this problem is the clipboard, used by every user to transfer information between applications. Clearly, due to the physical constraints for data input, most mobile users use this functionality to copy passwords, links or other content from one application to another. Apparently, the sensitivity of the content that is temporarily stored can easily be used to launch an attack [18,36]. Since there is no special permission for accessing the content of the clipboard, any application can sniff it and transmit it to a predefined location or modify it (e.g. injecting a malicious link). Clearly, this risk could be avoided if the applications had no Internet access or the user could define Internet access policies.

Apparently, the existence of such a channel, facilitates the leakage of other sensitive information. Another example is the access, without requesting any permission e.g. to local storage, to the drawable area of the wallpaper (reported by the authors, triaged and currently awaiting for a bug fix). While drawing on a canvas cannot be considered harmful, one has to consider that most users use personal photos as their wallpapers, which may depict their beloved, express their political or religious beliefs. Allowing an application to collect this information without user explicit consent could allow it to extract sensitive information, which apart from the aforementioned could include music and sexual preferences,

---

[7] https://www.elevenpaths.com/technology/tacyt/index.html.

relationship status etc. Clearly, if most users knew that this information could be mined and processed from apps without their explicit consent, they would be quite reluctant to use many of the photos that they currently do. Moreover, as shown in [4], this can be exploited to leak the user's unlock PIN or pattern.

It should also be highlighted that if users were able to block Internet access per application it is most certain that in many instances they would so. The reason is that most applications only need Internet access to display ads which for the vast majority of them is the only monetization source[8]. Apparently, if apps are not able to display ads, developers will have to result in other means for monetization in order to support their apps, e.g. shifting to the traditional paid model, which would radically change the Play store, as well as Google's monetization policy from Android. We argue that the answer to this question is not obvious, and there are several ways to avoid this dilemma, e.g. by providing unrestricted Internet access to applications only to fetch ads.

4.4 API Version Security Issues

One would expect that after the introduction of Marshmallow, all of the afore-mentioned functionality would be immediately provided to the systems that have the novel permission model installed. However, this is subject to the targeting API of the installed app. Practically, this means that apps may exploit this feature to extend their permissions. For instance, if an app is targeting an "old" API, prior to Marshmallow, then the app will request the permissions on instal-lation, and if the user accepts them, then once the app is loaded, the permissions have been granted, as in the pre-Marshmallow era, so the user has to disable the dangerous permissions manually and no granting screen will be displayed to the user. The issue is rather important as researchers have shown that permissions like SYSTEM_ALERT_WINDOW are automatically granted if they refer to older targeting APIs, allowing an adversary to create overlays that can lure the user to grant almost full control of the device to the adversary [23]. However, the overlay issues are far more severe and may apply to all Android versions [4].

4.5 User Profiling

While Android has been introducing many restrictions to unique identifiers, e.g. since Nougat most content of /proc has become inaccessible by apps, there are many ways that apps which use only normal permissions can profile the users.

The ACCESS_WIFI_STATE, as well as CHANGE_NETWORK_STATE and CHANGE_WIFI_STATE permissions have been removed in the new permission categoriza-tion. Automatically granting these permission allows an application to connect and disconnect from a WiFi. More interestingly, it allows the application to

---

[8] According to AppBrain (http://www.appbrain.com/stats/free-and-paid-android-ap lications) the ratio of free to paid apps is more than 10 at the time of writing. Free apps with in app purchases are considered free.

retrieve the information of the connected WiFi which can expose a lot of information [1]. On a first level of a nefarious scenario this could allow an application to enforce extra charges to the user by disconnecting from the WiFi and using a 3G/4G connection. Nonetheless, going a step further, one could determine the location of the user from the name of the connected WiFi, but more interestingly, the application can create a user profile as it has access to all stored networks. Apparently, collecting this information, one could correlate it with others to determine social connections using other sources of information such as time to infer e.g. how long two users stay in proximity, what times of day etc. harvesting users' relative location and potential relationship.

A lot of usage statics and preferences can be extracted by the apps using the GET_PACKAGE_SIZE permission, a normal permission as well. Using this permission, an application can profile a user as it can list all the installed applications and determine the user interests. Additionally, since this permission retrieves the space used by an application, an adversary could also infer how much an application is being used. Interestingly, the permission KILL_BACKGROUND_PROCESSES is also a normal permission, allowing it to kill other process, apart from system ones. Essentially, this permission can be used to sabotage other applications as they could shutdown, losing needed information or without notifying the user about e.g. an important event.

Finally, despite the upcoming changes to Android ID from Android O, apps can use a non user-resettable identifier which is app metadata. In this regard, an adversary can keep track of when apps were installed by reading the metadata of the /data directory which constitute a unique identifier.

5 Remedies

The most obvious change that is probably needed in the post Marshmallow era is to allow users to have full access to the underlying permissions. This would allow them to both review the permissions that they grant to each application; improving transparency, but also to revoke access on both normal permissions as well as categories from dangerous permission groups. This does not essentially have to confuse the user since for instance Android would automatically grant normal permissions, but request permission for each dangerous permission and not for a group. Such an interface could be conceived as the right hand side in Fig. 5, which showcases our approach in comparison with the current one. The user can easily see what are the granted permissions per application and revoke those when deemed necessary.

While the latter does not request many changes in the core of Android, a significant change should be introduced in the runtime permission model. As already discussed, applications request permissions to a resource at an irrelevant point, thus misleading users. While the developers may add an explanatory text of why they request a permission, the fact that the user cannot determine when it is actually used by the application does not create a trust relationship with it. For instance, a user cannot understand when an application needs to send an

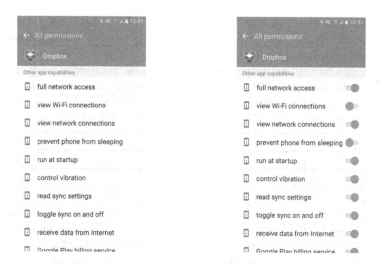

Fig. 5. Proposed interface for managing normal and dangerous permissions.

SMS, that might infer some additional cost. Such functionality might be needed once, e.g. for initialization and authorization of the application and never be used again, or be a part of a functionality that the user never uses. Having granted this permission prior to the actual request, authorizing arbitrary such actions, can lead to malicious applications exploiting this initial trust.

Going a step further, even normal permissions can lead to user profiling and expose sensitive user information, as outlined in the previous section. Therefore, Google has to consider what an application can infer from combinations of such permissions through communication between applications and alert the user of possible consequences.

6 Conclusions

The Android security for API levels prior to Marshmallow had several important issues that should be addressed, something that became apparent after many attacks in core libraries [16,30] and functionalities that had to be introduced to counter other attacks such as storage encryption or even setting the device to charge-only mode by default when connected to USB. Google's Android team, made a reasonable decision towards an implementation that would offer more and better protection to Android smartphone users of all ages and backgrounds. A good example is the presence of permission settings in the application manager, where users have real time access to specific groups of dangerous permissions, after an application is installed. However, major changes in software models that existed for several years can be easily accompanied by new security issues that may arise and new situations where end users may turn out not to be satisfied, nor actually protected.

This paper focused on highlighting several security issues that have risen since the introduction of the "Runtime Permission" model in the Android OS. Some of them may be addressed by re-organizing permission groups, and perhaps endorse a more "strict" permission policy in terms of "dangerous" and "normal" (not dangerous) permissions. Other issues regarding user notifications and especially what information is given to users are also quite important. Moreover, we detailed security and privacy issues which are either introduced or augmented by the new permission model. Undoubtedly, a core issue in all our apps is the unrestricted Internet access which provides applications with a communication channel that cannot be stopped or even filtered. As discussed, blocking this path may result to other sideeffects which may radically change Android market. Nevertheless, we believe that Android needs to incorporate more precise explanations to users and/or the ability to inform users in more detail. Finally, the runtime permission model should handle more sufficiently the need to inform users when a dangerous permission is required, by means of exact time and purpose. At its current implementation the proposed security model in Android leaves "more freedom" to Android developers to ask for permissions even when they do not need them and keep them for future uses. This combined with the "click once but permanent acceptance" of dangerous permissions, can lead to the destruction of what is meant as runtime permission and even more importantly what users expect by it. We argue that a possible solution to this problem would be to stop expecting developers to do the checks and request permissions in their programs but to force this operation to happen by the OS. Correspondingly, this could be accomplished by properly reconstructing Android's programming classes and interfaces involved in dangerous permissions so as to automatically request user permissions every time a dangerous resource is handled in code.

Acknowledgments. This work was supported by the European Commission under the Horizon 2020 Programme (H2020), as part of the *OPERANDO* project (Grant Agreement no. 653704). The authors would like to thank *ElevenPaths* for their valuable feedback and granting them access to Tacyt.

References

1. Achara, J.P., Cunche, M., Roca, V., Francillon, A.: WifiLeaks: underestimated privacy implications of the access_wifi_state Android permission. In: Proceedings of the 2014 ACM Conference on Security and Privacy in Wireless and Mobile Networks, pp. 231–236. ACM (2014)
2. Alepis, E., Patsakis, C.: Monkey says, monkey does: security and privacy on voice assistants. IEEE Access **5**, 17841–17851 (2017)
3. Alepis, E., Patsakis, C.: Theres wally! location tracking in Android without permissions. In: Proceedings of the 3rd International Conference on Information Systems Security and Privacy, ICISSP, vol. 1, pp. 278–284. INSTICC, ScitePress (2017)
4. Alepis, E., Patsakis, C.: Trapped by the UI: the Android case. In: Dacier, M., Bailey, M., Polychronakis, M., Antonakakis, M. (eds.) RAID 2017. LNCS, vol. 10453, pp. 334–354. Springer, Cham (2017). https://doi.org/10.1007/978-3-319-66332-6_15

5. Android Developer: Manifest.permission - System_Alert_Window. https://develop er.android.com/reference/android/Manifest.permission.html#SYSTEM_ALERT_ WINDOW. Accessed 28 Mar 2017

6. Android Source Code: platform_frameworks_base/core/res/AndroidManifest.xml (2017). https://github.com/Android/platform_frameworks_base/blob/master/cor e/res/AndroidManifest.xml

7. Balebako, R., Jung, J., Lu, W., Cranor, L.F., Nguyen, C.: Little brothers watching you: raising awareness of data leaks on smartphones. In: Proceedings of the Ninth Symposium on Usable Privacy and Security, p. 12. ACM (2013)

8. Barrera, D., Kayacik, H.G., van Oorschot, P.C., Somayaji, A.: A methodology for empirical analysis of permission-based security models and its application to Android. In: Proceedings of the 17th ACM Conference on Computer and Commu- nications Security, pp. 73–84. ACM (2010)

9. Bartel, A., Klein, J., Le Traon, Y., Monperrus, M.: Automatically securing permission-based software by reducing the attack surface: an application to Android. In: Proceedings of the 27th IEEE/ACM International Conference on Automated Software Engineering, pp. 274–277. ACM (2012)

10. Blasco, J., Chen, T.M.: Automated generation of colluding apps for experimental research. J. Comput. Virol. Hacking Tech. 1–12 (2017). https://doi.org/10.1007/ s11416-017-0296-4

11. Book, T., Pridgen, A., Wallach, D.S.: Longitudinal analysis of Android ad library permissions. arXiv preprint arXiv:1303.0857 (2013)

12. Book, T., Wallach, D.S.: A case of collusion: a study of the interface between ad libraries and their apps. In: Proceedings of the Third ACM Workshop on Security and Privacy in Smartphones and Mobile Devices, pp. 79–86. ACM (2013)

13. Davi, L., Dmitrienko, A., Sadeghi, A.-R., Winandy, M.: Privilege escalation attacks on Android. In: Burmester, M., Tsudik, G., Magliveras, S., Ilić, I. (eds.) ISC 2010. LNCS, vol. 6531, pp. 346–360. Springer, Heidelberg (2011). https://doi.org/10. 1007/978-3-642-18178-8_30

14. Diao, W., Liu, X., Zhou, Z., Zhang, K.: Your voice assistant is mine: how to abuse speakers to steal information and control your phone. In: Proceedings of the 4th ACM Workshop on Security and Privacy in Smartphones and Mobile Devices, pp. 63–74. ACM (2014)

15. Dimitriadis, A., Efraimidis, P.S., Katos, V.: Malevolent app pairs: an Android per- mission overpassing scheme. In: Proceedings of the ACM International Conference on Computing Frontiers, pp. 431–436. ACM (2016)

16. Durumeric, Z., Kasten, J., Adrian, D., Halderman, J.A., Bailey, M., Li, F., Weaver, N., Amann, J., Beekman, J., Payer, M., et al.: The matter of heartbleed. In: Pro- ceedings of the 2014 Conference on Internet Measurement Conference, pp. 475–488. ACM (2014)

17. Enck, W., Gilbert, P., Han, S., Tendulkar, V., Chun, B.G., Cox, L.P., Jung, J., McDaniel, P., Sheth, A.N.: TaintDroid: an information-flow tracking system for realtime privacy monitoring on smartphones. ACM Trans. Comput. Syst. (TOCS) **32**(2), 5 (2014)

18. Fahl, S., Harbach, M., Oltrogge, M., Muders, T., Smith, M.: Hey, you, get off of my clipboard. In: Sadeghi, A.-R. (ed.) FC 2013. LNCS, vol. 7859, pp. 144–161. Springer, Heidelberg (2013). https://doi.org/10.1007/978-3-642-39884-1_12

19. Faruki, P., Bharmal, A., Laxmi, V., Ganmoor, V., Gaur, M.S., Conti, M., Rajara- jan, M.: Android security: a survey of issues, malware penetration, and defenses. IEEE Commun. Surv. Tutor. **17**(2), 998–1022 (2015)

20. Felt, A.P., Chin, E., Hanna, S., Song, D., Wagner, D.: Android permissions demystified. In: Proceedings of the 18th ACM Conference on Computer and Communications Security, pp. 627–638. ACM (2011)

21. Felt, A.P., Greenwood, K., Wagner, D.: The effectiveness of application permissions. In: Proceedings of the 2nd USENIX Conference on Web Application Development, p. 7 (2011)

22. Felt, A.P., Ha, E., Egelman, S., Haney, A., Chin, E., Wagner, D.: Android permissions: user attention, comprehension, and behavior. In: Proceedings of the Eighth Symposium on Usable Privacy and Security, p. 3. ACM (2012)

23. Fratantonio, Y., Qian, C., Chung, S., Lee, W.: Cloak and Dagger: from two permissions to complete control of the UI feedback loop. In: Proceedings of the IEEE Symposium on Security and Privacy (Oakland), San Jose, CA, May 2017

24. Goodin, D.: Beware of ads that use inaudible sound to link your phone, TV, Tablet, and PC (2015). http://arstechnica.com/tech-policy/2015/11/beware-of-ads-that-use-inaudible-sound-to-link-your-phone-tv-tablet-and-pc/

25. Grace, M.C., Zhou, Y., Wang, Z., Jiang, X.: Systematic detection of capability leaks in stock Android smartphones. In: NDSS (2012)

26. Jeon, J., Micinski, K.K., Vaughan, J.A., Fogel, A., Reddy, N., Foster, J.S., Millstein, T.: Dr. Android and Mr. Hide: fine-grained permissions in Android applications. In: Proceedings of the Second ACM Workshop on Security and Privacy in Smartphones and Mobile Devices, pp. 3–14. ACM (2012)

27. Kelley, P.G., Consolvo, S., Cranor, L.F., Jung, J., Sadeh, N., Wetherall, D.: A conundrum of permissions: installing applications on an Android smartphone. In: Blyth, J., Dietrich, S., Camp, L.J. (eds.) FC 2012. LNCS, vol. 7398, pp. 68–79. Springer, Heidelberg (2012). https://doi.org/10.1007/978-3-642-34638-5_6

28. Kywe, S.M., Li, Y., Petal, K., Grace, M.: Attacking Android smartphone systems without permissions. In: 2016 14th Annual Conference on Privacy, Security and Trust (PST), pp. 147–156. IEEE (2016)

29. Orthacker, C., Teufl, P., Kraxberger, S., Lackner, G., Gissing, M., Marsalek, A., Leibetseder, J., Prevenhueber, O.: Android security permissions – can we trust them? In: Prasad, R., Farkas, K., Schmidt, A.U., Lioy, A., Russello, G., Luccio, F.L. (eds.) MobiSec 2011. LNICSSITE, vol. 94, pp. 40–51. Springer, Heidelberg (2012). https://doi.org/10.1007/978-3-642-30244-2_4

30. Peles, O., Hay, R.: One class to rule them all: 0-day deserialization vulnerabilities in Android. In: 9th USENIX Workshop on Offensive Technologies (WOOT 2015) (2015)

31. Poeplau, S., Fratantonio, Y., Bianchi, A., Kruegel, C., Vigna, G.: Execute this! analyzing unsafe and malicious dynamic code loading in Android applications. In: 21st Annual Network and Distributed System Security Symposium, NDSS 2014, San Diego, California, USA, 23–26 February 2014. The Internet Society (2014)

32. SnoopWall: Flashlight apps threat assessment report (2014). http://www.snoopwall.com/wp-content/uploads/2015/02/Flashlight-Spyware-Report-2014.pdf

33. Tsiakos, V., Patsakis, C.: AndroPatchApp: taming rogue ads in Android. In: Boumerdassi, S., Renault, É., Bouzefrane, S. (eds.) MSPN 2016. LNCS, vol. 10026, pp. 183–196. Springer, Cham (2016). https://doi.org/10.1007/978-3-319-50463-6_15

34. Wei, X., Gomez, L., Neamtiu, I., Faloutsos, M.: Permission evolution in the Android ecosystem. In: Proceedings of the 28th Annual Computer Security Applications Conference, pp. 31–40. ACM (2012)

35. Yang, L., Boushehrinejadmoradi, N., Roy, P., Ganapathy, V., Iftode, L.: Short paper: enhancing users' comprehension of Android permissions. In: Proceedings of the Second ACM Workshop on Security and Privacy in Smartphones and Mobile Devices, pp. 21–26. ACM (2012)

36. Zhang, X., Du, W.: Attacks on Android clipboard. In: Dietrich, S. (ed.) DIMVA 2014. LNCS, vol. 8550, pp. 72–91. Springer, Cham (2014). https://doi.org/10.1007/978-3-319-08509-8_5

Efficient Software Implementation of Laddering Algorithms Over Binary Elliptic Curves

Diego F. Aranha[1($\boxtimes$)], Reza Azarderakhsh[2], and Koray Karabina[2]

[1] University of Campinas, Campinas, Brazil
dfaranha@ic.unicamp.br
[2] Florida Atlantic University, Boca Raton, USA
{razarderakhsh,kkarabina}@fau.edu

Abstract. Designing efficient and secure implementations of Elliptic Curve Cryptography (ECC) has attracted enormous interest from both theoreticians and practitioners. The main contenders in terms of performance are curves defined over binary extension fields or large prime characteristic fields. In addition to the efficiency requirements, security advantages such as implementation simplicity and resistance to side-channel attacks are receiving increasing attention in research and commercial applications. In this paper, we keep pushing in this direction and study efficient implementation of regular scalar multiplication algorithms for binary curves equipped with efficient endomorphisms. Our focus is on implementing the Galbraith-Lin-Scott (GLS) family of binary curves by exploring the space of different models and laddering algorithms, for their high performance, reasonable implementation simplicity, lower memory consumption and side-channel resistance. Our results demonstrate that laddering implementations can be competitive with window-based methods by obtaining a new speed record for laddering implementations of elliptic curves on high-end Intel processors.

1 Introduction

Secure and efficient implementation of Elliptic Curve Cryptography (ECC) has received a lot of interest by researchers and implementers alike. The security of ECC cryptosystems relies on the hardness of the Elliptic Curve Discrete Logarithm Problem (ECDLP) conjectured as fully exponential, which consists in recovering the scalar $k \in \mathbb{Z}$ from the given points P and $Q = kP$ in some elliptic curve E defined over a finite field $\mathbb{F}_q$.

Scalar multiplication $(k, P \rightarrow kP)$ is the main operation required when evaluating ECC protocols and corresponds to adding point P to itself $k - 1$ times. The performance and security of a curve-based cryptosystem strictly relates to the choice of curve parameters, scalar multiplication algorithm, finite field arithmetic, and implementation quality. Algorithms for scalar multiplication can be broadly classified in *window-based methods*, composed of a precomputation step for computing small multiples of the input point, and a main loop exploiting this precomputation through table lookups; and simpler and more compact *laddering*

© Springer International Publishing AG 2017
S.S. Ali et al. (Eds.): SPACE 2017, LNCS 10662, pp. 74–92, 2017.
https://doi.org/10.1007/978-3-319-71501-8_5

methods [4, 23] that execute the same operation across all iterations. These algorithms can be further classified in fixed-base when the input is a known point G (generator), variable-base when the input is unknown point P and double-point when two points P and Q are simultaneously multiplied as $\ell P + mQ$ by scalars ℓ and m. These scenarios typically occur in key generation, key exchange and signature verification, respectively.

In practice, the main contenders in terms of performance are curves defined over large prime characteristic fields (*prime curves*), or over binary extension fields (*binary curves*). Performance is not the only metric, and security advantages such as implementation simplicity and resistance to side-channel attacks are receiving more attention in research and industry. In the prime case, for instance, Edwards curves [3] and FourQ [7] have provided most of the recent performance and/or security improvements by adopting more conservative or aggressive choices of parameters, respectively. In the binary case, recent advances firmly rely on exploiting efficient endomorphisms and optimized parameters in Koblitz [18,22] and Galbraith-Lin-Scott (GLS) [12,20] curves.

Thanks to many improvements introduced in modern processors as powerful vector instructions, binary curves arguably now enjoy better native support for their underlying field arithmetic in some micro-architectures. Combined with algorithmic developments such as the lambda coordinate system [20,21] and efficient endomorphisms, binary curves currently hold the speed record for the most efficient scalar multiplication in software targeting Intel desktop processors [19]. Despite advances in solving the ECDLP for these curves [10], binary curves are still considered secure for cryptographic applications [23] and were standardized by IEEE [13] and NIST [17].

In this paper, we study the efficient implementation of laddering algorithms for variable-base scalar multiplication under different models of elliptic curves defined over binary extension fields. Laddering algorithms offer some built-in side-channel protection because of their regularity, and implementation friendliness due to the simplicity of not requiring all coordinates of a point to be computed. The Montgomery ladder over the x-coordinate is the most popular algorithm pertaining to this class [16].

We target binary GLS curves equipped with efficient endomorphisms, allowing multi-dimensional laddering algorithms such as the DJB chain proposed by Bernstein in [2] to be used. The DJB algorithm is *uniform*, in the sense that all iterations in the main loop require the same number and type of field operations [6], and can be implemented in an *isochronous* way (constant time) because the number of loop iterations can be made constant. Recently, Azarderakhsh and Karabina proposed the AK laddering algorithm tailored for the computation of point multiplication on elliptic curves with efficiently computable endomorphisms. The AK algorithm can be faster than DJB but has a variable number of loop iterations (with small standard deviation). More recently, AK and DJB laddering algorithms have been employed by Costello et al. for the implementation of point multiplication and x-coodinate only key exchange on elliptic curves defined over prime fields [6]. The main contributions of this work are:

– Concrete strategies for efficiently implementing the Montgomery, DJB and AK variable-base laddering algorithms, minimizing the number of conditional operations for side-channel protection. As long as the efficiency of finite field arithmetic continues to improve due to progress in instruction sets, these overheads become significant and must be handled properly. Also, an efficient uniform algorithm for AK recoding is proposed and evaluated.

– Techniques for converting between binary GLS curves in the Weierstraß model to alternate models such as Huff and Edwards while keeping coefficients compact and efficient to operate with. Faster formulas for evaluating differential addition and doubling operations required by laddering algorithms are presented for these models, applying lazy reduction and other recent techniques from the literature [9].

– A set of GLS curve parameters at the 128-bit security level which maximize the efficiency of the proposed techniques, followed by a state-of-the-art implementation which demonstrate that laddering algorithms can be competitive with window-based methods while setting new speed records for laddering implementations.

The work is organized as follows. In Sect. 2, Weierstraß, Huff and Edwards elliptic curve models are introduced, together with efficient formulae and algorithms for converting from binary GLS curves in the Weierstraß model. In Sect. 3, the Montgomery, DJB and AK laddering algorithms for scalar multiplication are discussed together with improvements. Section 4 presents experimental results and discussion, and Sect. 5 concludes.

2   Binary GLS Curves

Let $E_{W,a,b}$ be an ordinary binary elliptic curve in short Weierstraß form defined by the equation

$$E_{W,a,b} : y^2 + xy = x^3 + ax^2 + b, \tag{1}$$

where $a, b \in \mathbb{F}_{2^m}$. The set of affine points $P = (x, y)$ with $x, y \in \mathbb{F}_{\mathbb{F}_{2^m}}$ that satisfy the above equation, together with the point at infinity $\mathcal{O}$, forms an additive abelian group with respect to the elliptic point addition operation. This group is denoted as $E_{W,a,b}(\mathbb{F}_{2^m})$ and its order can be written as $\#E_{W,a,b}(\mathbb{F}_{2^m}) = 2^m - t + 1$, where t is the *trace of Frobenius* and satisfies $|t| \leq 2^m$.

In order to define a Galbraith-Linn-Scott (GLS) curve [11,12], choose a quadratic extension $\mathbb{F}_{2^{2m}}$ of $\mathbb{F}_{2^m}$ as $\mathbb{F}_{2^{2m}} = \mathbb{F}_{2^m}[s]/(s^2 + s + 1)$ and pick a field element $a' \in \mathbb{F}_{2^{2m}}$ such that $Tr(a') = 1$, where Tr is the trace function from $\mathbb{F}_{2^{2m}}$ to $\mathbb{F}_{2^m}$ defined as $Tr : c \mapsto \sum_{i=0}^{2m-1} c^{2^i}$. It follows that $\#E(\mathbb{F}_{2^{2m}}) = (2^m + 1)^2 - t^2$. Let us define

$$E'/\mathbb{F}_{2^{2m}} : y^2 + xy = x^3 + a'x^2 + b, \tag{2}$$

with $\#E'_{W,a',b}(\mathbb{F}_{2^{2m}}) = (2^m - 1)^2 + t^2$. E' is the quadratic twist of $E_{W,a,b}$ which means that both curves are isomorphic over $\mathbb{F}_{2^{4m}}$ under the endomorphism $\phi : E \rightarrow E', (x, y) \mapsto (x, y + \sigma x)$, with $\sigma \in \mathbb{F}_{2^{4m}} \backslash \mathbb{F}_{2^{2m}}$ satisfying $\sigma^2 + \sigma = a + a'$.

Fix $a' = s$ and choose b such that $\#E'_{a',b}(\mathbb{F}_{2^{2m}}) = 2r$, where r is prime with $(2m - 1)$ bits. Let $a_1 = b^{-1/8}$, Eq. (2) is isomorphic over $\mathbb{F}_{2^{2m}}$ to

$$E''/\mathbb{F}_{2^{2m}} : Y^2 + a_1 XY = X^3 + a_1^2 sX^2 + 1/a_1^2, \qquad (3)$$

with isomorphism given by $\Phi : E' \to E'', (x, y) \mapsto (a_1^2 x, a_1^3 y)$ [24].

Let $\pi : E \to E$ be the Frobenius map and let ψ be the composite GLS endomorphism $\psi = \phi\pi\phi^{-1}$ given as $\psi(x, y) = (x^{2^m}, y^{2^m} + x^{2^m}s)$. Hankerson et al. showed in [12] that $\psi(P) = \lambda P$ for some $\lambda \in \mathbb{Z}$ satisfying $\lambda^2 + 1 \equiv 0 \pmod{r}$. For $k \in \mathbb{Z}$, the scalar multiplication kP can then be decomposed in $k_1 P + k_2 \psi(P)$ such that $k \equiv k_1 + k_2 \lambda \pmod{r}$.

Parameters. A concrete GLS curve targeting approximately the 128-bit security level can be found by choosing $m = 127$ and binary field $\mathbb{F}_{2^m}$ defined as $\mathbb{F}_2[z]/(f(z) = z^{127} + z^{63} + 1)$. Two possible choices for curve coefficient b defining curves E_1 and E_2, respectively, can be found below:

1. $b_1 = $ 0x540451444104015441015405405515101 in polynomial representation (hexadecimal form) with short 64-bit square root $\sqrt{b} = $ 0xE2DA921E91E38DD1. This parameter is widely used in the literature [18,20] to optimize a multiplication by b in the Montgomery ladder due to the short square root, and here is chosen for comparison with related work.
2. $b_2 = z^{85} + z^{21}$ in polynomial form with short root $b^{-1/8}$, introduced here to simplify curve coefficients when converted to other curve models.

Both concrete curves E_1 and E_2 have large 253-bit prime subgroup order r and thus satisfy common security requirements for the discrete logarithm setting.

The basic computation in each step of a laddering algorithm (LADD operation) is differential addition (DADD) and doubling (DOUB) evaluated over the base field where the curve is defined. Given points P_1 and P_2 on elliptic curve $E(\mathbb{F}_q)$ with known *difference* $P_0 = P_1 - P_2$, this operation computes point addition $P_1 + P_2$ and point doubling $2P_1$. In general, the formulas can be evaluated over a smaller set of coordinates. Let w be a rational function defined over elliptic curve $E(\mathbb{F}_q)$ given by the fraction of polynomials in the coordinate ring of E, with $w(P) = w(-P)$ [9]. For any points P_1, P_2 given by the values $w(P_1), w(P_2)$ and difference $w(P_1 - P_2)$, differential addition and doubling formulae again compute $w(P_1 + P_2)$ and $w(2P_1)$ in w-coordinates. A projective w-coordinate representation $w(P) = (W : Z)$ of a point P can also be defined to eliminate expensive inversions in curve arithmetic, and the corresponding affine representation can be simply recovered by computing $\frac{W}{Z}$.

Let $\boldsymbol{m}, \boldsymbol{s}, \boldsymbol{d}, \boldsymbol{r}, \boldsymbol{a}$ and $\boldsymbol{i}$ denote the costs of field multiplication, squaring, multiplication by short curve parameter, modular reduction by $f(z)$, addition and inversion in $\mathbb{F}_{2^{2m}}$, respectively. The *lazy reduction* technique evaluates an expression $(ab + cd)$ over a field $\mathbb{F}_q$ by accumulating the multiplication results before modular reduction, incurring a performance trade-off of $(\boldsymbol{a} - \boldsymbol{r})$. Because addition in a binary field is trivial, typically $\boldsymbol{r} > \boldsymbol{a}$ and the technique incurs a small speedup. Notation $[\cdot]_f$ here denotes an *explicit* modular reduction operation of a double-precision result, implying that multiplication and squaring results are automatically reduced otherwise. In the next subsections, we improve state-of-the-art differential addition and doubling formulas for several binary curve models presented in [9] by using lazy reduction and compare their relative performance.

2.1 Formulae for Weierstraß Curves

In Weierstraß curves, the w-coordinate representation $w(P)$ of a point P can be simplified to the x-coordinate $x(P)$. The formulae below compute the projective w-coordinate differential addition and doubling (LADD) operation among points $P_1 = (X_1 : Z_1)$ and $P_2 = (X_2 : Z_2)$, producing the results $(X_3 : Z_3) = (X_1 : Z_1) + (X_2 : Z_2)$ and $(X_4 : Z_4) = 2(X_1 : Z_1)$, given the difference point in projective coordinates $P_0 = (X_0 : Z_0) = (X_1 : Z_1) - (X_2 : Z_2)$:

$$A = (X_1 + Z_1), \ B = (X_2 + Z_2), \ T = [X_1 \cdot X_2 + Z_1 \cdot Z_2]_f,$$
$$Z_3 = (T + A \cdot B)^2 \cdot X_0, \ X_3 = T^2 \cdot Z_0,$$
$$Z_4 = (a_1 \cdot X_1 \cdot Z_1)^2, \ X_4 = A^4.$$

This formula was improved from [24] by using lazy reduction of $(X_1 X_2 + Z_1 Z_2)$ and can be used over the curve isomorphic to the set of parameters E_2 defined by Eq. (3). Total cost in this case is $(6m + 5s + d + 5a - r)$ by trading an additional modular reduction (r) by a double-precision addition (extra a). If $Z_0 = 1$, the formulae below can be used instead by switching to López-Dahab coordinates over curve E_1 defined by Eq. (2) with difference point $w(P_0) = x_0$ in affine coordinates [15], costing $(5m + 4s + d + 4a - r)$:

$$A = X_1 \cdot Z_2, \ B = X_2 \cdot Z_1, \ T = (X_2)^2, \ U = (Z_2)^2$$
$$X_4 = (T + U\sqrt{b_1})^2, \ Z_4 = T \cdot U$$
$$Z_3 = (A + B)^2, \ X_3 = [x_0 \cdot Z_4 + A \cdot B]_f.$$

Multiplication by b_1 is efficient because b_1 is chosen such that its square root is a 64-bit polynomial.

2.2 Formulae for Edwards Curves

Let $d_1, d_2 \in \mathbb{F}_{2^{2m}}$ with $d_1 \neq 0$ and $d_2 \neq d_1^2 + d_1$, the binary Edwards curve is the non-singular curve

$$E_{E,d_1,d_2} : (x + y)(d_1 + d_2(x + y)) = xy(1 + x)(1 + y). \tag{4}$$

When $Tr(d_2) = 1$, the curve is complete and there are no exceptions to the addition law. The Edwards model is birationally equivalent to the Weierstraß model

$$v^2 + uv = u^3 + (d_1^2 + d_2)u^2 + d_1^4(d_1^4 + d_1^2 + d_2^2) \tag{5}$$

under the map $(x, y) \longmapsto (u, v)$ and its inverse defined by [5]

$$u = (d_1^3 + d_1^2 + d_1 d_2)(x + y)/(xy + d_1(x + y)), \qquad (6)$$
$$v = (d_1^3 + d_1^2 + d_1 d_2)(d_1 + 1 + x/(xy + d_1(x + y)).$$

Since the curve used in this work has no rational points of order 4, it is not isomorphic to an Edwards curve with coefficients $d_1 = d_2$ and cannot enjoy the simpler arithmetic in that case.

We still obtain efficient arithmetic by selecting parameters of curve E_2 and choosing curve coefficients $d_1 = (s \cdot z^{84}) \in \mathbb{F}_{2^{2m}}$ and $d_2 = d_1^2 + d_1 + \sqrt{b}/d_1^2 \in \mathbb{F}_{2^{2m}}$. A subfield constant is thus obtained for evaluating the differential addition and doubling formula. Define function $w(x, y) = (x + y)/(d_1(x + y + 1))$ such that $w(P) = w(-P)$ for all affine points except when $x + y = 1$ [9]. Assuming that $w(P_1)$ and $w(P_2)$ are represented in projective coordinates $(W_1 : Z_1)$ and $(W_2 : Z_2)$, respectively, and given precomputed w-coordinate $z_0 = 1/w_0$ of difference point P_0, the formulae below compute differential addition and doubling with cost $(5m + 4s + d + 4a - r)$:

$$A = W_1 \cdot Z_1, \ B = W_1 \cdot Z_2, \ C = W_2 \cdot Z_1,$$

$$W_4 = A^2, \ Z_4 = (\sqrt[4]{d_1^4 + d_1^3 + d_1^2 d_2} W_1 + Z_1)^4,$$

$$W_3 = (B + C)^2, \ Z_3 = [B \cdot C + z_0 \cdot W_3]_f.$$

These formulae are faster than the almost complete formular given in [9] by $(r - a)$, due to lazy reduction. Compared to the affine Weierstraß formula, it apparently has the same cost, but the multiplication by the curve coefficient is slower because $(d_1^4 + d_1^3 + d_1^2 d_2)$ is a polynomial in $\mathbb{F}_{2^m}$ with degree 91 in our set of parameters E_2.

2.3 Formulae for Huff Curves

Let $h_a \neq h_b \in \mathbb{F}_{2^{2m}}$ the coefficients of the generalized binary Huff curve given by the set of coordinates satisfying the equation

$$E_{H,h_a,h_b} : h_a x(y^2 + fy + 1) = h_b y(x^2 + fx + 1). \qquad (7)$$

This equation is birationally equivalent to the Weierstrass curve

$$v(v + (h_a + h_b)fu) = u(u + h_a^2)(u + h_b^2). \qquad (8)$$

under the map $(x, y) \longmapsto (u, v)$ and its inverse defined by [8]

$$(x, y) = \left(\frac{h_b(u + h_a^2)}{v}, \frac{h_a(u + h_b^2)}{v + (h_a + h_b)fu} \right), \qquad (9)$$

$$(u, v) = \left(\frac{h_a h_b}{xy}, \frac{h_a h_b (h_a xy + h_b)}{x^2 y} \right).$$

In order to convert a GLS curve to the Huff curve model, we adapt the method in [8, Proposition 2] by defining $f = g(z) \cdot s$, where g is a polynomial of small degree such that $Tr(1/f) = Tr(s)$ and $Tr(f^8 b) = 0$. For simplicity, parameters h_a, h_b will be chosen as $h_b = 1$ and $h_a \in \mathbb{F}_{2^m}$ as the solution h_a^2 to equation $t^2 + \frac{1}{f^4 \sqrt{(b)}} t = 1$ in a subfield. This guarantees that the constant $\gamma = f^2 \frac{(h_a + h_b)^2}{h_a h_b}$ and its inverse $1/\gamma$ will have small degree and reside in a subfield, allowing fast multiplication by these constants.

We adapt the almost complete formulae from [9] to general binary Huff curves. By choosing $w(x, y) = (xy) \cdot \gamma$, and given the w-coordinate w_0 of difference point P_0 precomputed as $z_0 = 1/w_0$, we propose the following formulae for differential addition and doubling costing $(5\boldsymbol{m} + 4\boldsymbol{s} + \boldsymbol{d} + 4\boldsymbol{a} - \boldsymbol{r})$:

$$A = W_1 \cdot Z_1, \ B = W_1 \cdot Z_2, \ C = W_2 \cdot Z_1,$$
$$W_3 = A^2, \ Z_3 = (W_1/\gamma + Z_1)^4,$$
$$W_3 = (B + C)^2, \ Z_3 = [B \cdot C + z_0 \cdot W_3]_f.$$

These formula are again faster than [9] by $(\boldsymbol{r} - \boldsymbol{a})$ due to lazy reduction. Compared to the Edwards model, this formula is faster in our parameters because the multiplication by curve coefficient with cost $\boldsymbol{d}$ involves a multiplication by a polynomial of degree 54. This is equivalent to the cost of the Weierstraß formulae. There is another advantage of this curve model: it is easy to observe that $w(x, y) = xy\gamma = \frac{h_a}{u}$ for our choice of parameters, thus converting from the x-coordinate Weierstraß representation requires only an inversion and multiplication by a subfield constant. When working over w-coordinates only, this allows the GLS endomorphism to be computed as a simple 2^m-power over $\mathbb{F}_{2^{2m}}$ because h_a lies in a subfield.

At last, there are formulas in the binary Hessian model with this exact same cost [9], but which result in larger curve coefficients after conversion from Weierstrasß for our choices of parameters, so they are not discussed in this work.

3   Laddering Algorithms

Scalar multiplication is the performance-critical operation for protocols based on elliptic curves and the algorithms follow two general ideas. In window-based methods, a table of points containing small multiples $P_i = d_i P$ is precomputed, the scalar is recoded to another representation and the scalar multiplication follows by adding and doubling multiples obtained from the table according to the recoded scalar digits d_i. This strategy usually consumes more memory due to the precomputed table, and side-channel countermeasures are needed to prevent leaks from the recoding process or differences in memory access during table lookups. Laddering methods uniformly iterate a ladder step consisting of point doubling and addition over a smaller set of variables, reducing memory consumption. From the point of view of efficiency and simplicity, almost complete formulae as in the previous section which do not compute all coordinates are preferable and sufficient to prevent exceptional cases within the laddering. Side-channel countermeasures protect the selection of variables to be updated with conditional operations.

Below we summarize and propose optimizations for three different laddering algorithms: the original Montgomery ladder, Bernstein's double point multiplication algorithm based on the new binary chain and a recent double multiplication algorithm due to Azarderakhsh and Karabina. The algorithms heavily depend on three branchless operations depending on a bit condition: SELECT for selecting among two inputs, CSWAP for conditionally swapping variables, and CCOPY for conditionally copying the input to the output. These conditional operations are usually considered to be cheap, but their cost is becoming increasingly significant due to faster finite field and elliptic curve arithmetic, and more powerful instruction sets. Our proposed versions of the algorithms will then focus on simplifying conditional operations when merging two consecutive loop iterations.

3.1 Montgomery Ladder

A version of the Montgomery scalar multiplication based on the projective w-coordinate representation is given in Algorithm 1. The algorithm receives as input $w(P)$, the affine w-coodinate of P, and the integer scalar k. Two accumulator points $P_1 = (W_1 : Z_1)$ and $P_2 = (W_2 : Z_2)$ are initialized as $w(P)$ and $w(2P)$, respectively, which are doubled and added depending on the current bit of the key. Iteration j starts with accumulators $[w(lP), w((l+1)P)]$, where l is the integer represented by the j leftmost bits of k, and computes $[w(2lP), w((2l+1)P)]$ or $[w((2l+1)P), w((2l+2)P)]$. By induction, the last iteration produces $[kP, (k+1)P]$, where the first point is the result and the second point may be useful for recovering the full coordinates of the result. Following previous work, this version merges two consecutive iterations and only performs real swaps when necessary (consecutive bits are different).

When operating over Weierstraß curves with $w(P) = x(P)$, the y-coordinate y_1 of kP can be recovered from $(X_1 : Z_1) = w(P)$, $(X_2 : Z_2) = w((k+1)P)$ and $P = (x, y)$ with the following formula from [15]:

$$y_3 = (x + X_1/Z_1)[(X_1 + xZ_1)(X_2 + xZ_2) + (x^2 + y)(Z_1Z_2)](xZ_1Z_2)^{-1} + y.$$

Although not explictly mentioned in the literature, this formula can be used to fully recover $kP = (x_3, y_3)$ with cost of $(i + 10m + 1s + 6a)$, at a relatively small increase from the cost $(i + m)$ of computing $x_3 = X_1/Z_1$:

$$A = Z_1 \cdot Z_2, \; B = (X_1 + x \cdot Z_1), \; C = x \cdot Z_2, \; D = C \cdot X_1,$$
$$E = B \cdot (X_2 + C), \; F = (x^2 + y) \cdot A + E, \; G = (x \cdot A)^{-1}, \; H = F \cdot G,$$
$$x_3 = D \cdot G, \; y_3 = y + (x + x_3) \cdot H.$$

3.2 Two-Dimensional DJB Ladder

As described in Sect. 2, a scalar multiplication kP can be computed as $k_1P + k_2Q$, for $Q = \psi(P)$. Hence, two-dimensional laddering algorithms can be used to evaluate a single scalar multiplication exploiting endomorphisms. We briefly explain

Algorithm 1. Montgomery ladder using differential addition and doubling formulae (LADD). The auxiliary function CSWAP conditionally swaps the two first arguments depending on the value of the third parameter.

Input: $k = (k_{l-1}, \ldots, k_1, k_0) \in \mathbb{Z}$ such that $k > 0$ and $w(P)$, for $P \in E(\mathbb{F}_{2^{2m}})$
Output: $w(kP), w((k+1)P) \in E(\mathbb{F}_{2^{2m}})$
1: $(W_1 : Z_1) \leftarrow w(P)$
2: $(W_2 : Z_2) \leftarrow w(2P)$
3: $p \leftarrow 0$
4: **for** $j \leftarrow l - 2$ **downto** 0 **do**
5:    $c \leftarrow k_j \oplus p$
6:    $p \leftarrow k_j$
7:    $(W_1, W_2) \leftarrow \text{CSWAP}(W_1, W_2, c)$
8:    $(Z_1, Z_2) \leftarrow \text{CSWAP}(Z_1, Z_2, c)$
9:    $((W_1 : Z_1), (W_2 : Z_2)) \leftarrow \text{LADD}((W_1 : Z_1), (W_2 : Z_2), w(P))$
10: **end for**
11: $(W_1, W_2) \leftarrow \text{CSWAP}(W_1, W_2, p)$
12: $(Z_1, Z_2) \leftarrow \text{CSWAP}(Z_1, Z_2, p)$
13:**return** $(W_1 : Z_1) = w(kP), (W_2 : Z_2) = w((k+1)P)$

Bernstein's double point multiplication algorithm based on the new binary chain [2]. The chain for (k_1, k_2) is computed as follows. Let $(M, N) = (k_1, k_2)$ and $D = k_1 \bmod 2$. $C_D(0,0)$ is defined as the base case $(0,0), (1,0), (0,1), (1,-1)$. For $(M, N) \neq (0,0)$, $C_D(M, N)$ is defined recursively:

$$
\begin{aligned}
C_D(M, N) =\; & C_d(\lfloor M/2 \rfloor, \lfloor N/2 \rfloor), \\
& (M + (M + 1 \bmod 2), N + (N + 1 \bmod 2)), \\
& (M + (M \bmod 2), N + (N \bmod 2)), \\
& (M + (M + D \bmod 2), N + (N + D + 1 \bmod 2)), \quad \text{and}
\end{aligned}
$$

$$
d = \begin{cases}
0 & \text{if } (\lfloor M/2 \rfloor + M, \lfloor N/2 \rfloor + N) \bmod 2 = (0,1) \\
1 & \text{if } (\lfloor M/2 \rfloor + M, \lfloor N/2 \rfloor + N) \bmod 2 = (1,0) \\
D & \text{if } (\lfloor M/2 \rfloor + M, \lfloor N/2 \rfloor + N) \bmod 2 = (0,0) \\
1 - D & \text{if } (\lfloor M/2 \rfloor + M, \lfloor N/2 \rfloor + N) \bmod 2 = (1,1).
\end{cases}
$$

Building the new binary chain for the integers (k_1, k_2) requires a number of $\max(\lceil \log_2 k_1 \rceil, \lceil \log_2 k_2 \rceil)$ iterations, and at the each iteration three vectors are added to the sequence. Given two elliptic curve points $P, Q \in E(\mathbb{F}_q)$, the new binary chain for (k_1, k_2) allows us to compute $k_1 P + k_2 Q$ at a cost of two point additions and one point doubling per iteration. The algorithm generates a chain sequence specifying the input to the doubling and addition operations at each iteration and a sequence of differences which encodes the differences of the points that are the input points to the addition operations at each iteration [1].

Algorithm 2 presents our optimized version of the DJB laddering algorithm. The algorithm starts by computing the chain sequence, returning four bit sequences S_0, S_1, S_2, S_3 representing the recoded versions of the input scalars k_1 and k_2, a value f_a determining the first addition and the correct point f_i among three accumulators to be returned at the end of the algorithm. Accumulators $(W_0 : Z_0), (W_1 : Z_1), (W_2 : Z_2)$ are initialized in projective coordinates using the DADD and DOUB and later keep track of the multiples of P and Q inside the main loop. Accumulator $(W_2 : Z_2)$ starts with value $w(P + 2Q)$ or $w(2P + Q)$ depending on the chosen difference point and accumulator $(W_1 : Z_1)$ always starts with $w(2(P + Q))$. Differences w_{P+Q}, w_{P-Q} can be computed in affine coordinates sharing an inversion, to avoid slower projective representation of differences.

At the beginning of each iteration of our implementation, the condition bit t evaluates what operand will be copied to temporary variable $(W_4 : Z_4)$. This is needed because the DOUB operation inside the laddering can receive any of the three accumulators copied to $(W_3 : Z_3)$. Then the correct differences are copied to w_0 and w_1, followed by two differential additions using the chosen differences and a point doubling. These conditions were tediously derived and minimized from the bit combinations in the sequences S_0, S_1, S_2, S_3 to correctly position the inputs and outputs of the curve arithmetic operations. An advantage of this algorithm is always returning $(k+1)P = (k_1+1)P + k_2\psi(P)$ among the two other unused results, in a position depending on the parities of k_1 and k_2. This allows to recover the full coordinates of P using the same formulas in the previous subsection, increasing the scenarios in which the laddering can be applied.

3.3 Two-Dimensional AK Ladder

Let k_1 and k_2 be again two positive integers. In order to compute $k_1 P + k_2 Q$, the AK laddering algorithm starts with the initial values $d = k_1, e = k_2, \vec{R} = (P, Q)$, $\vec{u} = (1, 0), \vec{v} = (0, 1)$, and $\vec{\Delta} = (1, -1)$. Define also $R_u = \vec{u} \cdot \vec{R}, R_v = \vec{v} \cdot \vec{R}$, and $R_\Delta = \vec{\Delta} \cdot \vec{R}$. The initial values yield $R_u = P, R_v = Q, R_\Delta = R_u - R_v = P - Q$, and $dR_u + eR_v = k_1 P + k_2 Q$, and the values $d, e, \vec{u}, \vec{v}, \vec{\Delta}, R_u, R_v, R_\Delta$ are updated according to the rules in Table 1 so that $dR_u + eR_v = k_1 P + k_2 Q$ and $R_\Delta = R_u - R_v$ hold, $d, e > 0$, and $(d + e)$ decreases until $d = e$. When $d = e$, we have $k_1 P + k_2 Q = dR_u + eR_v = d(R_u + R_v)$ which can be computed using a single point multiplication algorithm with base $R_u + R_v$ and scalar d. Note that when $\gcd(k_1, k_2) = 1$, $(d + e)$ in the algorithm will decrease until $d = e = 1$ and we have $k_1 P + k_2 Q = R_u + R_v$ [1].

Algorithm 3 computes a recoded format for the scalars according to Table 1 in a branchless manner. The recoded sequence stores in each position a value among the four rules in the table. First conditions t and t' are computed in lines 3 and 4 as $d \overset{?}{\equiv} e \pmod 2$ and $d \overset{?}{\equiv} 0 \pmod 2$, respectively. Variable f is assigned to $|d - e|$ in line 6, values (d, e) are swapped before division by 2 (shifting to the right by 1) if the conditions for rules R_1' or R_2' apply, and d conditionally receives f to update the correct value, after which the swapping is restored in line 10. At the end of each iteration, the sequence is increased by one element storing the rule and the current length if incremented.

Algorithm 2. DJB laddering algorithm, employing the DADD and DOUB operations. The CHAIN computation returns recoded scalars and two additional values determining the first addition (f_a) and the correct point (f_i) to be returned at the end of the algorithm. Auxiliary functions SELECT conditionally selects among two arguments and CCOPY copies the input to the destination depending on the last parameter.

Input: Integers $k_1, k_2 > 0$ and $w(P), w(Q)$ for $P, Q \in E(\mathbb{F}_{2^{2m}})$
Output: $w(k_1 P + k_2 Q) \in E(\mathbb{F}_{2^{2m}})$
1: $S_0, S_1, S_2, S_3, f_a, f_i \leftarrow \text{CHAIN}(k_1, k_2)$
2: $(W_0 : Z_0) \leftarrow w(P + Q), w_P \leftarrow w(P), w_Q \leftarrow w(Q)$
3: $w_{P+Q} \leftarrow w(P + Q), w_{P-Q} \leftarrow w(P - Q)$
4: $(w_P, w_Q) \leftarrow \text{CSWAP}(w_P, w_Q, f_a \overset{?}{=} 1)$
5: $(W_2 : Z_2) \leftarrow \text{DADD}((w_{P+Q} : 1), (w_P : 1), w_Q)$
6: $(W_1 : Z_1) \leftarrow \text{DOUB}((W_0 : Z_0))$
7: $(w_P, w_Q) \leftarrow \text{CSWAP}(w_P, w_q, f_a \overset{?}{=} 1)$
8: **for** $j \leftarrow \max(\lceil \log_2 k_1 \rceil, \lceil \log_2 k_2 \rceil)$ **downto** 0 **do**
9:    $t \leftarrow S_{1,j} \oplus (S_{3,j} \wedge S_{0,j})$
10:   $w_0 \leftarrow \text{SELECT}(w_P, w_Q, \neg S_{3,j})$
11:   $w_1 \leftarrow \text{SELECT}(w_{P+Q}, w_{P-Q}, S_{2,j})$
12:   $(W_4 : Z_4) \leftarrow \text{SELECT}((W_1 : Z_1), (W_0 : Z_0), t)$
13:   $(W_3 : Z_3) \leftarrow \text{SELECT}((W_2 : Z_2), (W_4 : Z_4), \neg S_{0,j})$
14:   $(W_2 : Z_2) \leftarrow \text{DADD}((W_2 : Z_2), (W_4 : Z_4), w_0)$
15:   $(W_0 : Z_0) \leftarrow \text{DADD}((W_1 : Z_1), (W_0 : Z_0), w_1)$
16:   $(W_1 : Z_1) \leftarrow \text{DOUB}((W_3 : Z_3))$
17: **end for**
18: $R \leftarrow (W_0 : Z_0)$
19: $R \leftarrow \text{CCOPY}((W_1 : Z_1), f_i \overset{?}{=} 1)$
20: $R \leftarrow \text{CCOPY}((W_2 : Z_2), f_i \overset{?}{=} 2)$
21: **return** R

The authors of the algorithm discuss in [1] that, if k_1 and k_2 are ℓ-bit integers, then $k_1 P + k_2 Q$ can on average be computed in about 1.4ℓ point additions and 1.4ℓ point doublings. Moreover addition and doubling operations can be performed using differential addition and differential doubling formulas as the differences of the group elements to be added are known by construction. Algorithm 4 presents our implementation of the AK laddering approach by merging consecutive iterations. Expressions for the conditions determining the conditional operations at the beginning of each iteration were tediously evaluated and minimized to reduce the number of required conditional operations for a correct execution. In contrast with the previous laddering algorithms, the LADD operation now performs the laddering step with difference point in projective coordinates because the differences are not fixed in the AK algorithm, as it can be observed at the end of the conditional swap operations that R_Δ can be among the updated variables.

Algorithm 3. AK recoding, returning the sequence S and its length l according to the rules in Table 1. Auxiliary function CSWAP conditionally swaps the two arguments and SELECT returns one of the arguments based on the condition, respectively.

Input: Integers $k_1, k_2 > 0$
Output: Recoded sequence S and its length l
1: $d \leftarrow k_1, e \leftarrow k_2, i \leftarrow 0$
2: **while** $d \neq e$ **do**
3:    $t \leftarrow (d \overset{?}{\equiv} e) \pmod 2$
4:    $t' \leftarrow d \overset{?}{\equiv} 0 \pmod 2$
5:    $c \leftarrow (d - e)$
6:    $f \leftarrow \text{SELECT}(c, -c, (c < 0))$
7:    $(d, e) \leftarrow \text{CSWAP}(d, e, ((c < 0) \land t) \lor (\neg t \land \neg t'))$
8:    $d \leftarrow \text{SELECT}(d, f, t)/2$
9:    $d \leftarrow d/2$
10:   $(d, e) \leftarrow \text{CSWAP}(d, e, ((c < 0) \land t) \lor (\neg t \land \neg t'))$
11:   $S_i \leftarrow \text{SELECT}(\text{SELECT}(R_1, R'_1, (c < 0)), \text{SELECT}(R_2, R'_2, \neg t'), \neg t)$
12:   $i \leftarrow i + 1$
13: **end while**
14: **return** S, i

Table 1. Update rules for double point multiplication in the AK algorithm.

Rule	Condition	d	e	$\vec{u}$	$\vec{v}$	$\vec{\Delta}$	R_u	R_v	R_Δ
R1	$d \equiv e \pmod 2$ and $d > e$	$(d-e)/2$	e	$2\vec{u}$	$\vec{u} + \vec{v}$	$\vec{\Delta}$	$2R_u$	$R_u + R_v$	R_Δ
R1'	$d \equiv e \pmod 2$ and $d < e$	d	$(e-d)/2$	$\vec{u} + \vec{v}$	$2\vec{v}$	$\vec{\Delta}$	$R_u + R_v$	$2R_v$	R_Δ
R2	$d \equiv 0 \pmod 2$	$d/2$	e	$2\vec{u}$	$\vec{v}$	$\vec{u} + \vec{\Delta}$	$2R_u$	R_v	$R_u + R_\Delta$
R2'	$e \equiv 0 \pmod 2$	d	$e/2$	$\vec{u}$	$2\vec{v}$	$\vec{\Delta} + (-\vec{v})$	R_u	$2R_v$	$R_\Delta + (-R_v)$

4   Experimental Results and Discussion

In order to detect what curve model was more promising in terms of performance, we started the implementation from the differential addition and doubling formulas, because the operation counts for the multiple curve models were very similar. We largely followed and reused publicly available code[1] for finite field arithmetic from [19, 23] to enjoy optimizations for our high-end target platforms. This implementation employs compiler intrinsics to take advantage of 128-bit vector instructions for binary field arithmetic, especially the carryless multiplier available through instruction PCLMULQDQ to accelerate polynomial multiplication. The base binary field was defined as $\mathbb{F}_2^{127} \cong \mathbb{F}_2[z]/(z^{127} + z^{63} + 1)$ and its quadratic extension as $\mathbb{F}_{2^{254}} \cong \mathbb{F}_{2^{127}}[s]/(s^2 + s + 1)$. Curve arithmetic for the two

---

[1] SUPERCOP: https://bench.cr.yp.to.

Algorithm 4. AK laddering, employing a projective version of the LADD operation. The RECODE computation returns recoded scalars and the sequence length according to the recoding rules. The auxiliary function CSWAP conditionally swaps the two arguments depending on the value of the last condition.

Input: $k_1 > 0, k_2 > 0 \in \mathbb{Z}$ with $gcd(k_1, k_2) = 1$ and $w(P), w(Q)$ for $P, Q \in E(\mathbb{F}_{2^{2m}})$
Output: $w(k_1 P + k_2 Q) \in E(\mathbb{F}_{2^{2m}})$

1: $(S, l) \leftarrow \text{RECODE}(k_1, k_2)$
2: $R_u \leftarrow w(P), R_v \leftarrow w(Q), R_\Delta \leftarrow w(P - Q)$
3: $b'_0 \leftarrow 0, b'_1 \leftarrow 0, b'_2 \leftarrow 0$
4: **for** $j \leftarrow l - 1$ **downto** 0 **do**
5:    $b_0 = (S_j \overset{?}{=} R_2), b_1 = (S_j \overset{?}{=} R'_1), b_2 = (S_j \overset{?}{=} R'_2)$
7:    $c_0 \leftarrow b'_0 \oplus b_0, c_2 \leftarrow b'_2 \oplus b_2, c_1 \leftarrow (b'_1 \vee b'_2)$
6:    $c_1 \leftarrow c'_1 \oplus (b_1 \vee b_2)$
7:    $(R_v, R_\Delta) \leftarrow \text{CSWAP}(R_v, R_\Delta, (c_0 \wedge \neg c'_1) \vee (c_2 \wedge c'_1))$
8:    $(R_u, R_\Delta) \leftarrow \text{CSWAP}(R_u, R_\Delta, (c_0 \wedge c'_1) \vee (c_2 \wedge \neg c'_1))$
9:    $(R_u, R_v) \leftarrow \text{CSWAP}(R_u, R_v, c_1)$
10:    $(R_v, R_u) \leftarrow \text{LADD}_P(R_u, R_v, R_\Delta)$
11:    $b'_0 \leftarrow b_0, b'_1 \leftarrow b_1, b'_2 \leftarrow b_2$
12: **end for**
13: $(R_u, R_v) \leftarrow \text{CSWAP}(R_u, R_v, b'_1 \vee b'_2)$
14: $(R_u, R_\Delta) \leftarrow \text{CSWAP}(R_u, R_\Delta, b'_2)$
15: $(R_v, R_\Delta) \leftarrow \text{CSWAP}(R_v, R_\Delta, b'_0)$
16: $(R_u, R_v) \leftarrow \text{LADD}_P(R_u, R_v, R_\Delta)$
17: **return** R_u

sets of parameters described in Sect. 2 was implemented on top of the finite field arithmetic and the GLV recoding code for scalar decomposition was extended to work with the new curve parameters. Conditional operations were implemented based on the 128-bit version of the BLENDV instruction.

Our target platforms are an Intel Ivy Bridge Core i5-3510M running at 3.1 GHz, an Intel Haswell Core i7-4770 running at 3.4 GHz and an Intel Skylake Core i7-6700K clocked at 4 GHz, all three with Turbo Boost and HyperThreading disabled to make benchmarking more stable. The code was compiled with *gcc* 7.1.1, *icc* 17.0.4 and *clang* 4.0.1 with the optimization flags -O3 -march=native -fomit-frame-pointer in the three machines. Performance figures under different compilers were somewhat close, with *clang* producing marginally better results for the vectorized field arithmetic. Hence we decided to report only the numbers for the last compiler.

4.1   Laddering Steps

Table 2 presents our performance numbers for evaluating the differential addition and doubling formulae in the target platforms. Field operations within the routines were carefully scheduled to avoid dependencies and exploit the high throughput of vector instructions in the target platforms. Performance clearly increases in more recent microarchitecture families due to faster carryless multiplication instruction.

Differential addition and doubling was faster for all curve models in affine coordinates when compared to Weierstraß in projective coordinates due to the smaller number of multiplications, following our operation counts in Sect. 2. The implementations of the Huff model enjoyed a slightly better instruction scheduling for the field operations and were faster than Weierstraß in affine coordinates. The Edwards model was competitive with Weierstraß, but suffers from larger coefficients and an inefficient way of applying the GLS endomorphism spending expensive inversions to convert points from and to Weierstraß coordinates, which makes it less competitive in the big picture. This was much simpler for the Huff model, because our choice of parameters allows the GLS endomorphism to be applied with a single Frobenius application (Sect. 2.3), amounting to one field addition and some cheap word shuffling instructions. We observe that the Huff model was the best representation in terms of performance for the laddering step.

Table 2. Timings in clock cycles for evaluating the LADD operation in the Ivy Bridge, Haswell and Skylake platforms. Numbers were taken as the average of 10^4 executions and cycles were counted with help of the `rdtsc` instruction with TurboBoost and HyperThreading turned off.

Curve model	Cycles on Ivy	Cycles on Haswell	Cycles on Skylake
Weierstraß affine	630	225	168
Weierstraß projective	758	250	149
Huff	621	215	152
Edwards	643	223	178

4.2 Laddering Algorithms

The observations from Table 2 allow us to reduce the combinations of scalar multiplication algorithm and curve model to select only the most promising ones. Because we could not evaluate the GLS endomorphism in the Edwards model efficiently, we did not implement the two-dimensional DJB and AK laddering algorithms in this curve model. The DJB algorithm was then implemented for the Weierstraß and Huff models, where the GLS endomorphism can be efficiently applied, and the AK algorithm was implemented in the projective Weierstraß model due to the restrictions imposed by the difference point changing at every iteration (difference in projective coordinates). We present the execution times for scalar multiplication in Table 3 below. Following [6], implementations are classified in terms of resistance against timing attacks (TAR) in *uniform* (U) where the same number of field operations is executed at every laddering iteration, but the number of iterations may be variable; and *constant-time* (CT) when the two requirements are satisfied. Timings for DJB and AK include recoding routines, although this step is negligible only in the DJB chain.

Table 3. Results from related work and for our implementation for uniform (U) and constant-time (CT) scalar multiplication algorithms over binary and prime curves at the 128-bit security level. Performance figures are presented for Ivy Bridge (I), Haswell (H) or Skylake (S) platforms. Timings for Fourℚ in the Skylake processor were obtained by benchmarking code available by [7] in our platform (*). Our best numbers for each platform are highlighted in bold and best numbers overall in italic.

Related work (laddering/window)	Curve	TAR	Cycles on I	Cycles on H	Cycles on S
DJB laddering [6]	prime	CT	148,000	-	-
AK laddering [6]	prime	U	133,000	-	-
Fourℚ (window-based) [7]	prime	CT	*69,000*	56,000	46,467*
Montgomery ladder [18,23]	binary	CT	-	70,800	50,823
2-GLV double-and-add [19,20]	binary	CT	114,800	*48,312*	*38,044*
This work (laddering)	Curve	TAR	Cycles on I	Cycles on H	Cycles on S
Montgomery on Weierstraß	binary	CT	142,660	60,838	46,446
Montgomery on Huff	binary	CT	147,914	58,214	44,373
Montgomery on Edwards	binary	CT	150,483	60,083	46,538
DJB on Weierstraß	binary	CT	123,145	**50,851**	39,800
DJB on Huff	binary	CT	**122,541**	51,995	**38,658**
AK on Weierstraß	binary	U	124,267	55,524	41,492

The table demonstrates that binary curves are only competitive in Haswell and Skylake platforms supporting efficient vectorized binary field arithmetic through a very fast carry-less multiplier. Laddering approaches can be competitive with the window-based methods employed in Fourℚ [7] and 2-GLV double-and-add [19] if our techniques are employed. For the Weierstraß model, a direct comparison for the Montgomery Ladder algorithm between our implementation and [23] gives a 8.6% speedup on Haswell. We implemented formulas from Sect. 3.1 for y-coordinate recovery and the resulting cost was negligible, amounting to 333 cycles in Haswell and 312 cycles in Skylake, almost 4 times faster than the 1203 Skylake cycles in [23]. We strongly suspect that their implementation uses two inversions for computing both x and y coordinates.

In particular, performance figures for our implementation of the DJB algorithm in the Huff model were very close to speed records presented in [19], being slower by 5% and 1.6% in the Haswell and Skylake platforms, respectively. This is an interesting result, given that the laddering algorithms are simpler to implement with protection against side-channel attacks, and require smaller amounts of storage. These approaches are somewhat penalized by an affine point addition at the beginning of the laddering algorithm to compute difference points $w(P \pm Q)$. The AK laddering algorithm suffers from a slow recoding routine costing 6.4% and 8.7% of the whole scalar multiplication in the two platforms, respectively. This cost comes mostly from the side-channel protections in Algorithm 3 and the penalty could be alleviated if scalars were already generated in recoded form, given that the constant time requirement is not mandatory. We now discuss application of our techniques in the broader context of key exchange protocols.

4.3 Discussion

Our techniques can be applied for accelerating the curve-based Diffie-Hellman key exchange. In the ephemeral version of the protocol, two parties negotiate a shared key by first generating an ephemeral key pair (a, A) (respectively (b, B)) using a fixed-base scalar multiplication $A = aG$ of generator G (respectively $B = bG$), exchanging the resulting ephemeral public keys A and B and computing the variable-base scalar multiplication of the received public key by the ephemeral private key as $K = abG$.

After restricting the scalar multiplication approaches exclusively to laddering algorithms, there are a few options. The DJB algorithm in the Weierstraß and Huff model is well suited for the fixed-base scalar multiplication, because the affine point addition required for computing $w(G \pm \psi(G))$ can be precomputed and provided together with the curve parameters. The curve models also allow simple recovery of the y-coordinate to allow any receiving party to efficiently evaluate the GLS endomorphism and employ a two-dimensional laddering algorithm for its variable-base scalar multiplication. Notice that this is not true for the AK algorithm, which is more useful for the variable-base multiplication. In the latter case, subscalars can be generated in recoded form to avoid the high cost of the AK recoding. Table 4 reports our timings for implementing the ephemeral Diffie-Hellman key exchange using the proposed optimizations in three scenarios: for comparison with related work, the Montgomery laddering algorithm is used in the Weierstraß model; the DJB algorithm in the Huff model is used for the two scalar multiplications to achieve constant time execution; and side-channel security is relaxed by using the AK algorithm in the Weierstraß model for the second scalar multiplication with previously recoded subscalars.

We restrict the comparison to Haswell and Skylake platforms where binary curves enjoy faster vector instruction sets. Compared to the state-of-the-art in laddering implementations for the Skylake platform, our implementation of the standard Montgomery laddering in the Weierstraß model improves upon [23] by 2.9%, but is not competitive with the window-based method in [19]. The DJB algorithm in the Huff model increases the performance improvement to 21.3% and becomes close to window-based methods. Notice, however, that FourQ employs a large 7.5 KB precomputed table for accelerating the window-based fixed-base portion of the key exchange protocol, a technique from which we do not benefit in this work. We anticipate such an optimization would reach a new speed record for key exchange implementations in the target platform. The performance for key exchange can be slightly increased by using a combination of the DJB and AK laddering algorithms, if one is willing to sacrifice constant-time execution for uniform execution only.

Table 4. Results for related work and our implementations of the Diffie-Hellman key exchange, using different approaches for instantiating the protocol. Benchmarks are presented for Ivy Bridge (I), Haswell (H) or Skylake (S) platforms. Timings for FourQ in the Skylake processor were obtained by benchmarking code available by [7] in our platform (*). Our best numbers in each platform are highlighted in bold and best numbers overall in italic.

Related work (laddering/window)	Curve	TAR	Cycles on I	Cycles on H	Cycles on S
FourQ (window-based) [7]	prime	CT	*104,000*	*88,000*	*74,032**
2-GLV double-and-add [19]	binary	CT	120,000	96,624	76,088
Montgomery ladder [23]	binary	CT	-	-	95,702
This work (laddering)	Curve	TAR	Cycles on I	Cycles on H	Cycles on S
Montgomery on Weierstraß	binary	CT	295,828	121,676	92,890
DJB on Huff	binary	CT	245,682	**101,696**	75,318
DJB + AK on Weierstraß	binary	U	**243,188**	101,769	**74,440**

5   Conclusion

This work presented several contributions. First, we proposed tricks to convert GLS curves to alternative models and obtained parameters optimized for elliptic curve arithmetic. The latest formulas for differential addition and doubling in the Weiertraß, Huff and Edwards models were slightly improved by using lazy reduction and short coefficients allowed by the parameters. The resulting implementations were combined with efficient implementations of the Montgomery, DJB and AK algorithms to obtain efficient scalar multiplication based on laddering, achieving a new speed record in laddering algorithms for high-end Intel desktop processors and performance improvements for executing the Diffie-Hellman key exchange protocol.

As future work, we plan to extend our strategies to the recently proposed twisted μ_4-normal form binary curves [14] to enjoy their efficient arithmetic in the case of elliptic curves with endomorphisms. The entire code for our implementations is available at https://github.com/dfaranha/ladd-gls254 to allow reproducibility and facilitate further improvements by independent researchers.

Acknowledgements. The authors would like to thank the reviewers for their comments. This work is supported in parts by the Intel/FAPESP grant 14/50704-7 under project "Secure Execution of Cryptographic Algorithms", and the grants NIST-60NANB16D246, NSF CNS-1661557, and ARO W911NF-17-1-0311.

References

1. Azarderakhsh, R., Karabina, K.: A new double point multiplication algorithm and its application to binary elliptic curves with endomorphisms. IEEE Trans. Comput. **63**(10), 2614–2619 (2014)
2. Bernstein, D.J.: Differential addition chains, Preprint (2006)

3. Bernstein, D.J., Duif, N., Lange, T., Schwabe, P., Yang, B.: High-speed high-security signatures. J. Cryptograph. Eng. **2**(2), 77–89 (2012)

4. Bernstein, D.J., Lange, T.: Montgomery curves and the Montgomery ladder. In: Bos, J.W., Lenstra, A.K. (eds.) Topics In Computational Number Theory Inspired by Peter L. Montgomery. Cambridge University Press (2017, to appear). https://eprint.iacr.org/2017/293

5. Bernstein, D.J., Lange, T., Rezaeian Farashahi, R.: Binary edwards curves. In: Oswald, E., Rohatgi, P. (eds.) CHES 2008. LNCS, vol. 5154, pp. 244–265. Springer, Heidelberg (2008). https://doi.org/10.1007/978-3-540-85053-3_16

6. Costello, C., Hisil, H., Smith, B.: Faster compact Diffie–Hellman: endomorphisms on the x-line. In: Nguyen, P.Q., Oswald, E. (eds.) EUROCRYPT 2014. LNCS, vol. 8441, pp. 183–200. Springer, Heidelberg (2014). https://doi.org/10.1007/978-3-642-55220-5_11

7. Costello, C., Longa, P.: Fourℚ: four-dimensional decompositions on a ℚ-curve over the mersenne prime. In: Iwata, T., Cheon, J.H. (eds.) ASIACRYPT 2015. LNCS, vol. 9452, pp. 214–235. Springer, Heidelberg (2015). https://doi.org/10.1007/978-3-662-48797-6_10

8. Devigne, J., Joye, M.: Binary huff curves. In: Kiayias, A. (ed.) CT-RSA 2011. LNCS, vol. 6558, pp. 340–355. Springer, Heidelberg (2011). https://doi.org/10.1007/978-3-642-19074-2_22

9. Rezaeian Farashahi, R., Hosseini, S.G.: Differential addition on binary elliptic curves. In: Duquesne, S., Petkova-Nikova, S. (eds.) WAIFI 2016. LNCS, vol. 10064, pp. 21–35. Springer, Cham (2016). https://doi.org/10.1007/978-3-319-55227-9_2

10. Galbraith, S.D., Gaudry, P.: Recent progress on the elliptic curve discrete logarithm problem. Des. Codes Crypt. **78**(1), 51–72 (2016)

11. Galbraith, S.D., Lin, X., Scott, M.: Endomorphisms for faster elliptic curve cryptography on a large class of curves. J. Cryptol. **24**(3), 446–469 (2011)

12. Hankerson, D., Karabina, K., Menezes, A.: Analyzing the Galbraith-Lin-scott point multiplication method for elliptic curves over binary fields. IEEE Trans. Comput. **58**(10), 1411–1420 (2009). http://dx.doi.org/10.1109/TC.2009.61

13. Institute of Electrical and Electronics Engineers: Traditional public-key cryptography (IEEE Std 1363–2000 and 1363a–2004) (2004). http://grouper.ieee.org/groups/1363/

14. Kohel, D.: Twisted μ_4-normal form for elliptic curves. In: Coron, J.-S., Nielsen, J.B. (eds.) EUROCRYPT 2017. LNCS, vol. 10210, pp. 659–678. Springer, Cham (2017). https://doi.org/10.1007/978-3-319-56620-7_23

15. López, J., Dahab, R.: Fast multiplication on elliptic curves over $GF(2^m)$ without precomputation. In: Koç, Ç.K., Paar, C. (eds.) CHES 1999. LNCS, vol. 1717, pp. 316–327. Springer, Heidelberg (1999). https://doi.org/10.1007/3-540-48059-5_27

16. Montgomery, P.L.: Speeding the Pollard and elliptic curve methods of factorization. Math. Comput. **48**(177), 243–264 (1987)

17. National Institute of Standards and Technology: Recommended Elliptic Curves for Federal Government Use. NIST Special Publication (1999). http://csrc.nist.gov/groups/ST/toolkit/documents/dss/NISTReCur.pdf

18. Oliveira, T., Aranha, D.F., López, J., Rodríguez-Henríquez, F.: Fast point multiplication algorithms for binary elliptic curves with and without precomputation. In: Joux, A., Youssef, A. (eds.) SAC 2014. LNCS, vol. 8781, pp. 324–344. Springer, Cham (2014). https://doi.org/10.1007/978-3-319-13051-4_20

19. Oliveira, T., Aranha, D.F., Hernandez, J.L., Rodríguez-Henríquez, F.: Improving the performance of the GLS254 curve. In: CHES Rump Session (2016)

20. Oliveira, T., López, J., Aranha, D.F., Rodríguez-Henríquez, F.: Lambda coordinates for binary elliptic curves. In: Bertoni, G., Coron, J.-S. (eds.) CHES 2013. LNCS, vol. 8086, pp. 311–330. Springer, Heidelberg (2013). https://doi.org/10.1007/978-3-642-40349-1_18

21. Oliveira, T., López, J., Aranha, D.F., Rodríguez-Henríquez, F.: Two is the fastest prime: lambda coordinates for binary elliptic curves. J. Cryptograph. Eng. $4(1)$, 3–17 (2014)

22. Oliveira, T., López, J., Rodríguez-Henríquez, F.: Software implementation of Koblitz curves over quadratic fields. In: Gierlichs, B., Poschmann, A.Y. (eds.) CHES 2016. LNCS, vol. 9813, pp. 259–279. Springer, Heidelberg (2016). https://doi.org/10.1007/978-3-662-53140-2_13

23. Oliveira, T., López, J., Rodríguez-Henríquez, F.: The Montgomery ladder on binary elliptic curves. J. Cryptograph. Eng. (2017, to appear). https://eprint.iacr.org/2017/350

24. Stam, M.: On montgomery-like representations for elliptic curves over $GF(2^k)$. In: Desmedt, Y.G. (ed.) PKC 2003. LNCS, vol. 2567, pp. 240–254. Springer, Heidelberg (2003). https://doi.org/10.1007/3-540-36288-6_18

Analysis of Diagonal Constants in Salsa

Bhagwan N. Bathe[1(✉)], Bharti Hariramani[2(✉)], A.K. Bhattacharjee[2],
and S.V. Kulgod[1]

[1] Bhabha Atomic Research Centre, Mumbai, India
{bathebn,svkulgod}@barc.gov.in
[2] Bhabha Atomic Research Centre (CI), Homi Bhabha National Institute,
Mumbai, India
{bhartih,anup}@barc.gov.in

Abstract. In this paper, we study the effect of diagonal constants in the software oriented stream ciphers Salsa and Chacha. So far, there has not been any clear justification why such constants are chosen. We concentrate on differential cryptanalysis to evaluate how different constants affect the biases after a few rounds in these ciphers. We are using Measure of Uniformity in bias as a measure for differentiating constants as good or bad constants w.r.t. original constant. We have observed that after 4 rounds of Salsa20, for an Input Differential ($\mathcal{ID}$) at Most Significant Bit (MSB) of the third word of quarterround function, the specific patterns in constant involved in that quarterround function leads to increase or decrease in Measure of Uniformity in bias. The location of specific patterns in those diagonal constants varies with the change in last two rotation constants. We did not observe any pattern for ChaCha after 3 rounds. We have also observed a slight increase and decrease in time and data complexity for good and bad constants respectively as compared to an original constant. The designer constants are a good constant however it can be even better with a slight change in constant c_0 or c_3.

Keywords: Constants · Stream cipher · ChaCha · Salsa · Bias · Measure of Uniformity in bias · ARX Cipher · Input Differential · Output differential · Hamming distance

1 Introduction

Stream cipher, Salsa20 [4] was designed by Daniel Bernstein as a candidate for eStream [9] competition in 2006. It was submitted in both hardware and software category. Salsa20 was originally designed for 20 rounds of operations. Salsa20/12 and Salsa20/8 are reduced round versions of Salsa20. Salsa20 was designed for the 256-bit key, however, 128-bit and 80-bit key version are also available.

ChaCha20 [5] is a variant of Salsa20, which provides better diffusion and resistance against cryptanalytic attacks using less number of rounds as compared to Salsa20. Recent CHACHA20-POLY1305-AEAD [16] TLS 1.3 implementation includes ChaCha20 as a symmetric cipher. This, in turn, merits further analysis of both Salsa and ChaCha due to their similar structure.

© Springer International Publishing AG 2017
S.S. Ali et al. (Eds.): SPACE 2017, LNCS 10662, pp. 93–110, 2017.
https://doi.org/10.1007/978-3-319-71501-8_6

Related work. Since it had been published by Bernstein in eStream, significant amount of cryptanalysis [2,6,8,10–15,17,18] was done on both Salsa and ChaCha.

Although several attacks have been found on reduced round versions of the cipher, there is no attack better than exhaustive key search on either Salsa20/12 or Salsa20/20 till date. Most of the attacks are based on differential cryptanalysis where one can apply some input differences to the initial state and observe output differences after certain rounds. Since round function of both Salsa20 and ChaCha are reversible, it is possible to invert a few rounds from a final state to obtain further non-randomness. At SASC 2006, Crowley [8] presented a key recovery attack on Salsa20/5, where he had attacked the Salsa20 PRF directly; the resulting attack on the Salsa20 stream cipher followed straightforwardly. Tsunoo et al. [17] reported the significant bias in the fourth round of Salsa20, which was further used to break 8 rounds of Salsa20 with reduced complexity. Aumasson et al. at FSE 2008 [2] introduced a novel method based on Probabilistic Neutral Bits (PNBs). The work by Shi et al. [15] introduced the concept of Column Chaining Distinguisher (CCD) to achieve some incremental advancements over [2] for both Salsa and ChaCha. Maitra et al. [13] studied an interesting observation regarding round reversal of Salsa, but no significant cryptanalytic improvement could be obtained using this method. An important contribution of the authors in [13] is to correct some parameter values of [2] to obtain better attack complexity. Maitra [12] used a technique of Chosen IVs to obtain certain improvements over existing results. Choudhuri and Maitra [7] used multibit differentials to significantly improve the bias and attack the 6 rounds of Salsa and 5 rounds of ChaCha.

Salsa20 is an ARX-C type cipher. It uses three simple operations: addition modulo 2^n, bit rotation and exclusive or (XOR) with constants at its diagonal position of initial state matrix. It was previously [1] shown that ARX operations with the injection of constants can be used to implement any function. As mentioned in the Salsa20 security document [3]: '*Each Salsa20 column round affects each column, in the same way, starting from diagonal; each Salsa20 row round affects each row, in the same way, starting from the diagonal. Consequently shifting entire row along the diagonal has exactly the same effect on the output. The Salsa20 expansion function eliminates this shift structure by limiting the attacker's control over the hash function input. In particular, the input diagonal is always c_0 = 0x61707865, c_1 = 0x3320646e, c_2 = 0x79622d32, c_3 = 0x6b206574, which is different from all its nontrivial shifts. In other words, two distinct arrays with this diagonal are always in distinct orbits under the shift group*'. The constants are not invariant under rotation hence introduce the asymmetry. The precise value of the constant is not important as long as it is sufficiently asymmetric. The designer did not give any formal logic or explanation for selecting those constants however, it is suggested to change certain constants when being used with reduced key size version or used multiple times in compression function (Rumba). We believe that serious statistical analysis of constants should be carried out before selecting them.

Many government organizations use tweaked ciphers instead of proprietary designs as their security is well understood. Salsa20, being very efficient in software and hardware, is a promising candidate for tweaking. Possible choices for tweaking the design in Salsa20 are round function, rotation constants and diagonal constants.

Our Contribution. In this paper, we have studied the effect of randomly chosen diagonal constants on the overall security of the cipher. Our main strategy for evaluation is to use differential cryptanalysis. We introduced a new term, Measure of Uniformity in bias. It is Root Mean Square (RMS) value of variance from the mean value (Bias) observed over output differential matrix. We introduced some Input Differential ($\mathcal{ID}$) at an initial state and observed the Measure of Uniformity in bias after applying few rounds. We run this experiment for different sets of randomly chosen constants over uniform choices of Key and IV. After 4 rounds, we observed that for the different set of constants, we get different values of Measure of Uniformity in bias. Thus, the set of constants were divided into two categories i.e. good and bad constants w.r.t. original constant. Good constants are those for which the Measure of Uniformity in bias is low and vice versa for bad constants. So, the assumption that constants are chosen randomly may not be complete. We have done more statistical analysis of constants based on Measure of Uniformity in bias as well as published attacks on Salsa and ChaCha.

We have observed that there are a group of constants for which the Measure of Uniformity in bias is very near to each other. Those group of constants having similar Measure of Uniformity in bias has some pattern. Those patterns are observed in the last nibble i.e. 4 LSBs in one of the constant i.e. either c_0, c_1, c_2 or c_3. Among the four constants, similar patterns can be observed in any one of them which depends on the location of $\mathcal{ID}$. In general, if we create an $\mathcal{ID}$ at MSB of the third word of quarterround function, the patterns are observed in the corresponding value of constant involved in that quarterround function. Group is always formed by pair where the 4 LSBs of those particular constants are a complement to each other irrespective of other bits of constant. Group of constants with very low hamming distance have Measure of Uniformity in bias very near to each other except for some specific values at 4 LSBs of the particular constant.

In addition to diagonal constant, Salsa20 uses 4 different rotation constant in quarterround function. We have shown theoretically and experimentally that, there is a certain relation between the location of the pattern in a diagonal constant and the rotation constants. In particular, the location of nibble with a specific pattern in constant varies with the change in values of third and fourth rotation constants. It has been observed that addition (*modulo* 32) of third and fourth rotation constant point to the second bit of nibble (from RHS) with specific patterns.

Our result is based on a Measure of Uniformity in bias after four rounds of operations on Salsa20 with $\mathcal{ID}$ at MSB of 7th word. We studied the effect of constants on Multi-bit Output differential as in [7]. We did not observe any significant change in bias w.r.t. good or bad constants after 4 rounds in Salsa. We have also tested good and bad sets of constants for neutrality measures, forward bias, reverse bias and corresponding time as well as data complexity. It has been observed that there is a slight gain in time and data complexity for good constants and vice versa for bad constants. The constants being used by the designer are in fact near to a good set of constants but few better constants are also available.

Organization of the paper. The paper is organized in 5 Sections. In Sect. 2, Salsa, Chacha and differential cryptanalysis is described in brief. Section 2 also gives a brief description of hardware setup used for running our experiments. Section 3 gives the description of Measure of Uniformity in bias. Our experiments and observations are described in Sect. 4. Finally, we conclude in Sect. 5.

2 Specifications and Preliminaries

The notations to be used in this paper are presented in the Table 1.

Table 1. Notation

Notation	Description
X	The state matrix of the cipher of 16 words
$X^{(0)}$	Initial state matrix
$X^{(R)}$	State matrix after application of R round functions
x_i	i^{th} word of the state matrix (words arranged in row major)
$x_i[j]$	j^{th} bit of ith word
$x + y$	Addition of x and y modulo 2^{32}
$x \oplus y$	Bitwise XOR of x and y
$x \lll n$	Rotation of x by n bits to the left
Δx	XOR difference of x and x'. $\Delta x = x \oplus x'$
D	Measure of Uniformity in Bias
C_{ij}	No of times j^{th} bit of ith word changes i.e., bit counter
A_{ij}	Average of bit counter

2.1 Salsa

The core of the Salsa20 is a hash function with 64-byte input and 64-byte output. The hash function is used in a counter mode as a stream cipher. Salsa20 encrypts a 64-byte block plaintext by hashing the key, nonce, and block number and XORing the result with the plaintext. The initial state of cipher consists of 16 words represented as 4×4 matrix. Each element of the matrix is 32-bit words. The initial matrix can be defined as follows,

$$X^{(0)} = \begin{pmatrix} x_0^{(0)} & x_1^{(0)} & x_2^{(0)} & x_3^{(0)} \\ x_4^{(0)} & x_5^{(0)} & x_6^{(0)} & x_7^{(0)} \\ x_8^{(0)} & x_9^{(0)} & x_{10}^{(0)} & x_{11}^{(0)} \\ x_{12}^{(0)} & x_{13}^{(0)} & x_{14}^{(0)} & x_{15}^{(0)} \end{pmatrix} = \begin{pmatrix} c_0 & k_0 & k_1 & k_2 \\ k_3 & c_1 & v_0 & v_1 \\ t_0 & t_1 & c_2 & k_4 \\ k_5 & k_6 & k_7 & c_3 \end{pmatrix},$$

where,

c_0, c_1, c_2, c_3 are diagonal constants.

$k_0, \dots, k_7$ is 256-bits key

v_0, v_1 is 64-bits nonce

t_0, t_1 is 64-bits counter

Values of diagonal constants are fixed and predefined as c_0 = 0x61707865, c_1 = 0x3320646e, c_2 = 0x79622d32, c_3 = 0x6b206574. For the 128-bit version of Salsa, the key words are repeated twice and the constant values differ slightly. In this paper, we consider the 256-bit version for all the experiments. Further, we will refer to the nonce and counter words together as IV words.

Each Salsa20 round function consists of 4 simultaneous applications of quarterround. The quarterround function is performed on vector $\left(x_a^{(r)}, x_b^{(r)}, x_c^{(r)}, x_d^{(r)}\right)$ to update its values as defined below:

$$\left. \begin{aligned} x_b^{(r+1)} &= x_b^{(r)} \oplus ((x_a^{(r)} + x_d^{(r)}) \lll 7), \\ x_c^{(r+1)} &= x_c^{(r)} \oplus ((x_b^{(r+1)} + x_a^{(r)}) \lll 9), \\ x_d^{(r+1)} &= x_d^{(r)} \oplus ((x_c^{(r+1)} + x_b^{(r+1)}) \lll 13), \\ x_a^{(r+1)} &= x_a^{(r)} \oplus ((x_d^{(r+1)} + x_c^{(r+1)}) \lll 18). \end{aligned} \right\} \tag{1}$$

The Salsa20 round function is applied alternatively on columns and rows. Round function is applied on each of the four columns (x_0, x_4, x_8, x_{12}), (x_5, x_9, x_{13}, x_1), $(x_{10}, x_{14}, x_2, x_6)$ and $(x_{15}, x_3, x_7, x_{11})$ in odd numbered rounds, called as columnrounds. Round function is applied on each of the four rows (x_0, x_1, x_2, x_3), (x_5, x_6, x_7, x_4), $(x_{10}, x_{11}, x_8, x_9)$ and $(x_{15}, x_{12}, x_{13}, x_{14})$ in even numbered rounds, called as rowrounds. The consecutive rounds (a columnround and rowround) together are called a doubleround. The output matrix after R rounds is combined with initial matrix to generate 16 words (or 512 bits) keystream output as $Z = X^{(0)} + X^{(R)}$, where "+" symbolizes wordwise addition modulo 2^{32}, and $X^{(R)} = \text{round}^R(X^{(0)})$. Salsa20 is designed for $R = 20$, i.e. for 20 rounds however software portfolio of eSTREAM [9] has accepted Salsa20/12 version, where $R = 12$.

Each Salsa20 round is reversible as the state-transition operations are reversible, i.e., if $X^{(r+1)} = \text{round}(X^{(r)})$, then $X^{(r)} = \text{round}^{-1}(X^{(r+1)})$, where round^{-1} is the inverse of round. The inverse of the quarterround function on the vector $\left(x_a^{(r+1)}, x_b^{(r+1)}, x_c^{(r+1)}, x_d^{(r+1)}\right)$ is defined as:

$$\left. \begin{aligned} x_a^{(r)} &= x_a^{(r+1)} \oplus ((x_d^{(r+1)} + x_c^{(r+1)}) \lll 18), \\ x_d^{(r)} &= x_d^{(r+1)} \oplus ((x_c^{(r+1)} + x_b^{(r+1)}) \lll 13), \\ x_c^{(r)} &= x_c^{(r+1)} \oplus ((x_b^{(r+1)} + x_a^{(r)}) \lll 9), \\ x_b^{(r)} &= x_b^{(r+1)} \oplus ((x_a^{(r)} + x_d^{(r)}) \lll 7). \end{aligned} \right\} \tag{2}$$

2.2   ChaCha

ChaCha is a 256-bit stream cipher based on Salsa. ChaCha core was proposed by Bernstein as an improvement over Salsa core to increase diffusion over the same number of operations. It was designed to improve diffusion per round, conjecturally increasing resistance to cryptanalysis, while preserving and often improving time per round. ChaCha12 and ChaCha20 are analogous modifications of the 12-round and 20-round ciphers Salsa20/12 and Salsa20/20. ChaCha20 has the similar construction as that of Salsa20. Initial Matrix of ChaCha is as follows,

$$X^{(0)} = \begin{pmatrix} x_0^{(0)} & x_1^{(0)} & x_2^{(0)} & x_3^{(0)} \\ x_4^{(0)} & x_5^{(0)} & x_6^{(0)} & x_7^{(0)} \\ x_8^{(0)} & x_9^{(0)} & x_{10}^{(0)} & x_{11}^{(0)} \\ x_{12}^{(0)} & x_{13}^{(0)} & x_{14}^{(0)} & x_{15}^{(0)} \end{pmatrix} = \begin{pmatrix} c_0 & c_1 & c_2 & c_3 \\ k_0 & k_1 & k_2 & k_3 \\ k_4 & k_5 & k_6 & k_7 \\ t_0 & v_0 & v_1 & v_2 \end{pmatrix}$$

Similar to Salsa, the rightmost matrix shows the initial state that takes four predefined constants $c_0, \ldots, c_3$ (similar to Salsa), 256-bit key $k_0, \ldots, k_7$, 32-bit block counter t_0 and 96-bit nonce v_0, v_1, v_2. ChaCha builds the initial matrix with all attacker controlled input words at the bottom. The quarterround function on the vector $\left(x_a^{(r)}, x_b^{(r)}, x_c^{(r)}, x_d^{(r)} \right)$ is defined below:

$$\left. \begin{array}{l} x_{a'}^{(r)} = x_a^{(r)} + x_b^{(r)}; \quad x_{d'}^{(r)} = x_d^{(r)} \oplus x_{a'}^{(r)}; \quad x_{d''}^{(r)} = x_{d'}^{(r)} \lll 16; \\ x_{c'}^{(r)} = x_c^{(r)} + x_{d''}^{(r)}; \quad x_{b'}^{(r)} = x_b^{(r)} \oplus x_{c'}^{(r)}; \quad x_{b''}^{(r)} = x_{b'}^{(r)} \lll 12; \\ x_a^{(r+1)} = x_{a'}^{(r)} + x_{b''}^{(r)}; \quad x_{d'''}^{(r)} = x_{d''}^{(r)} \oplus x_a^{(r+1)}; \quad x_d^{(r+1)} = x_{d'''}^{(r)} \lll 8; \\ x_c^{(r+1)} = x_{c'}^{(r)} + x_d^{(r+1)}; \quad x_{b'''}^{(r)} = x_{b''}^{(r)} \oplus x_c^{(r+1)}; \quad x_b^{(r+1)} = x_{b'''}^{(r)} \lll 7; \end{array} \right\} \quad (3)$$

Chacha, like Salsa, uses 4 additions, 4 xors and 4 rotations to invertibly update four 32-bit state words. However, Chacha applies the operation in a different order. Unlike the Salsa quarterround, ChaCha quarterround gives each input word a chance to affect each output word and each word is updated twice. In each of the odd rounds, called columnround, we apply quarterround to the four columns (x_0, x_4, x_8, x_{12}), (x_1, x_5, x_9, x_{13}), $(x_2, x_6, x_{10}, x_{14})$, and $(x_3, x_7, x_{11}, x_{15})$. In each of the even rounds, called diagonalround, we apply quarterround to the diagonals $(x_0, x_5, x_{10}, x_{15})$, $(x_1, x_6, x_{11}, x_{12})$, (x_2, x_7, x_8, x_{13}), and (x_3, x_4, x_9, x_{14}). As before, we define $X^{(R)} = \text{round}^R(X^{(0)})$, and the keystream block $Z = X^{(0)} + X^{(R)}$. For ChaCha20, $R = 20$. As with Salsa, each round of ChaCha is reversible.

2.3   Differentials

Given two states $X^{(r)}, X'^{(r)}$, we denote the differential of individual words by $\Delta x_i^{(r)} = x_i^{(r)} \oplus x_i'^{(r)}$. For example, '$\Delta x_{13}^{(0)} = 2^5$' means that we have two initial states $X^{(0)}, X'^{(0)}$ that differ at the 5th bit of the 13th word.

From the perspective of cryptanalysis, we are interested in introducing a difference in the initial state (call it Input Differential or $\mathcal{ID}$) and then attempt to obtain certain biases corresponding to combinations of some output bits (call it Output Differential or $\mathcal{OD}$). In this direction, one can compute

$$\mathsf{Pr}(\Delta x_p^{(r)}[q] = 0 | \Delta x_i^{(0)} = 2^j) = \frac{1}{2}(1 + \varepsilon_d), \tag{4}$$

where the probability is estimated for a fixed key and all possible choices of nonces and counter words, other than the constraints imposed due to the input differences. Here, the bias is denoted by ε_d.

2.4   Hardware Setup

We are using The ANUPAM-AGGRA supercomputer for our experiments. The system consists of 8160 processor cores, 40960 Graphics Processing cores and 32 Terabytes of memory. The nodes of the system are interconnected by high speed Infiniband network with a bandwidth of 40 Gigabits per second. The peak performance of the system is 150 Teraflops and the sustained performance measured using the High Performance Linpack benchmark is 109 Teraflops. Scientific Linux 5.5 is used as the operating system along with OpenMPI, MVAPICH and MVAPICH2 libraries providing the parallel environment. We are using about 120 processor cores for our experiments. Most of the experiments are run for 2^{26} data samples and 4 rounds of Salsa20.

3   Measure of Uniformity in Bias

Security of ARX cipher is not well understood, but they are very efficient in software and hardware. There is always a trade-off between security and efficiency, but since this trade-off is not well understood, typically large number of rounds are preferred to provide larger security margin. Due to this, there are many published attacks on reduced round versions of ARX ciphers. Linear and differential cryptanalysis are the two major tools used against ARX ciphers. Salsa20 being an ARX cipher is also subjected to differential cryptanalysis. In differential cryptanalysis, input differential ($\mathcal{ID}$) is introduced at an initial state with intent to observe output differential ($\mathcal{OD}$) in a particular bit or group of bits as a distinguisher after applying few rounds. We observed that for the different set of diagonal constants, the bias in particular bit may increase or decrease. Hence, we have introduced a general term called Measure of Uniformity in bias ($\mathcal{D}$). It is Root Mean Square (RMS) value of variance from the mean value (Bias) observed over output differential matrix after applying few number of rounds, for some $\mathcal{ID}$. Measure of Uniformity in bias ($\mathcal{D}$) is calculated as,

$$\mathcal{D}_R^{\mathcal{ID}}(c_0, c_1, c_2, c_3) = \sqrt{\frac{\Sigma_{i=0}^{i=15}\Sigma_{j=0}^{j=31}(\frac{1}{2} - \frac{C_{ij}}{\mu})^2}{N}} \tag{5}$$

where,

$\mathcal{ID}$ = Input Differential
R = Number of Rounds
c_0, c_1, c_2, c_3 = Set of diagonal constants.
i = word location
j = bit location
C_{ij} = No of times j^{th} bit of ith word changes.
N = Number of output bits
μ = Number of operations

In above Eq. 5, number of operations represents randomly chosen key and IV for given $\mathcal{ID}$ and set of constants (c_0, c_1, c_2, c_3). Counter (C_{ij}) is normalized using number of operations (μ) and subtracted from theoretically expected value to represent the measure of bias. The RMS value of this bias is then calculated as a Measure of Uniformity in bias over N output bits. Details of an algorithm for calculation of Measure of Uniformity in bias $(\mathcal{D})$ for $\mathcal{ID}$ is as follows:

Input: $\mathcal{ID}$, R, (c_0, c_1, c_2, c_3), μ, N
Result: Measure of Uniformity in Bias $(\mathcal{D}_R^{\mathcal{ID}}(c_0, c_1, c_2, c_3))$
Set constant values to c_0, c_1, c_2, c_3;
loop=0;
while *While loop* $< \mu$ **do**
  Generate $X^{(0)}$ and $X'^{(0)}$, two valid initial states with a given $\mathcal{ID}$;
  Calculate $X^{(R)}$ and $X'^{(R)}$ i.e. state after applying $\mathcal{R}$ rounds;
  For each bit in $X^{(R)}$ and $X'^{(R)}$
  if $X_{ij}^{(R)} \oplus X_{ij}'^{(R)} == 0$ **then**
    Increment counter C_{ij};
  end
  Increment loop;
end
Calculate $A_{ij} = \frac{C_{ij}}{\mu}$ // Average of bit counter
Calculate $\mathcal{D}_R^{\mathcal{ID}}(c_0, c_1, c_2, c_3) = \sqrt{\frac{\Sigma_{i=0}^{i=15} \Sigma_{j=0}^{j=31} (\frac{1}{2} - A_{ij})^2}{N}}$ // Measure of Uniformity in bias

Algorithm 1: Calculates the Measure of Uniformity in bias for the random set of constants for a given $\mathcal{ID}$ after R rounds over N bits.

4   Experiments and Observations

Experiment 1. *Comparison among different sets of random constants.*

As per the designer, rotational invariance with some asymmetry is sufficient condition for choosing constant. However, we believe that this condition may not be sufficient. In order to evaluate correctness of his statement, we have calculated the Measure of Uniformity in bias for three different set of constants,

1. Designer constants,
2. Worst constants like all one or all zero constants,
3. Random constants.

The experiment (Algorithm 1) is run for each set of constants with 2^{26} uniformly distributed values of Key and IV. The experiment is repeated for $\mathcal{ID}$ in each bit of 7th word. 7th word is selected because many published results are based on $\mathcal{ID}$ at 7th word. Measure of Uniformity in bias is observed after four rounds of Salsa20. Results of an experiment are presented in Fig. 1.

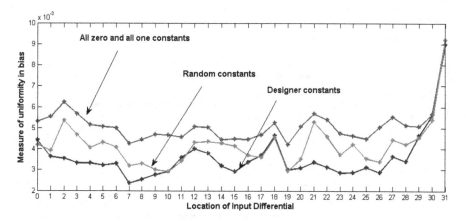

Fig. 1. Measure of Uniformity in bias with 4 set of constants

Observation 1. *Measure of Uniformity in bias is higher for worst constants. It is in the same range for random and designer constants. This observation is valid for $\mathcal{ID}$ at each bit of 7th word.*

Observation 1 indicates that designers statement about constant may not be complete. We need to do the serious statistical analysis of those constants before selecting them. There can be a certain set of constants which can be better or worst than designer constants. This leads to a definition of two categories of constants w.r.t. designer constants and they are as follows,

- Good constants: Whose Measure of Uniformity in bias is less than designer constants.
- Bad constants: Whose Measure of Uniformity in bias is more than designer constants.

Experiment 2. *Choosing optimal $\mathcal{ID}$ for evaluation.*

The aim of this experiment is to select optimal $\mathcal{ID}$ for further cryptanalysis. Most of the published attacks are based on $\mathcal{ID}$ in 7th word. So, we selected 7th word for creating an $\mathcal{ID}$. For $\mathcal{ID}$ in each bit of 7th word, we calculated Measure of Uniformity in bias for n sets of randomly chosen constants. Then for each bit, we calculated minimum, maximum and average of Measure of Uniformity in bias as follows,

- Min $\mathcal{D}_4^{7,k}$: Minimum Measure of Uniformity in bias among n set of random constants when $\mathcal{ID}$ is at $x_7[k]$.
- Max $\mathcal{D}_4^{7,k}$: Maximum Measure of Uniformity in bias among n set of random constants when $\mathcal{ID}$ is at $x_7[k]$.
- Average $\mathcal{D}_4^{7,k}$: Average Measure of Uniformity in bias among n set of random constants when $\mathcal{ID}$ is at $x_7[k]$.

Results of the above experiment are presented in Fig. 2.

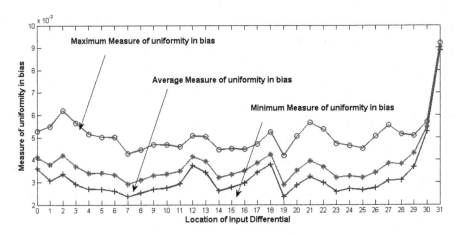

Fig. 2. Minimum, maximum and average Measure of Uniformity in bias for $\mathcal{ID}$ in 7th word

Observation 2. *Minimum, Maximum and Average Measure of Uniformity in bias is higher for $\mathcal{ID}$ at $x_7[31]$.*

Above observation implies that the Measure of Uniformity in bias is maximum when $\mathcal{ID}$ is created at the most significant bit (i.e. 31st or the leftmost bit). Hence for further work, $\mathcal{ID}$ $x_7[31]$ is selected.

Experiment 3. *Evaluation of the random set of constants w.r.t. designer constants with $\mathcal{ID}$ at MSB of 7th word.*

In this experiment, Measure of Uniformity in bias is calculated for a very large number of the randomly chosen set of constants with $\mathcal{ID}$ at MSB of 7th word. Each set is evaluated for 2^{26} uniformly distributed values of key and IV. Set of constants are then sorted as per increasing order of Measure of Uniformity in bias after four rounds of operations. The plot of such sorted data is shown in Fig. 3. Measure of Uniformity in bias for designer constant is taken as reference bias.

Observation 3. *There are certain values of uniformity in bias which are further away from reference bias in both positive and negative side (i.e. above and below reference bias value).*

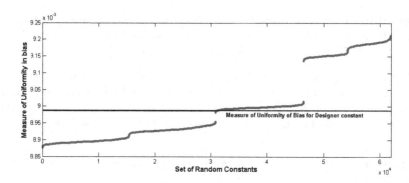

Fig. 3. Plot of the set of randomly chosen constant versus Measure of Uniformity in bias after 4 rounds for $\mathcal{ID}$ at $x_7[31]$. The set of random constants are sorted based on increasing order of Measure of Uniformity in bias.

Table 2. Patterns observed in the last nibble of c_3 for $\mathcal{ID}$ in $x_7[31]$

Group number	Nibble pattern in last byte of c_3	Range of measure of Uniformity in bias
1	$0x2, 0xd, 0x5, 0xa$	0.008877 to 0.008912
2	$0x1, 0x6, 0x9, 0xe$	0.008913 to 0.008955
3	$0x4, 0x3, 0xc, 0xb$	0.008981 to 0.009013
4	$0x7, 0x8$	0.009136 to 0.009166
5	$0xf, 0x0$	0.009167 to 0.009212

Observation 4. *The graph shows 5 steps. The flat portion of the graph indicates that the Measure of Uniformity in bias is very near to each other for some group of constants. It is observed that those groups are having some patterns in the last nibble (4 LSBs) of constant c_3. The group is formed by the pair of complementary nibbles. Following Table 2 shows those 5 groups with patterns and corresponding values of Measure of Uniformity in bias in increasing order.*

Constant c_3 and $x_7[31]$ are involved in same quarterround function during initial rounds. In order to analyze other constants for similar patterns, we extended the similar experiment for $\mathcal{ID}$ in x_8, k_6 and k_1. For $\mathcal{ID}$ in x_8, k_6 and k_1, we observed similar patterns in c_0, c_1, c_2 respectively. From this, we can say that if we create an $\mathcal{ID}$ at MSB of the third word of quarterround function, Measure of Uniformity in bias varies as per above patterns in corresponding constant. Since the third word for quarterround which involves constant c_1 and c_2 are keywords which are not user controlled hence, are not considered further. However, for c_0 and c_3, $\mathcal{ID}$ location is in user controlled bits like IV and counter.

Designer constant c_3 consist of $0x4$ at last nibble and hence belong to Group 3 in Table 2 and Fig. 3. As per definition of good and bad constants, Group 1 ($0x2$, $0xd$, $0x5$, $0xa$) & Group 2 ($0x1$, $0x6$, $0x9$, $0xe$) belong to set of good constants and Group 4 ($0x7$, $0x8$) & Group 5 ($0xf$, $0x0$) belongs to set of bad constants.

Observation 5. *Similar experiment has been carried out for one to five rounds. Some patterns were visible after 2nd and 3rd round but more clear results were obtained after 4th round. No pattern is observed after 5th round.*

For further experiments, we selected some set of constants from the good and bad category from experiment 3. Now onwards they will be referred as good and bad constants. Set of designer constant is taken as a reference. All our further experiments are based on designer constants, good constants and bad constants.

Experiment 4. *Calculation of Forward bias for the designer, good and bad constants.*

In Experiment 3, we sorted the constants w.r.t. Measure of Uniformity in Bias. Taking Measure of Uniformity in bias for designer constant as a reference, we can put the set of constants above the reference line into the set of bad constants and below the reference into the set of good constants. In order to reconfirm this segregation, we selected few constants from the set of good and bad constants and calculated forward bias (ε_d).

Let X, X' be two valid initial states with a given $\mathcal{ID}$ $\Delta_{i,j}^{(0)} = 1$, for which an $\mathcal{OD}$ $\Delta_{p,q}^{(r)}$ is observed after $r < R$ Salsa rounds. Thus, $\mathrm{Pr}(\Delta_{p,q}^{(r)} = 1|\Delta_{i,j}^{(0)}) = \frac{1}{2}(1+\varepsilon_d)$. In this experiment, forward bias (ε_d) is evaluated for $\mathcal{ID}$ at $\Delta_{7,31}^{(0)} = 1$ for designer constants, good constants and bad constants. After 4 rounds, we evaluated bias in both positive and negative direction. A Negative bias $(-\varepsilon_d)$ is referred as minimum bias while a positive bias $(+\varepsilon_d)$ is referred as maximum bias. With $\mathcal{ID}$ at $x_7[31]$, minimum bias occurs at output bit $x_1[12]$ and maximum bias at output bit $x_6[26]$. Figure 4 shows the plot of bias for the designer, good and bad constants.

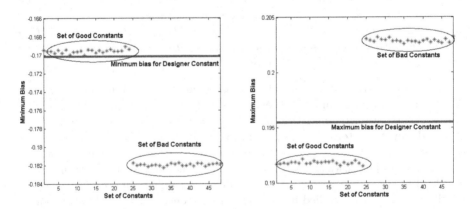

Fig. 4. Plot of constants versus bias. Line denotes reference as bias with designer constants (a) Left Figure: plot for constant versus minimum bias. (b) Right Figure: plot for constant versus maximum bias

Observation 6. *The location of bias is same for the designer, good and bad constants. For bad constants, the forward bias is more as compared to designer constants while it is less for good constants.*

Initially, an experiment was run for 2^{26} data samples on the designer, good and bad constants. Results were also confirmed for 2^{40} data samples for few selected constants.

Experiment 5. *Measure of Uniformity in bias for the designer, good and bad constants with a group of the hamming distance of one.*

The Hamming distance between two strings of equal length is the number of positions at which the corresponding symbols are different. In this experiment, we are analyzing variation in Measure of Uniformity in bias for the group of constants having very low hamming distance between them. For each constant in the set of designer, good and bad constants, we follow the procedure as defined below,

1. Calculate Measure of Uniformity in bias for selected constants with $\mathcal{ID}$ at $\Delta_{7,31}^{(0)} = 1$.
2. Flip one bit (hamming distance one) of selected constant and repeat step one.
3. Repeat step 2 for all possibilities of hamming distance one on selected constant.
4. Plot the Measure of Uniformity in bias for a group of the constant having hamming distance one.

The graph for one set of constants from designer, bad and good constants is shown in Fig. 5.

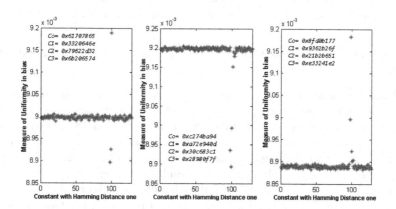

Fig. 5. Plot of constants with hamming distance one versus uniformity in bias. (a) Left Figure: plot for designer constants. (b) Middle Figure: plot for bad constants. (c) Right Figure: plot for good constant

Observation 7. *The Measure of Uniformity in bias for any group of constants with hamming distance one are very near to each other except for some cases. More importantly, those cases had occurred for patterns as per Observation 4. For example, for bad constants, the Measure of Uniformity in bias is maximum. After creating hamming distance one if last nibble changes to a group of good constants then the Measure of Uniformity in bias reduces significantly. We observed that for bad constants when the last nibble of constant c_3 becomes either $0x2$, $0x5$, $0xd$ or $0xa$ then Measure of Uniformity in bias becomes less. For good constants, if it is either $0xf$ or $0x0$, then Measure of Uniformity in bias becomes more.*

Observation 8. *One more important observation is that for designer constant, last nibble of constant c_3 ($0x6b206574$) is $0x4$. If hamming distance one is created at 0th bit of this constant, then nibble becomes $0x5$, thereby reducing the Measure of Uniformity in bias than that of designer constant. If hamming distance one is created at 2nd bit of this constant, then the last digit becomes $0x0$, thereby increasing the Measure of Uniformity in bias than that of designer constant. This is in line with our Observation 4 above.*

Experiment 6. *Effect of good and Bad constants on Multi-bit $\mathcal{OD}$.*

In [7] Choudhuri and Maitra have chosen multi-bit differentials as an extension of suitable single bit differentials with linear approximations, which is essentially a differential-linear attack. They obtained very high bias by the combination of many output bits (19 for Salsa and 21 for ChaCha) in Salsa after 6 rounds and in ChaCha after 5 rounds. In order to see the effect of random constants on their result, we extended similar experiment for the set of a designer, good and bad constants.

Observation 9. *We observed that there is a slight change in bias for bad and good constants in Salsa till round 4, but no significant change is observed in bias after round 5 in Salsa. We did not observe any significant change in bias for ChaCha.*

Experiment 7. *Relation between rotation constants and diagonal constants of Salsa20.*

Salsa20 quarterround function use two type of constants, diagonal constants and rotation constants. So far we have seen the effect of a change in diagonal constants on the overall security of cipher. Salsa20 use $7, 9, 13, 18$ as rotation constants in its quarterround function. In this experiment, we are analyzing the different diagonal constants with different rotation constants while creating $\mathcal{ID}$ at 31st bit of 7th word. Table 3 shows the results of this experiment.

With $\mathcal{ID}$ at $x_7[31]$, Measure of Uniformity in bias is increasing based on a certain pattern in the last constant i.e. c_3 after 4 round (as per Observation 4). With the change in rotation constant value, we still observe pattern on c_3 but at different bit locations.

Observation 10. *It has been observed that all the above Observations are valid for different values of rotation constants. However, the location of nibble with those specific patterns is different for different values of rotation constants.*

Table 3. Location of pattern with different rotation constant

x	y	z	w	Location of pattern on c_3	$(z+w)mod32$
28	18	21	12	0 to 3	1
10	28	5	1	5 to 8	6
27	16	20	20	7 to 10	8
21	6	20	22	9 to 12	10
8	20	11	1	11 to 14	12
7	9	21	25	13 to 16	14
5	15	3	12	14 to 17	15
7	9	9	10	18 to 21	19
8	20	11	10	20 to 23	21
8	20	11	16	26 to 29	27

In order to understand the relation between rotation constants and location of nibble with specific patterns, let us write the quarterround function in general form.

Let x, y, z, w be the rotation constants, then the quarterround function is as:

$$\left.\begin{aligned}
x_b^{(r+1)} &= x_b^{(r)} \oplus ((x_a^{(r)} + x_d^{(r)}) \lll x), \\
x_c^{(r+1)} &= x_c^{(r)} \oplus ((x_b^{(r+1)} + x_a^{(r)}) \lll y), \\
x_d^{(r+1)} &= x_d^{(r)} \oplus ((x_c^{(r+1)} + x_b^{(r+1)}) \lll z), \\
x_a^{(r+1)} &= x_a^{(r)} \oplus ((x_d^{(r+1)} + x_c^{(r+1)}) \lll w).
\end{aligned}\right\} \tag{6}$$

From our earlier experiment, We know that if we create $\mathcal{ID}$ at the third word (x_c) of quarterround, we get the pattern on first word (x_a) of quarterround. We can rewrite above quarterround operation in bit format as in [7]:

$$\left.\begin{aligned}
x_b^r[i+x] &= x_b^{r-1}[i+x] \oplus x_a^{r-1}[i] \oplus x_d^{r-1}[i] \oplus Carry_b[i] \\
x_c^r[i+y] &= x_c^{r-1}[i+y] \oplus x_a^{r-1}[i] \oplus x_b^r[i] \oplus Carry_c[i] \\
x_d^r[i+z] &= x_d^{r-1}[i+z] \oplus x_b^r[i] \oplus x_c^r[i] \oplus Carry_d[i] \\
x_a^r[i+w] &= x_a^{r-1}[i+w] \oplus x_c^r[i] \oplus x_d^r[i] \oplus Carry_a[i]
\end{aligned}\right\} \tag{7}$$

So x_a can be written as,

$$x_a^r[i+w]$$

$$= x_a^{r-1}[i+w] \oplus x_c^r[i] \oplus x_d^r[i] \oplus Carry_a[i]$$

$$= x_a^{r-1}[i+w] \oplus x_c^{r-1}[i] \oplus x_a^{r-1}[i-y] \oplus x_b^r[i-y] \oplus Carry_c[i-y] \oplus x_d^r[i] \oplus Carry_a[i]$$

$$= x_a^{r-1}[i+w] \oplus x_c^{r-1}[i] \oplus x_a^{r-1}[i-y] \oplus x_b^{r-1}[i-y] \oplus x_a^{r-1}[i-y-x] \oplus x_d^{r-1}[i-y-x] \oplus Carry_b[i-y-x] \oplus Carry_c[i-y] \oplus x_d^r[i] \oplus Carry_a[i]$$

$$= x_a^{r-1}[i+w] \oplus x_c^{r-1}[i] \oplus x_a^{r-1}[i-y] \oplus x_b^{r-1}[i-y] \oplus x_a^{r-1}[i-y-x] \oplus x_d^{r-1}[i-y-x] \oplus Carry_b[i-y-x] \oplus Carry_c[i-y] \oplus x_d^{r-1}[i] \oplus x_b^r[i-z] \oplus x_c^r[i-z] \oplus Carry_d[i-z] \oplus Carry_a[i]$$

$$= x_a^{r-1}[i+w] \oplus x_c^{r-1}[i] \oplus x_a^{r-1}[i-y] \oplus x_b^{r-1}[i-y] \oplus x_a^{r-1}[i-y-x] \oplus x_d^{r-1}[i-y-x] \oplus Carry_b[i-y-x] \oplus Carry_c[i-y] \oplus x_d^{r-1}[i] \oplus x_b^{r-1}[i-z] \oplus x_a^{r-1}[i-z-x] \oplus x_d^{r-1}[i-z-x] \oplus Carry_b[i-z-x] \oplus x_c^r[i-z] \oplus Carry_d[i-z] \oplus Carry_a[i]$$

$$= x_a^{r-1}[i+w] \oplus x_c^{r-1}[i] \oplus x_a^{r-1}[i-y] \oplus x_b^{r-1}[i-y] \oplus x_a^{r-1}[i-y-x] \oplus x_d^{r-1}[i-y-x] \oplus Carry_b[i-y-x] \oplus Carry_c[i-y] \oplus x_d^{r-1}[i] \oplus x_b^{r-1}[i-z] \oplus x_a^{r-1}[i-z-x] \oplus x_d^{r-1}[i-z-x] \oplus Carry_b[i-z-x] \oplus x_c^{r-1}[i-z] \oplus x_a^{r-1}[i-z-y] \oplus x_b^{r-1}[i-z-y] \oplus Carry_c[i-z-y] \oplus Carry_d[i-z] \oplus Carry_a[i]$$

$$= x_a^{r-1}[i+w] \oplus x_c^{r-1}[i] \oplus x_a^{r-1}[i-y] \oplus x_b^{r-1}[i-y] \oplus x_a^{r-1}[i-y-x] \oplus x_d^{r-1}[i-y-x] \oplus Carry_b[i-y-x] \oplus Carry_c[i-y] \oplus x_d^{r-1}[i] \oplus x_b^{r-1}[i-z] \oplus x_a^{r-1}[i-z-x] \oplus x_d^{r-1}[i-z-x] \oplus Carry_b[i-z-x] \oplus x_c^{r-1}[i-z] \oplus x_a^{r-1}[i-z-y] \oplus x_b^{r-1}[i-z-y] \oplus x_a^{r-1}[i-z-y-x] \oplus x_d^{r-1}[i-z-y-x] \oplus Carry_b[i-z-y-x] \oplus Carry_c[i-z-y] \oplus Carry_d[i-z] \oplus Carry_a[i]$$

Above equation indicates that $x_a^r[i+w]$ depends on $x_c^{r-1}[i]$ and $x_c^{r-1}[i-z]$ and hence, $x_a^r[i]$ will depend on $x_c^{r-1}[i-w]$ and $x_c^{r-1}[i-z-w]$. This relation gives the indication that the location of the pattern depends on two rotation constants, z and w.

Observation 11. *It has been observed that the location of the pattern depends on two rotation constants z and w i.e. third and fourth rotation constant. As shown in Table 3, $(z+w) \mod 32$ (last column) indicates the second bit of nibble with specific patterns. For rotation constants 7,9,21 and 25, the value of z and w is 21 and 25 respectively. So $(21+25) \mod 32 = 14$ which is second bit of the nibble (bit 13 to bit 16), with a specific pattern.*

4.1   Experiments and Observations for ChaCha

We carried out all above experiments for ChaCha also. We did not observe any patterns which can divide them into the set of good or bad constants. Surprisingly, patterns that we observed in Salsa does not show any significant results in ChaCha.

5   Conclusion

We have done the systematic statistical analysis based on Measure of Uniformity in bias for diagonal constants used by Salsa20 and ChaCha. Some significant results are observed for Salsa after 4 rounds but those results are not applicable to ChaCha. We have shown that there are some set of constants which are good and bad than designer constants. Constants c_3 or c_0 having 0x2, 0xd, 0x5, 0xa, 0x1, 0x6, 0x9, 0xe in the last nibble are good set of constants. Constants c_3 or

c_0 having $0x7$, $0x8$, $0x0$, $0xf$ in the last nibble are bad set of constants. We have also shown that for bad constants, the bias is more and for good constants, the bias is less. We have observed that the location of the pattern in a particular constant also depends on third and fourth rotation constant. The designer constants are near to a good set of constants however it can be even better with a slight change in constant c_0 or c_3. We do not claim that there is a weakness in original algorithm if we use the designer constants but we believe that using good constants can improve the security margin. We can use Measure of Uniformity in bias as a parameter while choosing random constants for tweaked design based on Salsa20.

Acknowledgments. The authors would like to thank anonymous reviewers for detailed comments. The authors are also thankful to Computer Division of Bhabha Atomic Research Centre for use of super computing facility.

References

1. Ashur, T., Liu, Y.: Rotational cryptanalysis in the presence of constants. IACR Cryptology ePrint Archive 2016, 826 (2016). http://eprint.iacr.org/2016/826
2. Aumasson, J.-P., Fischer, S., Khazaei, S., Meier, W., Rechberger, C.: New features of Latin dances: analysis of Salsa, ChaCha, and Rumba. In: Nyberg, K. (ed.) FSE 2008. LNCS, vol. 5086, pp. 470–488. Springer, Heidelberg (2008). https://doi.org/10.1007/978-3-540-71039-4_30
3. Bernstein, D.: Salsa20 security (2005). http://cr.yp.to/snuffle/security.pdf
4. Bernstein, D.J.: Salsa20 specification. eSTREAM Project algorithm description (2005). http://www.ecrypt.eu.org/stream/salsa20pf.html
5. Bernstein, D.J.: ChaCha, a variant of Salsa20. In: Workshop Record of SASC, vol. 8 (2008)
6. Hernandez-Castro, J.C., Tapiador, J.M.E., Quisquater, J.-J.: On the Salsa20 core function. In: Nyberg, K. (ed.) FSE 2008. LNCS, vol. 5086, pp. 462–469. Springer, Heidelberg (2008). https://doi.org/10.1007/978-3-540-71039-4_29
7. Choudhuri, A.R., Maitra, S.: Significantly improved multi-bit differentials for reduced round salsa and chacha. IACR Cryptology ePrint Archive 2016, 1034 (2016). http://eprint.iacr.org/2016/1034
8. Crowley, P.: Truncated differential cryptanalysis of five rounds of Salsa20. IACR Cryptology ePrint Archive 2005, 375 (2005). http://eprint.iacr.org/2005/375
9. The ECRYPT stream cipher project. eSTREAM portfolio of stream ciphers. http://www.ecrypt.eu.org/stream/
10. Fischer, S., Meier, W., Berbain, C., Biasse, J.-F., Robshaw, M.J.B.: Non-randomness in eSTREAM candidates Salsa20 and TSC-4. In: Barua, R., Lange, T. (eds.) INDOCRYPT 2006. LNCS, vol. 4329, pp. 2–16. Springer, Heidelberg (2006). https://doi.org/10.1007/11941378_2
11. Ishiguro, T., Kiyomoto, S., Miyake, Y.: Latin dances revisited: new analytic results of Salsa20 and ChaCha. In: Qing, S., Susilo, W., Wang, G., Liu, D. (eds.) ICICS 2011. LNCS, vol. 7043, pp. 255–266. Springer, Heidelberg (2011). https://doi.org/10.1007/978-3-642-25243-3_21
12. Maitra, S.: Chosen IV cryptanalysis on reduced round ChaCha and Salsa. Discret. Appl. Math. **208**, 88–97 (2016). http://www.sciencedirect.com/science/article/pii/S0166218X16300841

13. Maitra, S., Paul, G., Meier, W.: Salsa20 cryptanalysis: new moves and revisiting old styles. In: WCC 2015, the Ninth International Workshop on Coding and Cryptography, Paris, France, 13–17 April 2015 (2015). http://eprint.iacr.org/2015/217, http://eprint.iacr.org/2015/217
14. Mouha, N., Preneel, B.: A proof that the ARX Cipher Salsa20 is secure against differential cryptanalysis. IACR Cryptology ePrint Archive 2013, 328 (2013). http://eprint.iacr.org/2013/328
15. Shi, Z., Zhang, B., Feng, D., Wu, W.: Improved key recovery attacks on reduced-round Salsa20 and ChaCha. In: Kwon, T., Lee, M.-K., Kwon, D. (eds.) ICISC 2012. LNCS, vol. 7839, pp. 337–351. Springer, Heidelberg (2013). https://doi.org/10.1007/978-3-642-37682-5_24
16. https://tools.ietf.org/html/draft-ietf-tls-tls13-12
17. Tsunoo, Y., Saito, T., Kubo, H., Suzaki, T., Nakashima, H.: Differential Cryptanalysis of Salsa20/8 (2007). http://ecrypt.eu.org/stream/papersdir/2007/010.pdf
18. Velichkov, V., Mouha, N., De Cannière, C., Preneel, B.: UNAF: a special set of additive differences with application to the differential analysis of ARX. In: Canteaut, A. (ed.) FSE 2012. LNCS, vol. 7549, pp. 287–305. Springer, Heidelberg (2012). https://doi.org/10.1007/978-3-642-34047-5_17

Practical Fault Attacks on Minalpher: How to Recover Key with Minimum Faults?

Avik Chakraborti[1], Nilanjan Datta[2(✉)], and Mridul Nandi[1]

[1] Indian Statistical Institute, Kolkata, 203, B.T. Road, Kolkata 700108, India
avikchkrbrti@gmail.com, mridul.nandi@gmail.com
[2] Indian Institute of Technology, Kharagpur, Kharagpur 721302, West Bengal, India
nilanjan_isi_jrf@yahoo.com

Abstract. This work presents two *differential fault attacks* (or DFA) on Minalpher, a second round CAESAR candidate under practical fault model with as few faults as possible. Minalpher uses a new primitive called tweakable Even-Mansour, based on a permutation-based block-cipher proposed by Even and Mansour and to the best of our knowledge, no practical DFA has yet been reported on it. In the first DFA, only two random faults have been injected on two consecutive 4-bit nibbles (i.e. within total 8 bits) of a specific internal state. We show that (i) if both the faults are injected at the same nibble the key-space for the intermediate key can be reduced significantly from 2^{256} to 2^{32} and (ii) if the faults are injected at different positions, the key-space for the intermediate key can be reduced further to only 2^{16}. In the second DFA, we first consider two faults into a single nibble, which reduces the keyspace from 2^{256} to 2^{48}. Moreover, we show that one additional fault (i.e. total three faults) helps to reduce the key-space significantly to 2^8. We can compute the correct intermediate key by observing a few more plain-text, cipher-text pairs, which helps in computing valid cipher-text, tag pairs for any message and associated data under a fixed nonce.

Keywords: Minalpher · Fault · DFA · Tweakable Even Mansour · Nibble

1 Introduction

Fault attacks pose a serious threat in modern cryptographic implementations. In this type of attacks, the analyzed device is forced to operate under some unusual operating conditions (injecting faults through modifications of the power supply, clock source by injecting glitches) to produce erroneous outputs, by virtue of which secret informations (from internal states of a cipher to the entire secret key) can be revealed. Introduction of several hardwares like smart cards, mobile devices and many other devices associated with cryptographic applications requires fault resistance.

One of the most popular fault based attack, named as *differential fault analysis* (DFA) has been applied on DES by Biham and Shamir in [8]. Later DFA

© Springer International Publishing AG 2017
S.S. Ali et al. (Eds.): SPACE 2017, LNCS 10662, pp. 111–132, 2017.
https://doi.org/10.1007/978-3-319-71501-8_7

on both block-ciphers and stream-ciphers like AES [11,22,23,25], LED [20,21], Trivium [16,17], RC4 [9], Grain [3,5], Mickey 2.0 [2] have been proposed. AES proposed by Daemen and Rijnmen [10] is one of the most analyzed block-cipher. Lot of differential fault analysis have been done on AES. The first such attack has been proposed by [22]. To the best of our knowledge, the best fault analysis on AES has been Proposed by Tunshell *et al.* [25].

1.1 Fault Attacks on AE Schemes

Fault attacks are trivial to mount on block-cipher based AE scheme where the cipher-text blocks are affine functions of the plain-text and some intermediate block-cipher outputs. The standard technique for such an attack is, first mount a fault attack on the underlying block-cipher, and then trivially extend that attack due to the aforementioned property. In [23] Saha *et al.* have proposed a DFA on a CAESAR candidate APE. The attack reduces the key search space for APE-80 by injecting two 5-bit diagonal faults. Recently Dobraunig *et al.* [15] have developed a statistical fault attacks on several nonce-based authenticated encryption modes for AES. Their attack is applicable to the ISO/IEC standards GCM [13], CCM [26], EAX [7], and OCB [14], as well as several second-round candidates of the ongoing CAESAR competition like ELmD [12], CLOC [19], SILC [18]. All these attacks are based on the Statistical Fault Attacks by Fuhr *et al.*, which use a biased fault model and operate on collections of faulty ciphertexts.

1.2 Motivation of the Work

Central to our work is the second round CAESAR [1] candidate Minalpher, that uses a new primitive called tweakable Even-Mansour, based on a permutation-based block-cipher proposed by Even and Mansour. Minalpher has been well-evaluated and the designers has provided an extensive cryptanalysis report on it, however the analysis does not provide much information on the security of Minalpher against fault attacks. In [6], Yoshikawa and Nozaki presented a statistical fault analysis on Minalpher, capturing multiple correct and faulty cipher-texts to recover the correct secret key, using clock glitch. It is interesting to see that, there is no proper theoretical fault attacks on Minalpher has been yet reported and one can easily see that, the previous mentioned fault attack approaches no longer works for it. So, analyzing the fault resistance of Minalpher, is an interesting and non-trivial research problem.

1.3 Our Contribution

In this work, we investigate the resistance of Minalpher against fault attacks and demonstrate the vulnerability of the cipher against *differential fault attack* (DFA) under relaxed and practical fault model. Our results are two fold:

□ DFA WITH 2 SINGLE-NIBBLE FAULT INJECTED QUERIES. This analysis considers injection of two random faults both at two consecutive nibbles at a specific internal state of the cipher. We make one general encryption query and two fault injected encryption queries. Our analysis shows that,

- If both the faults are injected at the same location, the key space for the intermediate key can be reduced from 2^{256} to only 2^{32} with a practical time complexity of $O(2^{32})$.
- Further, if both the faults are injected at different locations (i.e., two different consecutive nibble positions), the key space for the intermediate key can be reduced further from 2^{256} to only 2^{16} with a reduced time complexity of $O(2^{16})$.

This key can be used further to forge a cipher-text for any message and associated data with the same nonce.

□ DFA WITH 3 SINGLE-NIBBLE FAULT INJECTED QUERIES. Here we consider the fault model with three random faults all injected at a single nibble of the cipher's internal state. We make one general encryption query and three fault injected encryption queries. In this case, we first observed that, two random faults (instead of three) injection at different nibble locations reduces the key space from 2^{256} to 2^{48} with a time complexity of $O(2^{48})$. More importantly, if we inject one more additional fault (total three faults) at a different location, the key space for the intermediate key can be reduced significantly from 2^{256} to 2^8. This analysis follows exactly the same procedure as the previous fault analysis mentioned for the first case. Note that, an earlier version of this result has been presented in DIAC [4].

1.4   Significance of the Work

This work presents the first DFA against Minalpher using only 2 and 3 faults, with an in-depth theoretical analysis. However, this result does not refute any standard security claims made by the designers but presents the behavior of Minalpher against differential fault attack. Minalpher uses a newly designed permutation in its structure, and this attack exploits the design of this permutation. This work not only mentions the fault attack against Minalpher, it also opens an avenue to update the underlying permutation that can resist on increase the complexity of differential fault attacks.

2   Preliminaries

2.1   Minalpher Authenticated Encryption Mode

Here we provide a complete technical description of Minalpher AEAD mode, with most of the notations and variable names borrowed from the original proposal [24]. Minalpher is based on a new primitive called Tweakable Even-Mansour mode (TEM), which essentially is a tweakable block cipher based on a 256-bit permutation P. It is described by an algorithm called TEM_Enc.

TEM_Enc takes as input a 128-bit secret key MK, a flag flag, a nonce N, two index i, j and a message M, with $|\text{flag}\|N| = 128$. The algorithm first computes $L = (MK\|\text{flag}\|N) \oplus P(MK\|\text{flag}\|N)$, and returns a ciphertext $C = \alpha^i(\alpha + 1)^j L \oplus P(M \oplus \alpha^i(\alpha + 1)^j L)$. Here α is a primitive element of $\mathbb{F}_{2^{256}}$ with some pre-defined primitive polynomial say $g(\alpha)$.

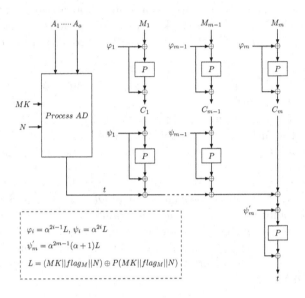

Fig. 1. Minalpher message processing and tag generation phase.

Now, we describe minalpher AEAD algorithm, defined through TEM_Enc: The minalpher AEAD algorithm takes as input MK, N and $M = (M_1, \ldots, M_m) \in (\{0,1\}^n)^m$ and returns the

- ciphertext $C = (C_1, \ldots, C_m)$ where

$$C_i = \text{TEM\_Enc}(MK, \text{flag}_M, N, 2i - 1, 0, M_i)$$

- tag $t = \text{TEM\_Enc}(MK, \text{flag}_M, N, 2m - 1, 1, C_m \oplus t_{m-1})$ where

$$t_i = t_{i-1} \oplus TEM\_Enc(MK, \text{flag}_M, N, 2i, 0, C_i), \quad i = 1, \ldots, m - 1$$

The above algorithm is pictorially depicted in Fig. 1.

2.2   Description of P

P is a 256-bit substitution permutation based permutation, which runs for 17.5 rounds. The 256-bit state can be viewed as two 2-D matrix A and B, where each of them are 4×8, 4-bit nibbles. The permutation state X_i at round i computed by

$$X_i = R(X_{i-1}) = M(T(S(X_i))) \oplus RC_{i-1}$$

for $1 \le i \le 17$, where RC_{i-1} is a constant depending upon the round i. The round function R is also shown in Fig. 2. It actually works on A^i and B^i, which are state representation of X_i. The final state X_{18} is computed by $X_{18} = T(S(X_{17}))$. Here the use of RC_{i-1} is omitted as it is not relevant for our attack. The sub-functions S, T and M are described below.

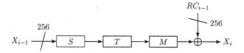

Fig. 2. R function

- **S Function.** This function is realized by a 4-bit Sbox s which replaces a nibble x by $s(x)$. S receives two 4×8 matrices A^{in}, B^{in} and applies s to all of the nibbles of both A^{in} and B^{in}, to produce the output A^{out} and B^{out}. The description of s is given by the Table 1 in the appendix.
- **T Function.** T receives two 4×8 nibble matrices A^{in} and B^{in} and outputs $A^{out} = SR^2(B^{in})$ and $B^{out} = SR^1(A^{in}) \oplus SR^2(B^{in})$ respectively. Here SR^1 and SR^2 are two positional matrices depicted in Fig. 3. By choice, SR^1 and SR^2 are inverse of each other.

Table 1. s Function

x	0	1	2	3	4	5	6	7	8	9	A	B	C	D	E	F
s(x)	B	3	4	1	2	8	C	F	5	D	E	0	6	9	A	7

0,0	0,1	0,2	0,3	0,4	0,5	0,6	0,7
1,0	1,1	1,2	1,3	1,4	1,5	1,6	1,7
2,0	2,1	2,2	2,3	2,4	2,5	2,6	2,7
3,0	3,1	3,2	3,3	3,4	3,5	3,6	3,7

SR^1

0,0	0,1	0,2	0,3	0,4	0,5	0,6	0,7
1,0	1,1	1,2	1,3	1,4	1,5	1,6	1,7
2,0	2,1	2,2	2,3	2,4	2,5	2,6	2,7
3,0	3,1	3,2	3,3	3,4	3,5	3,6	3,7

SR^2

0,6	0,7	0,1	0,0	0,2	0,3	0,4	0,5
1,4	1,5	1,0	1,1	1,7	1,6	1,2	1,3
2,3	2,2	2,4	2,5	2,6	2,7	2,0	2,1
3,2	3,3	3,6	3,7	3,0	3,1	3,5	3,4

0,3	0,2	0,4	0,5	0,6	0,7	0,0	0,1
1,2	1,3	1,6	1,7	1,0	1,1	1,5	1,4
2,6	2,7	2,1	2,0	2,2	2,3	2,4	2,5
3,4	3,5	3,0	3,1	3,7	3,6	3,2	3,3

Fig. 3. SR^1 and SR^2

- **M Function.** M takes as input A^{in} and B^{in} and multiplies each of the columns of A^{in} and B^{in} by the matrix described below to produce the output A^{out} and B^{out}. The matrix is as follows:

$$\begin{pmatrix} 1 & 1 & 0 & 1 \\ 1 & 1 & 1 & 0 \\ 0 & 1 & 1 & 1 \\ 1 & 0 & 1 & 1 \end{pmatrix}$$

2.3 Integrity Security Models

Let $\mathcal{AE} = (\mathcal{K}, \mathcal{E}, \mathcal{D}, \mathcal{V})$ be an authenticated encryption scheme, where $\mathcal{K}$ is the key generation algorithm, $\mathcal{E}$ is the encryption algorithm, $\mathcal{D}$ is decryption algorithm and $\mathcal{V}$ is the verification algorithm. We use a special symbol $\perp$ (abort) when the output of the verification algorithm is false. Denote uniform random sampling of x from a finite set X by $x \xleftarrow{\$} X$. The integrity security notion with both encryption and verification oracle access is defined as below.

Definition 1. *The INT-CTXT advantage of a distinguisher $\mathcal{D}$ with respect to $\mathcal{AE}$, is defined as*

$$\mathbf{Adv}_{\mathcal{AE}}^{INT\text{-}CTXT}(\mathcal{D}) = |Pr[K \xleftarrow{\$} \mathcal{K} : \mathcal{D}^{\mathcal{E}_K, \mathcal{V}_K} \neq \perp]|$$

We assume that $\mathcal{D}$ does not make a verification query (N, AD, C, T) if it ever obtained $(C, T) \leftarrow \mathcal{E}_K(N, AD, M)$ for some M. We use the notation $\mathbf{Adv}_{\mathcal{AE}}^{INT\text{-}CTXT}(q, l)$ to denote the supremum taken over all distinguishers making q queries with maximum message length as l bits.

By $\mathbf{Adv}_{\mathcal{AE}}^{INT\text{-}CTXT}(q, l) \leq 2^{-s}$, we mean $\mathcal{AE}$ has s bit INT-CTXT security against all adversaries making q queries with maximum query length l bits. In *nonce respect* settings $\mathcal{D}$ can not repeat N for distinct queries to $\mathcal{E}_K$. In *nonce misuse* settings $\mathcal{D}$ can repeat N for distinct queries to $\mathcal{E}_K$.

2.4 Security Claims for Minalpher

The designers of Minalpher proposed (Sects. 2.2 and 2.3 in [24]) the following claim.

Claim. Minalpher has 128-bit security for both privacy and integrity in the nonce respect settings as well as in nonce misuse settings.

2.5 Symbols and Notations

For any two $X, Y \in \{0, 1\}^{128}$, the xor operation is denoted by $X \oplus Y$. Let M_1 be a single block message. We denote φ_1, the key for computing $C_1 = \text{TEM\_Enc}(MK, flag_M, N, 1, 0, M_1)$ by $\varphi_1 = I\|K$, with $|I| = |K|$. Note that,

$\varphi_i = \alpha^{2i-1}L$, such that $L = \alpha^{-1}\varphi_1$. Both I, K are described by 4×8 nibble matrices. For any three $a, b, c \in \{0, 1\}^{128}$, we represent a, b and c by 4×8 nibble matrices. We use the notation $SN_{ij}^{a,b,c}$ to denote $SN^{-1}(a_{i,j} \oplus b_{i,j} \oplus c_{i,j})$. Let, the initial state of P is $State = LS \| RS$, with $|LS| = |RS|$. The state after S, T and M functions at round i is denoted by $State^{i,S} = LS^{i,S} \| RS^{i,S}$, $State^{i,T} = LS^{i,T} \| RS^{i,T}$ and $State^{i,M} = LS^{i,M} \| RS^{i,M}$ respectively. For the ease of understanding, we use SN, SR and MC instead of S, T and M respectively in the figures and the equation sets.

3   A Practical DFA with a Two Random Faults

This section briefly describes the attack techniques. In this work, we attempted to make the fault injection practical. We also aimed to decrease the number of faults and the attack complexity as low as possible. Thus, we simulated the fault propagation by programming for all the consecutive nibble positions (as injecting random faults into two consecutive 4-bit nibbles i.e., into a byte may be practical). Also note that, injecting random faults into two consecutive nibbles is almost the same as injecting random fault into a byte. The only difference is the need of nonzero fault injection into both the halves (first 4-bits and second 4-bits) of the byte. Thus, if the fault is random then with high probability, nonzero faults are injected into both the halves. We found 9 pairs of $((i, j), (i, j + 1))$ coordinates in the cipher's state such that, if we inject two faults (for two different encryption queries) into two of these 9 locations, the keyspace reduction and the time complexity of the attack are optimized. These 9 pairs of locations are described by the set

$$F = \{((0,0), (0,1)), ((0,4), (0,5)), ((1,0), (1,1)), ((1,6), (1,7)), ((2,2), (2,3)),$$
$$((2,3), (2,4)), ((2,6), (2,7)), ((3,2), (3,3)), ((3,4), (3,5))\}$$

We have computed the differential propagation for each of these locations in F and constructed the cipher-text differences. We can choose any two locations from F and the attack complexity are very much practical. We have for some pair of locations in $F \times F$, there are 4 *nonoverlapping* inactive nibbles for the cipher-text difference at $LS^{18,T}$. By *nonovelapping* nibble, we mean that this nibble is inactive for both the differential propagations. Otherwise there is an *overlap*. For example, if we inject both the faults at the same location say at $LS_{3,4}^{15,T}$ and $LS_{3,5}^{15,T}$, the overlaps will be minimum (4 nonoverlapped nibbles). In that case the intermediate keyspace is reduced from 2^{256} to 2^{32} with a time complexity of $O(2^{32})$. White cells in both Figs. 4a and b are inactive and at the same position and hence are nonoverlapping with each other.

However, if we inject faults at two different locations say $(LS_{3,4}^{15,T}, LS_{3,5}^{15,T})$ and $(LS_{3,2}^{15,T}, LS_{3,3}^{15,T})$, the overlaps will be maximum (no nonoverlapped nibbles).

(a) The Two Inactive Nibbles at $LS^{18,T}$ for the First Fault

(b) The Two Inactive Nibbles at $LS^{18,T}$ for the Second Fault

Fig. 4. Nonoverlapping inactives nibbles

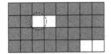 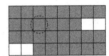

(a) The Two Inactive Nibbles at $LS^{18,T}$ for the First Fault

(b) The Two Inactive Nibbles at $LS^{18,T}$ for the Second Fault

Fig. 5. Overlapping inactives nibbles. The dashed circle denotes one overlap

In that case the intermediate keyspace is reduced significantly from 2^{256} to 2^{16} with a much reduced time complexity of $O(2^{16})$. White cells in both Figs. 5a and b are inactive and at different positions and hence all the nibbles in the state are overlapped by the same in the other state. We have observed that, for all $((i,j),(i,j+1)) \in F \times F$, either all 4 inactive nibbles are overlapping or none of them are overlapping. Now we describe the attack in following steps:

3.1 Make an Encryption Query and Two Fault Injected Encryption Queries

The attack first make an encryption query (N, AD, M_1) and receive (C_1, T_1), where M_1 is a single block message. The attack next make another encryption query (N, AD, M_1) and inject random faults f_1, f_2 at two consecutive nibbles $LS_{3,4}^{15,T}$ and $LS_{3,5}^{15,T}$ respectively to obtain the faulty cipher-text (C_1', T_1'). Let, $C_1 \oplus C_1' = A||B$, with $|A| = |B| = 128$. The difference relations for this fault are given in Fig. 6. Next, we make another encryption query (N, AD, M_1) and inject random faults f_1', f_2' at two consecutive nibbles $LS_{3,2}^{15,T}$ and $LS_{3,3}^{15,T}$ respectively to obtain the faulty cipher-text (C_1'', T_1'). Let, $C_1 \oplus C_1'' = A'||B'$, with $|A'| = |B'| = 128$. The difference relations for this fault are given in Fig. 7.

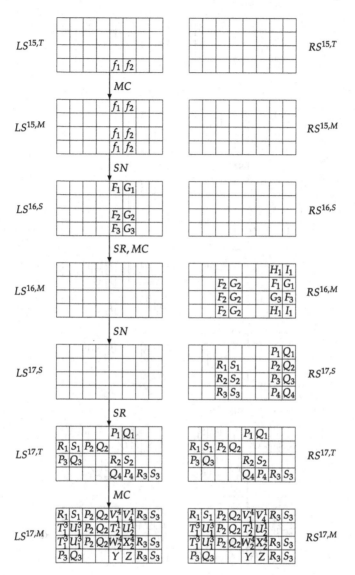

Fig. 6. Difference relations for the first fault. Here $H_1 = F_1 \oplus G_3, I_1 = G_1 \oplus F_3, T_i^j = R_i \oplus P_j, U_i^j = S_i \oplus Q_j, V_i^j = P_i \oplus Q_j, W_2^4 = R_2 \oplus Q_4, X_2^4 = S_2 \oplus P_4, Y = P_1 \oplus R_2 \oplus Q_4$ and $Z = Q_1 \oplus S_2 \oplus P_4$.

3.2 Construct the Difference Propagation and the Difference Relations

Observe the Differential Trail. The difference propagations and difference relations for the first fault at $LS_{3,4}^{15,T}$ and $LS_{3,5}^{15,T}$ are described by Figs. 8a and 6 respectively. The difference propagations and difference relations for the second

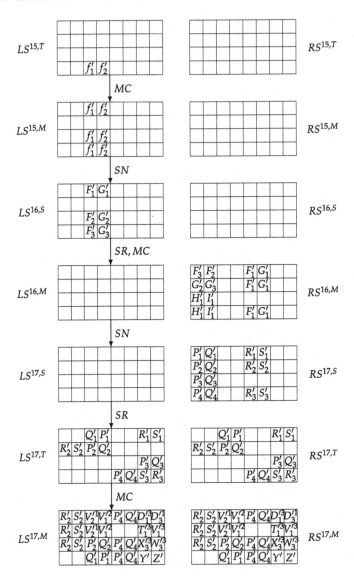

Fig. 7. Difference relations for the second fault. Here $H_1' = F_3' \oplus G_2'$, $I_1' = F_2' \oplus G_3'$, $T_i'^j = R_i' \oplus P_j'$, $U_i'^j = S_i' \oplus Q_j'$, $V_i'^j = P_i' \oplus Q_j'$, $W_3'^3 = R_3' \oplus Q_3'$, $X_3'^3 = S_3' \oplus P_3'$, $D_1'^3 = R_1' \oplus S_3'$, $D_3'^1 = R_3' \oplus S_1'$ $Y' = P_3' \oplus R_1' \oplus S_3'$ and $Z' = Q_3' \oplus S_1' \oplus R_3'$.

fault at $LS_{3,2}^{15,T}$ and $LS_{3,3}^{15,T}$ are described by Figs. 8b and 7 respectively. Note that all the values in Fig. 6 are random as we inject random faults in three nibble positions. Figure 13 in the appendix describes the backward propagation of the cipher-text differences along with the key mixing from $State^{18,T}$ to $State^{17,M}$. We form three sets of equations parallely for both faults from the difference relations to reduce the keyspace for I and K.

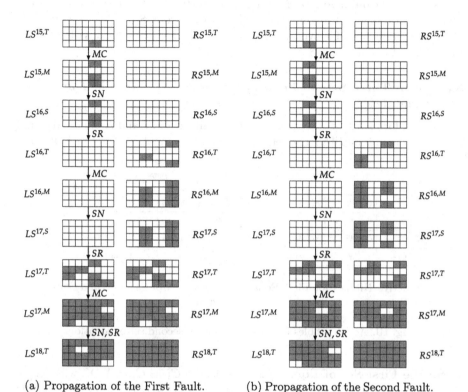

(a) Propagation of the First Fault.   (b) Propagation of the Second Fault.

Fig. 8. Difference propagation and backward propagation of I and K for the faults at $(LS^{15,T}_{3,4}, LS^{15,T}_{3,5})$ and $(LS^{15,T}_{3,2}, LS^{15,T}_{3,3})$.

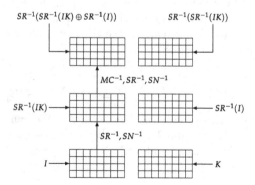

Fig. 9. Backward propagation of I and K.

Backward Propagation of I and K. Figure 9 describes how the effect of I and K are propagated in the backward direction from $State^{18,T}$ to $State^{16,M}$. Note that, influence of I over a $State$ means that $I_{i,j}$ is XOR-ed with $State_{i,j}$, for $1 \leq i \leq 4$ and $1 \leq j \leq 8$.

3.3 Form Three Sets of Equations to Filter Out Invalid I and K Candidates

The attack forms 3 sets of equations to filter out invalid I and K candidates and construct the unique $I\|K$. The sets of equations are mentioned in the Appendix.

$RS^{17,M}$

R_1	S_1	P_2	Q_2	V_1^4	V_4^1	R_3	S_3
T_1^3	U_1^3	P_2	Q_2	T_2^1	U_2^3		
T_1^3	U_1^3	P_2	Q_2	W_2^4	X_2^4	R_3	S_3
P_3	Q_3			Y	Z	R_3	S_3

$LS^{17,M}$

R_1	S_1	P_2	Q_2	V_1^4	V_4^1	R_3	S_3
T_1^3	U_1^3	P_2	Q_2	T_2^1	U_2^3		
T_1^3	U_1^3	P_2	Q_2	W_2^4	X_2^4	R_3	S_3
P_3	Q_3			Y	Z	R_3	S_3

(a) Active Nibbles for First Equation Set   (b) Active Nibbles for Second Equation Set

Fig. 10. Active nibbles for the first and the second set of equations

Form the First Set of Equations. We denote C_1 as $C_1 = X\|Y$, with $|X| = |Y| = 128$ and the 256 intermediate key φ_1 as $\varphi = I\|K$. By observing Fig. 10a we can form a set of 28 equations with each equation corresponding to an active nibble in $RS^{17,M}$. Below, we present few such equations to describe the attack procedure. The set of all of the equations are provided in appendix.

Filter Out the Invalid I Nibbles. For the first fault, consider the four nibbles corresponding to R_1 and P_3. Here, we can enumerate all 2^8 possible values of R_1 and P_3 and retrieve a value of I_{03}, I_{12}, I_{26} and I_{34} for each of the values of R_1 and P_3. Assuming that there is one solution x in an average of the equation $SN^{-1}(x) \oplus SN^{-1}(x \oplus a) = b$, we can reduce the key space for 4 nibbles of I to 2^8. The equations are given below:

$$R_1 = SN_{03}^{I,X,0} \oplus SN_{03}^{I,X,A}, \quad T_1^3 = SN_{12}^{I,X,0} \oplus SN_{12}^{I,X,A}$$
$$T_1^3 = SN_{26}^{I,X,0} \oplus SN_{26}^{I,X,A}, \quad P_3 = SN_{34}^{I,X,0} \oplus SN_{34}^{I,X,A}$$

Again consider the three active nibbles with P_2. We can enumerate P_2 to rescue the keyspace of I_{04}, I_{16} and I_{21} from 2^{12} to 2^4. Thus, the keyspace for the three I nibbles are reduced to 2^4 and we have to enumerate all the 2^4 values of I_{30} to reduce the keyspace for I_{04}, I_{16} I_{21} and I_{30} from 2^{16} to 2^8. The equations are given below:

$$P_2 = SN_{04}^{I,X,0} \oplus SN_{04}^{I,X,A}, P_2 = SN_{16}^{I,X,0} \oplus SN_{16}^{I,X,A}$$
$$P_2 = SN_{21}^{I,X,0} \oplus SN_{21}^{I,X,A}$$

We can enumerate all of the 2^{12} possible values of P_1, R_2 and Q_4 and retrieve a value of I_{06}, I_{10}, I_{22} and I_{37} for each P_1, R_2 and Q_4. valuesof these 4 nibbles of I to 2^{12}. The equations are given below:

$$V_1^4 = SN_{06}^{I,X,0} \oplus SN_{06}^{I,X,A}, \quad T_2^1 = SN_{10}^{I,X,0} \oplus SN_{10}^{I,X,A}$$
$$W_2^4 = SN_{22}^{I,X,0} \oplus SN_{22}^{I,X,A}, \quad Y = SN_{37}^{I,X,0} \oplus SN_{37}^{I,X,A}$$

Following the same procedure for all the equation we can reduce the keyspace from 2^{112} to $2^{8+8+8+8+4+4+8+8}$ i.e., 2^{56} using the 28 active I nibbles corresponding to the 28 equations. We can guess the remaining 4 nibbles and the total keyspace of I can be reduced from 2^{128} to $2^{56+16} = 2^{72}$. We denote this reduced keyspace by I_S. The time complexity of this step is $O(2^{12})$.

For the second fault, we can similarly observe the differential relation described in Fig. 7 and use the already reduced keyspace for I to reduce it further. In this case also, the key propagates in the backward direction in the same way as described in Fig. 9. Thus, same nibble appears in the same column for both the faults. As we, have reduced the keyspace for 6 of the columns of I from 2^{16} to 2^8 and two of the columns from 2^{16} to 2^{12}, we can further reduce the keyspace of I columns (i.e., 4 nibbles) from 2^8 to 1 for the 6 corresponding columns and 2^{12} to 2^8 for the 2 corresponding columns. This actually happens, as the active nibbles in $RS^{17,M}$ for the first fault overlaps with the same for the second fault. If this is not the case, for example, if both the faults are injected at $LS_{3,4}^{15,T}$ and $LS_{3,5}^{15,T}$, then for both the cases we have to enumerate all the 2^4 vaues of I_{30} in the reduced keyspace of I_{04}, I_{16} I_{21} and I_{30}. Thus, we can not reduce the keyspace for I_{04}, I_{16} I_{21} and I_{30} to 1 in this case. Hence, more overlaps will reduce the keyspace further.

Thus, in our case with faults injected at different positions, we can reduce the keyspace for I from 2^{128} to 2^{16}. More formally, we can deduce the reduction of the keyspace as $\frac{2^{72} \cdot 2^{72}}{2^{\#overlapped\ bits}} = \frac{2^{144}}{2^{128}} = 2^{16}$.

Note that, if we inject both the faults at $LS_{3,4}^{15,T}$ and $LS_{3,5}^{15,T}$. Then the keyspace for I can be reduced from 2^{128} to $\frac{2^{144}}{2^{128-16}} = 2^{32}$ as there are 4 non-overlapped nibbles.

Form the Second Set of Equations. The second set of equations are formed using Fig. 10b. In this state we form 28 equations with different IK nibbles corresponding to the active nibbles in $LS^{17,M}$. We provide a few of these equations below. The set of all of the equations are given in the appendix.

Filter Out the Invalid IK Nibbles. We follow exactly the same procedure described for filtering out invalid I nibbles. For example, we can enumerate all 2^8 possible values of R_1 and P_3 and retrieve a value of $IK_{06}, IK_{14}, IK_{23}$ and IK_{32} for each of the values of R_1 and P_3. We can reduce the key space for 4 nibbles of IK to 2^8. The equations are given below.

$$R_1 = SN_{06}^{IK,XY,0} \oplus SN_{06}^{IK,XY,AB}, \quad T_1^3 = SN_{14}^{IK,XY,0} \oplus SN_{14}^{IK,XY,AB}$$
$$T_1^3 = SN_{23}^{IK,XY,0} \oplus SN_{23}^{IK,XY,AB}, \quad P_3 = SN_{32}^{IK,XY,0} \oplus SN_{32}^{IK,XY,AB}$$

We can enumerate P_2 to rescue the keyspace of IK_{01}, IK_{10} and IK_{24} from 2^{12} to 2^4. Thus, the keyspace for the three IK nibbles are reduced to 2^4 and we have to enumerate all the 2^4 values of IK_{36} to reduce the keyspace for IK_{01}, IK_{10} IK_{24} and IK_{36} from 2^{16} to 2^8. The equations are given below.

$$P_2 = SN_{01}^{IK,XY,0} \oplus SN_{01}^{IK,XY,AB}, \quad P_2 = SN_{10}^{IK,XY,0} \oplus SN_{10}^{IK,XY,AB}$$
$$P_2 = SN_{24}^{IK,XY,0} \oplus SN_{24}^{IK,XY,AB}$$

We can enumerate all of the 2^{12} possible values of P_1, R_2 and Q_4 and retrieve a value of $IK_{02}, IK_{17}, IK_{26}$ and IK_{30} for each P_1, R_2 nd Q_4. Thus, we can reduce the key space of these 4 nibbles of I to 2^{12}. The equations are given below.

$$V_1^4 = SN_{02}^{IK,XY,0} \oplus SN_{02}^{IK,XY,AB}, \quad T_2^1 = SN_{17}^{IK,XY,0} \oplus SN_{17}^{IK,XY,AB}$$
$$W_2^4 = SN_{26}^{IK,XY,0} \oplus SN_{26}^{IK,XY,AB}, \quad Y = SN_{30}^{IK,XY,0} \oplus SN_{30}^{IK,XY,AB}$$

We can reduce the keyspace of IK from 2^{128} to 2^{16} by following the same reduction technique. We name this valid reduced keyspace for IK by IK_S. The time complexity of this step is $O(2^{12})$.

Note that, in this case also, injection of faults at the same position reduces the keyspace for IK can be reduced from 2^{128} to $\frac{2^{144}}{2^{128-16}} = 2^{32}$ as there are 16 non-overlapped nibbles. Also note that, invalid I and IK nibbles filtering can be computed parallely and total time complexity for these two steps are $O(2^{12})$.

Form the Third Set of Equations. The third set of equations are formed using Fig. 11. This set consists of 14 equations with each equation corresponding to each active nibble in $RS^{16,M}$. One such equation corresponding to the F_2 in $RS_{1,2}^{16,M}$ is given below. The remaining equations are formed by exactly the similar way given in the appendix.

$$F_2 = SN^{-1}(SN_{06}^{IK,XY,0} \oplus SN_{14}^{IK,XY,0} \oplus SN_{23}^{IK,XY,0})$$
$$\oplus SN^{-1}(SN_{06}^{IK,XY,AB} \oplus SN_{14}^{IK,XY,AB} \oplus SN_{23}^{IK,XY,AB})$$

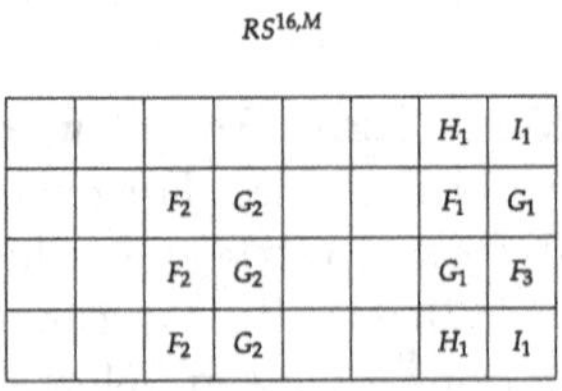

$RS^{16,M}$

				H_1	I_1
F_2	G_2			F_1	G_1
F_2	G_2			G_1	F_3
F_2	G_2			H_1	I_1

Fig. 11. Active nibbles for the third set of equations

Further Filtration of Invalid _IK_ Nibbles. We first enumerate all the 2^{16} filtered _IK_ nibbles and check them against each of the 14 equations. Both the RHS and LHS of the equations are assumed to be uniform and random. Thus, the probability that a $ik \in IK_S$ satisfies all the equations above is 2^{-32}, as for each of the fixed F_1, F_2, F_3, G_1, G_2 and G_3 assignment the probability that ik satisfies all the above equations is 2^{-56} and for each and their are 2^{24} possible values of F_1, F_2, F_3, G_1, G_2 and G_3. Thus we can uniquely compute the valid _IK_. Hence, the key space for _IK_ reduces from 2^{16} to 1. The time complexity of this step is $O(2^{16})$.

In the case of fault injection at the same position, the keyspace of _IK_ is reduced from 2^{32} to 1 using the same probability calculation. Thus the time complexity in this case will be $O(2^{32})$.

Find the Unique $I \| K$. Thus, we can form the set of 2^{16} $I \| K$ values and one of them is valid. We can find the valid key by making one more encryption query with the same N and A. The time complexity of this phase is $O(2^{16})$.

In the case of fault injection at the same position, the time complexity will be $O(2^{32})$ as there are 2^{32} possible I values.

Total Time Complexities of This Attack. The total time complexity required to uniquely compute _IK_ is $O(2^{16})$ for fault injections at two different positions and $O(2^{32})$ for fault injections at the same position. This time is required to reduce the keyspace for _IK_ by observing the third set of equations. The rest of the phases requires less time complexity than this phase. Note that, For all the time complexity analysis, we have used the O notation, as there are nominal overheads for some constant number of computations is addition to these computations.

3.4 Forge a Valid Ciphertext-Tag Pair for Any Message and Associated Data Under the Same Nonce

The attacker can forge a valid cipher-text-tag pair for any message M^* and associated data A^* under the same N. Now for the valid key $L = \alpha^{-1}\varphi_1$ ($\varphi_1 = I \| K$), the attacker can simulate the message processing phase, but to forge valid cipher-text-tag the attacker must compute the intermediate value t^* for A^* (described by the variable t in Fig. 1). This can be done by making an additional encryption query with N, A^* and empty message \$ to receive (C, T). Note that, t^* can be computed using the candidates in L_S. The message processing phase can now be simulated for any message M^* starting with t^* and to produce valid (C^*, T^*). Thus, one forging attempt can forge a valid cipher-text-tag pair.

4 A Practical DFA with a Three Random Faults at a Single Nibble Position

We have also considered another practical fault model with random faults injected at a single nibble. We have observed that, if the faults are injected at different positions, then with three random faults we can recover the intermediate key with a very low time complexity of $O(2^8)$. Here, we follow exactly the same procedure as describe in the previous section. More formally, this attack forms three sets of equations in a similar way to filter out invalid I and IK values. Thus, we simply provide results with respect to the number of faults, size of the reduced keyspace and the time complexity of the attack. We also provide the difference relations for the propagations of the first fault in Fig. 12. We simply omit the difference relations for the second and the third faults as they can be observed in a similar way. We also omit the attack description, as it is the same as that of the previous analysis except the active nibble positions in the internal cipher states. We first provide the attack complexities when only

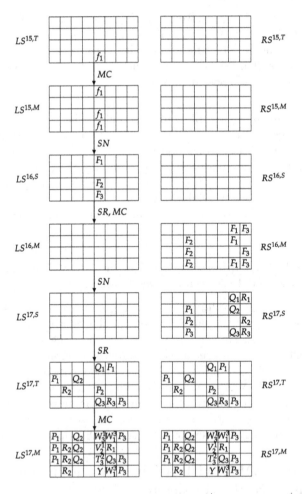

Fig. 12. Difference relation for the first fault. Here $T_i^j = R_i + P_j$, $V_i^j = P_i + Q_j$ and $W_i^j = R_i + Q_j$.

two random faults at different locations are injected for two different encryption queries. We next provide the attack complexities when three random faults at different locations are injected for three different encryption queries.

Attack Complexities with Two Random Faults. In this case, we make one general encryption query and two single nibble random fault injected encryption queries all with the same nonce, associated data and message. We have observed that, if the faults are injected at different locations, for example at $LS_{3,4}^{15,T}$ and $LS_{3,3}^{15,T}$, the keyspace of the intermediate key can be reduced from 2^{256} to 2^{48} with a time complexity of $O(2^{48})$. Figure 12 describes the faults propagation with fault injected at $LS_{3,4}^{15,T}$. This attack will work for faults at any two different locations at $LS^{15,T}$.

Attack Complexities with Three Random Faults. In this case, we make one general encryption query and three single nibble random fault injected encryption queries all with the same nonce, associated data and message. We have observed that, if the faults are injected at three different locations, for example at $LS_{3,4}^{15,T}, LS_{3,3}^{15,T}$ and $LS_{3,2}^{15,T}$, the keyspace of the intermediate key can be significantly reduced from 2^{256} to 2^8 with a time complexity of $O(2^8)$. This attack will work for faults at any three different locations at $LS^{15,T}$.

5 Conclusion

In this paper, we propose two differential fault analysis on Minalpher. Both the attacks we describe, recover the intermediate key. We have chosen two relaxed fault models, such that in the first model, we inject random faults into two consecutive nibbles (or 1 byte). We have analyzed several such fault locations and found 9 of them correspond to optimal attack complexities. In the second model, we analyzed all the single nibble positions and found that with three faults at different locations significantly reduces the attack complexities. Finally, we show that this intermediate key provides the attacker a significant power of forging a valid ciphertext-tag pair for any message and associated data pair under a fixed nonce. However, our attack does not refute the claim of the desginers of Minalpher, rather it shows the vulnerability of Minalpher if faults are injected under the two above fault models.

A Appendix

A.1 Backward Propagation of the Ciphertext Differences Along with the Keys

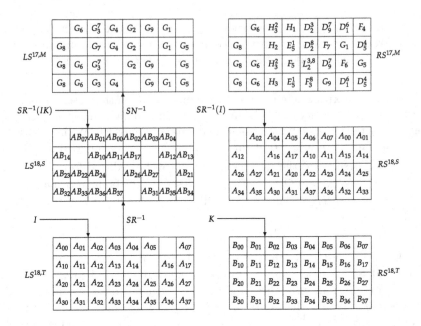

Fig. 13. Backward propagation of the ciphertext differences along with I and K

A.2 Three Sets of Equations for the First Fault

First Set of Equations

$$R_1 = SN_{03}^{I,X,0} \oplus SN_{03}^{I,X,A}, \quad T_1^3 = SN_{12}^{I,X,0} \oplus SN_{12}^{I,X,A}$$

$$T_1^3 = SN_{26}^{I,X,0} \oplus SN_{26}^{I,X,A}, \quad P_3 = SN_{34}^{I,X,0} \oplus SN_{34}^{I,X,A}$$

$$S_1 = SN_{02}^{I,X,0} \oplus SN_{02}^{I,X,A}, \quad U_1^3 = SN_{13}^{I,X,0} \oplus SN_{13}^{I,X,A}$$

$$U_1^3 = SN_{27}^{I,X,0} \oplus SN_{27}^{I,X,A}, \quad Q_3 = SN_{35}^{I,X,0} \oplus SN_{35}^{I,X,A}$$

$$P_2 = SN_{04}^{I,X,0} \oplus SN_{04}^{I,X,A}, \quad P_2 = SN_{16}^{I,X,0} \oplus SN_{16}^{I,X,A}$$

$$P_2 = SN_{21}^{I,X,0} \oplus SN_{21}^{I,X,A}$$

$$Q_2 = SN_{05}^{I,X,0} \oplus SN_{05}^{I,X,A}, \quad Q_2 = SN_{17}^{I,X,0} \oplus SN_{17}^{I,X,A}$$

$$Q_2 = SN_{20}^{I,X,0} \oplus SN_{20}^{I,X,A}$$

$$V_1^4 = SN_{06}^{I,X,0} \oplus SN_{06}^{I,X,A}, \quad T_2^1 = SN_{10}^{I,X,0} \oplus SN_{10}^{I,X,A}$$

$$W_2^4 = SN_{22}^{I,X,0} \oplus SN_{22}^{I,X,A}, \; Y = SN_{37}^{I,X,0} \oplus SN_{37}^{I,X,A}$$

$$V_4^1 = SN_{07}^{I,X,0} \oplus SN_{07}^{I,X,A}, \; U_2^3 = SN_{11}^{I,X,0} \oplus SN_{11}^{I,X,A}$$

$$X_2^4 = SN_{23}^{I,X,0} \oplus SN_{23}^{I,X,A}, \; Z = SN_{36}^{I,X,0} \oplus SN_{36}^{I,X,A}$$

$$R_3 = SN_{00}^{I,X,0} \oplus SN_{00}^{I,X,A}, \; R_3 = SN_{24}^{I,X,0} \oplus SN_{24}^{I,X,A}$$

$$R_3 = SN_{32}^{I,X,0} \oplus SN_{32}^{I,X,A}$$

$$S_3 = SN_{01}^{I,X,0} \oplus SN_{01}^{I,X,A}, \; S_3 = SN_{25}^{I,X,0} \oplus SN_{25}^{I,X,A}$$

$$S_3 = SN_{33}^{I,X,0} \oplus SN_{33}^{I,X,A}$$

Second Set of Equations

$$R_1 = SN_{06}^{IK,XY,0} \oplus SN_{06}^{IK,XY,AB}, \; T_1^3 = SN_{14}^{IK,XY,0} \oplus SN_{14}^{IK,XY,AB}$$

$$T_1^3 = SN_{23}^{IK,XY,0} \oplus SN_{23}^{IK,XY,AB}, \; P_3 = SN_{32}^{IK,XY,0} \oplus SN_{32}^{IK,XY,AB}$$

$$S_1 = SN_{07}^{IK,XY,0} \oplus SN_{07}^{IK,XY,AB}, \; U_1^3 = SN_{15}^{IK,XY,0} \oplus SN_{15}^{IK,XY,AB}$$

$$U_1^3 = SN_{22}^{IK,XY,0} \oplus SN_{22}^{IK,XY,AB}, \; Q_3 = SN_{33}^{IK,XY,0} \oplus SN_{33}^{IK,XY,AB}$$

$$P_2 = SN_{01}^{IK,XY,0} \oplus SN_{01}^{IK,XY,AB}, \; P_2 = SN_{10}^{IK,XY,0} \oplus SN_{10}^{IK,XY,AB}$$

$$P_2 = SN_{24}^{IK,XY,0} \oplus SN_{24}^{IK,XY,AB}$$

$$Q_2 = SN_{00}^{IK,XY,0} \oplus SN_{00}^{IK,XY,AB}, \; Q_2 = SN_{11}^{IK,XY,0} \oplus SN_{11}^{IK,XY,AB}$$

$$Q_2 = SN_{25}^{IK,XY,0} \oplus SN_{25}^{IK,XY,AB}$$

$$V_1^4 = SN_{02}^{IK,XY,0} \oplus SN_{02}^{IK,XY,AB}, \; T_2^1 = SN_{17}^{IK,XY,0} \oplus SN_{17}^{IK,XY,AB}$$

$$W_2^4 = SN_{26}^{IK,XY,0} \oplus SN_{26}^{IK,XY,AB}, \; Y = SN_{30}^{IK,XY,0} \oplus SN_{30}^{IK,XY,AB}$$

$$V_4^1 = SN_{03}^{IK,XY,0} \oplus SN_{03}^{IK,XY,AB}, \; U_2^3 = SN_{16}^{IK,XY,0} \oplus SN_{16}^{IK,XY,AB}$$

$$X_2^4 = SN_{27}^{IK,XY,0} \oplus SN_{27}^{IK,XY,AB}, \; Z = SN_{31}^{IK,XY,0} \oplus SN_{31}^{IK,XY,AB}$$

$$R_3 = SN_{04}^{IK,XY,0} \oplus SN_{04}^{IK,XY,AB}, \; R_3 = SN_{20}^{IK,XY,0} \oplus SN_{20}^{IK,XY,AB}$$

$$R_3 = SN_{35}^{IK,XY,0} \oplus SN_{35}^{IK,XY,AB}$$

$$S_3 = SN_{05}^{IK,XY,0} \oplus SN_{05}^{IK,XY,AB}, \; S_3 = SN_{21}^{IK,XY,0} \oplus SN_{21}^{IK,XY,AB}$$

$$S_3 = SN_{34}^{IK,XY,0} \oplus SN_{34}^{IK,XY,AB}$$

Third Set of Equations

$$F_2 = SN^{-1}(SN_{06}^{IK,XY,0} \oplus SN_{14}^{IK,XY,0} \oplus SN_{23}^{IK,XY,0})$$
$$\oplus SN^{-1}(SN_{06}^{IK,XY,AB} \oplus SN_{14}^{IK,XY,AB} \oplus SN_{23}^{IK,XY,AB})$$

$$F_2 = SN^{-1}(SN_{17}^{IK,XY,0} \oplus SN_{26}^{IK,XY,0} \oplus SN_{30}^{IK,XY,0})$$
$$\oplus SN^{-1}(SN_{17}^{IK,XY,AB} \oplus SN_{26}^{IK,XY,AB} \oplus SN_{30}^{IK,XY,AB})$$

$$F_2 = SN^{-1}(SN_{04}^{IK,XY,0} \oplus SN_{20}^{IK,XY,0} \oplus SN_{35}^{IK,XY,0})$$
$$\oplus SN^{-1}(SN_{04}^{IK,XY,AB} \oplus SN_{20}^{IK,XY,AB} \oplus SN_{35}^{IK,XY,AB})$$

$$G_2 = SN^{-1}(SN_{07}^{IK,XY,0} \oplus SN_{15}^{IK,XY,0} \oplus SN_{22}^{IK,XY,0})$$
$$\oplus SN^{-1}(SN_{07}^{IK,XY,AB} \oplus SN_{15}^{IK,XY,AB} \oplus SN_{22}^{IK,XY,AB})$$

$$G_2 = SN^{-1}(SN_{16}^{IK,XY,0} \oplus SN_{27}^{IK,XY,0} \oplus SN_{31}^{IK,XY,0})$$
$$\oplus SN^{-1}(SN_{16}^{IK,XY,AB} \oplus SN_{27}^{IK,XY,AB} \oplus SN_{31}^{IK,XY,AB})$$

$$G_2 = SN^{-1}(SN_{05}^{IK,XY,0} \oplus SN_{21}^{IK,XY,0} \oplus SN_{34}^{IK,XY,0})$$
$$\oplus SN^{-1}(SN_{05}^{IK,XY,AB} \oplus SN_{21}^{IK,XY,AB} \oplus SN_{34}^{IK,XY,AB})$$

$$H_1 = SN^{-1}(SN_{02}^{IK,XY,0} \oplus SN_{17}^{IK,XY,0} \oplus SN_{30}^{IK,XY,0})$$
$$\oplus SN^{-1}(SN_{02}^{IK,XY,AB} \oplus SN_{17}^{IK,XY,AB} \oplus SN_{30}^{IK,XY,AB})$$

$$F_1 = SN^{-1}(SN_{01}^{IK,XY,0} \oplus SN_{10}^{IK,XY,0} \oplus SN_{24}^{IK,XY,0})$$
$$\oplus SN^{-1}(SN_{01}^{IK,XY,AB} \oplus SN_{10}^{IK,XY,AB} \oplus SN_{24}^{IK,XY,AB})$$

$$G_1 = SN^{-1}(SN_{14}^{IK,XY,0} \oplus SN_{23}^{IK,XY,0} \oplus SN_{32}^{IK,XY,0})$$
$$\oplus SN^{-1}(SN_{14}^{IK,XY,AB} \oplus SN_{23}^{IK,XY,AB} \oplus SN_{32}^{IK,XY,AB})$$

$$H_1 = SN^{-1}(SN_{03}^{IK,XY,0} \oplus SN_{27}^{IK,XY,0} \oplus SN_{31}^{IK,XY,0})$$
$$\oplus SN^{-1}(SN_{03}^{IK,XY,AB} \oplus SN_{27}^{IK,XY,AB} \oplus SN_{31}^{IK,XY,AB})$$

$$I_1 = SN^{-1}(SN_{03}^{IK,XY,0} \oplus SN_{16}^{IK,XY,0} \oplus SN_{31}^{IK,XY,0})$$
$$\oplus SN^{-1}(SN_{03}^{IK,XY,AB} \oplus SN_{16}^{IK,XY,AB} \oplus SN_{31}^{IK,XY,AB})$$

$$G_1 = SN^{-1}(SN_{00}^{IK,XY,0} \oplus SN_{11}^{IK,XY,0} \oplus SN_{25}^{IK,XY,0})$$
$$\oplus SN^{-1}(SN_{00}^{IK,XY,AB} \oplus SN_{11}^{IK,XY,AB} \oplus SN_{25}^{IK,XY,AB})$$

$$F_3 = SN^{-1}(SN_{15}^{IK,XY,0} \oplus SN_{22}^{IK,XY,0} \oplus SN_{33}^{IK,XY,0})$$
$$\oplus SN^{-1}(SN_{15}^{IK,XY,AB} \oplus SN_{22}^{IK,XY,AB} \oplus SN_{33}^{IK,XY,AB})$$

$$I_1 = SN^{-1}(SN_{02}^{IK,XY,0} \oplus SN_{26}^{IK,XY,0} \oplus SN_{30}^{IK,XY,0})$$
$$\oplus SN^{-1}(SN_{02}^{IK,XY,AB} \oplus SN_{26}^{IK,XY,AB} \oplus SN_{30}^{IK,XY,AB})$$

References

1. (no editor): CAESAR Competition. http://competitions.cr.yp.to/caesar.html
2. Banik, S., Maitra, S.: A differential fault attack on MICKEY 2.0. In: Bertoni, G., Coron, J.-S. (eds.) CHES 2013. LNCS, vol. 8086, pp. 215–232. Springer, Heidelberg (2013). https://doi.org/10.1007/978-3-642-40349-1_13
3. Banik, S., Maitra, S., Sarkar, S.: A differential fault attack on the grain family of stream ciphers. In: Prouff, E., Schaumont, P. (eds.) CHES 2012. LNCS, vol. 7428, pp. 122–139. Springer, Heidelberg (2012). https://doi.org/10.1007/978-3-642-33027-8_8
4. Chakraborti, A., Nandi, M.: Differential fault analysis on Minalpher. Presented at DIAC (2015)
5. Banik, S., Maitra, S., Sarkar, S.: A differential fault attack on the grain family under reasonable assumptions. In: Galbraith, S., Nandi, M. (eds.) INDOCRYPT 2012. LNCS, vol. 7668, pp. 191–208. Springer, Heidelberg (2012). https://doi.org/10.1007/978-3-642-34931-7_12
6. Yoshikawa, M., Nozaki, Y.: Two stage fault analysis against a falsification detection cipher Minalpher. In: IEEE International Conference on Smart Cloud (2016)
7. Bellare, M., Rogaway, P., Wagner, D.: The EAX mode of operation. In: Roy, B., Meier, W. (eds.) FSE 2004. LNCS, vol. 3017, pp. 389–407. Springer, Heidelberg (2004). https://doi.org/10.1007/978-3-540-25937-4_25
8. Biham, E., Shamir, A.: Differential fault analysis of secret key cryptosystems. In: Kaliski, B.S. (ed.) CRYPTO 1997. LNCS, vol. 1294, pp. 513–525. Springer, Heidelberg (1997). https://doi.org/10.1007/BFb0052259
9. Biham, E., Granboulan, L., Nguyên, P.Q.: Impossible fault analysis of RC4 and differential fault analysis of RC4. In: Gilbert, H., Handschuh, H. (eds.) FSE 2005. LNCS, vol. 3557, pp. 359–367. Springer, Heidelberg (2005). https://doi.org/10.1007/11502760_24
10. Daemen, J., Rijmen, V.: The Design of Rijndael: AES - The Advanced Encryption Standard. Information Security and Cryptography. Springer, Heidelberg (2002). https://doi.org/10.1007/978-3-662-04722-4
11. Dusart, P., Letourneux, G., Vivolo, O.: Differential fault analysis on A.E.S. In: Zhou, J., Yung, M., Han, Y. (eds.) ACNS 2003. LNCS, vol. 2846, pp. 293–306. Springer, Heidelberg (2003). https://doi.org/10.1007/978-3-540-45203-4_23
12. Bossuet, L., Datta, N., Mancillas-López, C., Nandi, M.: ELmD: a pipelineable authenticated encryption and its hardware implementation. IEEE Trans. Comput. **65**, 3318–3331 (2016)
13. Viega, J., McGraw, D.: The use of Galois/Counter Mode (GCM) in IPsec Encapsulating Security Payload (ESP), RFC Editor, United States (2005)
14. Krovetz, T., Rogaway, P.: The software performance of authenticated-encryption modes. In: Joux, A. (ed.) FSE 2011. LNCS, vol. 6733, pp. 306–327. Springer, Heidelberg (2011). https://doi.org/10.1007/978-3-642-21702-9_18
15. Dobraunig, C., Eichlseder, M., Korak, T., Lomné, V., Mendel, F.: Statistical fault attacks on nonce-based authenticated encryption schemes. In: Cheon, J.H., Takagi, T. (eds.) ASIACRYPT 2016. LNCS, vol. 10031, pp. 369–395. Springer, Heidelberg (2016). https://doi.org/10.1007/978-3-662-53887-6_14
16. Hojsík, M., Rudolf, B.: Floating fault analysis of Trivium. In: Chowdhury, D.R., Rijmen, V., Das, A. (eds.) INDOCRYPT 2008. LNCS, vol. 5365, pp. 239–250. Springer, Heidelberg (2008). https://doi.org/10.1007/978-3-540-89754-5_19

17. Hojsík, M., Rudolf, B.: Differential fault analysis of Trivium. In: Nyberg, K. (ed.) FSE 2008. LNCS, vol. 5086, pp. 158–172. Springer, Heidelberg (2008). https://doi.org/10.1007/978-3-540-71039-4_10

18. Iwata, T., Minematsu, K., Guo, J., Morioka, S., Kobayashi, E.: SILC: SImple Lightweight CFB (2014). http://competitions.cr.yp.to/round1/silcv1.pdf

19. Iwata, T., Minematsu, K., Guo, J., Morioka, S., Kobayashi, E.: CLOC: compact low-overhead CFB (2014). http://competitions.cr.yp.to/round1/clocv1.pdf

20. Jeong, K., Lee, C.: Differential fault analysis on block cipher LED-64. In: (Jong Hyuk) Park, J.J., Leung, V., Wang, C.L., Shon, T. (eds.) Future Information Technology, Application and Service. LNEE, vol. 164, pp. 747–755. Springer, Dordrecht (2012). https://doi.org/10.1007/978-94-007-4516-2_79

21. Jovanovic, P., Kreuzer, M., Polian, I.: A fault attack on the LED block cipher. In: Schindler, W., Huss, S.A. (eds.) COSADE 2012. LNCS, vol. 7275, pp. 120–134. Springer, Heidelberg (2012). https://doi.org/10.1007/978-3-642-29912-4_10

22. Piret, G., Quisquater, J.-J.: A differential fault attack technique against SPN structures, with application to the AES and KHAZAD. In: Walter, C.D., Koç, Ç.K., Paar, C. (eds.) CHES 2003. LNCS, vol. 2779, pp. 77–88. Springer, Heidelberg (2003). https://doi.org/10.1007/978-3-540-45238-6_7

23. Saha, D., Kuila, S., Roy Chowdhury, D.: EsCAPe: diagonal fault analysis of APE. In: Meier, W., Mukhopadhyay, D. (eds.) INDOCRYPT 2014. LNCS, vol. 8885, pp. 197–216. Springer, Cham (2014). https://doi.org/10.1007/978-3-319-13039-2_12

24. Sasaki, Y., Todo, Y., Aoki, K., Naito, Y., Sugawara, T., Murakami, Y., Matsui, M., Hirose, S.: Minalpher v1 (2014). http://competitions.cr.yp.to/round1/minalpherv1.pdf

25. Tunstall, M., Mukhopadhyay, D., Ali, S.: Differential fault analysis of the advanced encryption standard using a single fault. In: Ardagna, C.A., Zhou, J. (eds.) WISTP 2011. LNCS, vol. 6633, pp. 224–233. Springer, Heidelberg (2011). https://doi.org/10.1007/978-3-642-21040-2_15

26. Whiting, D., Houeley, R., Ferguson, N.: Counter with CBC-MAC. Submission to NIST 2002 (2002). http://csrc.nist.gov/groups/ST/toolkit/BCM/modesdevelopment.html

eSPF: A Family of Format-Preserving Encryption Algorithms Using MDS Matrices

Donghoon Chang[1], Mohona Ghosh[2], Arpan Jati[1], Abhishek Kumar[1(✉)],
and Somitra Kumar Sanadhya[3]

[1] Indraprastha Institute of Information Technology, Delhi, India
{donghoon,arpanj,abhishekk}@iiitd.ac.in
[2] Indian Institute of Information Technology Design and Manufacturing,
Jabalpur, India
mohona@iiitdmj.ac.in
[3] Indian Institute of Technology, Ropar, India
somitra@iitrpr.ac.in

Abstract. The construction SPF, presented in Inscrypt-2016 was the first known SPN based format-preserving encryption algorithm. In this work, we significantly improve its performance and flexibility. We term this new construction as eSPF. Unlike SPF, all the basic transformations of eSPF are defined under the field $\mathbb{F}_p$. This allows us to use a MDS matrix instead of the binary matrix used in SPF. The optimal diffusion of MDS matrix leads to an efficient and secure design. However, this change leads to violations in the message format. To mitigate this, we propose a *discarding algorithm* to drop the symbols that are not the elements of the format thus preserving it.

We also present a concrete instantiation of eSPF for digits and its comparison with existing FPE algorithms like FFX and SPF. The performance analysis shows that the proposed design is at least 15 times faster than FFX for most of the practical applications.

Keywords: Format-preserving encryption · MDS matrix · SSN · Cryptanalysis · Substitution-permutation network

1 Introduction

Motivation. Maintaining the confidentiality of messages is one of the main goals of cryptography. Block ciphers are the most popular cryptographic primitives to fulfil this purpose. The conventional block ciphers such as AES [15] and DES [13] handle binary data of specific sizes, for example 128-bit for AES [15]. In many real world applications, it is desirable and essential to have the ciphertext follow the same format as the plaintext. Moreover, ciphertext length expansion is also not allowed in these situations. Encryption of Credit Card Numbers (CCN) or Social Security Numbers (SSN) are examples of such applications. Unfortunately, the conventional block ciphers and their modes such as ECB, CBC, CTR, etc. are not suitable for this purpose.

© Springer International Publishing AG 2017
S.S. Ali et al. (Eds.): SPACE 2017, LNCS 10662, pp. 133–150, 2017.
https://doi.org/10.1007/978-3-319-71501-8_8

Format-Preserving Encryption (FPE) refers to transformation of data that is formatted as a sequence of the symbols in such a way that the encrypted form of the data has the same format and length as the original data. Many financial or e-commerce databases contain CCN or SSN and for both practical and legal reasons, encryption of these values are important. However, these fields that need to be encrypted have fixed formats and a plain use of conventional block cipher will produce ciphertexts violating the specified format.

The problem of encryption over fixed formats was first investigated in the database community by Brightwell and Smith [11]. Schoroeppel and Orman proposed the Hasty Pudding Cipher [32] which first demonstrated an encryption scheme that worked for arbitrary domain. A few years later, Black and Rogaway [9] made the first systematic study of this problem and suggested some approaches to achieve the desired functionality. Being motivated by the real world application, many FPE designs have been proposed such as FFSEM [34], FFX [3], BPS [10], VFPE [33], FEA-1 and FEA-2 [25]. A special publication of NIST SP800-38G [20] specifies three modes of operation for format-preserving algorithms namely FF1, FF2 and FF3. Each of these modes employ an unbalanced Feistel structure and use AES-128 algorithm as the internal round function. FF1 and FF2 invokes AES-128 algorithm at least 11 times and FF3 invokes it eight times thus leading to high number of AES-128 invocations. Moreover, Bellare *et al.* [2] have been shown some message recovery attacks on FF1 and FF3. This was followed by an attack presented in [18] where Durak and Vaudenay presented a practical attack to the FF3 scheme. Apart from Feistel based FPE schemes another important mechanism of designing FPEs based on card shuffling was adopted in [23, 28–30]. In 2016, Chang *et al.* [12] proposed a new FPE algorithm SPF, based on a substitution permutation network (SPN) strategy. SPF is the first known SPN based FPE algorithm and it has been shown that it is almost 5 times faster than the other known FPE algorithms such as FF1, FF2 and FF3. However, the use of binary matrix in the linear layer of SPF has two limitations. Firstly, it doesn't allow SPF to be applied to formats of all sizes. Secondly, it restricts SPF to achieve maximal diffusion and hence the optimal efficiency. In this paper, we aim to address these limitations.

1.1 Our Contribution

We present a new substitution permutation design approach to construct efficient format-preserving encryption family. This is realized by using MDS matrix in the diffusion layer unlike SPF construction where binary matrix is used. As a result, higher diffusion is achieved in lesser number of rounds. Moreover, SPF construction doesn't work for format sizes which are multiples of 3 due to its design of the binary matrix. Our proposed construction does not have this limitation and works for any domain size. The other notable advantage of our proposed construction is that one instantiation may work for many formats.

We define the basic transformations for the proposed construction and a concrete instance for digits. The construction uses an iterated block cipher as the underlying building block. It consists of two algorithms - a non format preserving encryption scheme to generate the *keystream* and a *discarding algorithm* to ensure that the format is preserved.

The domain size of real-world applications of FPE motivates us to incorporate tweak in the proposed design. We propose a new *key scheduling and tweak scheduling algorithm* to realize our design goal. Further, we estimate a lower bound on the number of active S-boxes for different number of rounds for the proposed construction. The security of our design is then analyzed against differential, linear, square, related tweak and key scheduling attacks. Finally, we compare the efficiency of a concrete instance of our proposed construction for the most popular and widely used format - 'digit', with FFX and BPS and show that the proposed design is almost 15 times faster than FFX.

The rest of the paper is organized as follows. In Sect. 2, the important preliminaries are described. The proposed eSPF construction is presented in Sect. 3. The concrete instance of eSPF for digits is presented in Sect. 4. We analyze the security of the proposed scheme against the standard attacks in Sect. 5. This is followed by performance analysis of the same in Sect. 6. Finally, we conclude our work in Sect. 7.

2 Preliminaries

Let $\Sigma = \{0, 1, 2, \ldots, N - 1\}$ be the alphabet set, where $N \geq 2$. The size N of the set Σ is referred to as the 'format size' and the elements of Σ are referred to as 'symbols', for example, for digits, $N = 10$. Σ^* denotes the set of strings with elements from Σ. We assume that the plaintext contains symbols only from Σ. If this is not the case, suitable encoding and decoding functions could be used and then one can apply the "rank-then-encipher" approach [3] to use the methods described in this work.

2.1 The Notations Used in the Paper

The following notations have been used throughout the paper.

$|\Sigma|$	:	The number of elements in the set Σ.
$\boxplus_N$	:	Symbol wise addition modulo N.
$\lceil x \rceil$	:	Smallest integer just greater than x.
$S[i]$	:	i^{th} symbol of the string S from the left.
$S \parallel T$	:	Concatenation of two strings S and T.
$|S|_N$	:	Length of the string S in base N.
$\mathbb{F}_p$	:	Galois Field $GF(p)$ where p is prime.

2.2 Specification

An instance eSPF_r^N denotes a member of eSPF family that has format size N and consists of r-rounds. The input/output of each intermediate round is denoted as *state* [15]. Each *state* consists of $n = 16$ symbols. For ease of representation and discussion, we represent each *state* as a 4×4 two-dimensional array of symbols.

The transformation of an input string of length n over symbol set Σ to *state* is described by the function $\mathsf{STATE}(X)$ (Algorithm 1); while the inverse transformation of a *state* to produce a string over Σ^n is described by the function $\mathsf{STRING}(state)$ (Algorithm 2).

Algorithm 1. $\mathsf{STATE}(X)$
input : string X
output: *state*
1 **for** $i \leftarrow 0$ **to** $(n-1)$ **do**
2    $j \leftarrow i \bmod 4$;
3    $k \leftarrow \lfloor i/4 \rfloor$;
4    $state[j,k] \leftarrow X[i]$;
5 **return** *state*

Algorithm 2. $\mathsf{STRING}(state)$
input : *state*
output: string X
1 **for** $i \leftarrow 0$ **to** 3 **do**
2   **for** $j \leftarrow 0$ **to** 3 **do**
3       $n \leftarrow (i + j \times 4)$;
4       $X[n] \leftarrow state[i,j]$;
5 **return** X

3   The eSPF Construction

eSPF contains two components: a non format preserving encryption E_k and a *Discarding Algorithm (DA)*, followed by modular addition. To achieve diffusion in our encryption scheme, we use MDS matrix. MDS matrices have tremendous applications not only in the coding theory but also in the design of symmetric cryptographic primitives, for example, AES [15], Camellia [1], SQUARE [14] etc. owing to their highest possible branch number. This make them a natural choice for the diffusion layer since higher branch number ensures higher diffusion rate as well as lesser number of rounds, finally leading to a secure and efficient primitive construction.

Having an MDS matrix for diffusion functionality, requires the operations to be done over a finite field. This stringent requirement, limits the possible format size N to the cardinality of $\mathbb{F}_{p^b}$, where p is a prime and b is an integer. A suitable S-box and MDS matrix over the finite field $\mathbb{F}_{p^b}$ is then used to realize the substitution and permutation layer of our scheme.

As the operations are performed in $\mathbb{F}_{p^b}$, we need to perform a process to discard symbols which are not in format. This discarding process is equivalent of cycle-walking or using modular operation to ensure non-violation of the format. We show that the rate of discarding symbols in our case is low for practical scenarios and it does not affect the efficiency of our scheme significantly. Another important advantage of this construction is that, given one instance, the construction may be used for other formats as well, if their format size is smaller than or equal to p^b which is not possible in the SPF family.

3.1   The Round Transformations

Each round of eSPF consists of the following five following transformations which updates the internal state:

$$SB \circ SR \circ MC \circ KA \circ TA$$

SubBytes (SB): A SubBytes transformation $S : \mathbb{F}_{p^b} \rightarrow \mathbb{F}_{p^b}$ is used to create confusion in the cipher. It is a permutation consisting of a bijective mapping to each element of the state. Typically an S-box is the multiplicative inverse function in the field $\mathbb{F}_{p^b}$, i.e.,

$$S : x \rightarrow x^{-1}$$

This mapping is very popular and believed to be a good choice for designing differentially and linearly resistant cipher. However, another popular approach is to do a brute force search and choosing substitution layer based on analyzing the differential and linear properties along with the implementation cost. Many lighweight ciphers adopt the second approach.

ShiftRows (SR): This transformation shifts the rows cyclically over different offsets. Similar to AES, there is no shift over the first row, whereas symbols of second, third and fourth row are shifted left by one, two and three positions respectively.

MixColumns (MC): Permutation layer is used to introduce diffusion in the cipher to make sure that any local differences of an internal state before permutation layer propagates to the larger area of the state after this layer. In many modern ciphers, the linear diffusion layer is realized by using a $r \times r$ matrix that operates on the *state* column by column.

KeyAddition (KA): The key addition transformation modifies the *state* by adding round key symbol wise using modulo addition p^b.

TweakAddition (TA): Similar to KA step, given a sub tweak Tw_i and the current state S_i the tweak addition is a symbol wise addition modulo p^b.

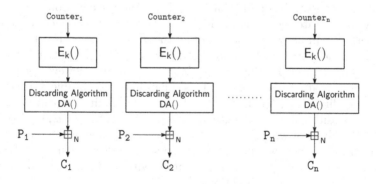

Fig. 1. Encryption of eSPF.

Algorithm 3. Enc $\text{SPF}_r^N(K, M, T, Tw)$	Algorithm 4. $\text{DA}(S)$
input : Key K, Message M, Counter T, Tweak Tw **output** : Ciphertext C	**input** : String S **output** : String S'

Algorithm 3. Enc $\text{SPF}_r^N(K, M, T, Tw)$

input : Key K, Message M,
        Counter T, Tweak Tw
output : Ciphertext C

1 Initialize two NULL strings Q, Q';
2 Initialize $\ell \leftarrow |M|_N$;
3 $state \leftarrow \text{STATE}(T)$;
4 KA($state, K$);
5 TA($state, Tw$);
6 **for** $j \leftarrow 1$ **to** $r - 1$ **do**
7 $\quad$ SubBytes($state$);
8 $\quad$ ShiftRow($state$);
9 $\quad$ MixColumns($state$);
10 $\quad$ KA($state, K_j$);
11 $\quad$ TA($state, Tw$);
12 SubBytes($state$);
13 ShiftRow($state$);
14 KA($state, K_j$);
15 TA($state, Tw$);
16 string $Q' \leftarrow \text{STRING}(state)$;
17 $Q \leftarrow \text{DA}(Q')$;
18 **for** $i \leftarrow 0$ **to** $(\ell - 1)$ **do**
19 $\quad$ $C[i] \leftarrow (M[i] \boxplus_N Q[i])$;
20 **return** C;

Algorithm 4. $\text{DA}(S)$

input : String S
output : String S'

1 Initialize a string $S' = \text{NULL}$;
2 For $i \leftarrow 1$ to n
3 $\quad$ **if** $S[i] \in \Sigma$
4 $\quad\quad$ $S' = S' || S[i]$;
5 $\quad$ **else**
6 $\quad\quad$ S' ;
7 **return** S';

The Operating Mode of eSPF. We adopt the Counter Mode [19] of operation for eSPF so that we can handle arbitrary length messages. For a large message block, the message will be divided into sub-blocks and the eSPF routine is invoked internally to generate the corresponding output block for a sequence of counters. The ciphertext will be concatenation of all the output blocks (Fig. 1).

The main advantages of counter-mode are parallel encryption/decryption and no requirement of padding, i.e., no length extension. However, *malleability* is the major limitation of this mode. This constraint is applicable to other block cipher modes like CBC, OFB etc. as well [31]. This limitation can be handled by using an additional message authentication protocol in our eSPF scheme, the design and analysis of which is currently beyond the scope of this work.

Algorithm 3 shows the encryption process of eSPF construction. The only difference between encryption and decryption will be the use of modular subtraction in place of modular addition.

3.2   Discarding Algorithm DA()

Let $\Sigma = \{0, 1, 2, \ldots, N - 1\}$ be the alphabet set of format size N. Let $\Sigma' = \{0, 1, 2, \ldots, N' - 1\}$, where Σ' is the alphabet set containing all the elements of $\mathbb{F}_{p^b}$ and $N' > N$. Since, each *state* of E_k contains n-symbols, the output of E_k is a string of n symbols. Let, the string Q' be the output of E_k, i.e., $Q' = q'_0 q'_1 q'_2 \cdots q'_{n-1}$ such that $q'_i \in \Sigma'$, for $0 \le i \le n - 1$. The output of *discarding algorithm* DA() will be a string Q, i.e., $Q = \text{DA}(Q) = q_0 q_1 q_2 \cdots q_{n'-1}$ such that $q_i \in \Sigma$ and $n' \le n$.

We are interested in finding the probability of occurrence of an arbitrary integer $a \in \Sigma$ at the k-th trial after the occurrence of elements of $(\Sigma' - \Sigma)$ in the first $k - 1$ trials.

Let X be the success event defined for the occurrence of a specific symbol $a \in \Sigma$ and the corresponding probability be $p_a = \frac{1}{N'}$. Let Z be a failure event defined as the occurrence of a symbol of set $(\Sigma' - \Sigma)$ and the corresponding probability p is $\frac{N'-N}{N'}$.

For $a \in \Sigma$, $\Pr[X = a] = p^{k-1} p_a$.

Thus, the total probability S of getting a can be estimated as:

$$S = \frac{1}{N'} + \frac{N'-N}{N'} \cdot \frac{1}{N'} + \frac{N'-N}{N'} \cdot \frac{N'-N}{N'} \cdot \frac{1}{N'} + \cdots \qquad (1)$$

After multiplication with $\frac{N'-N}{N'}$, Eq. 1 can be rewritten as

$$\frac{N'-N}{N'} \cdot S = \frac{N'-N}{N'} \cdot \frac{1}{N'} + \frac{N'-N}{N'} \cdot \frac{N'-N}{N'} \cdot \frac{1}{N'} + \cdots \qquad (2)$$

From Eqs. 1 and 2, $S = \frac{1}{N}$.

Without loss of generality, this can be shown for all elements of the set Σ and thus it can be concluded that the *discarding algorithm* does not impact the distribution of occurrence of symbols of Σ, i.e., it will not leak any additional information.

Discarding Rate: By discarding, we mean ignoring a symbol if it does not belong to alphabet set Σ. Let, p_r be the probability of not discarding an output symbol of E_k, i.e., $p_r = \frac{N}{N'}$, then the probability of discarding a symbol is $(1 - p_r)$.

Let, Z be a random variable with parameter n and p_r, where n denotes the number of independent trials and p_r is the success probability of the experiment. Then the random variable Z follows binomial distribution. Hence, the probability that Z contains a_0 symbol is $Pr(Z = a_0) = \binom{n}{a_0} p_r^{a_0} (1 - p_r)^{n-a_0}$ and expected value of a_0 is $n \times p_r$.

To minimize the discarding rate, the field $\text{GF}(p^b)$ and the corresponding set Σ' should be chosen carefully. The small difference between $(N' - N)$ will ensure a higher value for p_r. For example, if $N = 10$, $\mathbb{F}_{11}$ $(p = 11, b = 1, N' = 11)$ is the most suitable option. In this case the average value of a_0 is 14.55, i.e., on an average less than 1.45 symbols out of 16 symbols will be discarded by the discarding algorithm.

4   eSPF for Digits

In this section, we present eSPF_{10}^{10}, which is a concrete instantiation of our construction for digits. We choose, $\mathbb{F}_{11}$, i.e., $\text{GF}(11)$ for our construction. Thus, all the arithmetic operations are done modulo 11.

4.1 The S-Box

The S-box for $\mathbb{F}_{11}$ is shown in Table 1. To choose the S-box mapping, we analyzed all the possible mappings under different criteria such as maximal difference and linear probabilities and hardware implementation. Based on these, an optimal implementation of our S-box with logic gates is as follows:

$$y_0 = \{x_2\bar{x}_0 + x_3\} \quad y_1 = \{\bar{x}_1\bar{x}_2x_3 + \bar{x}_0\bar{x}_1\}$$
$$y_2 = \{x_0x_1 + \bar{x}_1x_3\} \quad y_3 = \{\bar{x}_0\bar{x}_1\bar{x}_3 + x_0\bar{x}_1x_2\}$$

where, our S-box can be represented as $y_n = S[x_n]$. The maximum differential probability and the maximum correlation for this S-box are $2^{-2.45}$ and $2^{-1.45}$ respectively.

Table 1. Representation of S-box for $\mathbb{F}_{11}$.

x	0	1	2	3	4	5	6	7	8	9	10
$S[x]$	2	0	10	6	3	8	9	4	7	5	1

4.2 The ShiftRows

The ShiftRows operation in this construction works exactly like AES.

4.3 The Permutation

In [22], Gupta et al. analyzed the format preserving diffusion layers for digits and showed that it is impossible to construct any cryptographically significant 4×4 matrices over the field $\mathbb{F}_{2^4}$ which yields a format preserving set of cardinality 10. Further, for an arbitrary format, non-existence of MDS matrix under some reasonable restrictions has been shown in [12]. Since, our motivation was to use a MDS matrix for optimal efficiency, based on the findings of [12,22], we decided to choose the diffusion layer such that it may violate the format size. The linear diffusion layer for our case is realized by the following 4×4 MDS matrix over GF(11).

$$M = \begin{pmatrix} 1 & 1 & 2 & 5 \\ 5 & 1 & 1 & 2 \\ 2 & 5 & 1 & 1 \\ 1 & 2 & 5 & 1 \end{pmatrix}$$

The branch number of this matrix is 5.

4.4 Key Addition

The key addition transformation is symbol wise modular addition for a state S_i and subkey K_i.

4.5 Tweak Addition

Inclusion of tweak for eSPF is motivated by the domain size of real world applications of FPE algorithms and birthday bound security of the associated block ciphers. Tweak is public and it is used to randomize the instance of the block cipher, i.e., different values of tweak correspond to different families of permutations. Its usage helps in case of FPE algorithms since now the same ciphertext (e.g., if the two credit card numbers will provide the same plaintext for encryption, say middle 6 digits) will look different to the attacker due to different values of the tweak and hence would be indistinguishable. The proposed construction works in counter mode and use of different counter value ensures variability over ciphertext. However, since in the real world applications of FPE algorithms, the length of messages is mostly short (single block messages), same counter value may be used to encrypt different messages. Further, as the domain sizes of various formats are also small, enough variability may not be achieved in some cases. To circumvent this issue, we are using a tweak in our design.

Initiated by the work of Liskov et al. [26], few tweakable block cipher designs have been proposed in literature. In [24], Jean et al. presented the generic TWEAKEY framework that can be used to convert any key alternating block cipher into a tweakable one and proposed three instantiations - Deoxys-BC, JoltiK-BC and KIASU-BC that were the first ad-hoc tweakable block ciphers based on AES.

Injection of tweak in eSPF construction follows the tweak injection method adopted in KIASU-BC [24], i.e., the the tweak will be added to the first two rows of the state. Considering the block size of $eSPF_{10}^{10}$ ($\approx 2^{56}$ and the security, we choose a 60-bit tweak Tw). Two subtweaks $Tw0$ and $Tw1$ will be generated by a Tw using (Algorithm 6). $Tw0$ and $Tw1$ will then be added to the first two rows of the state for each even and odd numbered rounds correspondingly.

4.6 Key Schedule

We propose a new scheduling algorithm (KSA) for $eSPF_{10}^{10}$. The key schedule algorithm takes the 128-bit key K as input and generates $(r+1)$ round subkeys as output. Let K be represented as $k_{127}k_{126}\ldots k_2 k_1 k_0$. We first divide the K into two bit string of equal size and find $K_0 = \text{STATE}(K \mod 11^{16})$. We iterate Step 5 to Step 9 of the Algorithm 5 to extract the remaining r subkeys. Addition of round constant i provides security against slide attack and the addition operation is chosen to introduce non-linearity. The shift operation ensures that all the bits of K will be used up to round 5. In [3] Bellare et al. estimated the lower bound of statistical distance between the uniform distribution on Z_p and the distribution obtained by $b \mod p$ after picking b randomly in Z_a as p/a where $a > p$. We estimate 2^{-72} ($a = 2^{128}$, $p = 11^{16} \approx 2^{56}$) as the statistical distance for digits. This bound suggests that the mod 11^{16} operation does not impact the distributions dramatically.

Algorithm 5. KSA(K)
input : Key K
output: Round Keys
$K_0, K_1, \ldots, K_r$
1 $x_1 \leftarrow k_{127}k_{126} \ldots k_{65}k_{64}$;
2 $y_1 \leftarrow k_{63}k_{62} \ldots k_1 k_0$;
3 $K_0 \leftarrow \mathsf{STATE}(K \mod 11^{16})$
4 **for** $i \leftarrow 1$ **to** r **do**
5 $\quad y_i \leftarrow ((y_i \lll 16) + x_i) \oplus i$;
6 $\quad x_i \leftarrow (x_i \ggg 33) \oplus y_i$;
7 $\quad K_i \leftarrow \mathsf{STATE}((x_i\|y_i)$ $\quad \mod 11^{16})$;
8 $\quad x_{i+1} \leftarrow x_i$;
9 $\quad y_{i+1} \leftarrow y_i$;
10 **return** $(K_0, K_1, \ldots, K_r)$;

Algorithm 6. TSA(Tw)
input : Tweak Tw
output: Round tweaks
$Tw0, Tw1$
1 $Tw_0 \leftarrow \mathsf{STATE}(Tw \mod 11^8)$;
2 $Tw \leftarrow (Tw \lll 30)$;
3 $Tw_1 \leftarrow \mathsf{STATE}(Tw \mod 11^8)$;
4 **return** $(Tw0, Tw1)$;

5 Security Analysis

In this section, we evaluate the security of eSPF_{10}^{10} construction against various standard attacks.

5.1 Differential and Linear Cryptanalysis

Differential [7] and linear cryptanalysis [27] are two of the most powerful techniques to analyze symmetric-key primitives. To resist the differential and linear attacks, we choose to design our transformations according to the wide trail design strategy [16] and estimate the lower bounds for active S-boxes for different rounds of eSPF_{10}^{10}.

Number of Active S-boxes: The diffusion layer of eSPF uses a 4×4 MDS matrix with branch number 5. Hence, any two round differential/linear characteristic has a minimum of 5 active S-boxes and any four round differential/linear characteristic has a minimum of 25 active S-boxes for eSPF. In Table 2, we mention the number of rounds (r) and the corresponding minimum number of active S-boxes (A_r) for eSPF. In FSE 2006, Granboulan et al. [21] presented a general framework for differential and linear cryptanalysis of block cipher when the block is not a bitstring. A $M \times M$ matrix Δ simulates the behavior of the S-box S over differences by $\Delta(S)_{a,b} = \#\{x|S(x+a) - S(x) = b\}$. The maximum entry of the matrix, i.e., $\mathsf{D}(S)$ is defined as:

$$\mathsf{D}(S) = \max_{(a,b) \neq \{0,0\}} \Delta(S)_{a,b}.$$

The corresponding maximum propagation probability is defined as differential probability, $\mathsf{DP}(S) = \mathsf{D}(S)/M$. The $\mathsf{D}(S)$ is equal to 2 for eSPF_{10}^{10} and the corresponding maximum $\mathsf{DP}(S)$ is equal to $2^{-2.45}$ ($\frac{2}{11} \approx 2^{-2.45}$).

Table 2. Minimum number of active S-boxes A_r for r rounds of eSPF.

r	1	2	3	4	5	6	8	10	12	16
A_r	1	5	6	25	26	30	50	55	75	100

In order to investigate the security against linear cryptanalysis of the S-box, firstly we calculate the distribution vector $\Lambda_0(S)_{\{a,b\}} = (\#\{x \in \mathbb{F}_{p^b} | \langle a, b | x, S(x) \rangle = u\})_{u \in \{Z\}}$, where $\langle a, b | x, y \rangle = \langle a | x \rangle - \langle b | y \rangle$ and $\langle a, x \rangle$ is scalar product of a and x. The distribution vector represents the behavior of the considered S-box. The random behavior can be defined as: $f_{a,b;u} = \frac{1}{M} \#(x, y) \in \mathbb{F}_{p^b} \times \mathbb{F}_{p^b} | \langle a, b | x, y \rangle = u$. The bias of the S-box represents the difference of behavior of S-box S and the random case and is defined as $\Lambda_S(S)_{a,b;u} = \Lambda_0(S)_{a,b;u} - f_{a,b;u}$. The highest bias measures the non linearity of the S-box. For eSPF_{10}^{10}, the maximal bias is equal to $\frac{2}{11} = 2^{-2.45}$ and the maximum correlation is $2^{-1.45}$.

Based on the above parameters, the probability of any single 6-round differential characteristic of eSPF_{10}^{10} is upper bounded by 2^{-73} and the maximum correlation of a 6-round linear trial is 2^{-43}. These bounds ensure that the data requirement to mount these attacks will exceed the available data $2^{55} (\approx 11^{16})$ for 6-rounds.

5.2 Square Attack

In this section, we describe a 7-round square attack [14] against eSPF. This attack is motivated by the attack shown in [17]. For our 7-round attack, we first construct a 4-round distinguisher. Consider a Λ-set of 11 plaintexts in which the first symbol takes all possible 11 values (active symbol) and the remaining symbols take any constant value that remains same throughout the set. Since, our construction involves tweak addition, in this attack, let us suppose that the attacker uses Λ-sets for the two subtweaks as well, i.e., one symbol of both the subtweaks (position being the same as that of the active symbol in the plaintexts) are active. Considering these, Fig. 2 shows the four round transformations of eSPF construction.

Let x_j, y_j, z_j, w_j denote the symbol values in round j after SubBytes, ShiftRows, MixColumns and KeyAddition and stage respectively. Let A[p] denote the pth symbol (column wise) in any intermediate state A where, $0 \leq p \leq 15$. Similarly, $A_j^i[p]$ denotes the pth symbol of ith state A in round j where, (where, $0 \leq i \leq 10$). In the pre-whitening stage, since Λ-sets of plaintexts and subtweaks are in control of the attacker, he chooses the plaintexts P^i and subtweaks TW_0^i (where, $0 \leq i \leq 10$) such that for each i the sum $(P^i + Tw_0^i)$ mod 11 is a constant. The state remains constant until S_1 where the first symbol becomes active again due to addition of the second sub-tweak Tw_1. In, round 2 consider state $S_2[0]$. Due to sub-tweak addition of $Tw_1[0]$, we have:

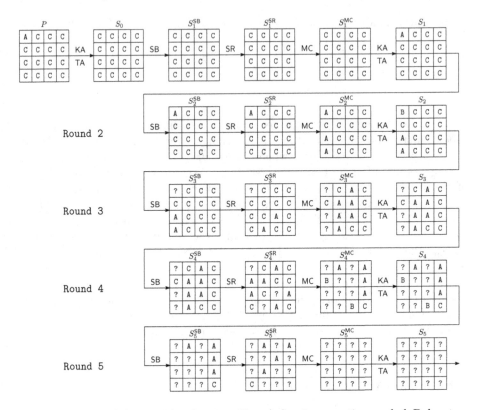

Fig. 2. A five round distinguisher for eSPF. Here A denotes an active symbol, B denotes that mod 10 sum of all values in that symbol is 0 and ? denotes unknown symbol.

$$w_2^i[0] = (z_2^i[0] + Tw_1^i[0]) \bmod 11$$

Since tweak symbol as well as the state symbol are active, if we add all the values in $w_2[0]$, then it can be shown that the sum mod 11 is always 0 as follows:

$$w_2^0[0] + w_2^1[0] + \ldots w_2^{10}[0] = \left(\sum_{i=0}^{10} z_2^i + \sum_{i=0}^{10} Tw_1^i\right) \bmod 11$$
$$= (55 + 55) \bmod 11 = 0$$

This shows that the set of values in the first symbol position after second round tweak addition forms a *balanced* set with probability 1. After SubBytes operation in round 3, the balanced set property is destroyed. Similar explanation can be given till state transformation after ShiftRows in round 4. After MixColumns operation in round 4, we get a completely unknown state. However, at state S_4^{MC}, consider the first column. Here, we have:

$$\sum_{i=0}^{10} z_5^i[0] + \sum_{i=0}^{10} z_5^i[3] = (\sum_{i=0}^{10} y_5^i[0] + \sum_{i=0}^{10} y_5^i[1] + 2\sum_{i=0}^{10} y_5^i[2] + 5\sum_{i=0}^{10} y_5^i[3]) \bmod 11 +$$

$$(\sum_{i=0}^{10} y_5^i[0] + 2\sum_{i=0}^{10} y_5^i[1] + 5\sum_{i=0}^{10} y_5^i[2] + \sum_{i=0}^{10} y_5^i[3]) \bmod 11$$

$$= (2\sum_{i=0}^{10} y_5^i[0] + 3\sum_{i=0}^{10} y_5^i[1] + 7\sum_{i=0}^{10} y_5^i[2] + 6\sum_{i=0}^{9} y_5^i[3]) \bmod 11$$

$$= (2\sum_{i=0}^{10} y_5^i[0] + 0) \bmod 11 = \text{ Even number}$$

Again in the right hand side of the above equation, since $y_5[1, 2, 3]$ are active cells, their sum over all 11 states is always going to be zero as discussed above. Hence, the additive sum of $Z_5[0] + Z_5[3]$ over all 11 states will always be an even number with probability 1; which will be preserved even after tweak addition in round 4. In the random case, the output will be even with a probability of $6/11$. Hence, a valid distinguisher is constructed. This four round attack can be extended up to seven rounds by adding one round in the backward and 2 rounds in the forward directions to recover the secret key.

5.3   Impossible Differential Cryptanalysis

Impossible Differential Cryptanalysis (IDC) [5] uses impossible differential characteristics to eliminate incorrect keys. Since the diffusion layer of eSPF construction is very similar to the AES algorithm, the basic 4 round impossible characteristics presented in [6] for AES algorithm and the proposed construction is same. The input and output characteristics for 4 rounds impossible characteristics is as follows:

$$(1, 0, 0, 0, 0, 0, 0, 0, 0, 0, 0, 0, 0, 0, 0, 0) \xrightarrow{4R} (0, 1, 1, 1, 1, 1, 1, 0, 1, 1, 0, 1, 1, 0, 1, 1)$$

More rounds can be appended before and after the 4 round impossible distinguisher. We found up to 6 rounds characteristics, which can be used for key-recovery attacks, but no such characteristics could be found when the number of round is greater than 6.

5.4   Key Related Attacks

Slide attacks [8] and related-key attacks [4] are the two most important types of key scheduling attacks. Our key scheduling algorithm for eSPF adds a round dependent counter in each round to prevent sliding of the subkeys. For related key attack to work, the attacker should be able to identify meaningful relationships between different subkeys so that a related key differential can be constructed over certain rounds. However, the non-linear addition operation and the modular function in our key scheduling algorithms do not allow an adversary to deduce all the other round keys (and the master key) from one round key by working through the key schedule. The modular function in particular also makes it very hard for an attacker to control the difference propagation through different round keys. Moreover, we also analyzed that each bit of the secret key K is used by the fifth round for all format size 10 or more. Hence, we believe that these features of the proposed KSA are sufficient to resist related key attacks.

5.5 Related Tweak Attack

Launching a related tweak attack to recover the secret key is easier for an attacker compared to related key attack. This is because the tweak value is a public entity and can be chosen by the attacker himself. This allows him to insert differences in the tweak input of the block cipher and construct related tweak differentials. Thus, it is imperative to assess the security of our schemes in this stronger related tweak setting.

We developed an automated program to count the number of active S-boxes and return an upper bound on the probability of the best related tweak truncated differentials. Table 3 lists the number of active S-boxes for the first 8-rounds of eSPF. It can be seen that the probability of any characteristic on more than 6 rounds is not higher than $2^{-36 \times 2.45} = 2^{-88.2}$ for eSPF. This bound ensures that the amount of data required to launch the attack will exceed the data available to an attacker (i.e., $11^{16} \approx 2^{53}$). Hence, our construction can resist any related tweak attack of practical complexity if the number of rounds is ≥ 6.

Table 3. Count of active S-box (A_r) and corresponding differential probability (P_r) over different rounds r of eSPF for related tweak differentials.

r	1	2	3	4	5	6	7	8
A_r	0	0	1	5	20	36	50	66
P_r	0	0	$2^{-2.45}$	$2^{-9.8}$	2^{-49}	$2^{-88.2}$	$2^{-122.5}$	$2^{-161.7}$

Considering the attacks discussed above as well as efficiency we recommend $r = 10$.

6 Performance

eSPF was designed with performance implementation costs in mind. In this section, we provide performance comparison of eSPF with FPE designs FFX and SPF.

6.1   Implementation

As eSPF is an AES-like block-cipher, the round-operations are best implemented using *table-lookups*. The reference implementation was done for 32-bit platform, but 64-bit processor support is ubiquitous and the implementation is also faster, so all the results are for the 64-bit implementation. Table 4 shows the implementation results.

Table 4. Execution speed in symbols/second and cycles/symbol for $eSPF_{10}^{10}$.

Processor	Clock speed	Speed for $eSPF_{10}^{10}$	
		Symbols/second	Cycles/symbol
Core i7 6700	3.4 GHz	201.2×10^6	16.8
Core i7 4770	3.4 GHz	168.1×10^6	20.2
Core i5 2400	3.1 GHz	44.8×10^6	70.5

The *lookup-table* based implementation of $eSPF_{10}^{10}$ round function required 4 tables with 64 entries of 32-bit integers. The round functions and the MOD (remainder) operation was combined. Each column required 4 table-lookups, as a result there were 16 table-lookups in total. PDEP and PEXT instructions, were used for various bit-manipulation operations needed, significantly improving the performance. Owing to the similarity with SPF for digits (which consists of 14 rounds), the performance gains for $eSPF_{10}^{10}$ would primarily be the result of reduced number of rounds, however the *discarding algorithm* would cause some performance degradation. The expected speedup can be estimated to be $((14 \div 10) \times (10 \div 11))$, which is about 1.27.

6.2   Performance of $eSPF_{10}^{10}$ Compared to FFX with Radix 10

Even for the smallest input sizes, FFX requires 11 invocations of AES-128 to encrypt messages containing about 52 symbols of radix 10. FFX needs 10 AES-128 invocations with a MOD operation which is quite expensive, and an extra AES-128. To test the expected performance, we used the inbuilt 128-bit integer support in gcc to perform MOD operations. On an Intel Core i7 4770 CPU at 3.4 GHz, the MOD operation was taking approximately 184 clock cycles at an average. We also tested an assembly version of a fast 128-bit MOD implementation for MSVC which took 296 clock cycles. On the same machine, it was found out that the AES-128 execution speed was 129 MiB/s by running openssl speed aes-128-cbc, which comes down to about 400 cycles per AES-128 invocation. As FFX uses 10 MOD operations and 11 AES-128 invocations, one FFX encrypt operation should take about $(184 \times 10) = 1840$ cycles for MOD and $(400 \times 11) = 4400$ cycles for AES, so in total it takes about 6240 cycles at least. So, FFX should run at about 120 cycles/symbol $(6240 \div 52)$ at max; this ignores any other performance loss due to copies, and other operations like $\mathsf{NUM}_{radix}()$, $\mathsf{STR}_{radix}()$ etc. So, eSPF is about **6 times faster** than FFX for similar parameters. Considering traditional applications of FPE such as encryption of SSN and CCN, eSPF would be around **30 and 15 times faster** than FFX respectively.

According to the definition of FFX, a large MOD (of size approximately $radix^{N/2}$, where N is the size of input string) operation is needed. As the MOD can get very large, efficient implementation would need to use *big-integer* libraries, which tend to be significantly slower (can be a few orders of magnitude, depending on parameters) than the AES-128, used. As a result the overall implementation can get very slow. This is not a problem in eSPF.

7   Conclusion

In this work, we present a new efficient format-preserving encryption construction based on substitution-permutation networks. We present a concrete instance of the proposed construction for format size 10. Further, to analyze the security of the presented design, we consider conventional cryptanalytic techniques as well as dedicated attacks. Finally, we compare the efficiency of the presented construction with existing schemes. The construction is approximately ten times faster than existing popular designs such as FFX and BPS for most of practical uses of FPE. A similar construction for other popular format size is an interesting open problem.

References

1. Aoki, K., Ichikawa, T., Kanda, M., Matsui, M., Moriai, S., Nakajima, J., Tokita, T.: *Camellia*: a 128-bit block cipher suitable for multiple platforms — design and analysis. In: Stinson, D.R., Tavares, S. (eds.) SAC 2000. LNCS, vol. 2012, pp. 39–56. Springer, Heidelberg (2001). https://doi.org/10.1007/3-540-44983-3_4
2. Bellare, M., Hoang, V.T., Tessaro, S.: Message-recovery attacks on Feistel-based format preserving encryption. Cryptology ePrint Archive, Report 2016/794 (2016). http://eprint.iacr.org/2016/794
3. Bellare, M., Ristenpart, T., Rogaway, P., Stegers, T.: Format-preserving encryption. In: Jacobson, M.J., Rijmen, V., Safavi-Naini, R. (eds.) SAC 2009. LNCS, vol. 5867, pp. 295–312. Springer, Heidelberg (2009). https://doi.org/10.1007/978-3-642-05445-7_19
4. Biham, E.: New types of cryptanalytic attacks using related keys. In: Helleseth, T. (ed.) EUROCRYPT 1993. LNCS, vol. 765, pp. 398–409. Springer, Heidelberg (1994). https://doi.org/10.1007/3-540-48285-7_34
5. Biham, E., Biryukov, A., Shamir, A.: Cryptanalysis of Skipjack reduced to 31 rounds using impossible differentials. In: Stern, J. (ed.) EUROCRYPT 1999. LNCS, vol. 1592, pp. 12–23. Springer, Heidelberg (1999). https://doi.org/10.1007/3-540-48910-X_2
6. Biham, E., Keller, N.: Cryptanalysis of reduced variants of Rijndael (1999, unpublished manuscript)

7. Biham, E., Shamir, A.: Differential cryptanalysis of DES-like cryptosystems. In: Menezes, A.J., Vanstone, S.A. (eds.) CRYPTO 1990. LNCS, vol. 537, pp. 2–21. Springer, Heidelberg (1991). https://doi.org/10.1007/3-540-38424-3_1
8. Biryukov, A., Wagner, D.: Advanced slide attacks. In: Preneel, B. (ed.) EURO-CRYPT 2000. LNCS, vol. 1807, pp. 589–606. Springer, Heidelberg (2000). https://doi.org/10.1007/3-540-45539-6_41
9. Black, J., Rogaway, P.: Ciphers with arbitrary finite domains. In: Preneel, B. (ed.) CT-RSA 2002. LNCS, vol. 2271, pp. 114–130. Springer, Heidelberg (2002). https://doi.org/10.1007/3-540-45760-7_9
10. Brier, E., Peyrin, T., Stern, J.: BPS: a format-preserving encryption proposal. NIST. http://csrc.nist.gov/groups/ST/toolkit/BCM/documents/proposedmodes/bps/bps-spec.pdf
11. Brightwell, M., Smith, H.: Using datatype-preserving encryption to enhance data warehouse security, vol. PP, pp. 141–149 (1997). http://csrc.nist.gov/niccs/1997
12. Chang, D., Ghosh, M., Gupta, K.C., Jati, A., Kumar, A., Moon, D., Ray, I.G., Sanadhya, S.K.: SPF: a new family of efficient format-preserving encryption algorithms. In: Chen, K., Lin, D., Yung, M. (eds.) Inscrypt 2016. LNCS, vol. 10143, pp. 64–83. Springer, Cham (2017). https://doi.org/10.1007/978-3-319-54705-3_5
13. Coppersmith, D., Holloway, C., Matyas, S.M., Zunic, N.: The data encryption standard. Inf. Secur. Tech. Rep. 2(2), 22–24 (1997)
14. Daemen, J., Knudsen, L., Rijmen, V.: The block cipher square. In: Biham, E. (ed.) FSE 1997. LNCS, vol. 1267, pp. 149–165. Springer, Heidelberg (1997). https://doi.org/10.1007/BFb0052343
15. Daemen, J., Rijmen, V.: The block cipher Rijndael. In: Quisquater, J.-J., Schneier, B. (eds.) CARDIS 1998. LNCS, vol. 1820, pp. 277–284. Springer, Heidelberg (2000). https://doi.org/10.1007/10721064_26
16. Daemen, J., Rijmen, V.: The wide trail design strategy. In: Honary, B. (ed.) Cryptography and Coding 2001. LNCS, vol. 2260, pp. 222–238. Springer, Heidelberg (2001). https://doi.org/10.1007/3-540-45325-3_20
17. Dobraunig, C., Eichlseder, M., Mendel, F.: Square attack on 7-round Kiasu-BC. In: Manulis, M., Sadeghi, A.-R., Schneider, S. (eds.) ACNS 2016. LNCS, vol. 9696, pp. 500–517. Springer, Cham (2016). https://doi.org/10.1007/978-3-319-39555-5_27
18. Betül Durak, F., Vaudenay, S.: Breaking the FF3 format-preserving encryption standard over small domains. Cryptology ePrint Archive, Report 2017/521 (2017). http://eprint.iacr.org/2017/521
19. Dworkin, M.: NIST Special Publication 800-38A: Recommendation for Block Cipher Modes of Operation-Methods and Techniques, December 2001
20. Dworkin, M.: Recommendation for block cipher modes of operation: methods for format-preserving encryption. NIST Special Publication, 800:38G
21. Granboulan, L., Levieil, É., Piret, G.: Pseudorandom permutation families over Abelian groups. In: Robshaw, M. (ed.) FSE 2006. LNCS, vol. 4047, pp. 57–77. Springer, Heidelberg (2006). https://doi.org/10.1007/11799313_5
22. Gupta, K.C., Pandey, S.K., Ray, I.G.: Format preserving sets: on diffusion layers of format preserving encryption schemes. In: Dunkelman, O., Sanadhya, S.K. (eds.) INDOCRYPT 2016. LNCS, vol. 10095, pp. 411–428. Springer, Cham (2016). https://doi.org/10.1007/978-3-319-49890-4_23
23. Hoang, V.T., Morris, B., Rogaway, P.: An enciphering scheme based on a card shuffle. In: Safavi-Naini, R., Canetti, R. (eds.) CRYPTO 2012. LNCS, vol. 7417, pp. 1–13. Springer, Heidelberg (2012). https://doi.org/10.1007/978-3-642-32009-5_1

24. Jean, J., Nikolić, I., Peyrin, T.: Tweaks and keys for block ciphers: the TWEAKEY framework. In: Sarkar, P., Iwata, T. (eds.) ASIACRYPT 2014. LNCS, vol. 8874, pp. 274–288. Springer, Heidelberg (2014). https://doi.org/10.1007/978-3-662-45608-8_15

25. Lee, J.-K., Koo, B., Roh, D., Kim, W.-H., Kwon, D.: Format-preserving encryption algorithms using families of tweakable blockciphers. In: Lee, J., Kim, J. (eds.) ICISC 2014. LNCS, vol. 8949, pp. 132–159. Springer, Cham (2015). https://doi.org/10.1007/978-3-319-15943-0_9

26. Liskov, M., Rivest, R.L., Wagner, D.: Tweakable block ciphers. In: Yung, M. (ed.) CRYPTO 2002. LNCS, vol. 2442, pp. 31–46. Springer, Heidelberg (2002). https://doi.org/10.1007/3-540-45708-9_3

27. Matsui, M.: Linear cryptanalysis method for DES cipher. In: Helleseth, T. (ed.) EUROCRYPT 1993. LNCS, vol. 765, pp. 386–397. Springer, Heidelberg (1994). https://doi.org/10.1007/3-540-48285-7_33

28. Morris, B., Rogaway, P.: Sometimes-recurse shuffle. In: Nguyen, P.Q., Oswald, E. (eds.) EUROCRYPT 2014. LNCS, vol. 8441, pp. 311–326. Springer, Heidelberg (2014). https://doi.org/10.1007/978-3-642-55220-5_18

29. Morris, B., Rogaway, P., Stegers, T.: How to encipher messages on a small domain. In: Halevi, S. (ed.) CRYPTO 2009. LNCS, vol. 5677, pp. 286–302. Springer, Heidelberg (2009)

30. Ristenpart, T., Yilek, S.: The mix-and-cut shuffle: small-domain encryption secure against N queries. In: Canetti, R., Garay, J.A. (eds.) CRYPTO 2013. LNCS, vol. 8042, pp. 392–409. Springer, Heidelberg (2013). https://doi.org/10.1007/978-3-642-40041-4_22

31. Rogaway, P.: Evaluation of Some Blockcipher Modes of Operation. http://www.cryptrec.go.jp/estimation/techrep_id2012_2.pdf

32. Schroeppel, R., Orman, H.: The hasty pudding cipher. AES candidate submitted to NIST, p. M1 (1998)

33. Sheets, J., Wagner, K.R.: Visa Format Preserving Encryption (VFPE). NIST Submission (2011)

34. Spies, T.: Feistel finite set encryption. NIST Submission, February 2008. http://csrc.nist.gov/groups/ST/toolkit/BCM/modes-development.html

Similarity Based Interactive Private Information Retrieval

Sashank Dara[1,2](✉) and V.N. Muralidhara[2]

[1] Cisco Systems Inc., Bangalore, India
sadara@cisco.com
[2] International Institute of Information Technology, Bangalore, Bangalore, India
murali@iiitb.ac.in

Abstract. *Private Information Retrieval (PIR)* schemes address users' privacy concerns while querying public databases. Two major advancements that are needed for designing practical privacy preserving applications are: *(i)* constant *communication complexity* and *(ii)* private retrieval of matching documents. In this paper, we propose a new family of interactive schemes namely ***SIMPIR***, that allow participating servers to interact with each other. Our methods are *similarity* based (i.e. the results could contain false positives but do not contain any false negatives). Importantly our approach has *constant* communication complexity agnostic of the size of database which is major improvement from known schemes. We achieve these results by slightly relaxing the traditional requirements of *PIR* schemes.

Keywords: Private information retrieval · Encryption switching protocols · Homomorphic encryption

1 Introduction

Private information retrieval (PIR) schemes enable a *User* to retrieve an item from a database *Server* without revealing the item to the *Server*. To understand the problem better, let's assume that Bob is trying to retrieve an element from a public database and he prefers that the database owner does not realize which element is being retrieved. Note that if Bob wants to hide his identity while retrieving the element he could simply use an anonymity service like *ToR* [1]. But Bob is interested in hiding the content of his query (and the element(s) subsequently retrieved) from the database itself. A *trivial* approach to address the issue is for Bob to download the whole database and query the downloaded database locally. However, there is a huge communication overhead in the trivial solution. *PIR* schemes have been proposed to address the problem in a non-trivial manner. Two major *PIR* approaches that exist are (i) *Information Theoretic (IT-PIR) schemes* and (ii) *Computational PIR (CPIR)* (discussed in detailed later).

Numerous real world applications have been identified for *PIR* schemes like private *domain name searching*, privately searching *patent databases*, privacy

© Springer International Publishing AG 2017
S.S. Ali et al. (Eds.): SPACE 2017, LNCS 10662, pp. 151–169, 2017.
https://doi.org/10.1007/978-3-319-71501-8_9

preserving *threat intelligence databases* etc. Let us consider a scenario where *Bob* would like to register for a domain name www.bob-garage.com. He needs to search whether such domain name is available. *Domain name front running* is a practice whereby an adversary (say a malicious domain registrar) mis-uses such insider information (from search queries) to pre-register domains for the sole purpose of re-selling them at higher price. To address this *Bob* could use a *PIR* scheme to privately search a public domain name database.

Traditional *PIR* schemes are based on the assumption that the *user* knows the *index (i.e. physical address)* of the element that is being retrieved. In practice, however, it is unrealistic to know the index of the element and retrieval is performed by keywords. For example, it is highly unlikely that *Bob* would know the *index* of the desired *domain name* in the server. To address such a problem a sub class of schemes called *PrivatE Retrieval by KeY words (PERKY)* are proposed. As discussed later, we identify that these schemes are not any efficient than *trivial* approach.

Also *PERKY* schemes proposed so far address *exact* string match and does not perform *similarity* match. For example, *Bob* may have to perform repeated searches for finding availability of *similar domains* like www.bob-garage.net, www.bob-garage.com, www.bob-garage.biz etc. So it would be useful to build *PIR* schemes that support *similarity* match.

For certain set of applications, it may be desirable to perform private searches based on entire documents. For example, *Alice* has come up with a creative solution for a problem and would like to patent it. *Alice* could perform a search on patent database like that of Google Patents to ensure her solution is novel and that no prior art exists. Hence it would be useful to build *PIR* schemes that could privately match the *similarity* of documents rather than just words.

In order to address these challenges we propose a family of efficient *similarity* based *private information retrieval (SIMPIR)* schemes with few relaxed requirements.

1.1   Key Contributions

In this paper, we propose *Computational Similarity PIR (C-SimPIR)*[1] scheme by using *encryption switching protocols*. We also introduce *Information Theoretic Similarity PIR(IT-SimPIR)* using *Secure Multi-Party Computation (MPC)* protocols and achieve better results.

- We propose *similarity* based *PIR* schemes. The results of retrieved records could contain false positives but do not contain false negatives.
- Our schemes have *constant* communication complexity irrespective of the size of database, where as best known previous result were $\mathcal{O}(\sqrt[d]{n})$ where d is dimension of database and n is total number of elements. We achieve this by relaxing few requirements and assumptions of traditional *PIR* schemes.

---

[1] A primitive construction and its applications in building privacy preserving threat intelligence services is under review in Elsevier Journal of Information Security and Applications.

- In the computational variety (*C-SimPIR*) scheme, we introduce a non-colluding trusted *auxiliary* server apart from the public database server, where as contemporary *CPIR* schemes are known for their simplicity in using a single server.
- In the information theoretic variety (*IT-SimPIR*) scheme, we introduce communication between non-colluding servers to perform *Secure Multi-Party Computation*, where as in contemporary *IT-PIR* schemes the servers do not communicate with each other.
- Our schemes are flexible enough to address private similarity match of keywords and also private similar document matching which is first of its kind.

2 Prior Art

We briefly recap both varieties of *PIR* schemes for benefit of the reader. Informally a *PIR* scheme enables a *User* to retrieve an element from the *database server* without revealing.

Computational PIR (CPIR). *CPIR* scheme's by large leverage homomorphic encryption schemes. Their security guarantees relies the hardness assumptions of underlying encryption schemes and on the computing resources available to the adversary [3,8,9,20].

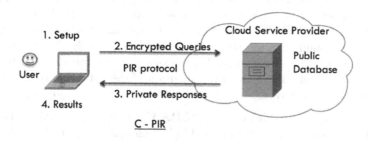

Fig. 1. Computational PIR

Note that the generic approach has a communication complexity of $\sqrt[d]{n}$ i.e. both the *query size* and the *response size* are function of size of the database n. With the explosion in the amount of data in modern databases, such schemes are highly impractical. Survey of *CPIR* schemes based on *locally decodable codes*, ϕ-hiding assumption *etc.* could be found in [25]. Moreover, *CPIR* schemes require only one *server* (as shown in Fig. 1) as opposed to *IT-PIR* schemes. Recently *CPIR* protocols using *BGV Fully Homomorphic Encryption* have been proposed that achieve $\mathcal{O}(\log \log n)$ in [15] they are single server based protocols.

C-SIMPIR schemes proposed by us deviate and assume the existence of multiple non-colluding servers in order to achieve **constant** communication complexity.

Information Theoretic PIR (IT-PIR). IT-PIR schemes leverage homomorphic properties of secret sharing schemes. They assume existence of multiple non-colluding replicas of database servers as shown in Fig. 2. Subsequently secret sharing techniques are applied on the input query for private retrieval of information. They do not rely on any limitations for computing resources available to the adversary and offer information-theoretic security [4,17,18,24].

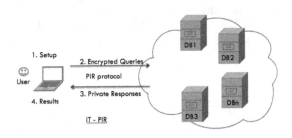

Fig. 2. Information Theoretic PIR

Hybrid Protocols. In order to leverage best of both *CPIR* and *IT-PIR* schemes hybrid PIR schemes have been proposed [14]. They leverage the recursive features of *CPIR* schemes and low communication and computation overheads of *IT-PIR* schemes. Our schemes are not in general comparable with hybrid schemes. Only similarity is our C-SIMPIR scheme (discussed later) uses multiple non-colluding servers. Their communication cost of input query is roughly $\mathcal{O}(n^2)$ where n is number of elements in the database. Their *response cost* is roughly $\mathcal{O}(l \times 6^{d-1} \times s)$ where l is number of servers and d is dimension of the database. Where as both our input *query cost* and *response cost* is constant which is major improvement.

Private Retrieval by Keyword (*PERKY*). Private retrieval by keyword (*PERKY*) protocols were first proposed in [10] and later extended in [23]. Informally, the goal is to retrieve an element from the database using a keyword itself rather than a physical address.

The main idea of these schemes is that the databases insert words $s_1, s_2, \ldots, s_n$ into a data structure which supports the search operations on words. *User*, conducts an *oblivious walk* on the data structure until the word w is found or the walk exhausts all possible n words in the database. If the element is found after few rounds in the *oblivious walk* the *user* will still execute the scheme until the last element, with arbitrary (dummy) queries. Otherwise, the *server* learns the search length for this specific keyword. If the element w does not exist in the database. *User* will not find the word even after a *walk* of n rounds. So in either case, this is the same as the *trivial* scheme, i.e. *User* retrieving all the n elements from the *Server*.

Where as our schemes are based on popular *data mining* techniques and do not suffer the above mentioned issues.

PIR techniques have been applied in many practical scenarios such as: web search, e-commerce, validation of the certificates, private LDAP lookups, anonymous communication *etc.* [18,19,22].

Related Areas. Cryptographic protocols such as: *Oblivious Transfer (OT)*, which guarantee that the database itself is kept private, or *Searchable Encryption*, which enables a *user* to search privately on encrypted data, are different. This is because in our setup, *Users* would like to query public databases by keeping their queries private.

3 Preliminaries

3.1 Homomorphic Encryption (HE)

Homomorphic encryption (HE) is a very useful tool in privacy preserving applications. Informally, such schemes allow one to perform operations on encrypted data without decrypting it. *Fully Homomorphic Encryption (FHE)* schemes are public key encryption (PKE) schemes that support both *additions* and *multiplications* on the encrypted data. *Partial Homomorphic Encryption (PHE)* schemes only one of them.

Apart from the typical *KeyGen, Encrypt, Decrypt* algorithms of PKE schemes, *PHE* schemes support special algorithms that allow addition (or multiplication) of two cipher texts without decrypting them.

Additive Homomorphic Encryption (AHE). *AHE* schemes have following interesting properties.

$$\mathcal{ENC}_{P_k}(a + b) = \mathcal{ENC}_{P_k}(a) + \mathcal{ENC}_{P_k}(b)$$
$$\mathcal{ENC}_{P_k}(a - b) = \mathcal{ENC}_{P_k}(a) - \mathcal{ENC}_{P_k}(b) \qquad (1)$$
$$\mathcal{ENC}_{P_k}(a) \times b = \mathcal{ENC}_{P_k}(a \times b)$$

By large *HE* schemes are well defined in algebraic structures like *finite fields* where subtraction is essentially addition (with additive inverse $a - b = a + (-b)$). Also Note that every *AHE* scheme also supports *homomorphic multiplication by scalar* (through repeated *homomorphic addition*); However, few schemes like *RING-LWE and Paillier* support such operation natively in a more efficient way [7,26]. We use this important property later in our schemes.

Multiplicative Homomorphic Encryption (MHE). *MHE* schemes have following property

$$\mathcal{ENC}_{P_k}(a \times b) = \mathcal{ENC}_{P_k}(a) \times \mathcal{ENC}_{P_k}(b) \qquad (2)$$

The popular *MHE* schemes being *ElGamal, RSA* etc. From a security point of view, the choice of *PHE* scheme (to be used in *PIR* later) should be based on its ability to achieve *indistinguishability* against *chosen-plaintext attack (IND-CPA)*. Informally it means an adversary could chose two plaintexts and obtain corresponding ciphertexts but cannot distinguish between them with any probability negligibly greater than $(1/2 + \epsilon(k))$, where $\epsilon(k)$ is a *negligible function* for security parameter k.

3.2   Encryption Switching Protocols (ESP)

Encryption Switching Protocols (ESP) are special kind of interactive two-party computation protocol which allows two players to obliviously convert an encryption of message m with a encryption scheme Π_1 to encryption of *same* message with another encryption scheme Π_2. These protocols were first introduced in [16,21]. Later both these approaches were proven to be error prone and much better protocols were proposed by *Couteau et al.* [11]. Their protocols convert ciphertext from *Paillier encryption scheme* to *ElGamal-like encryption scheme* bi-directionally. Subsequently much better variants have been proposed in their following work [12]. They also prove that *ESP* implies general two-party computation (2-PC).

We briefly mention simplified definitions and related algorithms of *ESP* protocols. Although details of exact algorithms are out of scope for this paper and readers recommended to refer [11] for such details.

Let $\mathcal{E}_1, \mathcal{E}_2$ be two encryption schemes with their respective algorithms (Setup, KeyGen, Enc, Dec). An encryption switching protocol (ESP) between $\mathcal{E}_1, \mathcal{E}_2$ has two algorithms (Share, Switch):

- Share(Pk, Sk): given the common keys Pk and Sk of both schemes, it outputs a secret shares of Sk i.e. (Sk_a, Sk_b). The parties A and B are configured with their respective Sk_a and Sk_b shares.
- $Switch((Pk, Sk_a, c), (Pk, Sk_b, c))$ is an interactive protocol that *switches* the encryption of the message m i.e. c under one encryption scheme $\mathcal{E}_1$ to its equivalent encryption c^1 (of the same message m) under another encryption scheme $\mathcal{E}_2$ (and vice versa).

Importantly both the parties A, B involved in the protocol are non-colluding.

We later use these protocols in building efficient *C-PIR* schemes.

3.3   Secret Sharing Schemes

Secret Sharing Schemes are interesting cryptographic primitives that enable *sharing* of a *secret* into multiple *shares* [5,27]. As per the standard security assumptions of *SSS*, if an adversary gains access to any number of shares less than defined threshold, it gains no information of the original secret value. They offer *information theoretic* security and has profound applications. Although both were first introduced independently *Shamir's Secret Sharing (SSS)* schemes [27] is considered more popular one.

We give a informal details of the two main algorithms in *SSS* schemes.

- Share(secret, t, n): Shares a given secret *secret* into n shares such that a threshold t share are required to reconstruct the secret.
- Reconstruct(secret$_i$, t, n): Given the shares i.e. $secret_i \forall i \in (1, n)$ this algorithm *reconstructs* the original *secret*.

SSS schemes have different *homomorphic properties* that could be performed in a non-interactive way. *Homomorphic Addition* could be performed on the individual *Shares* of a given *secret* without reconstructing it. Similarly *Homomorphic Multiplication by Scalar* could also be performed. Where as *Homomorphic Multiplication* requires an interactive protocol among the parties. A very good tutorial of different properties could be found here [6].

SSS schemes are the heart of *Secure Multi-Party Computation (MPC)* techniques that enable multiple parties to perform secure computations on their private inputs. A very good introduction of *MPC* and its different adversary models could be found here [13].

4 Private Differential Cosine Similarity

We briefly review popular *information retrieval* techniques based on *cosine similarity*. We then introduce the concept of *private differential cosine similarity* and leverage that subsequently in building efficient *PIR* schemes.

4.1 Term Frequency (tf) and Inverse Document Frequency (idf)

Term Frequency (tf) determines how frequently the word w appears in a given document d. *Inverse Document Frequency (idf)* determines how common the word appears in given set of documents. Combination of *tf* and *idf*, *tf-idf*, is the numerical statistical measure for each word w used by the search engines and the text mining applications.

$$tf(w, d) = f_{w,d}$$
$$idf(w, d, D) = |\{d \in D : w \in d\}|$$
$$tf\text{-}idf(w, d, D) = |tf(w, d) \times idf(w, d, D)|$$

There are many variants on how these measures are calculated, it is out of scope of this paper to describe them and we refer readers to [2] for more details.

4.2 Similarity

We formally define *similarity* of two documents as below.

Definition 1 (Similarity). *Let the database hold a set of documents $\mathcal{DB} = \{D_1, D_2, \ldots, D_n\}$. Let each document $D_i = [w_1, w_2 \ldots, w_n]$ i.e. each document D_i is a vector of n terms. Let $\mathcal{SIM}(D_1, D_2)$ be a similarity function for documents D_1, D_2 and $\mathcal{SF}$ is similarity factor then*

$$\mathcal{SIM}(D_1, D_2) = \mathcal{SF} \quad where \quad -1 \leqq \mathcal{SF} \leqq 1$$

If $\mathcal{SF} = -1$ then the documents are completely distinct.
If $\mathcal{SF} = 1$ the documents are exactly same.

Although defined w.r.t. *documents*, the same definition could be generalized for *arbitrary* strings of $(0,1)^l$. Rest of the paper we consider *document* level matching although the same definition could be extended for *keyword* level matching too.

Cosine similarity has been found useful to determine how similar two given documents [28] are. Documents are represented as vectors such that their components are *tf-idf* measures of each word.

Let $D1 = \{w_1, w_2 \ldots, w_n\}$, and $D2 = \{v_1, v_2, \ldots, v_n\}$ be two documents and w_i, v_i be their respective words. Let the vectors $D_a = [a_1, a_2, \ldots, a_n]$, and $D_b = [b_1, b_2, \ldots, b_n]$ be their *tf-idf* vectors such that $tf\text{-}idf(w_i) = a_i$ and $tf\text{-}idf(v_i) = b_i$.

Similarity Factor (SF) of two vectors D_a, D_b is defined as below.

$$\mathcal{SF} = \cos(\theta) = \frac{\sum_{i=1}^{i=n} a_i.b_i}{\sqrt{\sum_{i=1}^{i=n} a_i^2} \times \sqrt{\sum_{i=1}^{i=n} b_i^2}} \tag{3}$$

where similarity factor (SF) $\in \{-1, \ldots, 0, \ldots 1\}$

If the resulting *similarity factor* is -1 then the documents are completely distinct and if 1 the documents are exactly the same.

4.3   Private Differential Cosine Similarity

We define *differential cosine similarity (δ-sim)* as below

$$\delta\text{-}sim = \sum_{i=1}^{i=n} a_i.b_i - \mathcal{SF} \times \sqrt{\sum_{i=1}^{i=n} a_i^2} \times \sqrt{\sum_{i=1}^{i=n} b_i^2} \tag{4}$$

Although trivial but important observation is that δ-sim $= 0$ when the two documents are *similar* (as defined by *similarity factor (SF)*). For example, if the *User* prefers *exact match* of input document then *similarity factor (SF)* is set to 1. We further define *private differential cosine similarity (δ-psim)* on the ciphertext as below.

$$\delta\text{-}psim = \mathcal{ENC}_{P_k}(\delta\text{-}sim)$$
$$= \sum_{i=1}^{i=n} \mathcal{ENC}_{P_k}(a_i.b_i) - \mathcal{ENC}_{P_k}(\mathcal{SF} \times \sqrt{\sum_{i=1}^{i=n} a_i^2} \times \sqrt{\sum_{i=1}^{i=n} b_i^2}) \tag{5}$$

Similar observation is that, if the two documents are *similar* (as defined by *similarity factor (SF)*) then δ-psim $= \mathcal{ENC}_{P_k}(0)$. We later leverage this observation in achieving efficient *similarity based private information retrieval (SIMPIR)* schemes.

5 Similarity Based Private Information Retrieval (SIMPIR)

Informally, *SIMPIR* scheme should enable *User* to match *privately* an input document against a corpus of documents available in a public database.

5.1 Definition

We formally define a *similarity based private information retrieval scheme* and its desired properties. In later sections we propose different protocols that achieve them.

Definition 2 (SIMPIR). *A SIMPIR scheme, S, allows the user to find out for a given document D_u and some $j \in \{0, 1, \ldots, n\}$ where $D_j \in \mathcal{DB}_i$ $\forall i \in (1, l)$ server(s) and for predefined $\mathcal{SF}$ there is $\mathcal{SIM}(D_u, D_j) = \mathcal{SF}$ without leaking any information about D_u and $\mathcal{SF}$ to the database server(s) $\mathcal{DB}_i$.*

5.2 Properties

Security

- The *SIMPIR* scheme should achieve at least *Indistinguishability under chosen plaintext attacks (IND-CPA)*. Informally, an adversary should not be able to distinguish whether two different input documents are being privately queried.
- *Guessing Attacks:* An adversary should not be able to guess the document being retrieved with the probability $>1/n$ where n is total number of documents in the database.

Efficiency. Any *PIR* scheme should be efficient than *trivial* approach. A *trivial* scheme is where a *User* downloads the entire database of documents and subsequently computes the *similarity* locally. Efficiency is usually defined by the below parameters

- *Communication Complexity* of the scheme i.e. the amount of data retrieved by the *User* in order to determine if the element exists in the *database*. The *communication complexity* of the *trivial* scheme would be $O(|\mathcal{DB}|)$ and any valid *SIMPIR* scheme should be lesser.
- *Computational Complexity* of a *PIR* scheme is defined as the number of documents processed by the *database server* before it returns the response. Notice that this requirement is tightly linked with the *Security* of the scheme, if the *database server* does not process any record then an adversary could determine the *Users* input with probability $>1/n$. So the lower bound for any valid *SIMPIR* scheme should be $\Omega(n)$.

6   Computational Similarity PIR (C-SIMPIR)

Intuitively the *User* could encrypt the input vector using a *fully homomorphic encryption scheme (FHE)* and submit to the *Server* for finding relevant matches. The *Server* could evaluate the *differential similarity* blindfolded without decrypting the input. But unfortunately FHE schemes are quite expensive. So we have to achieve the same functionality using *partial homomorphic encryption schemes* that support either *addition* or *multiplication* on the ciphertext.

We first introduce the basic version of the protocol with *additive homomorphic encryption (AHE)* schemes alone. Later we provide an advanced version of our efficient *Computational SIMPIR* scheme and provide its analysis.

6.1   Basic Protocol

Informally, *User* encrypts the input document and *server* processes against all other documents blindfolded. This is achieved by leveraging the *additive homomorphic properties* of the encryption scheme. *User* subsequently retrieves the encrypted similarity quotients, decrypts them and calculates the *cosine similarity* in order to determine a match. We describe each of these steps of the algorithm below:

1. **DB_Preparation:** The *tf-idf* vectors for all the documents in the database server are calculated. Lets say for each document D_s its vector is $[b_1, b_2, \ldots, b_k]$ and its magnitude $||D_s|| = \sqrt{\sum_{j=1}^{j=k} b_j^2}$ is calculated.

2. **Query_Gen:** Let *user*'s document $D_u = [a_1, a_2, \ldots, a_k]$ for which the private *similarity* check need to be performed. An *additive homomorphic encryption (AHE)* is used to encrypt the *terms* of the document. Query vector $Q_u = [q_1, q_2, \ldots, q_k]$ is defined as below. *User* also sends $\mathcal{ENC}_{P_k}(\mathcal{SF} \times ||D_u||)$.

$$\mathcal{Q}_u = ([\mathcal{ENC}_{P_k}(a_1), \mathcal{ENC}_{P_k}(a_2), .., \mathcal{ENC}_{P_k}(a_k)]$$

3. **Response_Gen:** The *server* receives query vector, $\mathcal{Q}_u$, and calculates the *dot product* for each document in the database. This is done blindfold using *additive homomorphic* properties of the encryption scheme. Subsequently the response per each server's document D_s is calculated, this would be a constant $\mathcal{RES}$ is:

$$|Q_u.D_s| = \sum_{j=1}^{j=k} q_j.b_j = q_1.b_1 + q_2.b_2 + \ldots + q_k.b_k$$

$$= \mathcal{ENC}_{P_k}(a_1).b_1 + \mathcal{ENC}_{P_k}(a_2).b_2 + \ldots + \mathcal{ENC}_{P_k}(a_k).b_k$$

$$= \mathcal{ENC}_{P_k}(a_1.b_1) + \mathcal{ENC}_{P_k}(a_2.b_2) + \ldots + \mathcal{ENC}_{P_k}(a_k.b_k)$$

$$= \mathcal{ENC}_{P_k}(\sum_{j=1}^{j=k} a_j.b_j)$$

$$\mathcal{RES} = \mathcal{ENC}_{P_k}(\sum_{j=1}^{j=k} a_j.b_j) - \mathcal{ENC}_{P_k}(\mathcal{SF} \times ||D_u||) \times ||D_s||$$

$$= \mathcal{ENC}_{P_k}(\sum_{j=1}^{j=k} a_j.b_j) - \mathcal{ENC}_{P_k}(\mathcal{SF} \times ||D_u|| \times ||D_s||)$$

$$= \delta\text{-}psim$$

4. **Process_Res:** *User* retrieves the response $\mathcal{RES}$ and decrypts it. If it is 0 then the input document D_u matches with *Server*'s document D_s as defined by the *similarity factor (SF)*.

$$Match = \begin{cases} if\ \mathcal{DEC}_{S_k}(\delta\text{-}psim) = 0\ then\ \mathcal{SIM}(D_u, D_s) = \mathcal{SF} \\ else\ \ \mathcal{SIM}(D_u, D_s) \neq \mathcal{SF} \end{cases}$$

The above process has to be repeated for every document D_s in *DB*.

6.2   Analysis

Security

- The input document D_u is encrypted by the *User* using *AHE*. As long as the choice of *AHE* is probabilistic (for example *Paillier* scheme) which achieves indistinguishability under *chosen plaintext attacks* the *basic protocol* is secure under same level. More detailed proofs could be referred in [26].
- Also since the protocol is repeated for every document by the *User*, irrespective of a match found, an adversary cannot guess the *User*'s document with probability $(>1/n)$. For example, if the *User* finds a match after $k < n$ rounds and preempts the protocol, an adversary would know with good probability (i.e. $1 - (k/n)$) that the *Users* document D_u is in first k documents.

Efficiency

- The amount of data retrieved is $|\delta\text{-}psim|$ per document i.e. *constant* number of bits. So the *communication complexity* of basic protocol is efficient than *trivial* scheme i.e. downloading entire document (assuming on average $|D_i| > |\delta\text{-}psim|$ $\forall i \in (1, n)$).
  Also notice that the overall *communication complexity* is $O(|\delta\text{-}psim| \times n)$, where n is number of documents in the database.
- The overall *computation complexity* is $O(n)$ since the protocol is repeated for all the documents.

If the database is really large, the basic version, although efficient than *trivial* version, would still be inefficient for practical consumption. The *User* has to run the protocol for every input document.

6.3   Advanced Protocol

In order to address the efficiency challenges further we propose an advanced version of the protocol. Observe that only AHE scheme is used in the basic protocol. Instead if a FHE scheme was used, the *database server (DB)* could simply compute the product of all the δ-*psim* for a given document D_u.

The intuition is that even if one document D_k matches (with *Users* document D_u) then its respective δ-$sim_k = 0$ and subsequently the product of all the δ-*psims* would be 0. The resultant could be decrypted by the *User* to determine if there was a match as shown below.

$$\mathcal{RES} = \prod_{j=1}^{j=n} (\delta\text{-}psim_j) \quad \forall j \in (1, n)$$

$$Match = \begin{cases} if\ \mathcal{DEC}_{S_k}(\mathcal{RES}) = 0\ then\ D_u \in (DB) \\ else \quad D_u \notin (DB) \end{cases}$$

(6)

Unfortunately, FHE schemes are quite expensive for practical consumption still. Also *homomorphic multiplication* is not supported in AHE schemes due to which the *database server* cannot compute the product of all δ-*psims*. On the other hand we cannot perform the *basic protocol* using *multiplicative homomorphic encryption (MHE)* schemes to compute the product. In order to address this challenge, the trick is to convert the ciphertext from AHE to MHE *on-demand* using *encryption switching protocols (ESP)* as a sub protocol.

We assume the presence of a trusted *auxiliary server (AS)* that does not collude with the DB. *User* generates the relevant key pairs needed for ESP protocol and *shares* them with DB and AS as defined in Sect. 3.2. For a given *User* document D_u, the DB computes the δ-$psim_j^a$ for all the documents i.e. $j \in (1, n)$ as described in *basic protocol*. Observe the additional superscript a to denote that δ-$psim_j^a$ is resultant of *additive homomorphic encryption* scheme. The DB initiates the *switch* algorithm of *encryption switching protocol (ESP)* to *convert* the $(\delta$-$psim_j^a \rightarrow \delta$-$psim_j^m)$ i.e. *private differential similarity* encrypted under *multiplicative homomorphic encryption* without decrypting it. Subsequently DB computes the product $\prod_{j=1}^{j=n}(\delta$-$psim_j^m) \quad \forall j \in (1, n)$ through *homomorphic multiplication*. *User* retrieves the result and determines the match as defined in Eq. 6 (Fig. 3).

6.4   Analysis

Contemporary C-PIR schemes are known for their simplicity of being *single server* protocols. But with the assumption if this additional *auxiliary server (AS)*, we achieve a *constant* communication complexity and agnostic of size of the database. In practice AS could be a separate virtual machine owned by the *User* but not the *database* owner.

Security. Security requirements follow from the *basic protocol*. Additionally, as long as AS and DB are *non-colluding* the *security guarantees* of the *encryption switching protocols* hold good and could be referred in [11,12].

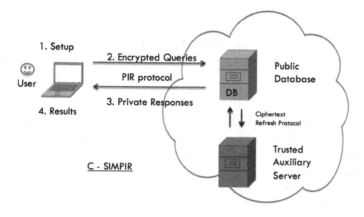

Fig. 3. Computational SIMPIR

Efficiency. The overall *Communication Complexity* is drastically simplified to *constant* number of bits i.e. *encryption* of 0 or *scalar* depending upon whether the *Users* input finds a match. The lower bound of *Computational Complexity* is still $\Omega(n)$ because all the documents are being processed. There is an additional overhead on the computation though due to the usage of *ESP* protocols.

7   Information Theoretic Similarity PIR (IT-SIMPIR)

IT-SIMPIR is conceptually similar to our *C-SIMPIR* protocols, except that we leverage the *homomorphic properties* of *secret sharing* schemes and *MPC* protocols. Informally, multiple replicas of database are made available $\mathcal{DB}_l \; \forall l \in (1, k)$. The input *tf-idf* document vector D_u is *secret shared* and sent to respective $\mathcal{DB}_l$ servers. Subsequently $Share(\delta\text{-}psim)_i$ is computed for each document by each server and returned. *User* subsequently reconstructs $\delta\text{-}psim$ from the shares to find a match.

7.1   Basic Protocol

The approach is conceptually similar to that of *basic protocol* of *C-SIMPIR* discussed in Sect. 6.1. In the interest of space we provide a high level overview of the *basic protocol* of *IT-SIMPIR* here and complete version in Appendix B.

User *secret shares* the document vector D_u and distributes across multiple *database servers* $\mathcal{DB}_i$. Each *database server* uses *additive homomorphic properties* of *secret sharing* schemes in order to calculate their respective *shares* of *private differential cosine similarity* i.e. $Share_i(\delta\text{-}sim)$. *User* retrieves all these *shares* in order to reconstruct $\delta\text{-}sim$ for each document to determine a match.

Security

- The input document D_u is *secret shared* by the *User* using *SSS*. As long as random polynomial is used to *secret share* each document an adversary

cannot distinguish between *shares* of different documents. Detailed proofs could be referred in [27].
- Also since the protocol is repeated for every document by the *User*, irrespective of a match found, an adversary cannot guess the *User*'s document with probability $(>1/n)$.

Efficiency

- The amount of data retrieved is $l \times |Share_i(\delta\text{-}psim)|$. The *basic protocol* need not be efficient than *trivial* approach. Also notice that the overall *communication complexity* is $O(l \times |Share_i(\delta\text{-}sim)| \times n)$, where n is number of documents in the database.
- The overall *computation complexity* is $O(n)$ since the protocol is repeated for all the documents.

7.2   Advanced Protocol

Notice that the participating *database servers* do not need to communicate among themselves this is same as classic *IT-PIR* schemes. But in order to achieve efficient schemes we make a newer assumption that the *DB* servers could communicate with each other without colluding. Under such assumptions, use *Secure Multi-Party Computation (MPC)* protocols.

We use the same intuition (as in *C-SIMPIR*) that even if one document D_k matches then its respective $\delta\text{-}sim_k = 0$ and subsequently the product of all the $\delta\text{-}sims$ would be 0 (Fig. 4).

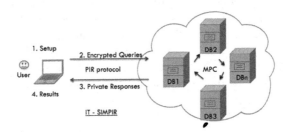

Fig. 4. Information Theoretic SIMPIR

For a given *User* document D_u, each $\mathcal{DB}_i$ server has a respective $Share_i(\delta\text{-}sim)$. Since the *homomorphic multiplication* of *SSS* schemes require interactivity, the $\mathcal{DB}_i$ collaboratively compute $\Pi_{j=1}^{j=k} Share_i(\delta\text{-}sim)$ and return their respective values. *User* reconstructs the final result.

$$\mathcal{RES} = reconstruct(\prod_{j=1}^{j=n}(\delta\text{-}sim_j)) \quad \forall j \in (1, n)$$

$$Match = \begin{cases} if\ (\mathcal{RES}) = 0\ then\ D_u \in (DB) \\ else\quad D_u \notin (DB) \end{cases}$$

(7)

Security

- The indistinguisability follows from security of *basic protocol*.
- Also since the protocol is based on *oblivious* product $(\delta\text{-}sim_j)$ of every document, irrespective of a match found, an adversary cannot guess the *User*'s document with probability $(>1/n)$.

Efficiency

- The amount of data retrieved is $l \times | \prod_{j=1}^{j=n} Share_i(\delta\text{-}psim)|$. The *basic protocol* need not be efficient than *trivial* approach. But notice that the overall *communication complexity* is constant and agnostic of number of documents in the database.
- The overall *computation complexity* is $\Omega(n)$ since the protocol is repeated for all the documents. There is an additional overhead of performing *MPC* protocol for product computation.

8   Limitations and Future Work

Cosine Similarity is prone to *false positives (fps)* i.e. two distinct documents could have same *tf-idf* vectors, so this might result in a *match* although documents are different. The rate of the *fps* highly depends on the high level applications and the content types being applied. For example, *fps* could be very rare for longer documents and more frequent when used for shorter *keyword* level matching. Another important nuance is calculation of *inverse document frequency (idf)* could be challenging. It is not known whether *idf* could calculated privately on a public database. So we assume *idf* value to be 1.

We presented the simplest possible *IT-SIMPIR* using *MPC* protocols. Advanced protocols based on scenarios like *k-out-of-l threshold, t-private, v-byzantine robust* and τ *independent* could be built on top of these as a natural extension in future. We would like to research on more variety of data mining techniques that could be used to build efficient *PIR* schemes. We would also like to experiment with practical implementations of *SIMPIR* schemes.

9   Conclusions

We introduced the concept of *similarity based private information retrieval (SIMPIR)* to address the privacy concerns of *Users* while querying public databases. We proposed both *computational (C-SIMPIR) and information theoretical (IT-SIMPIR)* variety protocols. Our methods are flexible to *privately* match either *keywords* or entire *documents* which is first of its kind. *Communication Complexity* of our protocols is *constant* and agnostic of size of the database which is significant improvement from previous known results. We hope our work would aide to develop practical systems that enable *Users* to privately query public databases.

Acknowledgments. We would like to thank Cisco Systems for supporting this work.

Appendix

A   Computational - SIMPIR

We present the complete version of the *advanced C-SIMPIR protocol* here.

1. **Setup:** The *User* configures creates the keypairs and *Shares* them among the *auxiliary server (AS)* and *database server (DB)* for *encryption switching protocols* to function.
2. **DB_Preparation, Query_Gen** are same as *basic protocol*.
3. **Response_Gen:** The *database server* generates δ-$psim^a$ for each document D_i in the database and initiates ciphertext *encryption switching protocol (ESP)* to *switch* the value to δ-$psim^m$. Subsequently $\prod_{j=1}^{j=n} \delta$-$psim^m$ is computed w.r.t all the documents.
4. **Process_Res:** *User* retrieves the response $\mathcal{RES}$ and decrypts it. If it is 0 then the input document D_u matches with *Server*'s document D_s as defined by the *similarity factor (SF)*.

$$Match = \begin{cases} if \; \mathcal{DEC}_{S_k}\left(\prod_{j=1}^{j=n} \delta\text{-}psim^m\right) = 0 \; then \; \mathcal{SIM}(D_u, D_s) = \mathcal{SF} \\ else \quad \mathcal{SIM}(D_u, D_s) \neq \mathcal{SF} \end{cases}$$

B   Information Theoretic - SIMPIR

We present the complete version of the *advanced IT-SIMPIR protocol* here.

1. **DB_Preparation:** The *tf-idf* vectors for all the documents are computed and replicated in k database servers $\mathcal{DB}_l$. Lets say for each document D_s its vector is $[b_1, b_2, \ldots, b_k]$ and its magnitude $||D_s|| = \sqrt{\sum_{j=1}^{j=k} b_j^2}$ is calculated.
2. **Query_Gen:** Let *user*'s document $D_u = [a_1, a_2, \ldots, a_k]$ for which the private *similarity* check need to be performed. An *Secret Sharing Scheme* is used to *share* the *terms* of the document. Query vector $\mathcal{Q}_u^i = ([q_1, q_2, \ldots, q_k]$ for $\mathcal{DB}_i$ is defined as below. *User* also computes respective *shares* of $(\mathcal{SF} \times ||D_u||)$ for each $\mathcal{DB}_i$.

$$\mathcal{Q}_u^i = ([Share_i(a_1), Share_i(a_2), .., Share_i(a_k)] \quad \forall i \in (1, l) \; servers$$

3. **Response_Gen:** Each *database server* $(\mathcal{DB}_i)$ receives its respective query vector, $\mathcal{Q}_u^i$, and computes the *dot product* for each document in the database. This is done blindfold using *additive homomorphic* properties of the *secret sharing scheme*. Subsequently the response per each server's document D_s is calculated, this would be a constant $\mathcal{RES}$ is:

$$|Q_u.D_s| = \sum_{j=1}^{j=k} q_j.b_j = q_1.b_1 + q_2.b_2 + \ldots + q_k.b_k$$

$$= Share_i(a_1).b_1 + Share_i(a_2).b_2 + \ldots + Share_i(a_k).b_k$$

$$= Share_i(\sum_{j=1}^{j=k} a_j.b_j)$$

$$\mathcal{RES} = Share_i(\sum_{j=1}^{j=k} a_j.b_j) - Share_i(\mathcal{SF} \times ||D_u||) \times ||D_s||$$

$$= Share_i(\sum_{j=1}^{j=k} a_j.b_j) - Share_i(\mathcal{SF} \times ||D_u|| \times ||D_s||)$$

$$= Share_i(\delta\text{-}sim)$$

Subsequently MPC protocol is initiated among all the *database servers* $(\mathcal{DB}_i)$ in order to compute their respective share of $Share_i(\prod_{j=1}^{j=n}(\delta\text{-}sim_j))$.

4. **Process_Res:** *User* retrieves the all the respective shares of the $\mathcal{RES}$ from the *database servers* $\mathcal{DB}_i$ and reconstructs δ-*sim*. If it is 0 then the input document D_u matches with *Server*'s document D_s as defined by the *similarity factor (SF)*.

$$\delta\text{-}sim = reconstruct(Share_i(\delta\text{-}sim))\forall i \in (1, l)$$

$$Match = \begin{cases} if\ (\delta\text{-}psim) = 0\ then\ \mathcal{SIM}(D_u, D_s) = \mathcal{SF} \\ else\ \ \ \mathcal{SIM}(D_u, D_s) \neq \mathcal{SF} \end{cases}$$

The deviation from original assumptions of *IT-PIR* schemes is that in our protocols the servers communicate with each other in a non-colluding way to perform *MPC* protocols.

References

1. https://www.torproject.org/ (2016)
2. Term frequency - inverse document frequency (2016). https://en.wikipedia.org/wiki/Tf-idf
3. Aguilar-Melchor, C., Barrier, J., Fousse, L., Killijian, M.O.: Xpire: Private information retrieval for everyone. Technical report, Cryptology ePrint Archive, Report 2014/1025 (2014)
4. Beimel, A., Ishai, Y., Malkin, T.: Reducing the servers computation in private information retrieval: PIR with preprocessing. In: Bellare, M. (ed.) CRYPTO 2000. LNCS, vol. 1880, pp. 55–73. Springer, Heidelberg (2000). https://doi.org/10.1007/3-540-44598-6_4
5. Blakley, G.R.: Safeguarding cryptographic keys. In: Proceedings of the National Computer Conference 1979, vol. 48, pp. 313–317 (1979)
6. Bogdanov, D.: Foundations and properties of Shamir's secret sharing scheme. University of Tartu, Institute of Computer Science, 1 May 2007

7. Brakerski, Z., Vaikuntanathan, V.: Fully homomorphic encryption from ring-LWE and security for key dependent messages. In: Rogaway, P. (ed.) CRYPTO 2011. LNCS, vol. 6841, pp. 505–524. Springer, Heidelberg (2011). https://doi.org/10.1007/978-3-642-22792-9_29

8. Chang, Y.-C.: Single database private information retrieval with logarithmic communication. In: Wang, H., Pieprzyk, J., Varadharajan, V. (eds.) ACISP 2004. LNCS, vol. 3108, pp. 50–61. Springer, Heidelberg (2004). https://doi.org/10.1007/978-3-540-27800-9_5

9. Chor, B., Gilboa, N.: Computationally private information retrieval. In: Proceedings of the twenty-Ninth Annual ACM Symposium on Theory of Computing, pp. 304–313. ACM (1997)

10. Chor, B., Gilboa, N., Naor, M.: Private information retrieval by keywords. Citeseer (1997)

11. Couteau, G., Peters, T., Pointcheval, D.: Encryption switching protocols. Technical report, Cryptology ePrint Archive, Report 2015/990 (2015). http://eprint.iacr.org

12. Couteau, G., Peters, T., Pointcheval, D.: Secure distributed computation on private inputs. In: Garcia-Alfaro, J., Kranakis, E., Bonfante, G. (eds.) FPS 2015. LNCS, vol. 9482, pp. 14–26. Springer, Cham (2016). https://doi.org/10.1007/978-3-319-30303-1_2

13. Cramer, R., Damgård, I.: Multiparty computation, an introduction. In: Catalano, D., Cramer, R., Di Crescenzo, G., Darmgård, I., Pointcheval, D., Takagi, T. (eds.) Contemporary Cryptology, pp. 41–87. Springer, Heidelberg (2005). https://doi.org/10.1007/3-7643-7394-6_2

14. Devet, C., Goldberg, I.: The best of both worlds: combining information-theoretic and computational PIR for communication efficiency. In: De Cristofaro, E., Murdoch, S.J. (eds.) PETS 2014. LNCS, vol. 8555, pp. 63–82. Springer, Cham (2014). https://doi.org/10.1007/978-3-319-08506-7_4

15. Dong, C., Chen, L.: A fast single server private information retrieval protocol with low communication cost. In: Kutyłowski, M., Vaidya, J. (eds.) ESORICS 2014. LNCS, vol. 8712, pp. 380–399. Springer, Cham (2014). https://doi.org/10.1007/978-3-319-11203-9_22

16. Gavin, G., Minier, M.: Oblivious multi-variate polynomial evaluation. In: Roy, B., Sendrier, N. (eds.) INDOCRYPT 2009. LNCS, vol. 5922, pp. 430–442. Springer, Heidelberg (2009). https://doi.org/10.1007/978-3-642-10628-6_28

17. Goldberg, I.: Improving the robustness of private information retrieval. In: IEEE Symposium on Security and Privacy, SP 2007, pp. 131–148. IEEE (2007)

18. Henry, R., Olumofin, F., Goldberg, I.: Practical PIR for electronic commerce. In: Proceedings of the 18th ACM Conference on Computer and Communications Security, pp. 677–690. ACM (2011)

19. Kikuchi, H.: Private revocation test using oblivious membership evaluation protocol. In: 3rd Annual PKI R&D Workshop. Citeseer (2004)

20. Kushilevitz, E., Ostrovsky, R.: Replication is not needed: single database, computationally-private information retrieval. In: FOCS, p. 364. IEEE (1997)

21. Lim, H.W., Tople, S., Saxena, P., Chang, E.C.: Faster secure arithmetic computation using switchable homomorphic encryption. IACR Cryptology ePrint Archive 2014/539 (2014)

22. Mittal, P., Olumofin, F.G., Troncoso, C., Borisov, N., Goldberg, I.: PIR-Tor: scalable anonymous communication using private information retrieval. In: USENIX Security Symposium (2011)

23. Olumofin, F., Goldberg, I.: Privacy-preserving queries over relational databases. In: Atallah, M.J., Hopper, N.J. (eds.) PETS 2010. LNCS, vol. 6205, pp. 75–92. Springer, Heidelberg (2010). https://doi.org/10.1007/978-3-642-14527-8_5

24. Olumofin, F., Goldberg, I.: Revisiting the computational practicality of private information retrieval. In: Danezis, G. (ed.) FC 2011. LNCS, vol. 7035, pp. 158–172. Springer, Heidelberg (2012). https://doi.org/10.1007/978-3-642-27576-0_13

25. Ostrovsky, R., Skeith, W.E.: A survey of single-database private information retrieval: techniques and applications. In: Okamoto, T., Wang, X. (eds.) PKC 2007. LNCS, vol. 4450, pp. 393–411. Springer, Heidelberg (2007). https://doi.org/10.1007/978-3-540-71677-8_26

26. Paillier, P.: Public-key cryptosystems based on composite degree residuosity classes. In: Stern, J. (ed.) EUROCRYPT 1999. LNCS, vol. 1592, pp. 223–238. Springer, Heidelberg (1999). https://doi.org/10.1007/3-540-48910-X_16

27. Shamir, A.: How to share a secret. Commun. ACM **22**(11), 612–613 (1979)

28. Singhal, A.: Modern information retrieval: a brief overview. IEEE Data Eng. Bull. **24**(4), 35–43 (2001)

A Secure and Efficient Implementation of the Quotient Digital Signature Algorithm (qDSA)

Armando Faz-Hernández[✉], Hayato Fujii, Diego F. Aranha, and Julio López

Institute of Computing, University of Campinas,
1251 Albert Einstein, Cidade Universitária, Campinas, São Paulo, Brazil
{armfazh,dfaranha,jlopez}@ic.unicamp.br, hayato@lasca.ic.unicamp.br

Abstract. Digital signatures provide a means to publicly authenticate messages sent over an insecure channel. Recently, the Quotient Digital Signature Algorithm (qDSA) was introduced aiming key-compatibility with the Diffie-Hellman X25519 function. Due to the novelty of qDSA, there remains a need for an optimized implementation that allows identifying the real impact of this new algorithm. In this work, we focus on the secure and efficient implementation of qDSA. By leveraging the use of precomputation on the right-to-left Joye's algorithm, we reduced the running time of signature generation by 30–35%, and the running time of the verification procedure by 19%. In addition, for increased security, we show a verification method that validates qDSA signatures unequivocally. All of these improvements were included into an optimized software library targeting 32–bit ARM and 64–bit Intel architectures. The improved performance achieved in these platforms, it positions qDSA as a competitive alternative for deploying digital signatures efficiently and securely.

Keywords: qDSA · Digital signatures · Elliptic curve cryptography · Secure software · Montgomery curves

1 Introduction

Digital signatures are public-key cryptographic schemes used to authenticate messages sent over a public channel; thus, anyone with the knowledge of the signer's public-key is able to verify whether a signed message comes from a reliable source. Digital signatures also provide other security services such as data integrity, authentication, and non-repudiation. One of the most relevant applications of digital signatures is the certification of public keys in the Public-Key Infrastructure (PKI). In this scenario, a trusted authority issues and signs a

The authors acknowledge support during the development of this research from Intel and FAPESP under project *"Secure Execution of Cryptographic Algorithms"* (grant 14/50704-7), and from LG Electronics Inc. under project *"Efficient and Secure Cryptography for IoT"*. The fourth author was partially supported by a research productivity grant from CNPq.

© Springer International Publishing AG 2017
S.S. Ali et al. (Eds.): SPACE 2017, LNCS 10662, pp. 170–189, 2017.
https://doi.org/10.1007/978-3-319-71501-8_10

digital certificate that binds a public key to its owner; then, whenever an entity claims to be the owner of a public key, the digital certificate must be presented; therefore, anybody with the knowledge of the authority's public key is able to verify the signature of the certificate that attests this relationship.

In the last decades, several digital signature algorithms have been standardized. In 1998, the National Institute of Standards and Technology (NIST) approved the use of the Digital Signature Algorithm (DSA) [24] and the RSA digital signature [34]. Later in 2000, NIST also adopted the use of a digital signature algorithm that relies on the computational intractability of the elliptic curve discrete logarithm problem, such a method is known as the Elliptic Curve Digital Signature Algorithm (ECDSA) [17,25]. Since their standardization, these algorithms have been widely used in secure communication protocols, such as the Transport Layer Security (TLS) protocol [33].

More recently, cutting-edge cryptographic research is in pursuit of efficient digital signature algorithms. The introduction of the Edwards Digital Signature Algorithm (EdDSA) [2] is an example of the latest progress. EdDSA uses Edwards curves, which belong to a special family of elliptic curves whose point addition formulas are more efficient than the formulas used for an arbitrary curve in the short Weierstrass model. Ed25519 [18] is an instance of EdDSA addressing the 128-bit security level. Particularly, Ed25519 uses an Edwards curve derived from the Montgomery curve known as Curve25519 [1]. This latter curve was intended to accelerate the key exchange protocol leading to the Diffie-Hellman X25519 function [41]. Although Ed25519 and X25519 can be used in conjunction benefiting from the common prime field arithmetic, the keys used in each protocol are not entirely compatible.

To make this compatibility possible, novel alternatives were derived such as the XEdDSA signature scheme [30]. In the past few months, an alternative approach was proposed by Renes and Smith [32], who introduced a new signature scheme based on Curve25519. They named this scheme as the Quotient Digital Signature Algorithm (qDSA) because scalar point multiplications are performed on an algebraic variety generated by the quotient of an algebraic curve.

The most salient properties of qDSA are: first, it allows to use X25519's keys (without modification) for signing; and second, elliptic curve operations are performed using only the x-coordinate of points (provided by the use of Montgomery elliptic curves). On the opposite side, given a qDSA signature, it is easy to obtain a second signature that also passes the verification procedure. Although this fact does not represent an attack per se, it does open a breach to a misuse of the cryptographic scheme that could potentially become an effective attack [7,8]. Therefore, there is a need for methods that allows verifying qDSA's signatures unequivocally.

Contributions. In view of the current scenario, our main contribution focuses on the secure and efficient software implementation of qDSA. On the security side, we provide a verification method that validates (without ambiguity) the correct signature of a message, and we also analyze the overheads on space and time introduced by our approach. On the efficiency side, we show a technique that accelerates the key generation, signing, and verification procedures. This speedup was achieved as a consequence of employing precomputed look-up tables during the evaluation of the right-to-left Joye's algorithm [19], using a similar approach to the one introduced by Oliveira et al. [29]. Due to the novelty of qDSA, there is a need for an optimized implementation beyond the one developed by qDSA's authors [32]. For this reason, we focus on the development of a software library that supports both 32-bit ARM processors (Cortex M4, Cortex A7 and Cortex A15 micro-architectures) and 64–bit Intel processors (Haswell and Skylake micro-architectures). For all of these architectures, we use optimized prime field arithmetic and elliptic curve operations leading to an efficient and secure implementation of the qDSA signature scheme. The source code is available at: [http://github.com/armfazh/qdsa-space17].

Regarding the scalar point multiplication algorithm presented in [29], it requires the use of points that are in small subgroups of the elliptic curve, i.e. low-order points. An attacker can leverage the use of low-order points to weaken the security of a implementation; for example, by means of side-channel attacks [9], or by exploiting vulnerabilities on unsecure implementations, like the ones found in some cryptographic currencies [37]. For this reason and as a side result, we describe a technique that avoids low-order points during the calculation of scalar point multiplications.

The remainder of this document is divided as follows. In Sect. 2, we review the qDSA scheme and the parameters used in our implementation. In Sect. 3, we show how to accelerate the calculation of fixed-point multiplications. In Sect. 4, we present a new verification procedure. In Sect. 5, we report the results of the performance benchmark of our software library. Finally, in Sect. 6, we point out some concluding comments.

2   The Quotient Digital Signature Algorithm

The Quotient Digital Signature Algorithm (qDSA) is a Schnorr-like signature scheme [35] that operates over a Kummer variety $\mathcal{K}$. This variety comes from the quotient of an elliptic (or hyper-elliptic) curve E as $\mathcal{K} = E/\langle\pm1\rangle$, i.e. for the case of elliptic curves, the points $P, -P \in E$ are mapped to a single element in $E/\langle\pm1\rangle$. Although this mapping does not preserve the group structure of E, it is still possible to compute multiplications by integers. When qDSA is instantiated with elliptic curves the Kummer variety resultant is a one-dimensional projective space $\mathbb{P}^1(\mathbb{F}_p)$, also known as the x-line (see [6,32] for more details).

In this section, we revisit elliptic curve operations on Montgomery curves; then, we detail the qDSA signature scheme together with the instance generated from Curve25519's parameters.

2.1   Arithmetic of Montgomery Curves

Let $\mathbb{F}_p$ be a prime field, a Montgomery elliptic curve is defined over $\mathbb{F}_p$ as:

$$E_{A,B}/\mathbb{F}_p: \quad By^2 = x^3 + Ax^2 + x, \tag{1}$$

where $A, B \in \mathbb{F}_p$, $A^2 \neq 4$, and $B \neq 0$. The set of solutions of this equation forms a commutative group having as identity the element $\mathcal{O}$, which is known as the point at infinity. Hence, given two points P and Q, we can obtain a third point R such that $R = P + Q$. The inverse of a point $P = (x, y)$ is obtained as $-P = (x, -y)$. For these curves, the order of the group is always divisible by four [22]. Given an n-bit integer k and a point P, the scalar point multiplication is defined as $kP = \text{sgn}(k) \sum_{i=0}^{n-1} 2^i k_i P$, where k_i is the i-th bit of $|k|$.

For adding points, Montgomery found efficient formulas that operate over the x-coordinate of points [22]. In order to apply these operations the elliptic curve must be embedded on a projective space. Let $\mathbb{P}^2(\mathbb{F}_p)$ be a projective space of dimension two, then the projective representation of a point $P = (x_P, y_P)$ is $(\lambda X_P : \lambda Y_P : \lambda Z_P)$, such that $\lambda \neq 0$, $x_P = X_P/Z_P$, and $y_P = Y_P/Z_P$. Montgomery noted that, in the projective space, a point addition can be calculated using only the x-coordinate of the points. Therefore, the following function maps elliptic curve points to elements in the Kummer variety $E/\langle \pm 1 \rangle$ as follows:

$$
\begin{array}{ccc}
E & \to E/\langle \pm 1 \rangle \cong \mathbb{P}^1(\mathbb{F}_p) \\
(X_P : Y_P : Z_P) & \mapsto & (X_P : Z_P) \\
\mathcal{O} & \mapsto & (1 : 0)
\end{array}
\tag{2}
$$

Let $P = (X_P : Z_P)$ and $Q = (X_Q : Z_Q)$ be two points mapped into the Kummer variety. Montgomery devised a formula for computing differential additions (DADD); thus, given P, Q, and $R = P - Q$ (all in projective coordinates) the differential addition formula computes $P +_R Q = (X_{P+_R Q} : Z_{P+_R Q})$ as follows:

$$
\begin{aligned}
X_{P+_R Q} &= Z_R(X_P X_Q - Z_P Z_Q)^2, \\
Z_{P+_R Q} &= X_R(X_P Z_Q - Z_P X_Q)^2.
\end{aligned}
\tag{3}
$$

For the particular case when the points to be added are equal, we have a point doubling (DOUB) denoted as $2P = (X_{2P} : Z_{2P})$ and calculated as follows:

$$
\begin{aligned}
X_{2P} &= (X_P^2 - Z_P^2)^2, \\
Z_{2P} &= 4X_P Z_P(X_P^2 + AX_P Z_P + Z_P^2).
\end{aligned}
\tag{4}
$$

Based on (3) and (4), Montgomery also introduced an algorithm for computing scalar point multiplications. The well-known Montgomery ladder algorithm (Algorithm 1) computes the x-coordinate of kP, given the x-coordinate of P and an n-bit integer scalar k. The cost of Algorithm 1 is mainly determined by the number of operations performed in each iteration; hence, Montgomery ladder algorithm takes one doubling operation and one differential addition per bit of k.

Algorithm 1 uses an auxiliary function CSWAP(b, U, V), which interchanges the values of U and V whenever $b = 1$, otherwise points are not modified. Since this function could introduce a time variability in its execution, CSWAP must be securely implemented by adding countermeasures that prevent of, for example, timings attacks [4,20]. Consequently, we implemented CSWAP using

---

Algorithm 1. Montgomery Ladder Algorithm.

Input: $k \in \mathbb{Z}$ such that $k > 0$, and $P = (X_P : Z_P)$.
Output: $kP = (X_{kP} : Z_{kP})$.
1: Let $(k_{n-1} = 1, \ldots, k_0)_2$ be the binary representation of k.
2: Initialize $Q_0 \leftarrow 2P$, $Q_1 \leftarrow P$.
3: **for** $i \leftarrow n - 2$ **to** 0 **do**
4:    $(Q_0, Q_1) \leftarrow \text{CSWAP}(k_i \oplus k_{i+1}, Q_0, Q_1)$
5:    $(Q_0, Q_1) \leftarrow (\text{DOUB}(Q_0), \text{DADD}(Q_0, Q_1, P))$ $//Q_0 \leftarrow 2Q_0, Q_1 \leftarrow Q_0 +_P Q_1$
6: **end for**
7: $(Q_0, Q_1) \leftarrow \text{CSWAP}(k_0, Q_0, Q_1)$
8: **return** Q_0 $//$Return also Q_1 for y-coordinate recovery.

Boolean operations; thus, assuming U and V are n-bit strings CSWAP is computed as follows:

$$
\begin{aligned}
(U', V') &= \text{CSWAP}(b, U, V) \\
&= \big((\neg M \wedge U) \oplus (M \wedge V), (M \wedge U) \oplus (\neg M \wedge V)\big),
\end{aligned}
\tag{5}
$$

where M is an n-bit mask initialized to $(111\ldots1)_2$, i.e. n ones, if $b = 1$; otherwise $M = (000\ldots0)_2$, i.e. n zeros.

2.2   Instantiating qDSA with Montgomery Curves

Domain Parameters of qDSA. Given an integer number N, the size of public keys is fixed to N bits and the signature's size is $2N$ bits. The following set represents the domain parameters of the signature scheme:

$$
\mathcal{D} = \{N, p, E_{A,B}, \ell, G, H\},
\tag{6}
$$

where: p is a large prime number such that $N \approx \log_2(p)$, $E_{A,B}$ is a Montgomery elliptic curve defined over $\mathbb{F}_p$, this curve has a large prime subgroup of order ℓ, G is a point of order ℓ, and H is a hash function producing $2N$–bit digests.

A qDSA Instance. Due to the performance features offered by the elliptic curve named Curve25519 [1], it can also be used to produce an efficient instance of qDSA; thus, $\mathcal{D}$ is specified as:

- Since $p = 2^{255} - 19$, we have $N = 256$.
- The Curve25519 is defined over $\mathbb{F}_p$ as $E_{486662,1}$.
- This curve forms a group of order 8ℓ, where

$$
\ell = 2^{252} + 27742317777372353535851937790883648493
\tag{7}
$$

  is a prime number.
- A point $G = (x_G, y_G)$ of order ℓ is fixed as $x_G = 9$ and $y_G = \sqrt{39420360} \in \mathbb{F}_p$ such that y_G is odd.
- Regarding the cryptographic hash function, the authors of qDSA selected an extendable-output function belonging to the Secure Hash Algorithm v3 (SHA3) standard [26]; therefore, they selected H as the SHAKE128 function fixing its output size to 512 bits.

2.3   Digital Signature Operations

The qDSA scheme consists of three algorithms: key generation (Algorithm 2), signature generation (Algorithm 3), and signature verification (Algorithm 4). This latter procedure requires an auxiliary function (Algorithm 5) that it will be revised in Sect. 4.

Algorithm 2. Key generation.

Input: $\mathcal{D}$, the domain parameters.
Output: $(d_0, d_1) \in \{0,1\}^{2N}$ is a private key, and $x_Q \in \mathbb{F}_p$ is a public key.

1: $d \xleftarrow{\$} \{0,1\}^N$
2: $(h_{2N-1}, \ldots, h_0)_2 \leftarrow H(d)$
3: $d_0 \leftarrow (h_{2N-1}, \ldots, h_N)_2$
4: $d_1 \leftarrow (h_{N-1}, \ldots, h_0)_2$
5: $Q = (X_Q : Z_Q) \leftarrow d_0 G$ //Alg. 7.
6: $x_Q \leftarrow X_Q/Z_Q$
7: **return** (d_0, d_1) and x_Q

Algorithm 3. Signature generation.

Input: (d_0, d_1) and x_Q are the signer's keys; and $M \in \{0,1\}^*$ is a message.
Output: $(x_R \parallel s)$ is the signature of M, where $x_R \in \mathbb{F}_p$ and $s \in \{0,1\}^N$.

1: $r \leftarrow H(d_1 \parallel M) \bmod \ell$
2: $R = (X_R : Z_R) \leftarrow rG$ //Alg. 7.
3: $x_R \leftarrow X_R/Z_R$
4: $h \leftarrow H(x_R \parallel x_Q \parallel M)$
5: $s \leftarrow r - hd_0 \bmod \ell$
6: **return** $(x_R \parallel s)$

Algorithm 4. Signature verification.

Input: x_Q is the public key of the signer, $(x_R \parallel s)$ is a signature, and $M \in \{0,1\}^*$ is a message.
Output: True, if the signature is valid; otherwise, False.

1: $Q \leftarrow (x_Q : 1)$
2: $h \leftarrow H(x_R \parallel x_Q \parallel M) \bmod \ell$
3: $R_0 \leftarrow sG$ //Alg. 7.
4: $R_1 \leftarrow hQ$ //Alg. 1.
5: **return** Check(x_R, R_0, R_1) //Alg. 5.

Algorithm 5. Check $x_R \in \{x(P \pm Q)\}$.

Input: $x_R \in \mathbb{F}_p$, and (P, Q) are elliptic curve points in projective coordinates.
Output: True, if $x_R \in \{x(P \pm Q)\}$; otherwise, False.

1: Let $f(x) \leftarrow f_2 x^2 + f_1 x + f_0$ such that f_i are defined as in Equation (10).
2: **if** $f(x_R) = 0$ **then**
3:      **return** True
4: **else**
5:      **return** False
6: **end if**

By analyzing the elliptic curve operations required by qDSA, it was noted that the running time is dominated by the computation of scalar point multiplications. Consequently, we focused on the acceleration of this operation. Notice that a multiple of the base point G is calculated in each qDSA operation. Since G is fixed for the entire scheme, then we can precompute a table that stores some multiples of G. Hence, a scalar multiplication algorithm can be modified to look up in the table and to retrieve multiples of G for calculating kG; this scenario is commonly known as a fixed-point multiplication, and it will be addressed in the next section.

3   Accelerating Fixed-Point Multiplications

In the open literature, there exist specialized algorithms that accelerate the calculation of fixed-point multiplications. In the general setting, the most used algorithm is the Comb technique [21], which arranges the bits of k in a matrix form, then the point multiplication algorithm interprets bit-columns as indexes to look up in the precomputed table. Several fixed-point multiplication algorithms were derived from the Comb technique, for example [10, 11, 14, 15], among others.

Comb-based algorithms have in common that indexes are directly derived from the bits of the scalar. This implies that when the scalar is secret, every access to the look-up table must be protected; otherwise, an attacker could extract some bits of the scalar by correlating variations in the latency of access to the cache memory. This kind of attack is known as a cache attack [40], which in practice have been a successful method for recovering secret keys from insecure implementations of tabled-based algorithms.

A common countermeasure to protect look-up table queries consists on using a uniform accessing pattern. Hence, in spite of it occurs variations on the latency of cache memory accessing, the attacker will not be able to determine from which part of the table the requested entry was retrieved. However, in some cases the cost of adding countermeasures impacts negatively on the performance of point multiplication. A desirable solution for this scenario would be an algorithm that uses non-secret indexes for accessing to the look-up table. In the following section, we will show an algorithm that satisfies these conditions.

3.1 A Fixed-Point Multiplication Algorithm with Non-secret Indexes

In 2007, Joye presented right-to-left algorithms to compute scalar point multiplications [19]. As their name suggests, these algorithms scan the bits of the scalar from the least- to the most-significant bit, unlike conventional methods such as the double-and-add algorithm or the Montgomery ladder algorithm. Moreover, Joye's algorithm uses a regular execution pattern of elliptic curve operations and without using dummy operations, these features aid on the prevention of timings attacks [20] and fault-based attacks [3, 42]. Joye's algorithm has been applied on the implementation of both Weierstrass curves [13] and Koblitz binary curves [28, 38].

More recently, Oliveira et al. [29] adapted the right-to-left Joye's algorithm to use precomputed look-up tables with the purpose of accelerating fixed-point multiplications (see Algorithm 6). The central operation of Algorithm 6 is to add some precomputed multiples of G in two accumulators, namely Q_0 and Q_1. The bits of the scalar k determine which accumulator must be updated in such a way that, at the i-th iteration, Algorithm 6 accumulates the point $2^i G$ into Q_0 using a differential addition (with Q_1 as the difference) whenever $k_i \oplus k_{i-1} = 0$; otherwise, it accumulates $2^i G$ into Q_1 also using a differential addition (but this time with Q_0 as the difference). Observe that Algorithm 6 is composed of evaluations of differential additions, since no point doublings are required at all. Notice that in either case, one operand of the differential addition is known in advance. Hence, assuming Q is the known point, the differential addition can be calculated saving one multiplication (as it was proposed in [29]). Let $R = P - Q$

Algorithm 6. Right-to-left fixed-point multiplication algorithm (cf. [29]).

Input: (k, G, S), where $k \in \mathbb{Z}_\ell$ and $k \neq 0$; G is a point of order ℓ; and S is a point of order 4 such that $S \notin \langle G \rangle$.
Precomputation: A look-up table storing $(\mu_0, \ldots, \mu_{n-1})$ as defined in Eq. (9).
Output: $8kG = (X_{8kG} : Z_{8kG})$.

1: Let $(k_{n-1}, \ldots, k_0)_2$ be the n-bit binary repr. of k such that $n = \lfloor \log_2(\ell) \rfloor + 1$.
2: Initialize $Q_0 \leftarrow S$, $Q_1 \leftarrow G - S$, and define $k_{-1} = 0$.
3: **for** $i \leftarrow 0$ **to** $n - 1$ **do**
4:     $(Q_0, Q_1) \leftarrow \mathrm{CSWAP}(k_i \oplus k_{i-1}, Q_0, Q_1)$
5:     $Q_0 \leftarrow \mathrm{DADD}^*(\mu_i, Q_0, Q_1)$ $// Q_0 \leftarrow Q_0 +_{Q_1} 2^i G$
6: **end for**
7: $Q_1 \leftarrow \mathrm{DOUB}(Q_1)$
8: $Q_1 \leftarrow \mathrm{DOUB}(Q_1)$
9: $Q_1 \leftarrow \mathrm{DOUB}(Q_1)$
10: **return** Q_1

---

and $\mu = (x_Q + 1)(x_Q - 1)^{-1} \in \mathbb{F}_p$; then, we denote with DADD^* the following formula:

$$X_{P+_R Q} = Z_R \left[(X_P + Z_P) + \mu (X_P - Z_P) \right]^2,$$
$$Z_{P+_R Q} = X_R \left[(X_P + Z_P) - \mu (X_P - Z_P) \right]^2. \tag{8}$$

To compute scalar point multiplications Algorithm 6 requires a precomputed table storing one entry per bit of the scalar. Let $n = \lfloor \log_2(\ell) \rfloor + 1$, then the look-up table will store the values $(\mu_0, \ldots, \mu_{n-1})$, where μ_i is defined as:

$$\mu_i = (x_i + 1)(x_i - 1)^{-1} \in \mathbb{F}_p, \text{ such that } (x_i, y_i) = 2^i G. \tag{9}$$

Remark 3.1. To retrieve a point from the look-up table, the index used is actually a counting variable, and most importantly, this index is not derived from the secret scalar. Thus, a query is performed by directly choosing the correspondent value from the table. This enables a faster execution in contrast to Comb-based methods which require a secure (and sometimes costly) look-up table accessing.

By using Oliveira et al.'s algorithm, we expect an increase on the performance of fixed-point multiplications. Note that in each iteration, only one differential addition is processed in contrast with the (left-to-right) Montgomery ladder and the right-to-left Joye's algorithm, which require an extra point doubling per iteration. Before applying Oliveira et al.'s algorithm in the calculation of fixed-point multiplications, in the following section, we will introduce a set of modifications to avoid the use of low-order points.

3.2 Circumventing the Use of Low-Order Points

Attention is required during the initialization of the accumulators Q_0 and Q_1 in Algorithm 6, since the formula for differential point addition is not complete. This means that for adding $P +_R Q$ such that $R = P - Q$, the differential addition formula fails whenever $R \in \{ \mathcal{O}, (0,0) \}$.

We recall that the goal of Algorithm 6 in Oliveira et al.'s work [29] is to calculate the point $8kG$ required by the Diffie-Hellman X25519 function. For this reason, Algorithm 6 initializes accumulators with $Q_0 \leftarrow S$ and $Q_1 \leftarrow G - S$ such that $S \notin \langle G \rangle$. For the case of Curve25519, S was chosen as a point of order four (i.e. $4S = \mathcal{O}$). Thus, Algorithm 6 will compute $S + kG$, and after applying three consecutive point doublings, the point S will vanish resulting in $8kG$. Although this procedure is correct, some vulnerabilities could appear due to a misuse of low-order points [9,37]. Therefore, it is imperative to protect the implementation against this potential threat.

To avoid the use of low-order points, we show a technique that accomplishes this requirement. Our technique relies on the observation that if the order of G is odd, like in the case of Curve25519; then, the point S is not required any more. Notice that replacing S by $\mathcal{O}$ in Algorithm 6 causes a failure when the least-significant bit of k is zero; nonetheless, it always computes the correct point multiplication whenever k is odd. This observation indicates that Algorithm 6 with $S = \mathcal{O}$ computes scalar point multiplications only for odd scalars. Therefore, we introduce a modification in Algorithm 6 that supports even and odd scalars, and avoids using low-order points.

Let ℓ be the order of G. The key observation is that if ℓ is odd, then the parity of an element in $\{1, \ldots, \ell - 1\}$ determines a bijection between the disjoint sets of even and odd elements.

Proposition 3.1. *Let ℓ be an odd number. For any value a such that $0 < a < \ell$ define $b = \ell - a$; we have that if a is even, then b is odd.*

Proof. First, note that b is bounded as $0 < b < \ell$. Since $a < \ell$, then $b = \ell - a > 0$. Suppose $b \geq \ell$, then by the definition of b we have that $\ell - a \geq \ell$, i.e. $a \leq 0$, which is a contradiction, since $a > 0$; thus, $0 < b < \ell$. Now, since ℓ is odd and a is even, then there exist some $i, j \in \mathbb{Z}$ such that $b = \ell - a = 2i + 1 - 2j = 2(i - j) + 1$; showing that b is odd. $\qquad \square$

Using this proposition, we can calculate kG as $k'G$, for $k' = \ell - k$, whenever the scalar k is even. Note that if this operation was computed using points in the affine space, then the point $k'G$ must be inverted to obtain kG. Fortunately, this is not required since we are operating with elements in the Kummer variety, which maps kG and $k'G$ to the same element in $E/\langle \pm 1 \rangle$. All of these observations led to Algorithm 7, which supports both even and odd scalars, and does not require low-order points in the computation of the fixed-point multiplication.

Among the changes made, Algorithm 7 starts by computing $r = \ell - k$ and then selects the scalar between r and k. This selection could introduce a time variability in its execution, and consequently, it must be processed using a regular execution pattern. This task can be achieved using the CSWAP function as shown in line 2 of Algorithm 7. Thus after computing a conditional swapping, r will be odd allowing to start the main-loop from the second iteration.

Finally, we apply Algorithm 7 to compute multiples of G during the qDSA signature scheme. Since the fixed-point multiplication appears in all operations of the qDSA scheme, we improve the running time of the entire scheme. Section 5 reveals the impact on performance obtained by our software implementation.

Algorithm 7. Our proposed right-to-left fixed-point multiplication algorithm without using low-order points.

Input: (k, G), where $k \in \mathbb{Z}_\ell$ and $k \neq 0$; and G is a point of odd-order ℓ.
Precomputation: A look-up table storing $(\mu_0, \ldots, \mu_{n-1})$ as defined in Eq. (9).
Output: $kG = (X_{kG} : Z_{kG})$.

1: $r \leftarrow \ell - k$
2: $(k, r) \leftarrow \text{CSWAP}(k_0, k, r)$
3: Let $(r_{n-1}, \ldots, r_0 = 1)_2$ be the n-bit binary repr. of r such that $n = \lfloor \log_2(\ell) \rfloor + 1$.
4: Initialize $Q_0 \leftarrow G$, $Q_1 \leftarrow G$.
5: **for** $i \leftarrow 1$ **to** $n - 1$ **do**
6: $\quad (Q_0, Q_1) \leftarrow \text{CSWAP}(r_i \oplus r_{i-1}, Q_0, Q_1)$
7: $\quad Q_0 \leftarrow \text{DADD}^*(\mu_i, Q_0, Q_1)$ $\qquad\qquad$ //$Q_0 \leftarrow Q_0 +_{Q_1} 2^i G$
8: **end for**
9: $(Q_0, Q_1) \leftarrow \text{CSWAP}(r_{n-1}, Q_0, Q_1)$
10: **return** Q_1 $\qquad\qquad$ //Return also Q_0 for y-coordinate recovery.

4   A New qDSA Signature Verification Method

Given an alleged signature $(x_R \parallel s)$ of a message M, the qDSA signature verification procedure must determine whether x_R is the x-coordinate of $R_0 + R_1$, where $R_0 = sG$ and $R_1 = hQ$ for h defined as in Algorithm 4. For that purpose, the authors of qDSA provided Algorithm 5, which checks a weaker relation. Such a method accepts the signature whenever $f(x_R) = 0$, where f is the quadratic polynomial $f(x) = f_2 x^2 + f_1 x + f_0$, such that:

$$
\begin{aligned}
f_2 &= (x_{R_0} - x_{R_1})^2, \\
f_1 &= -2(x_{R_0} x_{R_1} + 1)(x_{R_0} + x_{R_1}) - 4A\, x_{R_0}\, x_{R_1}, \\
f_0 &= (x_{R_0} x_{R_1} - 1)^2.
\end{aligned}
\tag{10}
$$

This method works since one of the roots of f is x_R, however one disadvantage of this approach is that there is another value x' that also passes the verification procedure. Specifically, x' is the other root of f and corresponds to the x-coordinate of $R_0 - R_1$. Therefore, M has another valid signature $(x' \parallel s)$.

Although a low adversarial advantage can be exploited from this relaxed verification method, it has a high risk to introduce a misuse of the cryptographic scheme, such as the ones reported in [7,8,16]. To avoid potential issues in future implementations, we looked for an efficient method that verifies qDSA signature of a message unequivocally.

4.1   Unequivocal Techniques for Signature Verification

Let x_S and x_D be the x-coordinate of $R_0 + R_1$ and $R_0 - R_1$, respectively. Given an alleged signature $(x_R \parallel s)$, we look for a relation that allows us to determine whether $x_R = x_S$ from the coordinates of R_0 and R_1, instead of verifying whether $x_R \in \{x_S, x_D\}$ as Algorithm 5 does. Thus, inspired by Montgomery's insights [22], we derive the following equivalences:

$$x_S + x_D = \beta/\alpha, \tag{11}$$

$$x_S \times x_D = \gamma/\alpha, \tag{12}$$

$$x_S - x_D = \delta/\alpha, \tag{13}$$

such that α, β, γ and δ are defined as follows[1]:

$$
\begin{aligned}
\alpha &= (x_{R_0} - x_{R_1})^2, \\
\beta &= 2(x_{R_0} x_{R_1} + 1)(x_{R_0} + x_{R_1}) + 4A x_{R_0} x_{R_1}, \\
\gamma &= (x_{R_0} x_{R_1} - 1)^2, \\
\delta &= -4B y_{R_0} y_{R_1}.
\end{aligned}
\tag{14}
$$

The coefficients of f can be derived by solving Eq. (11) for x_D, and plugging in this into Eq. (12), what results in a second-degree polynomial function of x_S. Thus, f can also be written as $f(x) = \alpha x^2 - \beta x + \gamma$. We note that solving Eq. (11) for x_S and substituting this into Eq. (12) yields into a second-degree polynomial function of x_D that has the same coefficients as f. This means that both x_S and x_D are the roots of f. Therefore, f does not help to distinguish between x_S and x_D.

Our key idea is to obtain a (linear) polynomial that has a zero in x_S. For that end, we start by solving Eq. (13) for x_S and substituting this into Eq. (12); thus we obtain $g_0(x) = \alpha x^2 - \delta x - \gamma$. Analogously, we apply the same procedure, but this time solving for x_D, and we obtain $g_1(x) = \alpha x^2 + \delta x - \gamma$. So far, we have that $g_0 \neq g_1$, which means that by using g_0, we are now able to distinguish between x_S and x_D, since $g_0(x_S) = 0$ and $g_0(x_D) \neq 0$. However, g_0 has zeros in x_S and in $-x_D$. Now, using $f(x) = (x - x_S)(x - x_D)$ and $g_0(x) = (x - x_S)(x + x_D)$, we show how to unequivocally identify x_S. Note that $f(x_S) = 0$ and $g_0(x_S) = 0$; therefore, we define:

$$
\begin{aligned}
h_0(x) &= (f + g_0)/x = 2\alpha x - \delta - \beta, \text{ and} \\
h_1(x) &= f - g_0 = (\delta - \beta)x + 2\gamma,
\end{aligned}
\tag{15}
$$

such that x_S is a zero of both h_0 and h_1. Listing 4.1 shows a SageMath [31] computer script that validates the formulas used in this section. In summary, either h_0 or h_1 aids to determine the validity of an alleged signature.

Our signature verification method proceeds as follows: given $(x_R \parallel s)$, it calculates α, β, and δ from the coordinates of R_0 and R_1; then, it declares a signature as valid if $h_0(x_R) = 0$ (alternatively, it calculates γ instead of α and accepts the signature if $h_1(x_R) = 0$). We have shown two relations that allow to   ·
verify a signature unequivocally.

4.2   Trade-Off Analysis of Our Signature Verification Method

In contrast to the original signature procedure, our method requires calculating the δ term, which implies the knowledge of the y-coordinate of both $R_0 = sG$ and $R_1 = hQ$.

---

[1] To avoid inversions, these terms can also be calculated using projective coordinates.

```
1   QQ = Rationals()
2   R.<x1,y1,x2,y2,A,B> = PolynomialRing(QQ,6,"x1,y1,x2,y2,A,B")
3   I = R.ideal([
4       B*y1**2-x1**3-A*x1**2-x1,
5       B*y2**2-x2**3-A*x2**2-x2 ])
6   FQuo = Frac(R.quotient(I))
7   evaluate = lambda F,X: FQuo(F.subs(x=X).rational_simplify())
8
9   def addMontgomery(X1,Y1,X2,Y2):
10      global A, B
11      Xs = B*((Y1-Y2)/(X1-X2))**2-A-X1-X2
12      Ys = (2*X1+X2+A)*(Y2-Y1)/(X2-X1)-B*(Y2-Y1)**3/(X2-X1)**3-Y1
13      return Xs,Ys
14
15  xs,ys = addMontgomery(x1,y1,x2,y2)
16  xd,yd = addMontgomery(x1,y1,x2,-y2)
17
18  alpha   =  (x1-x2)**2
19  betta   =  2*(x1*x2+1)*(x1+x2)+4*A*x1*x2
20  gamma   =  (x1*x2-1)**2
21  delta   =  -4*B*y1*y2
22
23  relAdd = FQuo(xs+xd)
24  relPro = FQuo(xs*xd)
25  relDif = FQuo(xs-xd)
26  # Verifying Relations
27  assert( relAdd == betta/alpha )
28  assert( relPro == gamma/alpha )
29  assert( relDif == delta/alpha )
30  # Renes&Smith's f polynomial and testing its zeros
31  f = alpha*x**2-betta*x+gamma
32  assert( evaluate(f,xs) == evaluate(f,xd) == 0 )
33  # Defining g0 and g1 and testing their zeros
34  g0 = alpha*x**2-delta*x-gamma
35  g1 = alpha*x**2+delta*x-gamma
36  assert( evaluate(g0, xs) == evaluate(g0,-xd) == 0 )
37  assert( evaluate(g1,-xs) == evaluate(g1, xd) == 0 )
38  # Defining h0 and h1 and testing their zeros
39  h0 = 2*alpha*x-delta-betta
40  h1 = (delta-betta)*x+2*gamma
41  assert( evaluate(h0,xs) == evaluate(h1,xs) == 0 )
```

Listing 4.1: SageMath script for the validation of formulas in $\mathbb{Q}$.

One can use the Okeya-Sakurai's [27] method for recovering the y-coordinate of $R_0 = sG$ and $R_1 = hQ$. This technique requires some auxiliary points, namely $R_2 = (s+1)G$ and $R_3 = (h+1)Q$, which are also computed by the Montgomery ladder algorithm (Algorithm 1). Thus, following Theorem 2 of [27], we have:

$$y_{R_0} = [(x_{R_0}x_G + 1)(x_{R_0} + x_G + 2A) - 2A - (x_{R_0} - x_G)^2 x_{R_2}](2By_G)^{-1},$$
$$y_{R_1} = [(x_{R_1}x_Q + 1)(x_{R_1} + x_Q + 2A) - 2A - (x_{R_1} - x_G)^2 x_{R_3}](2By_Q)^{-1}; \quad (16)$$

then, δ can be written as $\delta = -4By_{R_0}y_{R_1} = (By_Gy_Q)^{-1}T$, where T is:

$$T = - \left[(x_{R_0}x_G + 1)(x_{R_0} + x_G + 2A) - 2A - (x_{R_0} - x_G)^2 x_{R_2}\right]$$
$$\times \left[(x_{R_1}x_Q + 1)(x_{R_1} + x_Q + 2A) - 2A - (x_{R_1} - x_G)^2 x_{R_3}\right]. \quad (17)$$

Algorithm 8. Unequivocally qDSA Verification Procedure.

Input: $(x_R \parallel s)$ is a signature, $M \in \{0,1\}^*$ is a message, and $(x_Q \parallel y_{Q(0)})$ is the public key of the signer.
Constants: (x_G, y_G) are the affine coordinates of the generator $G \in E_{A,B}$.
Output: True, if the signature is valid; otherwise, False.
1: $h \leftarrow H(x_R \parallel x_Q \parallel M) \mod \ell$
2: $Q \leftarrow (x_Q : 1)$, $R_0 \leftarrow sG$, $R_1 \leftarrow hQ$
3: $\{y', y''\} \leftarrow \pm\sqrt{B^{-1}(x_Q^3 + Ax_Q^2 + x_Q)} \in \mathbb{F}_p$.
4: Set $y_Q \leftarrow y'$, if $y' \equiv y_{Q(0)} \mod 2$; otherwise, $y_Q \leftarrow y''$.
5: Calculate α, β, and δ as in Eq. (14).
6: **if** $h_0(x_R) = 0$ **then** $//h_0$ as defined in Eq. (15).
7:     **return** True
8: **else**
9:     **return** False
10: **end if**

The most important thing to be noticed here is that $y_G y_Q$ must be known by the verifier. There are several alternatives to obtain such value:

– The simplest one is to append $y_G y_Q$ (or $(By_G y_Q)^{-1}$) to the public key; hence the calculation of δ is straightforward, however the public-key's size doubles.
– Alternatively, the public key could contain an extra bit $y_{Q(0)}$, which is the least-significant bit of y_Q; thus, the verification procedure calculates $\{y', y''\} = \pm\sqrt{B^{-1}(x_Q^3 + Ax_Q^2 + x_Q)}$; then, if $y' \equiv y_{Q(0)} \mod 2$, it sets $y_Q \leftarrow y'$; otherwise it assigns $y_Q \leftarrow y''$. After that, it calculates $y_G y_Q$. Note that y_G must be also known, fortunately, this is a fixed parameter of the scheme. This method has the advantage that the public key size is not increased significantly; for example using Curve25519, $(x_Q \parallel y_{Q(0)})$ fits in 256 bits. However, the cost of verification increases by computing one square-root and a few multiplications. This approach is summarized in Algorithm 8.

We want to remark that for verifying a qDSA signature unambiguously, it is mandatory that the verification method knows the y-coordinate of G (which is a fixed parameter) and the y-coordinate of Q as inputs.

5   Performance Results and Comparisons

We focused on the development a software library that supports the 32-bit ARM architecture, which is designed for embedded devices, and the 64-bit Intel architecture, which is wide-spread distributed from commodity computers to high-end servers. For measuring execution times, we use the clock cycle counter available in each architecture. Besides that on Intel processors, the advanced hardware technologies Intel Turbo Boost, Intel Speed Step, and Intel Hyper-Threading were disabled to obtain stable and reproducible measurements.

5.1 Performance of Prime Field Arithmetic

For the arithmetic operations over $\mathbb{F}_{2^{255}-19}$, we use an optimized library for Cortex M4 ARM-based processors taken from [12]; and for the 64-bit Intel processors, we use the optimized library available in [29]. In Table 1, we summarize the clock cycle measurements of the arithmetic operations.

Table 1. Latency (in clock cycles) of the arithmetic operations on $\mathbb{F}_{2^{255}-19}$. The last columns list the ratio of the latency between square and multiplication, and the ratio between inversion and multiplication.

Architecture	Micro-architecture	Processor model	Arithmetic operations					Ratios	
			Add	Mul	Sqr	Inv	Sqrt	S/M	I/M
32-bit	Cortex M4	Teensy 3.2	85	278	250	66,637	132,416	0.90	239.7
	Cortex A7	Odroid XU4	49	290	233	63,095	132,785	0.80	217.6
	Cortex A15	Odroid XU4	36	225	139	41,978	97,242	0.62	186.6
64-bit	Intel Haswell	Core i7-4770	8	64	48	14,925	29,344	0.75	233.2
	Intel Skylake	Core i7-6700K	6	48	39	11,090	22,598	0.81	231.0

The 32–bit implementation of the integer multiplier uses the full consecutive operand caching technique [36], which in turn utilizes multiply-and-accumulate instructions (`UMLAL/UMAAL` instructions). The scheduling of these instructions was ordered in such a way that reduces the presence of carry values during the evaluation of the product. The 64–bit implementation of the integer multiplier followed the operand scanning technique, which is highly compatible with the `MULX` instruction. For Skylake, the latency of the multiplier was improved even more, by using the newest integer addition instructions (`ADCX/ADOX` instructions).

5.2 Performance of Our Optimized Implementation of qDSA

First of all, we want to highlight the acceleration introduced by the right-to-left fixed-point multiplication algorithm presented in Sect. 3. To that end, we measured the percentage of improvement introduced by Algorithm 7 in the execution time of the qDSA operations. Table 2 shows the timings obtained on a Cortex M4 and on an Intel Haswell processor.

As it can be noted, the timings for computing qDSA operations were significantly reduced; the impact was more evident on the key generation and the signing procedures achieving, respectively, a 35–40% and 30–34% reduction in the execution time. Likewise the verification procedure was accelerated by 19%.

Regarding memory footprint, the last row of Table 2 shows the overhead introduced by integrating the use of precomputation. The code's size (including the 8 KB table stored in ROM) of our implementation was increased by around 36% and 44% on the 64-bit and 32-bit platforms, respectively. We recall

Table 2. Performance comparison of the qDSA operations by replacing the Montgomery ladder algorithm (Algorithm 1) by the right-to-left fixed-point multiplication algorithm (Algorithm 7). For each processor, the third column shows the percentage of improvement achieved. Entries represent 10^3 clock cycles, except the last row.

Processor	ARM Cortex M4			Intel Haswell		
Scalar point mult.	Algorithm 1	Algorithm 7	Savings	Algorithm 1	Algorithm 7	Savings
Key generation	927.9	604.9	34.8%	171.5	103.8	39.5%
Signing	1,059.1	736.2	30.5%	197.3	130.1	34.1%
Verification	1,746.2	1,422.8	18.5%	347.3	279.5	19.5%
Code size (bytes)	20,898	30,058	−43.8%	30,037	41,000	−36.4%

Table 3. Summary of the performance rendered by our optimized implementation. Table entries show the latency, reported in 10^3 clock cycles, of each qDSA operation.

qDSA operation	ARM (32-bit)			Intel (64-bit)	
	Cortex M4	Cortex A7	Cortex A15	Haswell	Skylake
Key generation	604.9	538.8	366.5	103.8	86.8
Signing	736.2	652.1	422.7	130.1	114.6
Verification (Algorithm 4)	1,422.8	1,271.7	870.6	279.5	231.1
Verification (Algorithm 8)	1,555.2	1,404.4	967.8	309.6	253.5

that computations aided by precomputation always incur on trade-offs between space and time; hence, the best approach will depend on several engineering aspects.

The inclusion of the optimized prime field arithmetic in conjunction with the use of the fixed-point multiplication algorithm reduced considerably the execution time in comparison to the original implementation given by qDSA's authors [32]. In Table 3, we summarize the timings of our qDSA implementation measured in several ARM and Intel platforms.

Table 3 also shows the latency of the proposed verification method (Algorithm 8) described in Sect. 4. Recall that our method must calculate one square-root and a few multiplications to recover the y-coordinate of the public key. The use of our method has an overhead increment from 8% to 10% in the execution time. This timing penalty is compensated by the security benefits that our verification method provides, besides it prevents some issues that could appear in future applications of qDSA.

In Table 4, we show a performance comparison of qDSA with other digital signature algorithms. As can be seen, the qDSA's signing procedure has a better performance than RSA and DSA signature schemes. In addition, qDSA generates signatures as fast as ECDSA does; however, the qDSA's verification procedure is faster than ECDSA's verification. This positions qDSA as a more efficient alternative for deploying digital signatures in contrast with standardized signature algorithms.

Table 4. Performance comparison of qDSA and other digital signature schemes.

Signature scheme	Instance	32-bit ARM Cortex A7		64-bit Intel Haswell	
		Sign/sec	Verify/sec	Sign/sec	Verify/sec
RSA[a]	2048	41.3	1,596.9	1,618	36,576
DSA[a]	2048	146.3	137.9	2,071	1,883
ECDSA[a]	P-256	940.5	250.7	25,344	10,198
EdDSA	Ed25519	3,414.6[b]	1,840.9[b]	48,701[c]	17,167[c]
qDSA[d]	Curve25519	2,148.0	1,001.6	25,109	12,109

[a]Timings taken using OpenSSL library (v.1.0.2) [39].
[b]Moon's implementation [23] using the prime field arithmetic from [12].
[c]Moon's implementation [23] compiled for 64-bit architectures.
[d]This work.

From the comparison table, one can observe that, in both architectures, the calculation of Ed25519 signatures is approximately twice as fast as the calculation of qDSA signatures. One of the reasons for this performance gap relies on the properties of the elliptic curve model used by each scheme, which imposes certain limitations on the point multiplication algorithms.

On Edwards curves, the point addition formula is complete and unified. This allows to associate point additions in many different ways, like in the Comb-based algorithms; and because of that, the fixed-point multiplication algorithms for Edwards curves have more degrees of freedom on their construction. For example, it allows the use of larger look-up tables; this property has been reflected in state-of-the-art implementations of Ed25519; for instance, Moon's [23] implementation uses a look-up table of 24 KB, whereas Chou's [5] implementation increased look-up table's size to 30 KB for further speed up.

On the other hand, the point addition formula for Montgomery curves is not complete, meanwhile the differential point addition depends on the coordinates of an auxiliary third point. These facts restrict point multiplication algorithms to be, in fact, addition-chain evaluations; for example, the Montgomery ladder algorithm (Algorithm 1) or the right-to-left Joye's algorithm [19]. With the introduction of precomputation in the right-to-left method, the look-up table size depends now on the size of ℓ (the order of the main elliptic curve subgroup), since the look-up table stores the sequence $(\mu_0, \ldots, \mu_{n-1})$ where $n = \lfloor \log_2(\ell) \rfloor + 1$. Thus, for the case of Curve25519, the look-up table used in our implementation is not larger than 8 KB, which is a third of the table size used in Ed25519's implementations.

Alternatively, qDSA can be also implemented using Edwards curves (through a birational equivalence with Montgomery curves [6]) for obtaining a performance closer to the Ed25519's one; however, note that our implementation uses a smaller look-up table, which is a relevant factor that must be noticed when targeting memory-constrained architectures. We left the Edwards approach as a future work.

6   Closing Remarks

The novel Quotient Digital Signature Algorithm was designed with the aim to provide key compatibility with Diffie-Hellman functions based in Montgomery curves. These curves are also employed for performing the signature operations of qDSA; hence, the implementation of qDSA benefits from reusing the prime field and the elliptic curve arithmetic that support the Diffie-Hellman protocol.

Like other elliptic curve based schemes, the performance-critical operation of qDSA is the calculation of scalar point multiplications. To attend to this issue, we revisited the fixed-point multiplication proposed by Oliveira et al. [29]. One advantage of this algorithm is the use of precomputed tables, which reduces the execution time of point multiplications. However, this algorithm operates with low-order points during its computation, and it must be recalled that an improper utilization of these points could open a breach to vulnerabilities.

For that reason and with the aim to provide not only an efficient but also a secure implementation, we showed modifications on Oliveira et al.'s algorithm that circumvent the use of low-order points. We noticed that whenever k is odd, the x-coordinate of kP can be calculated without requiring low-order points; and in the case k is even, the x-coordinate of $-kP$ is calculated instead. In both cases, the x-coordinate resultant will be the same, since in the Kummer variety, scalar multiplication is performed regardless the scalar's sign. Our observations led to Algorithm 7 which computes fixed-point multiplications on Montgomery curves faster and does not require low-order points.

Additionally, we derived a new method to verify qDSA signatures unequivocally. Our method was inspired by Montgomery's work and revealed than the public key must contain not only the x-coordinate of Q, but also its y-coordinate; with this information the verifier will be able to validate signatures unequivocally. This requirement introduces a trade-off between time and space. On the one hand, if the public key contain both coordinates, then the verification procedure will remain as efficient as the original method; however, the public key's size is increased to double. On the other hand, in order to avoid increasing the size of keys, the y-coordinate can be encoded into a bit value; nonetheless, the execution time of the verification procedure increases by 8–10% with respect to the original method. We remark that opting by the either alternative enables the unequivocally verification of qDSA signatures, which further prevents against potential vulnerabilities and the misuse of the original method.

According to the timings obtained in the performance benchmark, it can be concluded that, for the evaluated platforms, qDSA can be considered as competitive alternative for deploying digital signatures.

Acknowledgments. The authors want to thank the anonymous reviewers of SPACE 2017 conference for the comments given to this research project.

References

1. Bernstein, D.J.: Curve25519: new Diffie-Hellman speed records. In: Yung, M., Dodis, Y., Kiayias, A., Malkin, T. (eds.) PKC 2006. LNCS, vol. 3958, pp. 207–228. Springer, Heidelberg (2006). https://doi.org/10.1007/11745853_14
2. Bernstein, D.J., Duif, N., Lange, T., Schwabe, P., Yang, B.Y.: High-speed high-security signatures. J. Cryptogr. Eng. **2**(2), 77–89 (2012). https://doi.org/10.1007/s13389-012-0027-1
3. Biehl, I., Meyer, B., Müller, V.: Differential fault attacks on elliptic curve cryptosystems. In: Bellare, M. (ed.) CRYPTO 2000. LNCS, vol. 1880, pp. 131–146. Springer, Heidelberg (2000). https://doi.org/10.1007/3-540-44598-6_8
4. Brumley, D., Boneh, D.: Remote timing attacks are practical. In: Proceedings of the 12th Conference on USENIX Security Symposium, USENIX Association, pp. 1–13, August 2003. https://www.usenix.org/conference/12th-usenix-security-symposium/remote-timing-attacks-are-practical
5. Chou, T.: Sandy2x: new curve25519 speed records. In: Dunkelman, O., Keliher, L. (eds.) SAC 2015. LNCS, vol. 9566, pp. 145–160. Springer, Cham (2016). https://doi.org/10.1007/978-3-319-31301-6_8
6. Costello, C., Smith, B.: Montgomery curves and their arithmetic. J. Cryptogr. Eng. (Special Issue on Montgomery Arithmetic) 1–14 (2017). http://dx.doi.org/10.1007/s13389-017-0157-6
7. Egele, M., Brumley, D., Fratantonio, Y., Kruegel, C.: An empirical study of cryptographic misuse in Android applications. In: Proceedings of the 2013 ACM SIGSAC Conference on Computer and Communications Security, CCS 2013, pp. 73–84. ACM, New York (2013). http://doi.acm.org/10.1145/2508859.2516693
8. Fahl, S., Harbach, M., Muders, T., Baumgärtner, L., Freisleben, B., Smith, M.: Why Eve and Mallory love Android: an analysis of Android SSL (in)security. In: Proceedings of the 2012 ACM Conference on Computer and Communications Security, CCS 2012, pp. 50–61. ACM, New York (2012). http://doi.acm.org/10.1145/2382196.2382205
9. Fan, J., Gierlichs, B., Vercauteren, F.: To infinity and beyond: combined attack on ECC using points of low order. In: Preneel, B., Takagi, T. (eds.) CHES 2011. LNCS, vol. 6917, pp. 143–159. Springer, Heidelberg (2011). https://doi.org/10.1007/978-3-642-23951-9_10
10. Faz-Hernández, A., Longa, P., Sánchez, A.H.: Efficient and secure algorithms for GLV-based scalar multiplication and their implementation on GLV-GLS curves (extended version). J. Cryptogr. Eng. **5**(1), 31–52 (2015). https://doi.org/10.1007/s13389-014-0085-7
11. Feng, M., Zhu, B.B., Zhao, C., Li, S.: Signed MSB-set comb method for elliptic curve point multiplication. In: Chen, K., Deng, R., Lai, X., Zhou, J. (eds.) ISPEC 2006. LNCS, vol. 3903, pp. 13–24. Springer, Heidelberg (2006). https://doi.org/10.1007/11689522_2
12. Fujii, H., Aranha, D.F.: Curve25519 for the cortex-M4 and beyond. In: Progress in Cryptology - LATINCRYPT 2017: 5th International Conference on Cryptology and Information Security in Latin America 2017, Proceedings. LNCS, Springer International Publishing, September 2017, to appear
13. Goundar, R.R., Joye, M., Miyaji, A., Rivain, M., Venelli, A.: Scalar multiplication on Weierstraß elliptic curves from Co-Z arithmetic. J. Cryptogr. Eng. **1**(2), 161 (2011). https://doi.org/10.1007/s13389-011-0012-0

14. Hamburg, M.: Fast and compact elliptic-curve cryptography. Cryptology ePrint Archive, Report 2012/309, May 2012. http://eprint.iacr.org/2012/309
15. Hedabou, M., Pinel, P., Bénéteau, L.: A comb method to render ECC resistant against Side Channel Attacks. Cryptology ePrint Archive, Report 2004/342, December 2004. http://eprint.iacr.org/2004/342
16. Jager, T., Schwenk, J., Somorovsky, J.: Practical invalid curve attacks on TLS-ECDH. In: Pernul, G., Ryan, P.Y.A., Weippl, E. (eds.) ESORICS 2015. LNCS, vol. 9326, pp. 407–425. Springer, Cham (2015). https://doi.org/10.1007/978-3-319-24174-6_21
17. Johnson, D., Menezes, A., Vanstone, S.: The elliptic curve digital signature algorithm (ECDSA). Int. J. Inf. Secur. 1(1), 36–63 (2001). https://doi.org/10.1007/s102070100002
18. Josefsson, S., Liusvaara, I.: Edwards-Curve Digital Signature Algorithm (EdDSA). RFC 8032, January 2017. https://dx.doi.org/10.17487/rfc8032
19. Joye, M.: Highly regular right-to-left algorithms for scalar multiplication. In: Paillier, P., Verbauwhede, I. (eds.) CHES 2007. LNCS, vol. 4727, pp. 135–147. Springer, Heidelberg (2007). https://doi.org/10.1007/978-3-540-74735-2_10
20. Kocher, P.C.: Timing attacks on implementations of Diffie-Hellman, RSA, DSS, and other systems. In: Koblitz, N. (ed.) CRYPTO 1996. LNCS, vol. 1109, pp. 104–113. Springer, Heidelberg (1996). https://doi.org/10.1007/3-540-68697-5_9
21. Lim, C.H., Lee, P.J.: More flexible exponentiation with precomputation. In: Desmedt, Y.G. (ed.) CRYPTO 1994. LNCS, vol. 839, pp. 95–107. Springer, Heidelberg (1994). https://doi.org/10.1007/3-540-48658-5_11
22. Montgomery, P.L.: Speeding the pollard and elliptic curve methods of factorization. Math. Comput. 48(177), 243–264 (1987). https://doi.org/10.2307/2007888
23. Moon, A.: Implementations of a fast Elliptic-curve Digital Signature Algorithm, March 2012. https://github.com/floodyberry/ed25519-donna
24. NIST: Digital Signature Standard (DSS). Technical report FIPS 186–1, National Institute for Standards and Technology, December 1998
25. NIST: Digital Signature Standard (DSS). Technical report FIPS 186–2, National Institute of Standards and Technology, January 2000. http://csrc.nist.gov/publications/fips/archive/fips186-2/fips186-2.pdf
26. NIST: SHA-3 Standard: Permutation-Based Hash and Extendable-Output Functions. Technical report FIPS-202, National Institute of Standards and Technology, August 2015. http://dx.doi.org/10.6028/NIST.FIPS.202
27. Okeya, K., Sakurai, K.: Efficient elliptic curve cryptosystems from a scalar multiplication algorithm with recovery of the y-coordinate on a montgomery-form elliptic curve. In: Koç, Ç.K., Naccache, D., Paar, C. (eds.) CHES 2001. LNCS, vol. 2162, pp. 126–141. Springer, Heidelberg (2001). https://doi.org/10.1007/3-540-44709-1_12
28. Oliveira, T., Aranha, D.F., López, J., Rodríguez-Henríquez, F.: Fast point multiplication algorithms for binary elliptic curves with and without precomputation. In: Joux, A., Youssef, A. (eds.) SAC 2014. LNCS, vol. 8781, pp. 324–344. Springer, Cham (2014). https://doi.org/10.1007/978-3-319-13051-4_20
29. Oliveira, T., López, J., Hışıl, H., Faz-Hernández, A., Rodríguez-Henríquez, F.: How to (pre-)compute a ladder. In: Selected Areas in Cryptography - SAC 2017: 24th International Conference, Ottawa, Ontario, Canada, 16–18 August 2017, Revised Selected Papers, Springer International Publishing, August 2017, to appear
30. Perrin, T.: The XEdDSA and VXEdDSA Signature Schemes. Technical report, Open Whisper Systems, October 2016. https://whispersystems.org/docs/specifications/xeddsa/xeddsa.pdf

31. The Sage Developers: SageMath, the Sage Mathematics Software System (Version 7.6) (2017). http://www.sagemath.org
32. Renes, J., Smith, B.: qDSA: small and secure digital signatures with curve-based Diffie-Hellman key pairs. In: Advances in Cryptology - ASIACRYPT 2017: 23nd International Conference on the Theory and Application of Cryptology and Information Security, Hong Kong, China, 3–7 December 2017, December 2017, to appear
33. Rescorla, E., Dierks, T.: The Transport Layer Security (TLS) Protocol Version 1.2. RFC 5246, August 2008. https://dx.doi.org/10.17487/rfc5246
34. Rivest, R.L., Shamir, A., Adleman, L.: A method for obtaining digital signatures and public-key cryptosystems. Commun. ACM **21**(2), 120–126 (1978). https://doi.org/10.1145/359340.359342
35. Schnorr, C.P.: Efficient signature generation by smart cards. J. Cryptol. **4**(3), 161–174 (1991). https://doi.org/10.1007/BF00196725
36. Seo, H., Kim, H.: Consecutive operand-caching method for multiprecision multiplication, revisited. J. Inf. Commun. Convergence Eng. **13**(1), 27–35 (2015). https://doi.org/10.6109/jicce.2015.13.1.027
37. Spagni, R.: Disclosure of a Major Bug in CryptoNote Based Currencies, May 2017. Announment on https://getmonero.org/2017/05/17/disclosure-of-a-major-bug-in-cryptonote-based-currencies.html
38. Taverne, J., Faz-Hernández, A., Aranha, D.F., Rodríguez-Henríquez, F., Hankerson, D., López, J.: Speeding scalar multiplication over binary elliptic curves using the new carry-less multiplication instruction. J. Cryptogr. Eng. **1**(3), 187 (2011). https://doi.org/10.1007/s13389-011-0017-8
39. The OpenSSL Project: OpenSSL: The Open Source toolkit for SSL/TLS, April 2003. www.openssl.org
40. Tromer, E., Osvik, D.A., Shamir, A.: Efficient cache attacks on AES, and countermeasures. J. Cryptol. **23**(1), 37–71 (2010). https://doi.org/10.1007/s00145-009-9049-y
41. Turner, S., Langley, A., Hamburg, M.: Elliptic Curves for Security. RFC 7748, January 2016. https://dx.doi.org/10.17487/rfc7748
42. Yen, S.M., Joye, M.: Checking before output may not be enough against fault-based cryptanalysis. IEEE Trans. Comput. **49**(9), 967–970 (2000). https://doi.org/10.1109/12.869328

Variable-Length Bit Mapping and Error-Correcting Codes for Higher-Order Alphabet PUFs

Vincent Immler[1]([✉]), Matthias Hiller[1], Qinzhi Liu[1,2], Andreas Lenz[3], and Antonia Wachter-Zeh[3]

[1] Fraunhofer Institute for Applied and Integrated Security (AISEC), Garching bei München, Germany
{vincent.immler,matthias.hiller,qinzhi.liu}@aisec.fraunhofer.de
[2] RWTH Aachen University, Aachen, Germany
[3] Institute for Communications Engineering, Technical University of Munich (TUM), Munich, Germany
andreas.lenz@mytum.de, antonia.wachter-zeh@tum.de

Abstract. Device-specific physical characteristics provide the foundation for Physical Unclonable Functions (PUFs), a hardware primitive for secure storage of cryptographic keys. So far, they have been implemented by either directly evaluating a binary output or by mapping outputs from a higher-order alphabet to a fixed-length bit sequence. However, the latter causes a significant bias in the derived key when combined with an equidistant quantization.

To overcome this limitation, we propose a variable-length bit mapping that reflects the properties of a Gray code in a different metric, namely the *Levenshtein* metric instead of the classical Hamming metric. Subsequent error-correction is therefore based on a custom insertion/deletion correcting code. This new approach effectively counteracts the bias in the derived key already at the input side.

We present the concept for our scheme and demonstrate its feasibility based on an empirical PUF distribution. As a result, we increase the effective output bit length of the secret by over 40% compared to state-of-the-art approaches while at the same time obtaining additional advantages, e.g., an improved tamper-sensitivity. This opens up a new direction of Error-Correcting Codes (ECCs) for PUFs that output responses with symbols of higher-order output alphabets.

Keywords: Physical Unclonable Functions · Fuzzy extractor · Secrecy leakage · Coding theory · Quantization · Varshamov-Tenengolts (VT) code

1 Introduction

For a variety of applications, PUFs provide cryptographic keys with an increased level of security when compared to previous approaches, e.g., keys stored in non-volatile memory that can be extracted while the device is powered off. Most

© Springer International Publishing AG 2017
S.S. Ali et al. (Eds.): SPACE 2017, LNCS 10662, pp. 190–209, 2017.
https://doi.org/10.1007/978-3-319-71501-8_11

PUFs are implemented in silicon, such as the Ring Oscillator (RO) [1] or SRAM PUF [2]. Other more specialized approaches include the Coating PUF [3] which additionally provides tamper-evidence, i.e., a property that is required to determine if the device has been physically tampered with. At their core, all PUFs output quasi-continuous physical measurement data that is processed by a quantization and error correction to generate reliable keys.

For the ease of implementation, most PUFs map these quasi-continuous values to a single-bit response, as it is the case for the RO PUF. However, this discards large portions of the information provided by the PUF response. It was shown, e.g., for the Coating PUF, that a multi-bit quantization step increases the output entropy and also facilitates a first error reduction step [3].

So far, the non-uniformly distributed input data of the quantization is mapped to symbols by a fixed-length bit mapping. Depending on the selected type of quantization this has several drawbacks. For equiprobable quantization, helper data vectors leak significant amounts of secret information and also the tamper-sensitivity is poor, i.e., physical changes in the underlying PUF structure may not necessarily cause a change in the output of the quantization [4]. For an equidistant quantization, the resulting binary sequence is heavily biased and causes secrecy leakage in the helper data of a subsequent ECC.

To address this issue, we follow the information-theoretical intuition of quantizing values with different probabilities of occurrence to binary sequences of varying length, i.e., values that occur more often are assigned a shorter binary representation and vice-versa. A good compression algorithm maps a non-uniform sequence to a shorter uniformly distributed sequence. Therefore, the output binary data is nearly unbiased and the underlying equidistant quantization does not leak secret information. Moreover, for tamper-evident PUFs, an equidistant quantization is more sensitive towards physical attacks [4].

Unfortunately, following this idea comes at the expense that a large body of previous work on error correction [5–13] can no longer be applied to the quantized bit sequence of a PUF. This is owed to the fact that if noise exceeds the tolerance of the quantization scheme, the *length* of the considered sequence changes. A change in length is either called an *insertion* if it gets longer, or a *deletion* if it gets shorter. For more advanced cases not specifically considered in the paper, they may occur also at the same time.

In contrast, commonly known ECCs are directed towards correcting *substitution* errors, typically by taking into account the Hamming distance of sequences. Since one insertion or deletion does not only affect the erroneous symbol itself, but also shifts all subsequent symbols, codes in the Hamming metric are not able to efficiently correct insertion or deletion errors.

The challenge therefore is to use codes capable of correcting errors that stem from variable-length bit mappings within the context of PUFs, i.e., they must address common design issues of PUF key derivation schemes such as reliability and secrecy leakage in the helper data. To do so, we leverage the properties of Varshamov-Tenengolts (VT) codes [14–16] that are able to correct insertion and deletion errors. In fact, we use a variation of the original VT codes that also covers substitution errors.

To further elaborate on our scheme, let us briefly introduce the PUF system model, as illustrated in Fig. 1. The upper part represents the enrollment of the PUF, i.e., the point in time when it is initialized in a secure environment and helper data is created to enable later error correction. The lower part depicts the reconstruction in the field where the PUF key is extracted again to serve as secret input for cryptographic applications. As part of this processing chain, the PUF values are affected by noise which makes it necessary to compensate for this influence by suitable schemes, e.g., a combination of quantization and ECC. In this work, we focus on the specifics of this algorithmic part.

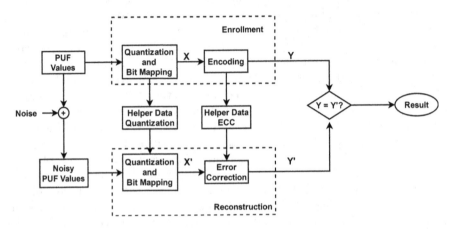

Fig. 1. PUF system model with enrollment and reconstruction. X is the quantized PUF response and Y the secret bit sequence. Added noise is denoted as $(\cdot)'$.

1.1 Contributions

In short, this work presents the following three contributions:

- A variable-length bit-mapping scheme that is well-adjusted in terms of the Levenshtein distance to the properties of an equidistant quantization.
- First application of codes with insertion and deletion error-correcting capability in the domain of PUFs including necessary code modifications.
- Practical design and comparison to state-of-the-art approaches, showcasing a gain of over 40% in effective output secret bits while at the same time improving tamper-sensitivity and ensuring sufficient reliability.

1.2 Organization

A brief outline of our paper is as follows. Related work is discussed in Sect. 2, while the required background information on insertion/deletion-correcting codes is reviewed in Sect. 3. Subsequently, we introduce our custom VT based key derivation scheme in Sect. 4. This new scheme is then evaluated in Sect. 5. Eventually, we conclude our work in Sect. 6.

1.3 Notation

Unless specifically noted otherwise, random variables and their distributions are represented by capital letters, whereas numbers and specific realizations of random variables are denoted as small letters. Subscripts refer to indices of vectors, and superscripts show the length of vectors (in either symbols or bit). $\mathcal{C}_{\text{VT}}$ is the ECC and c stands for the n-bit codeword with m information bits and r parity bits.

For the helper data W^*, a quantized PUF response X^v with either superscript v as the symbol-wise length with alphabet size q or superscript n as length in bit, the mutual information between PUF response and helper data $I(X^v; W^*)$ measures the information leakage. The min-entropy definition for $\tilde{H}_\infty(X^v|W^*)$ is given in [6]:

$$I(X^v; W^*) = H(X^v) - H(X^v|W^*) \leq v \cdot \log_2(q) - \tilde{H}_\infty(X^v|W^*), \qquad (1)$$

$$\tilde{H}_\infty(X^v|W^*) = -\log_2\left(\underset{w^*}{E} \left[\max_{x^v} \underset{X^v|W^*}{\Pr} [x^v|w^*] \right] \right). \qquad (2)$$

2 State of the Art

We align our work with two other domains. In Sect. 2.1, we discuss previous work on quantization schemes and bit mappings. Subsequently, in Sect. 2.2 we briefly consider other ECC proposals for PUFs and explain why they cannot be applied to our setting.

2.1 Quantization Schemes and Bit Mappings

A common approach for generating secret keys from PUFs with continuous output values is to apply an equiprobable quantization as in [3] or [17]. The Probability Density Function (PDF) over all analog PUF responses is divided into intervals of equal probability and each interval is mapped to a symbol from a higher-order alphabet as illustrated in Fig. 2a. In order to decrease the probability of an erroneous quantization value, an offset is stored during enrollment that shifts the PUF response to the center of its corresponding quantization interval. However, as shown in [4], equiprobable quantization with these correcting vectors causes significant helper data leakage and requires precise knowledge of the distribution of the sampled PUF values. Hence, investigating other schemes is necessary.

Other equiprobable quantization schemes implement a partitioning scheme to avoid helper data leakage but again require precise knowledge of the distribution [18]. Also, for equiprobable approaches, tamper-sensitivity varies significantly due to the varying size of the quantization intervals [4]. Equidistant quantization intervals mitigate these effects but come at the downside of biased quantized PUF outputs. Here, the PDF is divided into intervals of equal width but different probability as shown in Fig. 2b. As a consequence, a suboptimal assignment of the interval boundaries relative to the PDF only has a minor impact on the resulting entropy of the quantized output.

For both cases, the resulting symbols can be represented with a Gray code bit mapping, i.e., neighboring intervals differ only in a single bit position in terms of the Hamming distance. This results in a practical scheme for an equiprobable quantization, neglecting the challenge of precisely knowing the PDF. However, when combining equidistant quantization with fixed-length binary outputs and a linear fuzzy extractor scheme, significant amounts of secret information are leaked by the helper data due to the induced bias [19].

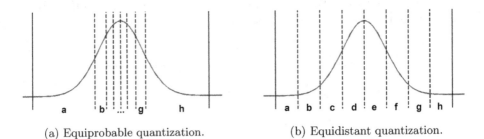

(a) Equiprobable quantization.   (b) Equidistant quantization.

Fig. 2. Visualization of equiprobable and equidistant quantization schemes.

2.2 Error-Correcting Codes for PUFs

A significant amount of work was carried out in the domain of PUFs ranging from formalizing PUFs [20] to generic ECC constructions, and protocols [21] in addition to analyses in terms of implementation and information efficiency [19,22].

As outlined before, previous work is mostly specifically tailored towards PUFs with a binary alphabet. The strong focus on these PUFs has been a valid requirement due to their large availability. While generally being suitable to provide a sufficient reliability, these schemes suffer from other shortcomings mostly related to helper data leakage that is caused by biased PUF data, as explained in [23]. Schemes targeting PUFs that provide higher-order alphabets must take these possible effects into account, too.

While lacking the opportunity to use existing ECC constructions, we still need to check if suitable ideas from the binary or fixed-length domain could be applied to our scenario, e.g., to prevent helper data leakage and bias. To remove this leakage, various debiasing schemes were proposed.

Index-Based Syndrome coding (IBS) [8] is a debiasing technique that also improves the reliability by indexing only reliable PUF response bits. However, the quantized input values all have the same reliability for equidistant quantization such that IBS is not applicable for the discussed scenario.

The scheme presented in [24] improves the von Neumann (VN) corrector [25]. For i.i.d. PUF response bits, pairs of consecutive zeros or ones occur with different probabilities, while pairs (1, 0) and (0, 1) have the same probability.

However, the approach is intended for PUFs with small output alphabets. It evaluates groups of elements that occur with the same probability but differ in their sequence, such that an increasing number of elements decreases the probability of these equiprobable events. In [26], it was recently extended to ternary outputs using reliability information. However, it cannot be efficiently applied to higher-order alphabets. The multi-bit symbol approach in [27] is especially suited for PUFs with high bit error probabilities >20%. It is not explicitly designed for bias reduction but can also handle biased inputs efficiently as well. However, please note that it still has binary inputs and cannot compensate for insertion/deletion errors so that it cannot by applied under our constraints.

As a result, none of the discussed techniques provide a promising foundation to efficiently derive keys from PUFs with higher-order alphabets. To the best of our knowledge, the case of a variable-length bit mapping for PUFs has not been considered beforehand. We are aware of the threat of helper data manipulation attacks [28]. However, for the presented work, we are interested in discussing more fundamental properties of variable-length bit mappings and the corresponding ECCs.

3   Preliminaries

This section briefly introduces the two concepts that form the theoretical foundation of our proposed scheme. First, the Levenshtein distance is presented and its applicability to quantify the distortion caused by insertion/deletion errors is discussed. Second, VT codes are covered as a code class to deal with errors of this type.

3.1   Insertion/Deletion Errors and Levenshtein Distance

Let us briefly consider the following example: let $X = [1, 0, 1, 0, 1, 0, 1]$ be the designated bit sequence and $X' = [1, 1, 0, 1, 0, 1]$ a shorter received sequence where a deletion occurred at the second position of X. Since the Hamming distance is not defined between vectors of unequal length, one could artificially pad X' with a zero which results in $d_H(X, [X', 0]) = 6$. This large distance highlights that it is impractical to rate deletions (and similarly, insertions) with the help of the Hamming metric.

To better reflect the nature of the error, Levenshtein [29] defined the distance $d_L(X, X')$ as the smallest number of insertions, deletions, and substitutions that are required to transform X' into X. Hence, $d_L(X, X') = 1$ for the given example. In the following, we review VT codes that form a class of codes that can correct errors in the Levenshtein metric.

3.2   VT Codes for Insertion/Deletion Error Correction

Varshamov-Tenengolts (VT) codes have been introduced to address insertion and deletion errors and correct a single insertion or deletion [15, 30]. For a fixed integer $a \in \{0, \dots, n\}$, a binary VT code of length n is defined as the set of all vectors $C^n = (c_1, c_2, \dots, c_n) \in \{0, 1\}^n$ such that:

$$\sum_{i=1}^{n} i \cdot c_i \equiv a \pmod{n+1}. \tag{3}$$

The integer a is called the checksum (or syndrome). VT codes are conjectured to be optimal in the sense that they have the largest cardinality of all single-deletion correcting codes [30]. The largest code sizes are obtained for $a = 0$. The size of the code for $a = 0$ is at least $\frac{2^n}{n+1}$ and its redundancy therefore at most $\lceil \log_2(n+1) \rceil$ bits. Please note that this basic construction is unable to correct substitutions and only works when the type of error is already known, i.e., the length of the received word must be provided.

The procedure to construct *systematic* VT-like codes according to [31] is as follows: For a binary input sequence $(x_1, \dots, x_m)$, the corresponding codeword has the form $(c_1, \dots, c_n)$ where $x_1 = c_{i_1}, x_2 = c_{i_2}, \dots, x_m = c_{i_m}, 1 \le i_1 < i_2 < \dots < i_m \le n$. The bits c_k, where $k \notin \{i_1, i_2, \dots, i_m\}$ are called parity bits. For a codeword of length n, the number of parity-check bits is $r = \lceil \log_2(n-1) \rceil + 1$ and they are located at positions $k = 2^l$, where $0 \le l \le r - 2$, and at position n.

For M such that $2n \le M \le \min(n + 2^{r-1}, 2^r)$, the parity-check bits $(p_1, \dots, p_r)$ are chosen according to

$$\sum_{l=1}^{r-1} p_l \cdot 2^{l-1} + p_r \cdot n + \sum_{j=1}^{m} i_j \cdot x_j \equiv 0 \pmod{M}. \tag{4}$$

Please note, that "systematic" in this setting does not imply that the *first* m bits contain the information, they are distributed to positions which are not a power of 2 or equal to n. Extending this systematic encoding with the capability to also correct one substitution error comes at the expense of storing one additional redundancy bit.

In our PUF use case, only parts of the codewords are transmitted since the parity bits are stored as public helper data. The helper data is assumed not to be corrupted, so we can retrieve it without errors, similarly to [32]. However, the message bits may contain errors at unknown positions as they are drawn from the noisy PUF.

The standard systematic VT code cannot be employed in PUFs, because when recovering the response from the PUF, the positions where to insert the parity-check bits cannot be determined. It is therefore necessary to fully separate parity-check bits from the message containing secret information. This is explained in Sect. 4.2.

4   Variable-Length Bit Mapping and New VT-Like Code

We first introduce the variable-length bit mapping of equidistant quantization intervals and discuss how to encode them into VT-like codewords.

4.1 Variable-Length Bit Mapping for Equidistant Quantization

Ideally, the bit mapping is such that the obtained sequence is not biased, i.e., the 1s and 0s are uniformly distributed. In addition, the bit mapping should support the subsequent error correction in terms of low distance changes from one to another quantization interval. At the same time this improves tamper-sensitivity, as errors that result in a larger distance to the designated value are almost certainly caused by a physical attack and therefore – as part of its intended purpose – should cause the device to fail.

To achieve low distance changes for neighboring intervals in Hamming distance, i.e., $d_H = 1$, one would use a Gray code [33]. However, it cannot be applied in our case, since this scheme only works for fixed-length bit mappings. Another disadvantage of fixed-length bit mappings is that some patterns of 1s and 0s would occur more likely, i.e., cause a bias. To overcome these limitations, we propose a new variable-length bit mapping scheme, as shown in Fig. 3b.

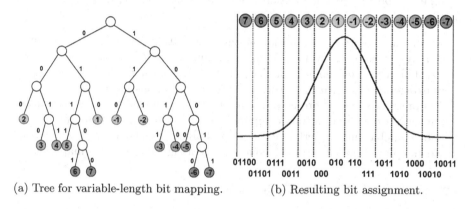

(a) Tree for variable-length bit mapping.   (b) Resulting bit assignment.

Fig. 3. Proposed variable-length bit mapping for equidistant quantization.

In order to preserve the entropy of the quantization, i.e., when mapping its symbols to the binary domain, the quantization procedure requires a uniquely decodable code, e.g., it should be prefix-free. Therefore, we build a binary tree to explicitly assign symbols to a variable-length bit mapping that differs only in $d_L = 1$ for neighboring intervals. Hence, it is the Levenshtein counterpart to the Gray code. Notice that a Huffman code is not an eligible candidate here as it neither ensures a debiasing characteristic due to the lack of same-probability of 0s and 1s, nor is the constraint of $d_L = 1$ for neighboring intervals considered.

The example displayed for 14 intervals of Fig. 3a is explained by following the conventions of graph theory. Let $\mathcal{G} = (\mathcal{V}; \mathcal{E})$ be the graph $\mathcal{G}$, whereas $\mathcal{V}$ represents the set of vertices and $\mathcal{E}$ the set of edges. The effective vertices are numbered from ± 1 to ± 7 to indicate the vertices's corresponding quantization interval to the left and right of the PDF's mean.

This construction follows the principle of a prefix-free code, where each effective vertex is connected to only one other vertex by one edge. For the resulting symbols of adjacent quantization intervals, the desired distance of $d_L = 1$ is achieved. By traversing the graph either to the left or right, bit 1 or 0 is incorporated in the pattern. Unfortunately, we have not yet found a way to generalize this construction. The resulting bit mapping for the case of 14 intervals as represented by Fig. 3b is therefore given in Table 1.

Table 1. Example for variable-length encoding with Levenshtein distance 1 between adjacent intervals. The colors are matched to Fig. 3b.

Symbol	7	6	5	4	3	2	1	−1	−2	−3	−4	−5	−6	−7
Binary	01100	01101	0111	0011	0010	000	010	110	111	1011	1010	1000	10010	10011

The new bit mapping is well-suited for the application based on the following perspective:

- As long as the input distribution is symmetric, 0s and 1s are balanced, since equally probable intervals have an equal number of 1s and 0s.
- It fulfills the requirement that adjacent intervals only differ by one insertion/deletion/substitution error, i.e., adjacent intervals have $d_L = 1$.
- It is prefix-free, i.e., it preserves the information provided by the quantization but with less redundant bits compared to a fixed-length bit mapping.
- It has a debiasing property, i.e., more probable symbols are assigned shorter bit mappings and less probable symbols are assigned longer bit mappings.

4.2   Systematic VT-Like Code Construction for PUFs

This section introduces a code to address a single insertion, deletion or substitution error that originates to a quantization error and subsequently stems from the bit mapping as introduced in Sect. 4.1. We propose a VT-like code construction for the situation that the parity-check bits are not transmitted within the input bit stream and are thus error-free. Our code construction is as follows:

$$\mathcal{C}_{\mathrm{VT}} := \left\{ (x_1, \cdots, x_m, p_1, \cdots, p_r) : \sum_{i=1}^{m} i x_i + \sum_{j=1}^{r} 2^{j-1} p_j \equiv 0 \pmod{2m+1} \right\},$$

(5)

where m information bits and r parity-check bits together for a codeword of length $n = m + r$. The redundancy of this code construction is $\lceil \log(2m+1) \rceil$ and smaller than the redundancy of the systematic construction from [31]. In the following, we will show how $\mathcal{C}_{\mathrm{VT}}$ can correct one deletion, insertion, or substitution error. The decoding procedure is similar to the decoding of classical VT codes [30].

First consider an example with a single deletion. Assume that the π-th bit in the original bit sequence was deleted, which has λ_0 0s to the left of it, ρ_0 0s to the right of it, λ_1 1s left of it and ρ_1 1s right of it. Therefore, $\pi = 1 + \lambda_0 + \lambda_1$. Let ω be the Hamming weight the received bit stream, i.e., $\omega = \lambda_1 + \rho_1$. Evaluating the sums in Eq. 5, the deficiency Δ of the new checksum compared to the original one is

$$\Delta = -(\pi \cdot x_\pi + \sum_{i=\pi+1}^{m} x_i) \pmod{(2 \cdot m + 1)} \tag{6}$$

When a 1 was deleted, the checksum deficiency is given by

$$\Delta = -(\pi + \rho_1) \tag{7}$$
$$= -(1 + \lambda_0 + \lambda_1 + \rho_1) \tag{8}$$
$$= -(1 + \lambda_0 + \omega) \tag{9}$$
$$\equiv 2 \cdot m + 1 - (1 + \lambda_0 + \omega) \pmod{2 \cdot m + 1} \tag{10}$$

To recover the initial input, one needs to insert a 1 at the right side of λ_0 0s in the received sequence. When a 0 was deleted, the new checksum is ρ_1 less than the original, i.e., $\Delta = 2 \cdot m + 1 - \rho_1$. To recover, one needs to insert a 0 on the left side of ρ_1 1s. The case for insertion errors can be solved in a similar manner.

For substitution errors, the error pattern where the 0 flips to 1 gives a deficiency Δ of the position number, i.e., π. Vice-versa, if 1 changes to 0, the deficiency Δ is the value of $2m + 1 - \pi$. The range of values for the checksum deficiency Δ for insertion, deletion, and substitution errors is given in Table 2.

Table 2. Checksum deficiency Δ vs. error pattern

Error type	Error pattern	Δ	Range of Δ
Insertion	Insert 0	ρ_1	$[0, \omega]$
Insertion	Insert 1	$\pi + \rho_1 = \omega + \lambda_0$	$[\omega, m + 1]$
Deletion	Delete 0	$-\rho_1 + 2m + 1$	$[2m + 1 - \omega, 2m] \cup \{0\}$
Deletion	Delete 1	$-\rho_1 - \pi + 2m + 1$	$[m + 1, 2m - \omega]$
Substitution	Flip 0 to 1	π	$[1, m]$
Substitution	Flip 1 to 0	$2m + 1 - \pi$	$[m + 1, 2m]$

The table shows that the range of the two cases of insertions overlap in ω. The error correction here can be explained as follows: for an insertion error, if $\Delta = \omega$, there is either a 0 or 1 inserted in the beginning. For this case, we delete the first bit to correct the insertion error. Algorithm 1 shows the decoding procedure for our proposed VT-like code construction. It generalizes the systematic decoding process of the previously discussed example.

In Algorithm 1, l_I denotes the length information $m \pmod 3$ which is stored as helper data. It allows to identify the error type. Recall that X' is the output of the measured PUF values and Y' is the corrected secret.

Algorithm 1. VT-like Systematic Decoding Algorithm for PUFs

    Data: $l_I =$ (Length information)

    $\Delta =$ (Checksum deficiency)

    $X' =$ (noisy PUF response)

    $m' =$ (bit length for reference PUF response)

    Result: $Y' =$ (corrected secret bit sequence)

1 **if** $m' \equiv l_I$ (mod 3) **then**

      /* substitution error or error-free,i.e., $m' = m$ */

2   **if** $\Delta = 0$ **then**

3 | No error ;   // $Y' \leftarrow X'$

4   **else**

5   **if** $\Delta > m'$ **then**

6 | $X'[2\,m' + 1 - \Delta] = 1$;   // substitution error from 1 to 0

7   **else**

8 | $X[\Delta] = 0$;   // substitution error from 0 to 1

9   **end**

10   **end**

11    $Y' \leftarrow X'$

12 **else if** $m' + 1 \equiv l_I$ (mod 3) **then**

      /* deletion error, i.e., $m' = m - 1$ */

13   **if** $\Delta = 0$ **then**

14 | $Y' \leftarrow X'$ with 0 inserted at the end

15   **else**

16   **if** $\Delta > 2 \cdot m' + 3 - \omega$ **then**

17 | insert 0 at left side of ρ_1 1's on the right ;   // $\rho_1 = 2\,m' + 3 - \Delta$

18   **else**

19 | insert 1 at right side of λ_0 0's on the left ; // $\lambda_0 = 2\,m' + 2 - \omega - \Delta$

20   **end**

21     $Y' \leftarrow X'$

22   **end**

23 **else**

      /* insertion error, i.e., $m' = m + 1$ */

24   **if** $\Delta = 0$ **then**

25 | $Y' \leftarrow X'$ with 0 deleted at the end

26   **else**

27   **if** $\Delta > \omega$ **then**

28 | delete 1 at the right side of λ_0 0's on the left ;   // $\lambda_0 = \Delta - \omega$

29   **else**

30 | delete 0 at the left side of ρ_1 1's on the right ;   // $\rho_1 = \Delta$

31   **end**

32     $Y' \leftarrow X'$

33   **end**

34 **return** Y'

We increase argument of the modulo operation to $2m + 1$ to also guarantee substitution error correction. If we only have insertion or deletion errors, we use the following code definition which has one bit less redundancy:

$$\{(x_1 \cdots x_m, p_1 \cdots p_r)| \sum_{i=1}^{m} i \cdot x_i + \sum_{j=1}^{r} 2^{j-1} \cdot p_j \equiv 0 \pmod{m + 1}\}. \tag{11}$$

4.3   Helper Data

Our coding scheme stores two types of helper data, the length indicator information l_I and the parity bits p^r. We could also directly store the length m in l_I. However, this significantly reduces the number of possible sequences which is equivalent to a large helper data leakage. The VT-like code can only correct a single insertion, deletion or substitution such that we only need to correctly indicate whether the length of the sequence was increased by one, decreased by one or remained the same. This can also be represented by $m \pmod 3$ which reveals less information than providing the precise length.

In addition, the parity information is stored as helper data according to [32]. It was shown in [34] that the other linear schemes have a higher efficiency for the Hamming metric while the parity approach in [32] is less efficient and has a higher secrecy leakage. However, the other schemes apply an XOR operation between parts of the helper data and the PUF response. An insertion or deletion error destroys the mapping such that error correction is no longer possible. This makes the parity approach currently the only applicable scheme.

4.4   Toy Size Example

In the following toy example, we demonstrate the encoding and decoding of our VT-like code. Based on PUF nodes with $x^8 = [5, 4, -3, -6, 7, -1, 2, 4]$. The symbols are encoded according to the bit mapping presented in Sect. 4.1, i.e.,

$$\text{enc}(x^8) = [(0111), (0011), (1011), (10010), (01100), (110), (000), (0011)]. \tag{12}$$

Afterwards, 4 symbols are combined to one VT codeword. The first 4 symbols are encoded to a binary sequence of length 17. Therefore $l_I(x^4) = 17 \equiv 2 \pmod 3$. The left half of Eq. 5 is

$$\sum_{i=1}^{17} i \, x_i = 2 + 3 + 4 + 7 + 8 + 9 + 11 + 12 + 13 + 16 = 85 \equiv 15 \pmod{35}. \tag{13}$$

The parity bits are a binary representation of $35 - 15 = 20$, so $p^6 = (010100)$. For the second part of the PUF response, we analogously calculate the helper data $l_I = 15 \equiv 0 \pmod 3$ and $p^6 = (001111)$.

To demonstrate deletion and insertion error correction, let us assume that during reconstruction one quantization error occurred in the third symbol and another one in the seventh symbol, such that $x'^8 = [5, 4, -2, -6, 7, -1, 3, 4]$. Therefore the third symbol is encoded to (111) instead of (1011), which corresponds to one deletion error. Computing $l_1(x'^4) = 1 \equiv 16 \pmod 3$ shows that the one bit was deleted:

$$\Delta = \sum_{i=1}^{m} i\, x'_i + \sum_{j=1}^{r} 2^{j-1}\, p_j = 81 + 20 = 101 \equiv 31 \pmod{33 + 2}. \tag{14}$$

$\Delta = 2 \cdot (16 + 1) + 1 - \rho_1$, therefore we have $\rho_1 = 4$ and insert 0 on the left of 4 1s in the right. Thus, we were able to detect the position of the deletion and correct the error. For the second half, let us assume that the third symbol shifted from 2 to 3 such that (0010) is forwarded instead of (000). Now $l_1(x'^4) = 1$. Since $I(x^4) = 0$, one insertion occurred. $\Delta = 13$, so according to line 28 of Algorithm 1, we delete the 1 at the right side of $13 - 7 = 6$ 0s.

5   Evaluation

To allow a fair comparison to the state of the art, the results in this section have been simulated according to the scenario in [3]. We therefore used the following parameters: The device contains 128 PUF nodes with Gaussian distributed PUF responses with $\mu = 1.8 \cdot 10^{-13}$ and $\sigma = 3.6 \cdot 10^{-15}$. Individual measurements of the nodes are affected by Gaussian distributed, mean-free noise with $\sigma_N = 2 \cdot 10^{-16}$.

5.1   Reliability

In the following, two mechanisms are considered to improve the reliability of the PUF system. First, we evaluate the effects of the quantization. Afterwards, the specifics of the VT-like code are analyzed in terms of number of secret bits and reliability.

Error Reduction by Quantization. As a baseline, we first evaluate the performance of a system that only relies on a quantization without any further error correction or leakage mitigation steps. Following [4], the equidistant quantization is applied to the PUF response of each individual node. The width of the quantization intervals is set to

$$Q_w = 2 \cdot y \cdot \sigma_N. \tag{15}$$

As mentioned beforehand, by storing a helper data vector, the quantization scheme itself has an error tolerance of $[-y \cdot \sigma_N, +y \cdot \sigma_N]$, i.e., as long as the error does not exceed this interval no error will occur. Here, y is a parameter that determines the reliability. This is illustrated in Fig. 4a with a yellow arrow indicating the interval Q_w. Later, we will combine this quantization with Reed–Solomon (RS) codes with different code parameters [35].

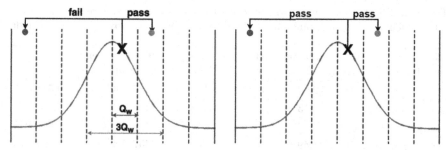

(a) Quantization and VT-like code as ECC.   (b) Quantization and RS code as ECC.

Fig. 4. Comparison of equidistant quantizations with differing subsequent ECCs. In (a), only shifts by small errors are correct, as it is the preferred case to improve tamper-sensitivity. In contrast, (b) corrects any shift to arbitrary intervals, as long as the overall error-threshold of the RS code is not exceeded. (Color figure online)

Error Reduction by VT-Like Code. Figure 4a illustrates the difference of the noise tolerance between the pure quantization and the combination of quantization with error correction. After error correction using the VT-like code, the noise tolerance has tripled to $3 \cdot Q_w$ for one value. Therefore, same values of y now offer a much better reliability compared to a pure quantization.

However, for each segment of nodes still only one error can be corrected due to the properties of the constructed code. This limitation is preferred, as a physical attack which causes a large increase in Levenshtein distance from the reference value should *not* be corrected. Heavily distorted measurement values occur from noise only with small probability, so multiple errors outside of the $[-y \cdot \sigma_N, +y \cdot \sigma_N]$ interval should cause the system to fail, thereby improving tamper-sensitivity.

In the following, we add a hat ($\hat{\cdot}$) to probabilities that refer to corrected values after the VT-decoding. We calculate the error probability P_n of a node by integrating over the PDF of the noise. Then we apply the VT-like code for error correction to obtain the corresponding error probability for a segment, if more than one node is corrupted with $d_L = 1$. Finally, for an error-free device, all of its segments must be correct. The node error probability is calculated by the PDF of a Gaussian distribution with $\mathcal{N}(\mu, \sigma)$ as follows:

$$P_n = 1 - \int_{-y \cdot \sigma_N}^{+y \cdot \sigma_N} \mathcal{N}(0, \sigma_N).$$

Without error correction, a segment with m nodes will pass the authentication process only if all its nodes are quantized correctly. This corresponds to a segment error probability P_s of

$$P_s = 1 - (1 - P_n)^m. \tag{16}$$

In this paper, the aim is to correct the error when the encoded value shifts into adjacent intervals. Hence, per segment, only one node with $d_L = 1$ must be

Table 3. Effect of varying parameters of the quantization and resulting data for entropy, length of bit mapping, and reliability. The entropy is given in bits per node.

Number of intervals	Min entropy	Shannon entropy	Bits per node	Bits per device	97% confidence interval	P_d
12 ($y = 4.95$)	2.26	2.92	3.27	419	[406, 430]	9.5×10^{-5}
14 ($y = 4.24$)	2.47	3.13	3.36	430	[417, 443]	2.8×10^{-3}
16 ($y = 3.71$)	2.65	3.33	3.51	449	[433, 466]	2.6×10^{-2}
18 ($y = 3.30$)	2.81	3.49	3.73	478	[457, 500]	1.2×10^{-1}
20 ($y = 2.97$)	2.96	3.64	3.92	502	[482, 517]	3.1×10^{-1}

corrected. The probability $\hat{P}_n$ that a single node is correct after correction is:

$$\hat{P}_n = 1 - \int_{-3 \cdot y \cdot \sigma_N}^{+3 \cdot y \cdot \sigma_N} \mathcal{N}(0, \sigma_N). \tag{17}$$

The error probability $\hat{P}_s$ after VT error correction is

$$\hat{P}_s \leq 1 - \left(m(1 - P_n)^{m-1}(P_n - \hat{P}_n) + (1 - P_s) \right) \tag{18}$$

$$= 1 - \left(m(1 - P_n)^{m-1}(P_n - \hat{P}_n) + (1 - P_n)^m \right) \tag{19}$$

The probability in (17) assumes that only adjacent intervals differ in one bit, i.e., a single insertion/deletion/substitution error. However, in the process of building the codebook, one cannot avoid that nearby intervals other than the adjacent ones also differ in only one bit.

Hence, the probability of the analytically computed error rate upper bounds the error probability and simulated results should slightly outperform the calculations. This difference can be practically observed, whereas the margin is larger for a higher error-rate and smaller for a lower error-rate. For a device with ν segments, the overall device error probability $\hat{P}_d$ is finally given by

$$\hat{P}_d = 1 - (1 - \hat{P}_s)^\nu. \tag{20}$$

If no error correction is carried out, $\hat{P}_d$ and $\hat{P}_s$ will be replaced by P_d and P_s.

As listed in Table 3, we observe for a device with 128 nodes that increasing y leads to an improved reliability at the expense of loss in entropy and shortened length of the bit sequence. Therefore, a designer's goal is to maximize the number of secret bits while meeting the reliability requirement.

5.2   Information Leakage Caused by ECC

To determine the amount of leakage between encoded sequence X^v helper data $W = (L_I, P^*)$, we select one of our later results from Table 4 that meets the reliability requirements and has the largest number of effective secret bits. For other selected parameters, the calculation is similar.

The first source of leakage is caused by the stored length information l_I. It is stored for each segment and may have 3 possible values only. Therefore $I(X^v; L_I)$ is considered as worst-case if rounded-up, i.e.,

$$I(X^v; L_I) \leq H(L_I) \leq \lceil \log_2(3) \rceil = 2 \text{bits}$$

The second source of leakage is based on the parity bits P^* of the VT code. For a segment with $v = 128$ node values, the maximum entropy of these parity bits is therefore considered as information leakage $I(X^v; P^*)$. Please note, for the subsequent calculation, the maximum length of the segment is used as upper bound for the leaked bits. For the specific example, the code size determines the maximum entropy, i.e., here, resulting in the size of P^*. The remaining multiplicative factor of 2 and additive component $+1$ is due to the structure of the code, cf. Eq. (5):

$$I(X^{128}; P^*) \leq H(P^*) \tag{21}$$
$$\leq \lceil \log_2(2m + 1) \rceil \tag{22}$$
$$= \lceil \log_2(2 \cdot 5 \cdot 128 + 1) \rceil \tag{23}$$
$$= 11 \text{ bits} \tag{24}$$

Hence, the overall number of leaked bits based on a worst-case assumption is

$$I(X^{128}; W^*) \leq 2 + 11 = 13 \text{ bits} \tag{25}$$

Concerning the min-entropy that is extracted on average from a device, we consider each node with $y = 4.94$ (resulting in 12 quantization intervals) which leads to a min-entropy of 2.26 bit per node, according to Table 3. This gives

$$\tilde{H}_\infty(X^v) = 2.26 \cdot 128 = 289.3 \text{ bits} \tag{26}$$

Hence, for a device with 128 nodes, the number of overall effective secret bits is

$$\tilde{H}_\infty(X^v) - I(X^v; W^*) = 289.3 - 13 = 276.3 \text{ bits} \tag{27}$$

5.3   Comparison of Fuzzy Commitment and VT-Like Codes

In the following, we compare a fuzzy commitment scheme based on an RS code and our VT-like code. The results for the RS code are given in Table 4. For the VT-like code, the results are summarized in Table 5. In either case, we make use of the min-entropy per node that we obtain from the quantization histogram as listed in Table 3. The values for y range from 3 to 5 and result in 2.26 to 2.96 bits of min-entropy per node.

From the comparison of Tables 4 and 5, we observe a sufficient reliability for both approaches. The VT-like entries with a lower numbers of effective bits have been added for explanatory reasons. In terms of effective secret bits, the VT-like

Table 4. Evaluation of RS codes for PUFs with $v = 128$ output symbols. P_n and P_d are node and device error probabilities. Effective secret bit already account for the information leakage of the helper data.

y	z	RS code parameters	P_n (before RS)	P_d (before RS)	$\hat{P}_n$ (after RS)	$\hat{P}_d$ (after RS)	Effective secret bits
5	8	(15, 13, 3)	5.73×10^{-7}	7.34×10^{-5}	4.60×10^{-12}	4.79×10^{-10}	≈ 192
3.71	8	(15, 11, 5)	2.05×10^{-4}	2.59×10^{-2}	7.83×10^{-10}	6.89×10^{-8}	≈ 178
3	4	(31, 23, 8)	2.67×10^{-3}	2.90×10^{-1}	3.72×10^{-9}	3.42×10^{-7}	≈ 195

Table 5. Evaluation of error probability and information leakage for the proposed VT-like code. P_s and P_d are segment and device error probabilities for a PUF with $v = 128$ output symbols. Leakage $I(X^v; W^*)$ is given in terms of bit.

y	Nodes per segment	P_s (before VT)	$\hat{P}_s$ (after VT)	$\hat{P}_d$ (after VT)	$I(X^v; W^*)$ (in bits)	Effective secret bits	Comparison against RS
4.95	4	3×10^{-6}	3.3×10^{-12}	1.1×10^{-10}	≤ 256	≈ 33.3	
4.95	8	6×10^{-6}	1.6×10^{-11}	2.5×10^{-10}	≤ 144	≈ 145.3	
4.95	16	1.2×10^{-5}	6.6×10^{-11}	5.3×10^{-10}	≤ 80	≈ 209.3	
4.95	32	2.4×10^{-5}	2.7×10^{-10}	1.1×10^{-9}	≤ 44	≈ 245.3	
4.95	64	4.7×10^{-5}	1.1×10^{-9}	2.2×10^{-9}	≤ 24	≈ 265.3	
4.95	128	9.5×10^{-5}	4.5×10^{-9}	4.5×10^{-9}	≤ 13	≈ 276.3	$\leftarrow$
4.24	4	8.8×10^{-5}	2.9×10^{-9}	9.4×10^{-8}	≤ 256	≈ 59.8	
4.24	8	1.8×10^{-4}	1.4×10^{-8}	2×10^{-7}	≤ 144	≈ 171.8	
4.24	16	3.5×10^{-4}	5.9×10^{-8}	5×10^{-7}	≤ 80	≈ 235.8	
4.24	32	7.1×10^{-4}	2×10^{-7}	1×10^{-6}	≤ 44	≈ 271.8	

code outperforms the RS code by over 40%. Moreover, its expected implementation is simplified as no operations in Galois fields are required. Furthermore, instead of the burst error-correction by the RS code, the VT-like code maintains a better tamper-sensitivity since mostly adjacent intervals are corrected. Another advantage is that its bit mapping introduces less bias and therefore leaks less information.

Considering Table 5 more closely, we observe that for smaller segments with less nodes, a better reliability is achieved. However, at the same time more information is leaked by the helper data. In the simulation of 1.2×10^7 devices, no device failed, which gives a confident error rate $\ll 1 \times 10^{-6}$.

6   Conclusion

The majority of previous fuzzy extractor schemes is limited to binary PUF outputs and therefore impractical to use for higher-order alphabets. Moreover, the few existing works considering higher-order alphabets are limited to fixed-length bit mappings and equiprobable quantization.

This work introduces a variable-length bit mapping and a corresponding error correction scheme for an equidistant quantization. Its impact is manifold:

it relieves designers of PUF systems of previously existing constraints regarding the selection of the quantization scheme, it results in a more efficient scheme and therefore a longer effective secret bit output, and also improves other desired properties such as tamper-sensitivity.

For the practical scenario considered, we are able to increase the number of effective secret bits by 40% while at the same time not requiring complex finite field operations as it would be the case for an RS decoder. While the results are already promising, we consider this only as a first step towards a more efficient use of higher-order alphabet PUFs.

Acknowledgements. The authors from Fraunhofer AISEC have been supported by the Fraunhofer Internal Programs under Grant No. MAVO 828 432. A. Lenz and A. Wachter-Zeh have been supported by the Technical University of Munich–Institute for Advanced Study, funded by the German Excellence Initiative and European Union Seventh Framework Programme under Grant Agreement No. 291763. Many thanks to Aysun Önalan for preparing the numbers of the RS-based fuzzy commitment scheme.

References

1. Suh, G.E., Devadas, S.: Physical unclonable functions for device authentication and secret key generation. In: ACM/IEEE Design Automation Conference (DAC) (2007)
2. Guajardo, J., Kumar, S.S., Schrijen, G.-J., Tuyls, P.: FPGA intrinsic PUFs and their use for IP protection. In: Paillier, P., Verbauwhede, I. (eds.) CHES 2007. LNCS, vol. 4727, pp. 63–80. Springer, Heidelberg (2007). https://doi.org/10.1007/978-3-540-74735-2_5
3. Tuyls, P., Schrijen, G.-J., Škorić, B., van Geloven, J., Verhaegh, N., Wolters, R.: Read-proof hardware from protective coatings. In: Goubin, L., Matsui, M. (eds.) CHES 2006. LNCS, vol. 4249, pp. 369–383. Springer, Heidelberg (2006). https://doi.org/10.1007/11894063_29
4. Immler, V., Hennig, M., Kürzinger, L., Sigl, G.: Practical aspects of quantization and tamper-sensitivity for physically obfuscated keys. In: Workshop on Cryptography and Security in Computing Systems (CS2) (2016)
5. Juels, A., Wattenberg, M.: A fuzzy commitment scheme. In: ACM Conference on Computer and Communications Security (CCS) (1999)
6. Dodis, Y., Reyzin, L., Smith, A.: Fuzzy extractors: how to generate strong keys from biometrics and other noisy data. In: Cachin, C., Camenisch, J.L. (eds.) EUROCRYPT 2004. LNCS, vol. 3027, pp. 523–540. Springer, Heidelberg (2004). https://doi.org/10.1007/978-3-540-24676-3_31
7. Bösch, C., Guajardo, J., Sadeghi, A.-R., Shokrollahi, J., Tuyls, P.: Efficient helper data key extractor on FPGAs. In: Oswald, E., Rohatgi, P. (eds.) CHES 2008. LNCS, vol. 5154, pp. 181–197. Springer, Heidelberg (2008). https://doi.org/10.1007/978-3-540-85053-3_12
8. Yu, M., Devadas, S.: Secure and robust error correction for physical unclonable functions. IEEE Des. Test Comput. **27**(1), 48–65 (2010)
9. Maes, R.: Physically unclonable functions: constructions, properties and applications. Dissertation (2012)

10. Hiller, M., Merli, D., Stumpf, F., Sigl, G.: Complementary IBS: application specific error correction for PUFs. In: IEEE International Symposium on Hardware-Oriented Security and Trust (HOST), pp. 1–6 (2012)

11. Puchinger, S., Müelich, S., Bossert, M., Hiller, M., Sigl, G.: On error correction for physical unclonable functions. In: International ITG Conference on Systems, Communications and Coding (SCC), February 2015

12. Hiller, M., Yu, M., Sigl, G.: Cherry-picking reliable PUF bits with differential sequence coding. IEEE Trans. Inf. Forensics Secur. **11**(9), 2065–2076 (2016)

13. Puchinger, S., Müelich, S., Bossert, M., Wachter-Zeh, A.: Timing attack resilient decoding algorithms for physical unclonable functions. In: International ITG Conference on Systems, Communications and Coding (SCC), February 2017

14. Tenengolts, G.: Nonbinary codes, correcting single deletion or insertion (corresp.). IEEE Trans. Inf. Theory **30**(5), 766–769 (1984)

15. Varshamov, R.R., Tenengolts, G.M.: Codes which correct single asymmetric errors. Automatika i Telemekhanika (1965). (in Russian)

16. Levenshtein, V.: Binary codes capable of correcting deletions, insertions and reversals. Doklady Akademii Nauk SSR **163**(4), 845–848 (1965). (in Russian)

17. Günlü, O., Iscan, O.: DCT based ring oscillator physical unclonable functions. In: IEEE International Conference on Acoustics, Speech and Signal Processing (ICASSP), pp. 8248–8251 (2014)

18. Stanko, T., Andini, F.N., Skoric, B.: Optimized quantization in zero leakage helper data systems. IEEE Trans. Inf. Forensics Secur. (2017)

19. Delvaux, J., Gu, D., Verbauwhede, I., Hiller, M., Yu, M.-D.M.: Efficient fuzzy extraction of PUF-induced secrets: theory and applications. In: Gierlichs, B., Poschmann, A.Y. (eds.) CHES 2016. LNCS, vol. 9813, pp. 412–431. Springer, Heidelberg (2016). https://doi.org/10.1007/978-3-662-53140-2_20

20. Armknecht, F., Maes, R., Sadeghi, A.-R., Standaert, F.-X., Wachsmann, C.: A formalization of the security features of physical functions. In: IEEE Symposium on Security and Privacy (S&P), pp. 397–412 (2011)

21. Colombier, B., Bossuet, L., Fischer, V., Hely, D.: Key reconciliation protocols for error correction of silicon PUF responses. IEEE Trans. Inf. Forensics Secur. **12**, 1988–2002 (2017)

22. Hiller, M., Yu, M.-D.M., Pehl, M.: Systematic low leakage coding for physical unclonable functions. In: ACM Symposium on Information, Computer and Communications Security (ASIACCS) (2015)

23. Ignatenko, T., Willems, F.M.: Information leakage in fuzzy commitment schemes. IEEE Trans. Inf. Forensics Secur. **5**(2), 337–348 (2010)

24. Maes, R., van der Leest, V., van der Sluis, E., Willems, F.: Secure key generation from biased PUFs: extended version. J. Cryptogr. Eng. **6**(2), 121–137 (2016)

25. von Neumann, J.: Various techniques used in connection with random digits. In: Applied Math Series (1951)

26. Suzuki, M., Ueno, R., Homma, N., Aoki, T.: Multiple-valued debiasing for physically unclonable functions and its application to fuzzy extractors. In: Guilley, S. (ed.) COSADE 2017. LNCS, vol. 10348, pp. 248–263. Springer, Cham (2017). https://doi.org/10.1007/978-3-319-64647-3_15

27. Yu, M., Hiller, M., Devadas, S.: Maximum likelihood decoding of device-specific multi-bit symbols for reliable key generation. In: IEEE International Symposium on Hardware-Oriented Security and Trust (HOST), pp. 38–43 (2015)

28. Delvaux, J., Verbauwhede, I.: Key-recovery attacks on various RO PUF constructions via helper data manipulation. In: Design, Automation Test in Europe Conference Exhibition (DATE) (2014)

29. Levenshtein, V.I.: Binary codes capable of correcting deletions, insertions, and reversals. Soviet physics doklady (1966)
30. Sloane, N.J.A.: On single-deletion-correcting codes. In: Codes and Designs, pp. 273–292. de Gruyter (2002)
31. Saowapa, K., Kaneko, H., Fujiwara, E.: Systematic deletion/insertion error correcting codes with random error correction capability. In: Defect and Fault Tolerance in VLSI Systems (1999)
32. Davida, G.I., Frankel, Y., Matt, B.J.: On enabling secure applications through off-line biometric identification. In: IEEE Symposium on Security and Privacy (S&P), pp. 148–157 (1998)
33. Gray, F.: Pulse code communication. US Patent 2,632,058 (1953)
34. Delvaux, J., Gu, D., Verbauwhede, I., Hiller, M., Yu, M.: Secure sketch metamorphosis: tight unified bounds. IACR eprint archive (2015)
35. MacWilliams, F.J., Sloane, N.J.A.: The theory of error-correcting codes. North-Holland, Amsterdam (1977)

Mutual Friend Attack Prevention in Social Network Data Publishing

Kamalkumar R. Macwan$^{(\boxtimes)}$ and Sankita J. Patel

Sardar Vallabhbhai National Institute of Technology,
Surat 395007, Gujarat, India
kamal.macwan@yahoo.com, sankitapatel@gmail.com

Abstract. Due to increasing demand of publishing social network data, privacy has raised more concern for data publisher. There are different risks and attacks still exist that can breach user privacy. Online social network such as Facebook, Google Plus and LinkedIn provide a feature that allows finding out number of mutual friends (NMF) between two users. Adversary can use such information to identify individual user and his/her connections. As published dataset itself reveals mutual friends information for each connection, it becomes very easy for an adversary to re-identify the individual user.

Existing anonymization techniques for mutual friends attack are based on edge anonymization. It performs edge anonymization operation without considering the NMF-requirement of other edges that results into more edge insertion operations. Due to that, the data utility of anonymized dataset is very low. In this paper, we propose the anonymization approach that works on the mutual friend sequence. It ensures that, there exist at least k elements in mutual friend sequence that holds same value. The vertex selection process to increase the number of mutual friend (NMF) for one edge reduces the mutual friend anonymization requirement for other edges too. The experimental results demonstrate that the proposed anonymization approach preserve the privacy and the utility of the published dataset against mutual friend attack.

Keywords: Social network data publishing · Mutual friend attack · k-NMF · Data utility

1 Introduction

Recently, social networking platforms have become very popular among people to post and share information and to get connected, too. Users can create their profile and maintain their connections on social networking sites. According to Facebook statistics, they have over 1.94 billion monthly and 1.15 billion daily users [1]. As this data becomes increasingly easy to access and collect, many web providers publish this data for the research purpose. Social network analysis is being used in marketing, modern sociology, geography, economics, information

© Springer International Publishing AG 2017
S.S. Ali et al. (Eds.): SPACE 2017, LNCS 10662, pp. 210–225, 2017.
https://doi.org/10.1007/978-3-319-71501-8_12

science and also in various fields [2]. However, publishing original social network data has privacy threat. Adversary may try for documented threats that include identity theft, digital stalking and personalized spam [3]. The publicly available user information can be used to train predictive models which can infer user's private information and also predict user's behaviour. Many works have been proposed for the privacy preserving social network publication [2–4].

1.1 Privacy Preserving Data Publishing

There are three types of users involved to make the data publicly available. Data owners are the users who share information on social networks, service providers are responsible to gather and manage the social network data and third parties who are interested in making use of the data. Although third parties are interested in user's data for marketing, advertisement or collecting and re-selling it, some of them may have malevolent intentions. The combination of multiple datasets and some background information can infer user privacy. The field of research on privacy preserving data publishing studies how to publish data in a way that it maintains user's privacy whose records are being published, while keeping the released dataset rich enough for data-mining purposes.

Most research on data disclosure focuses on protecting individuals from the release of sensitive attributes which could be embarrassing or harmful, if released. The objective of privacy preservation model is to prevent an individual user from being identified by their published data. To prevent identity disclosure, one common approach is to publish social data without disclosing the identity of individual. Due to availability of user information from various sources, adversary can use background knowledge of individual such as degree [5], neighbourhood graph [2], and so on to re-identify the individual. So, simply removing the user identity from published data is not sufficient to maintain user privacy [6,7].

Simple solution to maintain privacy is to make data anonymous. K-anonymity approach was the first carefully studied model for data anonymity [8]; the k-anonymity privacy assurance guarantees that a published record can be identified as one of no fewer than k individuals. The k-anonymity problem has traditionally been researched from the perspective of sensitive data disclosure– a commonly cited domain is that of medical records released for data mining purposes, where it is important to be able to link diseases to demographic data, without revealing that an individual has a particular disease.

1.2 Mutual Friend Attack

Social networking platform helps to search new friends, make new connections and to maintain their connections. Most social networking sites, such as Facebook, Twitter and LinkedIn provide facility to see friend list (connections) and list of mutual friends too. Such information is very useful to search new friends and to verify user identity. One can directly see the list of mutual friends shared with any user on Facebook. Adversary can also get the number of mutual friends of two users by intersecting their friend list.

Here, we present link disclosure prevention approach based on the number of mutual friends (NMF) of two individual users. Figure 1 shows an example of the mutual friend attack. The original social network G is shown in Fig. 1(a). Figure 1(b) represents the published dataset of same social network by replacing the user identities with anonymous character.

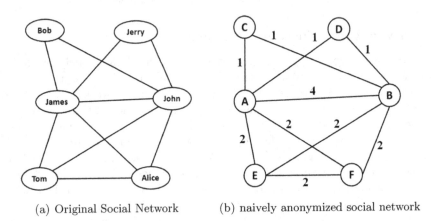

(a) Original Social Network   (b) naively anonymized social network

Fig. 1. Example of published social network

Each link that connects two vertices is assigned with a number that represents the number of mutual friends between the two end vertices. So, in order to commit the mutual friend attack, the adversary only needs to retrieve the number of mutual friends of two victims. Based on this kind of simple background knowledge, an adversary can issue the attack on the published social network to re-identify the edge corresponding to the relationship between two victims. For example, James and John are friends, and they have 4 mutual friends. Adversary can retrieve such information and try it to map these users with vertices of published dataset. Since no other edge than (A, B) contains weight as 4, adversary can uniquely re-identify the edge (A, B) to (James, John) or (John, James). By applying such information step by step, the adversary can uniquely re-identity every users from the published dataset.

1.3   Motivation

Information regarding number of mutual friends between two users are easily available on social networking platforms. So, to protect the privacy of relationship from the mutual friend attack, privacy-preserving model, k-anonymity on the number of mutual friends (k-NMF Anonymity) is introduced [9]. There should be at least k number of edges that have the same number of mutual friends. In mutual friend attack, weight assigned to edge represents the number of common connections. So, in order to change the edge weight, number of common connection should be changed. K-NMF approach proposed in [9] handles one edge at a time. Edge insertion operation that brings favourable change in multiple edges may reduce percentage edge difference in anonymized data.

The rest of the paper is organized as follows: Sect. 2 presents an overview of the existing work related to the problem domain. Section 3 briefly explains the proposed work for k-NMF anonymization. Section 4 considers the experimental evaluation of the proposed work. Various experimental results presented in this section describe the effectiveness of proposed approach. Finally, Sect. 5 states the contributions of this work and demonstrates several possible directions for future research.

2   Background and Related Work

We model a social network $G = (V, E)$ as a simple, undirected graph and it contains no multiple egdes, where V is a set of vertices representing individual users and $E \subseteq V \times V$ is the set of edges representing the relationship between individuals. Each edge is assigned with mutual friend value. Let f be the mutual friend sequence for G, in which entries are in descending order, i.e. $f_1 \geq f_2 \geq f_3 \geq ... \geq f_m$.

2.1   Preliminaries

Definition 1 *(NMF of an edge). It is defined as the number of mutual friends between two users. For a given graph, it is calculated as number of common neighbour vertices between two end vertices. For example, an edge e between v_1 and v_2 vertices, the NMF value of the edge e is the number of common neighbour vertices of v_1 and v_2.*

Definition 2 *(Mutual Friend Sequence). For given social network $G(V, E)$, set of edge is defined as $E = (v_1, v_2)$ where $v_1 \in V$ and $v_2 \in V$. Mutual friend sequence f is a vector that contains NMF value for each edge $e \in E$.*

Definition 3 *(Mutual Friend Attack). Given a social network $G(V, E)$ and published anonymized network $G'(V', E')$, adversary can get the number of mutual friends for edge e as f_e. Mutual friend attack will identify an edge $e' \in E'$ from G' that satisfy $f_{e'} = f_e$.*

Definition 4 *(k-Anonymous Sequence [5]). A sequence vector z is k-anonymous, if for any entry with value as v, there exist at least k-1 other entries with the same value as v.*

If there is only one edge $e' \in E'$ that satisfy the condition for mutual friend attack, adversary can map e' to e with high confidence. Suppose there are k candidate edges for mutual friend attack, the probability to map edge e with candidate edges is no more than $\frac{1}{k}$. Our main goal is to make original graph k-NMF anonymous for given anonymous parameter k. To make graph k-NMF anonymous, mutual friend sequence should be converted into k-NMF anonymous sequence.

2.2 Literature Survey

The major goal of privacy preservation is to hide sensitive information of individual. Privacy attacks re-identify the individual user or relationship between two users by joining published dataset with some external dataset to model the background knowledge of users. A privacy breach occurs when some sensitive information about an individual is disclosed to an adversary. It poses various threats and it also damages the image and reputation of an individual. Therefore, published data should be ensured to provide privacy before it is released to third parties. Privacy breaches in social networks can be categorized into three types [4, 10].

1. Identity disclosure: Identity disclosure occurs when an individual behind a record is exposed. A simple way of defining identity disclosure is to say that an adversary can map victim with query with full certainty.
2. Sensitive link disclosure: It occurs when an adversary is able to find out the existence of a sensitive relationship between two users.
3. Sensitive attribute disclosure: Sensitive attribute disclosure takes place when an adversary is able to determine the true value of a sensitive user attribute.

One of the fundamental issues when releasing social network data is avoiding disclosure of individuals' sensitive information while still permitting certain analysis on the network. A straightforward approach of naive anonymization is not sufficient [6, 7], since background knowledge of individuals' such as degree [5], neighbourhood graph [11], and so on, provides additional information which can be used by adversaries to re-identify the individuals from the published dataset.

Some proposed work [7, 12] consider group of vertices as a single super-vertex or partitions the graph into local substructure and treats each substructure as a single unit to be anonymized. Although these approaches provide better link privacy by hiding connection information between users, it decreases the utility of published dataset. Ying and Wu [13] includes edge addition, edge deletion and edge swap operations for anonymization operation to protect against link disclosure. They focus on the change caused in the eigenvalues (spectrum) of the network. Zheleva and Getoor [10] performs edge deletion and node merging operations to protect sensitive relationship among the individuals. As the anonymized dataset hides so much useful information, it is not impressive for aggregate user query.

Zhou and Pei [11] proposed a method to prevent 1-neighborhood attacks by identifying neighbourhood configuration. Such attacks just focus on connectivity among vertices in the subgraph. But, it does not consider the vertex degree of neighbours. So, it fails to stand against friendship attacks. Zou [14] proposed k-automorphism approach against subgraph attack by inserting many new vertices and edges. Inserted new vertices and edges to protect any arbitrarily large subgraph decrease the utility of social graph. Zhang [15] proposed an approach to reduce the probability of the existence of an edge between two users by edge swap and edge deletion operations. He assumes vertex degree as a vertex description attribute. Although the probability of an edge connecting victim with his/her friend is small, it is possible they can be uniquely re-identified by their friendship information. Tai [16] introduced a friendship attack, in which the adversary uses the degrees of two vertices to re-identify victim. As these works focus on the vertex degree, it cannot achieve the k-NMK anonymity, which focuses on the number of common neighbours of two vertices. Thus, it fails to preserve user privacy against mutual friend attack. K-NMF approach proposed in [9] handles one edge at a time. In our approach, we have made edge insertion operation favourable for multiple edges to have increment in their NMF values that results into less percentage edge difference in anonymized data.

3 Proposed Work

In this section, we aim to anonymize number of mutual friend (NMF) sequence of social graph by edge insertion operation only. First step towards this operation is to organize the entire NMF sequence into different groups. There should be at least k entries in each group to meet k-anonymity requirement. Next step is to anonymize edges to achieve same NMF value in each group. We first anonymize the edges which have high NMF values, and due to that many low NMF values will also be set. We have implemented one common data structure to store NMF values and to keep track of updated NMF values.

3.1 Mutual Friend Sequence Partition

The goal of this step is to have target NMF value for each element of mutual friend sequence of original social network. The entire NMF sequence is organized into different groups. After that, for each group we will convert all element value to some common mutual friend value. As we want to restrict our graph modification operation to edge insertion only, first element in each partition will be considered as target value for that partition.

Here, we consider MF sequence f is sorted in descending order. To have at least k entries in MF sequence to share same values, we will keep at least k elements in each group. After putting first k edges into one group, next step is to check whether next successive element should be merged into current group or to start another group. The decision should be made based on two different partition cost for that element.

Algorithm 1 shows the steps for NMF sequence partition. For given social graph $G(V, E)$, the edge set $<v_1, v_2>$ is given as input to k-anonymization sequence partition algorithm. In each iteration, it calculates two partitions cost and make a decision of optimal partitioning. For given $f_e = \{5, 5, 5, 4, 4, 3, 3, 3, 3, 2, 2, 1, 1\}$, to have 4-NMF anonymous sequence, first 4 elements are placed into first group. Now, at 5th position, two partition cost is calculated. First partition cost named as PC_1 considers the case to merge that element '4' into current partition. To satisfy k-anonymity, next k edges after that element(i.e. $\{3, 3, 3, 3\}$) should be in new group. Second partition cost PC_2 is to start another group from that element only. Hence, PC_1 calculate the cost

Algorithm 1. k-NMF Sequence Partition

MF_Seq = [ ];
for each edge $< v_1, v_2 >$ in edge set **do**
   $count$ = mutual_friend(v_1,v_2)
   insert $count$ in MF_Seq f in descending order
end for
last_partition_index = 0;
for $i=k$ to $No\_of\_edges - k$ **do**
   PC_1 = MF_Seq[last_partition_index] - MF_Seq[i];
   PC_2 = 0;
   for $j=i+1$ to $i+k$ **do**
      PC_1 = PC_1 + MF_Seq[i + 1] - MF_Seq[j];
      PC_2 = PC_2 + MF_Seq[i] - MF_Seq[j − 1];
   end for
   if $PC_2 < PC_1$ **then**
      last_partition_index = i;
      $i = i + k$;
   else
      $i++$;
   end if
end for

to anonymize $k + 1$ edges by merging the current element in old group while PC_2 is cost for k edges by keeping them in new group. So, if PC_2 is less than PC_1, then only the partition will be made and new group will be created. For 5th position (element 4), value of PC_1 is 1 while PC_2 is 3. So, that element is merged into current group only. Following the same procedure for other elements, entire NMF sequence is divided into different partitions. Likewise, for any NMF sequence, we iteratively calculate this partition cost at different positions and follow the same procedure to have optimal partition. For given MF sequence in f_e, we get $\{\{5, 5, 5, 4, 4\}, \{3, 3, 3, 3\}, \{2, 2, 1, 1\}\}$ as the final 4-NMF sequence partition result. At each position, it looks ahead k edges to take a decision to merge the current edge with old group or to start a new group. Hence, the time complexity of Algorithm 1 is $\mathcal{O}(k|E|)$.

3.2 k-NMF Based Edge Anonymization

Here, we consider how to anonymize an edge by edge insertion operation to meet k-NMF anonymity requirement. Entire MF sequence is divided into different groups as a result of k-NMF sequence partition. Let g_f be the target NMF of the group, then to anonymize edge $<u, v>$, the NMF value of edge $<u, v>$ should be increased to g_f. To achieve the target g_f value for each edge, number of mutual friends for that edge should be increased.

As the anonymization operation performs edge insertion operation, it affects NMF of other edges too. For any new inserted edge $<m, n>$, NMF value of all the edges between them and their mutual friends are increased by 1. Therefore, the vertex selection decision for edge insertion operation should be in favor of NMF requirement of affecting edges too. k-NMF based edge anonymization operation contains four steps and each step is briefly described below.

1. **k-NMF requirement set implementation:** To implement k-NMF requirement set, we make an entry for all elements of NMF sequence along with it's target value. Consider, for each element e of group g, g_e is the value of that element (NMF value) and g_t is value of first element (target NMF value) in that group. We implement a common data structure for all elements and make a NMF requirement entry for each element in it. For each non-zero value of $g_t - g_e$, we make an entry of $(g_e, g_t - g_e)$ as a (key, value) pair in k-NMF requirement data structure. For example, for given social network in Fig. 2(a) and for 3-NMF sequence anonymization partition in Fig. 2(b), data structure for the same is shown in Table 1. It contains two fields: key and value. Key referrers to NMF value of edge and value represents the increment for that key to conform k-NMF anonymity.

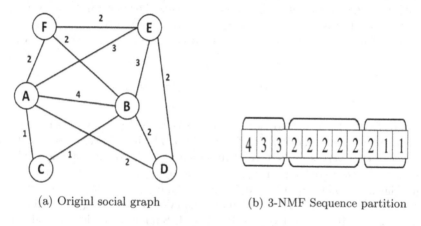

(a) Originl social graph   (b) 3-NMF Sequence partition

Fig. 2. Example of 3-NMF sequence partition

Table 1. 3-NMF Requirement data structure

Key	Values
3	1 , 1
1	1 , 1

2. **Candidate generation:** Here, we select optimal candidate vertices pair to add new edge between them to increment the key by 1. We access the keys from NMF requirement data structure in decreasing order for anonymization operation. Each key basically represents the NMF value of edges for given social network. For a single key, there are many candidate edges. We create

edge set E_S for key y such that, $\forall\ e \in E_S$, NMF$(e) = y$. For given social network in Fig. 2(a) and from k-NMF requirement shown in Fig. 2(b), edge set for key value 3 is defines as $E_S = \{(A, E), (B, E)\}$. Now, next task is to generate candidate vertices for all the edges of edge set. We search the candidate vertices for edge (u, v) in a Breadth First Search (BFS) manner to preserve the graph topological properties. Candidate vertices for edge (u, v) contains all neighbour vertices of end-vertex u and v. Moreover, it should not create a complete triangle. It means it should be neighbour of vertex u or v, not both. For given social graph in Fig. 2(a), for edge set $E_S = \{(A, E), (B, E)\}$, candidate vertex set is defined as $C_S = \{C, C\}$.

3. **Candidate selection:** Once the candidate vertex list is generated for edge set, we can add new edge between one of the vertex of $(u, v) \in E_S$ and $w \in C_S$ to increase the NMF value of edge (u, v) by 1. This new edge insertion operation increases the NMF value of other edges too. Each candidate vertex has its own impact on existing social network dataset in terms of NMF values. So, it is required to select the suitable vertex for this edge insertion operation. k-NMF requirement data structure constructed in previous step is useful to calculate the impact of each candidate vertex. For the candidate vertex w, if new inserted edge is (w, x) where $x = u$ or v and $MF_{(w,x)}$ is the set of mutual friends of vertices w and x, then the impact value, $IV(w, x)$ can be defined as :

$$IV(w, x) = \sum_{n=1}^{|MF_{(w,x)}|} f(MF_n) \tag{1}$$

where $f(MF_n) = 1$, if NMF$(MF_n) \in$ key set of k-NMF anonymization requirement data structure, otherwise $f(MF_n) = 0$. The impact value represents the effect of that vertex on k-NMF requirement. So, the vertex having maximum impact value is selected for edge insertion operation. For given social graph in Fig. 2(a), for $C_S = \{C\}$ and for edge $(A, E) \in E_S$, the impact value of new inserted edge (C, E), is calculated as $IV(C, E) = MF_{(A,E)} + MF_{(A,C)} + MF_{(B,E)} + MF_{(B,C)} = 1 + 1 + 1 + 1 = 4$. Similarly, the impact value of C for edge (B, E) is also 4. So, we can go for any option as both have the same impact value.

4. **Update k-NMF requirement set:** After a new edge is inserted, we need to update the k-NMF requirement data structure. Although, selected candidate is supportive to k-NMF requirement, the change should be reflected in data structure for further edge insertion operation. For all affected edge (w, x), consider $l = MF(w, x)$. If $l \in$ key_set(requirement data structure) then replace the entry (l, value) by $(l + 1, \text{value-1})$. This shows that the value of the key is incremented by 1 in order to reach the target value. The entry will be discarded, if it is reaches to the target value. The same procedure is carried out for each affected edge. For a new inserted edge (x, y), a new entry should be inserted with target value as nearest target NMF value.

Algorithm 2 basically contains four steps of edge modification operation for k-NMF sequence anonymization. The function define_MF_Inc_Set() gathers

Algorithm 2. k-NMF Sequence Anonymization Algorithm

define_MF_Inc_Set();
while MF_Inc_Set != empty **do**
   $key \leftarrow \max(\text{MF\_Key}) \in \text{MF\_Inc\_set}$
   create edge set, $E_S = <v_1, v_2>$ where $\text{MF}(v_1, v_2)=key$
   for each edge $<v_1, v_2> \in E_S$ **do**
     create cand_vertices set C_S
     for each $u \in C_S$ **do**
       select $x \in C_S$ where Impact_Value(x)=MAX;
     end for
   end for
   select edge $<v_1, v_2>$ and x where Impact_Value(x, v)=MAX;
   perform the edge insertion operation
   update MF_Inc_Set
end while
while MF_Inc_Set != empty **do**
   select candidate_vertex z where dist$(v_1, z) >3$ and dist$(v_2, z) >3$
   update MF_Inc_Set
end while

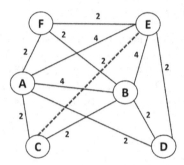

Fig. 3. 3-NMF anonymized social graph

$<key, value>$ requirement for each edge and store it in one data structure as shown in Table 1. Figure 3 shows 3-NMF anonymized social graph for original social graph shown in Fig. 2(a). Algorithm 2 generates a candidate set C_S for edge (u, v) from the neighbours of end vertices. Candidate selection operation create a new triangle by inserting new edge (x, w). So, the shortest path length (SPL) between $x \in (u, v)$ and w will decrease from 2 to 1. Selected candidate vertices from 2-hop neighbours decrease their SPL to 1. If these steps for 1-hop and 2-hop cannot successfully anonymize the highest key value, we select candidate vertices from distance ≥ 3. By the Breadth-First search, the time complexity to get $neig(u)$ and $neig(v)$ is $\mathcal{O}(|V| + |E|)$. Candidate generation operation takes $\mathcal{O}(|V|)$ time. In candidate selection step, it calculates impact value for each candidate vertex. This operation takes $\mathcal{O}(|E||V|)$ time. Therefore, the running time for each candidate set is $\mathcal{O}(|E||V|^2)$. It takes $\mathcal{O}(1)$ time for candidate selection from distance ≥ 3. For E edges, k-NMF requirement set have $\mathcal{O}(|E|)$ entries. So, the total time complexity of proposed algorithm is $\mathcal{O}(|E|^2|V|^2)$.

4   Experimental Results

In this section, we present our experimental study on real dataset to evaluate the performance of the proposed k-NMF sequence anonymization algorithm. We evaluate the utility of anonymized social network graph by computing their graph topological properties. We have also compared effectiveness of k-anonymization approach with existing approaches. The experiments are conducted on an Intel Core, 2 Quad CPU, 3.20 GHz machine with 4GB main memory running Windows 7 OS. We have used *Networkx* package [17] to calculate graph topological properties in python.

4.1   Datasets

We conduct our experiments on two datasets: Facebook and Hamsterster. Both datasets contains undirected graphs without self-loop and multiple edges. These datasets is available at network repository [18].

1. **SOCFB-USFCA72:** This dataset is extracted from Facebook. It represents social friendship network consisting of people (nodes) with edges representing friendship ties. It contains 58,228 nodes and 214,078 edges.
2. **SOC-HAMSTERSTER:** This network also represents friendships and family links(edges) between users(nodes). It contains 2426 nodes and 16,630 edges.

4.2   Evaluation Metrics

Anonymization methods convert original dataset $G = (V, E)$ into anonymized dataset $G' = (V', E')$. In order to check the usefulness of dataset, we evaluate some graph structural properties. Evaluation metrics [5, 11, 16, 19, 20] are listed here:

- **Average Clustering Coefficient (ACC):** It is a measure of the degree to which vertices in a graph tend to cluster together. It is calculated as the average of local clustering coefficient of all the vertices:

$$ACC_{G(V,E)} = \frac{1}{|V|} \sum_{v \in V} C_v \tag{2}$$

Here, local clustering of vertx v_i is calculated as follows:

$$C_i = \frac{2|e_{jk} : v_j, v_k \in N_i, e_{jk} \in E|}{k_j(k_j - 1)} \tag{3}$$

where N_i represents the neighbors of vertex v_i and k_i is the degree of vertex v_i.

- **Average Path Length (APL):** It is defined as the average number of steps along the shortest paths for all possible pairs of network nodes.

$$APL_{G(V,E)} = \frac{1}{|V|(|V|-1)} \sum_{u,v \in V, u \neq v} d(u,v) \tag{4}$$

where $d(u,v)$ is the shortest path length of vertices u and v.
- **Average Betweenness (BW):** It is defined as the average of betweenness centrality of all nodes. It is equal to the number of shortest paths from all vertices to all others that pass through that node. The betweenness centrality of a vertex v is calculated as follows:

$$g(v) = \sum_{s \neq v \neq t} \frac{\sigma_{st}(v)}{\sigma_{st}} \tag{5}$$

where σ_{st} is the number of shortest path from vertex s to vertex t and $\sigma_{st}(v)$ is the total number of those paths that pass through vertex v length of vertices u and v. The normalization of betweenness centrality is calculated as follows:

$$norm(g(v)) = \frac{g(v) - min(g)}{max(g) - min(g)} \tag{6}$$

- **Percentage of Changed Edges (PCE):** It evaluates the number of added edges in the social network. Our anonymization approach considers only edge insertion operations. So, this metric is calculated as follows:

$$PCE_{G,G'} = \frac{|E' - E|}{|E|} \tag{7}$$

where E' and E is the number of edges in anonymized and original social network respectively.

The metrics listed above are widely used to evaluate the performance of privacy preserving algorithms. Also, the utility of anonymized dataset is inspected in different aspects through these metrics. The first three metrics are related to structure of social network. The closer the value of anonymized network to original network, the utility of anonymized dataset is maintained. For PCE metric, smaller values indicate better performance.

4.3 Experimental Evaluation

We use utility metrics listed in Sect. 4.2 as the performance metrics. The effect of anonymization parameter k on different metrics are shown in Fig. 4. For this experiment, we have used extracted dataset from Facebook. Candidate vertex selection for edge insertion is based on BFS traversal. The value of average path length (APL) decreases (Fig. 4(a)) and clustering coefficient (CC) increases (Fig. 4(b)) as the value of k increases. Figure 4(b) shows that there is a negligible

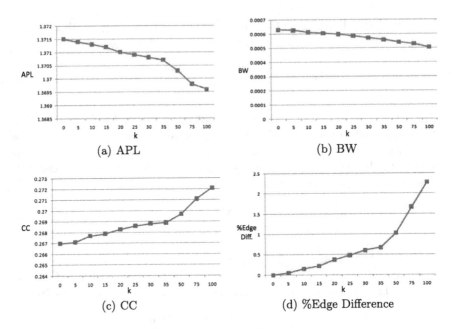

(a) APL

(b) BW

(c) CC

(d) %Edge Difference

Fig. 4. Properties of k-NMF social network

change in betweenness (BW). Its value remains same for any value of k. The more number of edge insertion operations are required with increasing value of anonymization parameter k. Therefore, as shown in Fig. 4(d) percentage edge change in anonymized dataset also increase with increasing value of k. Although the value of k is reached up to 100, the changes in structural properties are not greater than 1%.

4.4   Comparison with Existing Approach

Here, we have compared results of our proposed approach with BFSEA algorithm for Hamsterster dataset. Comparison in terms of all four utility metrics are shown in Fig. 5. As our proposed approach considers the requirement for other edges too, it performs comparatively small number of graph modification operations. That results into less deviation in graph topological properties (Fig. 5(a), (b), (c)). Anonymization approach performs the optimal edge insertion operation that can increment NMF value of other required edges too. So, as depicted in Fig. 5(d), there is a significant improvement in percentage of changed edges for our approach.

BFSEA algorithm takes $\mathcal{O}(|E||V|^2)$ time to execute anonymization algorithm [9]. Our proposed approach calculates impact value for each candidate vertex. Therefore, the time complexity of our proposed anonymization approach is $\mathcal{O}(|E|^2|V|^2)$. Figure 6 shows running time comparison of both approaches for Hamsterster dataset. As time complexity of BFSEA algorithm is lower than our

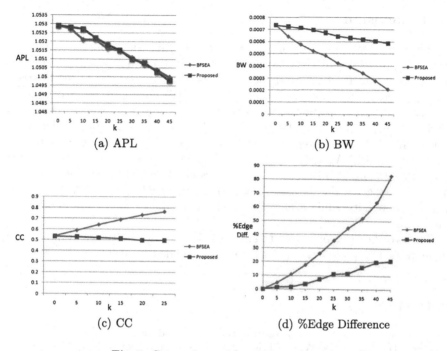

(a) APL

(b) BW

(c) CC

(d) %Edge Difference

Fig. 5. Comparison with existing approach

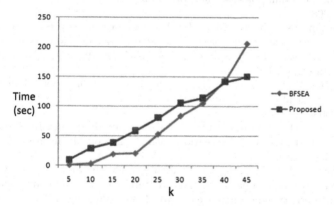

Fig. 6. Running time comparison with BFSEA algorithm

approach, running time is also lesser for BFSEA algorithm. But, the time complexity for both the algorithm contains number of edges in the social network. Figure 5(d) shows that as the value of k increased, there is high increment in percentage of inserted edge for BFSEA algorithm compared to our proposed approach. So, the less number of edges are inserted for our proposed approach, the execution time is lesser for higher values of anonymization parameter k.

5   Conclusion

In this paper, we propose a more efficient anonymization approach that protects the published social network dataset against mutual friend attack. BFS search algorithm used for candidate vertex selection is helpful to retain structural properties in anonymized social dataset. We have implemented separate data structure that highlights requirement for different NMF values. This information is very useful in candidate vertex selection operation. Single edge insertion operation fulfils the requirement for other edges too. So, it results into very small deviation in APL, CC and BW value. The experimental results demonstrate that the number of inserted edge is lesser compared to existing approach. Hence, it preserves the data usefulness of anonymized dataset. We can ensure k-NMF anonymity while preserving much of the data utility in original social dataset.

This work can be extended to ensure k-degree anonymity based on k-NMF anonymity. The proposed approach can be extended for neighbourhood attack also.

References

1. Facebookstatistics: http://nvestor.fb.com/ Accessed on May 2017
2. Zhou, B., Pei, J., Luk, W.S.: A brief survey on anonymization techniques for privacy preserving publishing of social network data. ACM Sigkdd Explor. Newsl. **10**(2), 12–22 (2008)
3. Wu, X., Ying, X., Liu, K., Chen, L.: A survey of privacy-preservation of graphs and social networks. In: Aggarwal, C., Wang, H. (eds.) Managing and Mining Graph Data, pp. 421–453. Springer, Heidelberg (2010). https://doi.org/10.1007/978-1-4419-6045-0_14
4. Liu, K., Das, K., Grandison, T., Kargupta, H.: Privacy-preserving data analysis on graphs and social networks, In: Next Generation Data Mining, pp. 415–431. CRC Press (2008)
5. Liu, K., Terzi, E.: Towards identity anonymization on graphs. In: Proceedings of the 2008 ACM SIGMOD International Conference on Management of Data, pp. 93–106. ACM (2008)
6. Backstrom, L., Dwork, C., Kleinberg, J.: Wherefore art thou r3579x? Anonymized social networks, hidden patterns, and structural steganography. In: Proceedings of the 16th International Conference on World Wide Web, pp. 181–190. ACM (2007)
7. Hay, M., Miklau, G., Jensen, D., Towsley, D., Weis, P.: Resisting structural re-identification in anonymized social networks. Proc. VLDB Endowment **1**(1), 102–114 (2008)
8. Sweeney, L.: K-anonymity: a model for protecting privacy. Int. J. Uncertainty Fuzziness Knowl.-Based Syst. **10**(05), 557–570 (2002)
9. Xindong, W., Zhu, X., Gong-Qing, W., Ding, W.: Privacy preserving social network publication against mutual friend attacks. IEEE Trans. Data Priv. **7**(2), 71–77 (2014)
10. Zheleva, E., Getoor, L.: Preserving the privacy of sensitive relationships in graph data. In: Bonchi, F., Ferrari, E., Malin, B., Saygin, Y. (eds.) PInKDD 2007. LNCS, vol. 4890, pp. 153–171. Springer, Heidelberg (2008). https://doi.org/10.1007/978-3-540-78478-4_9

11. Zhou, B., Pei, J.: Preserving privacy in social networks against neighborhood attacks. In: 2008 IEEE 24th International Conference on Data Engineering, pp. 506–515. IEEE (2008)
12. He, X., Vaidya, J., Shafiq, B., Adam, N., Atluri, V.: Preserving privacy in social networks: a structure-aware approach. In: Web Intelligence and Intelligent Agent Technologies, WI-IAT 2009. IEEE/WIC/ACM International Joint Conferences on, vol. 1, pp. 647–654. IET (2009)
13. Ying, X., Wu, X.: Randomizing social networks: a spectrum preserving approach. In: Proceedings of the 2008 SIAM International Conference on Data Mining, pp. 739–750. SIAM (2008)
14. Zou, L., Chen, L., Tamer Özsu, M.: K-automorphism: a general framework for privacy preserving network publication. Proc. VLDB Endowment 2(1), 946–957 (2009)
15. Zhang, L., Zhang, W.: Edge anonymity in social network graphs. In: International Conference on Computational Science and Engineering CSE 2009, vol. 4, pp. 1–8. IEEE (2009)
16. Tai, C.-H., Yu, P.S., Yang, D.-N., Chen, M.-S.: Privacy-preserving social network publication against friendship attacks. In: Proceedings of the 17th ACM SIGKDD International Conference on Knowledge Discovery and Data Mining, pp. 1262–1270. ACM (2011)
17. Networkx: http://networkx.lanl.gov/ Accessed on Mar 2017
18. Rossi, R.A., Ahmed, N.K.: The network data repository with interactive graph analytics and visualization. In: Proceedings of the Twenty-Ninth AAAI Conference on Artificial Intelligence (2015)
19. Cheng, J., Fu, A.W., Liu, J.: K-isomorphism: privacy preserving network publication against structural attacks. In: Proceedings of the 2010 ACM SIGMOD International Conference on Management of data, pp. 459–470. ACM (2010)
20. Tai, C.-H., Yu, P.S., Yang, D.-N., Chen, M.-S.: Structural diversity for privacy in publishing social networks. In: Proceedings of the 2011 SIAM International Conference on Data Mining, pp. 35–46. SIAM (2011)

Short Integrated PKE+PEKS in Standard Model

Vishal Saraswat[1(✉)] and Rajeev Anand Sahu[2]

[1] R.C. Bose Centre for Cryptology and Security, Indian Statistical Institute,
Kolkata, India
vishal_v@isical.ac.in
[2] Département d'Informatique, Université Libre de Bruxelles, Brussels, Belgium
rajeev.sahu@ulb.ac.be

Abstract. At SeCrypt 2015, Buccafurri et al. [BLSS15] presented an
integrated public-key encryption (PKE) and public-key encryption with
keyword search (PEKS) scheme (PKE+PEKS) whose security relies on
the Symmetric eXternal Diffie-Hellman (SXDH) assumption but they did
not provide a security proof. We present a construction of PKE+PEKS
and prove its security in the standard model under the SXDH assumption. We prove that our scheme is both IND-PKE-CCA secure, that is,
it provides message confidentiality against an adaptive chosen ciphertext adversary, and IND-PEKS-CCA secure, that is, it provides keyword
privacy against an adaptive chosen ciphertext adversary. Ours is the
first secure PKE+PEKS construction to use asymmetric pairings which
enable an extremely fast implementation useful for practical applications.
Our scheme has much shorter ciphertexts than the scheme in [BLSS15]
and all other publicly known PKE+PEKS schemes. Finally, we compare our scheme with other proposed PEKS and integrated PKE+PEKS
schemes and provide a relative analysis of various parameters including
assumption, security and efficiency.

Keywords: PKE+PEKS · Searchable encryption · Asymmetric pairings (type 3) · Provable security · Standard model · SXDH

1 Introduction

The primary goal in cryptography is message-privacy which is usually achieved
by the encryption techniques. In practice, a recipient may wish to filter the
messages that come to her inbox based on the message content, or a user may
wish to download some encrypted files from a server whose content satisfies
certain criterion. In cryptography, this functionality is achieved by searching
on the encrypted data (that is, *searchable encryption*). Boneh et al. [BDOP04]
introduced a method of searching for certain keyword(s) in data encrypted using
public key encryption (PKE) and called it *public key encryption with keyword*

Second author is supported by the Brussels Region INNOVIRIS project SeCloud.

S.S. Ali et al. (Eds.): SPACE 2017, LNCS 10662, pp. 226–246, 2017.
https://doi.org/10.1007/978-3-319-71501-8_13

search (PEKS). Since then, applications of PEKS have been realized in various issues such as the design of spam filter, searchable cloud storage, time released encryption (TRE) etc.

The main advantage of this primitive is that it allows one to delegate to a third party the capability of "searching on public key encrypted data" without impacting privacy. Suppose a bank uses a third party cloud service provider (CSP) to facilitate the banking services to its account holders. To prevent fraudulent transactions, the bank must put some checks on the transactions being conducted and needs constant monitoring of the transaction "contents". For example, for a certain account holder with address in the zipcode 20500 in DC, USA, the bank may put checks as

- if the transaction location zipcode is not 20500 but the state is DC and country is USA, a sms alert must be sent to the account holder informing them of the activity outside home zipcode.
- if the transaction location state is not DC but the country is USA, a sms alert must be sent to the account holder informing them of activity outside home state and a red alert must be sent to the bank, and
- if the transaction country is not USA, the transaction must not be processed further until intervention from the bank.

However, to protect the privacy of the users, the CSP must not be able to get any information about the transactions that any of the account holders conduct. Using a PEKS, the bank can enable the CSP with the ability to test whether the zipcode, state and country values are certain values or not and then act accordingly without learning anything else about the transaction. More generally, the bank can specify a few "keywords" that the CSP can search for, but learn nothing else about the transactions.

The primitive of PEKS basically acts as a "search" function on a PKE scheme but does not retrieve any data by itself. So, in practice, a PEKS scheme is always used together with an underlying PKE scheme and such a combination of these two schemes is called *integrated PKE and PEKS* and is denoted as PKE+PEKS.

The generic approaches that simply combine a PKE scheme and a PEKS scheme (as described in [BDOP04]) work as follows. Let (pk_R, sk_R) be a receiver's (public-key, private-key) pair. A sender encrypts a message-keyword pair (M, W) as $C_M = PKE(M, pk_R) \| C_W = PEKS(W, pk_R)$. The mail server on receiving the ciphertext $C_M \| C_W$ parses C_W and tests it with its trapdoors $t_{W'}$ and if the result is 'TRUE', it forwards C_M to the receiver, who then decrypts it using its private key sk_R. Note that in such a generic approach, the server acts only on the second component C_W and the receiver acts only on the first component C_M.

The basic objective of security in an encryption scheme is *data-privacy*. To achieve this property the standard notions like indistinguishability against-chosen-plaintext attack (IND-CPA) and chosen-ciphertext attack (IND-CCA) have been formalized [GM84,BDPR98,BF01]. The latter one is stronger. For the PKE+PEKS scheme the privacy must be achieved for both, the message (that is, data) and the keyword. Hence, the strongest security notion for a PKE+PEKS scheme corresponds to the idea to achieve CCA-security for both the message and the keyword, that is, IND-PKE-CCA and IND-PEKS-CCA.

Further, we must consider the security of the whole system PKE+PEKS rather than that of each of the components PKE and PEKS independently. As pointed out by Baek et al. [BSS06], Zhang and Imai [ZI07] and Abdalla et al. [ABN10], a PKE+PEKS scheme formed from a CCA secure PKE scheme and a CCA secure PEKS scheme may not remain CCA secure as a whole system. This is shown as follows: an adversary with a target ciphertext $C_M \| C_W$ can produce another valid ciphertext $C_M \| C_{W'}$ where $C_{W'}$ is a valid PEKS of some keyword W' and retrieve the plaintext M and thus breaking the CCA security of the PKE+PEKS scheme. So, a unified security model for the joint CCA-security of PKE+PEKS is desired.

1.1 Related Work

The related work on the subject of this paper is reasonably current and exhaustive in related work section of [BLSS15] and we reproduce almost verbatim from [BLSS15].

Abdalla et al. [ABC+05] have defined computational and statistical relaxations of perfect consistency for a PEKS scheme and showed that the BDOP PEKS scheme [BDOP04] is computationally consistent. They have also proposed a new statistically consistent scheme. Moreover, they have provided a transform of an anonymous identity-based encryption (IBE) scheme to a PEKS scheme that, unlike the BDOP PEKS scheme, gives consistency. Baek et al. [BSS06] have formally defined a combined scheme for PKE and PEKS (denoted as PKE/PEKS) based on the BDOP PEKS scheme and the variation of ElGamal encryption scheme with the randomness reuse technique [Kur02]. Parallel to these works, various other researchers have also studied the design and efficiency of the PEKS schemes including [BW06,FP07,ZI07,BSS08,ABN10]. Crescenzo and Saraswat [DS07] have constructed the first PEKS scheme which was not based on bilinear forms. Various other works [SVEG10,INHJ11,SR14] have studied the application aspects of PEKS.

Boneh et al. [BDOP04] formalized the security precisely for the PEKS scheme with IND-PEKS-CPA notion. Later Baek et al. [BSS08] combined PKE and PEKS with a joint security notion. But as their idea covered only data privacy and not the keyword privacy, the notion lacks completeness. Zhang and Imai [ZI07] first extended the security notion to achieve both data privacy and keyword privacy. The security notion for data privacy is IND-PKE-CCA, which is achieved in their scheme using a tag-based CCA-secure PKE scheme, and for keyword privacy the notion is IND-PEKS-CPA, which they have achieved using a CPA-secure PEKS scheme. Further their scheme achieves non-malleability with respect to the PKE component only and not with respect to the PEKS component. Hence their construction has IND-PKE-CCA security for data privacy but only IND-PEKS-CPA security for keyword privacy. Also, the joint security of their construction is built up on the key separation strategy, that is, using different keys for different cryptographic operations. Hence the construction suffers from double key size, which increases key-maintenance overheads unnecessarily during the practical implementations. However, none of the works [BSS08, ZI07] prove the joint security of a PKE+PEKS scheme in strongest notion, that is, 'IND-PKE+PEKS-CCA security'. One reason for why they are unable to give an IND-PEKS-CCA security for their schemes is that the adversary in their model is not given access to a test oracle [ABN10]. In [ABN10], Abdalla et al. introduced a new combined CCA-security notion on the standard model with a privilege to the adversary to access both, decryption oracle and test oracle. To achieve the CCA security for the PKE+PEKS scheme, they have followed the idea of [DK05], and combined two schemes, a tag-based CCA-secure PKE scheme and a tag-based CCA-secure PEKS scheme, but this idea leads to increase the computational overhead of the resulting PKE+PEKS scheme which is not appreciated at the practical platform. Additionally, their construction also suffers from double key size due to the adoption of key separation strategy. Recently, [CZLZ14] have minimized the key size of their PKE+PEKS scheme using a single key pair for both PKE and PEKS operations. They have defined data privacy and keyword privacy for PKE+PEKS schemes separately and claimed that the PKE+PEKS scheme is said to achieve the joint CCA-security if it attains keyword privacy and data privacy simultaneously.

1.2   Our Contribution

We present a construction of an efficient integrated PKE+PEKS scheme with short ciphertexts and prove its security in the standard model. We prove that our scheme is IND-PKE-CCA secure, that is, provides message confidentiality against an adaptive chosen ciphertext adversary, and also achieves IND-PEKS-CCA security, that is, provides keyword privacy against an adaptive chosen ciphertext adversary, under the SXDH assumption.

Up till now, although there have been lot of research on searchable encryption, the only fully secure schemes [ABN10, CZLZ14, BLSS15] are inefficient to be practical enough to be used in implementation. We propose a state of art efficient, computationally and bandwidth-wise, fully secure practical scheme which, we believe, can be used in real applications.

At SeCrypt 2015, Buccafurri et al. [BLSS15] presented an integrated public-key encryption (PKE) and public-key encryption with keyword search (PEKS) scheme (PKE+PEKS) whose security relies on the SXDH assumption. Their scheme is relatively efficient and our scheme improves upon it. Our scheme has much shorter ciphertexts and uses fewer number of the pairings. Please see Tables 1 and 2 for detailed comparison with [BLSS15] and other PEKS schemes.

Also, in comparison to the scheme in [CZLZ14], our construction has shorter public keys, shorter secret keys, shorter ciphertexts and a much improved efficiency in terms of computation. Further, we provide a unified proof of the overall security of the whole system in a much tighter way. Also, our scheme uses one unified framework for the full PKE+PEKS scheme—the security of the scheme relies on one single hardness assumption and we use the same bilinear pairing map throughout the scheme, instead of using different groups/maps/structures at different stages of the scheme which makes the implementation of our scheme much simpler both on hardware and on software.

We use the method of Paterson et al. [PSST11] of using bit prefix and a one-time signature to enable us to use the same key-pair for our integrated PKE+PEKS scheme and to obtain the joint security for our scheme. To obtain the short size and efficiency, we use the short IBE and IBS schemes of [JR13] which use asymmetric pairings to enable an extremely fast implementation useful for practical applications.

1.3   Outline of the Paper

The rest of this paper is organized as follows. In Sect. 2, we introduce some related mathematical definitions, problems and assumptions. In Sect. 3, we formally define an integrated public key encryption (PKE) and public key encryption with keyword search (PEKS) scheme (PKE+PEKS) and a unified security model for it. Our proposed PKE+PEKS scheme is presented in Sect. 4. In Sect. 5, we analyse the security of our scheme and in Sect. 6, we do an efficiency comparison with the state-of-art. Finally, in Sect. 7, we conclude our work and point a few improvements that can be made while implementing our scheme.

2   Preliminaries

In this section, we introduce some relevant definitions, mathematical problems and assumptions. Note that these definitions are standard and we reproduce these almost verbatim from [BLSS15] to maintain consistency and easier comparison.

2.1   Notations

We denote by $y \leftarrow A(x)$ the operation of running a randomized or deterministic algorithm $A(x)$ and storing the output to the variable y. If X is a set, then $v \xleftarrow{\$} X$ denotes the operation of choosing an element v of X according to the uniform random distribution on X. We say that a given function $f : N \rightarrow [0,1]$ is *negligible in n* if $f(n) < 1/p(n)$ for any polynomial p for sufficiently large n. For a group G and $g \in G$, we write $G = \langle g \rangle$ if g is a generator of G.

2.2   Bilinear Maps

Let G_1, G_2 and G_T be multiplicative cyclic groups of the same prime order q. A map $e : G_1 \times G_2 \rightarrow G_T$ is called a *cryptographic bilinear map* or a *pairing* if it satisfies the following properties:

Bilinearity: For all $(g_1, g_2) \in G_1 \times G_2$ and for all $a, b \in \mathbb{Z}_q$, $e(g_1^a, g_2^b) = e(g_1, g_2)^{ab}$.
Non-Degeneracy: There exists $(g_1, g_2) \in G_1 \times G_2$ such that $e(g_1, g_2) \neq 1$, the identity of G_T.

Computability: There exists an efficient algorithm to compute $e(g_1, g_2) \in G_T$, for all $(g_1, g_2) \in G_1 \times G_2$.

A pairing $e : G_1 \times G_2 \rightarrow G_T$ is called a *symmetric* or a *Type 1* pairing if $G_1 = G_2$ otherwise it is called *asymmetric*. Asymmetric pairings are further categorized into *Type 2* and *Type 3* pairings. If there exists an efficiently computable isomorphism between G_1 and G_2 then the pairing is referred to as Type 2, whereas if there is no efficiently computable isomorphism between G_1 and G_2, then the pairing is referred to as Type 3.

2.3   Symmetric eXternal Diffie-Hellman (SXDH) Assumption

Definition 1. Let G be a multiplicative cyclic group and g be its generator. Let $a, b, c \in \mathbb{Z}_q^\times$ be randomly chosen and kept secret. Given $g, g^a, g^b, g^c \in G$, the *decisional Diffie-Hellman problem* (DDHP) in the group G is to decide if $g^{ab} = g^c$.

Definition 2. The *DDH assumption* holds in a group G if there is no efficient polynomial time algorithm which can solve DDHP in G. Specifically, let $\mathcal{A}$ be a DDH adversary for a group G which takes as input a generator $g \in G$, and three elements $g_1 = g^a$, $g_2 = g^b$, $g_3 = g^c$ of the group G, and outputs 1 if $g_3 = g^{ab}$ and 0 otherwise. Further, let the advantage of $\mathcal{A}$ be defined as

$$\mathbf{Adv}_{\mathcal{A}} = |Pr[\mathcal{A}(g, g^a, g^b, g^{ab}) = 1]| - |Pr[\mathcal{A}(g, g^a, g^b, g^c) = 1]|$$

where $g \xleftarrow{\$} G^\times$, $a \xleftarrow{\$} \mathbb{Z}_q^\times$, $b \xleftarrow{\$} \mathbb{Z}_q^\times$ and $c \xleftarrow{\$} \mathbb{Z}_q^\times$. We say that (t, ε)-*DDH assumption* holds in the group G if any DDH adversary running in time t has an advantage at most ε.

Definition 3. Given two cyclic groups G_1 and G_2, we say the *Symmetric eXternal Diffie-Hellman* (SXDH) assumption holds if the DDH assumption is true in both the groups G_1 and G_2.

3   Integrated PKE and PEKS Scheme (PKE+PEKS)

Here we reproduce almost verbatim from [BLSS15] the formal definition of an integrated public-key encryption (PKE) and public-key encryption with keyword search (PEKS) scheme (PKE+PEKS).

In PEKS, three parties called *sender*, *receiver* and *server* are involved. The sender is a party that creates and sends encrypted keywords, which we call *PEKS ciphertexts*. The receiver is a party that creates trapdoors and sends them to the server to find the data that it wants. The server is a party that receives PEKS ciphertexts and performs search upon receiving trapdoors from the receiver.

3.1   Formal Definition of PKE+PEKS

A PKE+PEKS scheme comprises of six algorithms: *Setup, KeyGen, Encrypt, Decrypt, TokenGen* and *Test*.

Params ← **Setup**(1^k): This is the system initialization algorithm run by the receiver which takes as input a security parameter 1^k and outputs public parameters *Params*. In all the algorithms from here onward, *Params* will be considered as an implicit input.

(pk_X, sk_X) ← **keyGen**(X): This is the key generation algorithm run by a user X which takes input *Params* and outputs a key pair (pk_X, sk_X). For the receiver $X = R$, the key pair is its (public key, private key) pair (pk_R, sk_R) and for a sender $X = S$, the key pair is its (verification key, signing key) pair (vk_S, sk_S).

$\mathcal{U}$ ← **Encrypt**(pk_R, m, w): This is a randomized algorithm run by the sender and takes input *Params*, the receiver's public key pk_R, a message m and a keyword w, and outputs the joint PKE+PEKS ciphertext $\mathcal{U}$.

m ← **Decrypt**$(pk_R, sk_R, \mathcal{U})$: This is a deterministic algorithm run by the receiver and takes input *Params*, the receiver's public key pk_R and the secret key sk_R and a ciphertext $\mathcal{U}$, and outputs a message m or $\bot$.

t_w ← **TokenGen**(pk_R, sk_R, w): This is a randomized algorithm run by the receiver and takes input *Params*, the receiver's public key pk_R and the secret key sk_R and a keyword w, and outputs a token t_w which it gives to the server.

b ← **Test**$(pk_R, t_w, \mathcal{U})$: This is a deterministic algorithm run by the server and takes input *Params*, the receiver's public key pk_R, a token t_w and a ciphertext $\mathcal{U}$, and outputs a bit $b \in \{0, 1\}$ or $\bot$.

From now on, where the context is clear, the inputs *Params* and the keys will be assumed to be implicit and we will not write them explicitly in the algorithms.

3.2   Security Model for PKE+PEKS

Joint data and keyword privacy for PKE+PEKS schemes is defined via the following experiment.

Setup: On input a security parameter 1^k, the challenger $\mathcal{C}$ runs *KeyGen*(1^k) to generate the public parameter *Params* and the system key pair (pk, sk) and gives the adversary $\mathcal{A}$ the public key pk.

Phase 1: $\mathcal{A}$ can adaptively make three types of queries:

  – Decryption query $\langle u \rangle$: $\mathcal{C}$ responds with m ← *Decrypt*(sk, u).
  – Token query $\langle w \rangle$: $\mathcal{C}$ responds with t_w ← *TokenGen*(sk, w).
  – Test query $\langle u, w \rangle$: $\mathcal{C}$ responds with *Test*$(u, t_w$ ← *TokenGen*$(sk, w))$.

Challenge: $\mathcal{A}$ outputs two messages m_0^* and m_1^* and two keywords w_0^* and w_1^*. $\mathcal{C}$ picks a random bit $b \xleftarrow{\$} \{0, 1\}$ and sends u^* ← *Encrypt*(pk, m_b^*, w_b^*) to $\mathcal{A}$ as the challenge ciphertext.

Phase 2: $\mathcal{A}$ can adaptively make more queries as in Phase 1 subject to the restrictions that it is not allowed to make

- Decryption query $\langle u^* \rangle$,
- Token queries $\langle w_0^* \rangle$ and $\langle w_1^* \rangle$, and
- Test queries $\langle u^*, w_0^* \rangle$ and $\langle u^*, w_1^* \rangle$.

$\mathcal{C}$ responds the same way as in Phase 1.

Guess: $\mathcal{A}$ outputs its guess (b^*) for (b).

Definition 4. The adversary succeeds in breaking the data privacy or the keyword privacy if $b^* = b$. We denote this event by $Succ_{\mathcal{A}}$ and define $\mathcal{A}$'s advantage as

$$Adv_{\mathcal{A}}(1^k) \stackrel{\text{def}}{=} |Pr[Succ_{\mathcal{A}}] - 1/2|.$$

We say a PKE+PEKS scheme is IND-PKE+PEKS-CCA secure, that is, the scheme achieves data privacy and keyword privacy simultaneously against an adaptive chosen ciphertext adversary, if $Adv_{\mathcal{A}}(1^k)$ is negligible. A PKE+PEKS scheme is said to be $(t, q_w, q_t, q_d, \varepsilon)$-IND-PKE+PEKS-CCA secure, if for all t-time adversaries making at most q_w token queries, at most q_t test queries, and at most q_d decryption queries have advantage at most ε.

Definition 5 (Data Privacy). We may define a game for just data privacy, if $w_0^* = w_1^*$ and the adversary has no restriction on Token queries and Test queries in the above game. The adversary succeeds in breaking the data privacy if $b^* = b$. We denote this event by $Succ_{\mathcal{A}}^{dp}$ and define $\mathcal{A}$'s advantage as

$$Adv_{\mathcal{A}}^{dp}(1^k) \stackrel{\text{def}}{=} |Pr[Succ_{\mathcal{A}}^{dp}] - 1/2|.$$

A PKE+PEKS scheme is said to have $(t, q_w, q_t, q_d, \varepsilon)$-data privacy if for all t-time adversaries making at most q_w token queries, at most q_t test queries, and at most q_d decryption queries have advantage at most ε against its data privacy. Informally, we say a PKE+PEKS scheme has data privacy if there is no PPT adversary having non-negligible advantage in 1^k in the above experiment.

Definition 6 (Keyword Privacy). We may define a game for just keyword privacy, if $m_0^* = m_1^*$ and the adversary has no restriction on Decryption queries in the above game. The adversary succeeds in breaking the keyword privacy if $b^* = b$. We denote this event by $Succ_{\mathcal{A}}^{kp}$ and define $\mathcal{A}$'s advantage as

$$Adv_{\mathcal{A}}^{kp}(1^k) \stackrel{\text{def}}{=} |Pr[Succ_{\mathcal{A}}^{kp}] - 1/2|.$$

A PKE+PEKS scheme is said to have $(t, q_w, q_t, q_d, \varepsilon)$-keyword privacy if for all t-time adversaries making at most q_w token queries, at most q_t test queries, and at most q_d decryption queries have advantage at most ε against its keyword privacy. Informally, we say a PKE+PEKS scheme has keyword privacy if there is no PPT adversary having non-negligible advantage in 1^k in the above experiment.

Remark 1. Note that our joint CCA-security notion for PKE+PEKS embodies both IND-PKE-CCA security and IND-PEKS-CCA security in the joint sense and is relatively unified and standard than previous ones considered in [CZLZ14, BLSS15].

4   Proposed Scheme

We present here our efficient and CCA secure integrated PKE+PEKS scheme. As described in Sect. 3, our scheme consists of the following algorithms: *Setup*, *KeyGen*, *Encrypt*, *Decrypt*, *TokenGen* and *Test*.

Setup: A receiver R wishing to receive joint PKE+PEKS messages uses a group generation algorithm for which the SXDH assumption holds to generate the public parameters of the system:

$$G := (q, G_1, G_2, G_T, e)$$

where G_1, G_2, and G_T are cyclic groups of prime order q and

$$e : G_1 \times G_2 \to G_T$$

is a Type 3 pairing. The receiver R then chooses two cryptographic collision resistant hash functions

$$H : \{0,1\}^* \to \mathbb{Z}_q^\times \quad \text{and} \quad J : \{0,1\}^* \to G_T.$$

Finally, R publishes the public parameters of the system as

$$Params = (G, H, J).$$

(These may be considered as part R's public key, but for sake of clarity we keep these separate.)

KeyGen: To generate the keys for the system, the receiver does the following:

- samples two random generators $g_1 \xleftarrow{\$} G_1^\times$ and $g_2 \xleftarrow{\$} G_2^\times$;
- samples $b, c, d, e, u, l, m, n, p \xleftarrow{\$} \mathbb{Z}_q^\times$;
- computes
    - $f_1 = g_1^b$,
    - $f_2 = g_2^c$,
    - $v_1 = g_1^{d-bl}$,
    - $v_2 = g_1^{e-bm}$,
    - $v_3 = g_1^{c-bn}$, and
    - $k = e(g_1, g_2)^{u-bp}$;
- sets the public key $pk_R = (g_1, f_1, v_1, v_2, v_3, k)$; and
- sets the master secret $sk_R = (g_2, f_2, l, m, n, p, d, e, u)$.

Encrypt: To encrypt a message $M \in G_T$ with a keyword $w \in \{0,1\}^*$ for the receiver R, a sender S does the following:

- samples two random generators $\tilde{g}_1 \xleftarrow{\$} G_1^\times$ and $\tilde{g}_2 \xleftarrow{\$} G_2^\times$;
- samples $\tilde{b}, \tilde{c}, \tilde{d}, \tilde{e}, \tilde{u}, \tilde{l}, \tilde{m}, \tilde{n}, \tilde{p} \xleftarrow{\$} \mathbb{Z}_q^\times$;
- computes
    - $\tilde{f}_1 = \tilde{g}_1^{\tilde{b}}$,
    - $\tilde{f}_2 = \tilde{g}_2^{\tilde{c}}$,

- $\tilde{v}_1 = \tilde{g}_1^{\tilde{d} - \tilde{b}\tilde{l}}$,
- $\tilde{v}_2 = \tilde{g}_1^{\tilde{e} - \tilde{b}\tilde{m}}$,
- $\tilde{v}_3 = \tilde{g}_1^{\tilde{c} - \tilde{b}\tilde{n}}$, and
- $\tilde{k} = e(\tilde{g}_1, \tilde{g}_2)^{\tilde{u} - \tilde{b}\tilde{p}}$;

- sets the verification key $vk_S = (\tilde{g}_1, \tilde{f}_1, \tilde{v}_1, \tilde{v}_2, \tilde{v}_3, \tilde{k})$; and
- sets the signing key $sk_S = (\tilde{g}_2, \tilde{f}_2, \tilde{l}, \tilde{m}, \tilde{n}, \tilde{p}, \tilde{d}, \tilde{e}, \tilde{u})$;
- sets $\text{V} = J(vk_S)$

- picks $x, y, z, \text{TAG}_\text{M}, \text{TAG}_\text{W} \xleftarrow{\$} \mathbb{Z}_q$;
- computes
  - $i_\text{V} = H(0\|\text{V})$ and $i_\text{W} = H(1\|\text{W})$;
  - $C_{\text{M}0} = \text{M} \cdot k^x$, $C_{\text{M}1} = g_1^x$, $C_{\text{M}2} = f_1^x$, and $C_{\text{M}3} = v_1^x v_2^{x i_\text{V}} v_3^{x \text{TAG}_\text{M}}$;
  - $C_{\text{W}0} = \text{V} \cdot k^y$, $C_{\text{W}1} = g_1^y$, $C_{\text{W}2} = f_1^y$, and $C_{\text{W}3} = v_1^y v_2^{y i_\text{W}} v_3^{y \text{TAG}_\text{W}}$;
  - $h = H(C_\text{M} \| C_\text{W})$;
  - $R_\sigma = \tilde{g}_2^z$, $S_\sigma = \tilde{f}_2^z$, $T_\sigma = \tilde{g}_2^{\tilde{u} + z(\tilde{d} + h\tilde{e})}$, $W_{\sigma 1} = \tilde{g}_2^{-\tilde{p} - z(\tilde{l} + h\tilde{m})}$, and $W_{\sigma 2} = \tilde{g}_2^{-z\tilde{n}}$;
- sets
  - $C_\text{M} = (C_{\text{M}0}, C_{\text{M}1}, C_{\text{M}2}, C_{\text{M}3}, \text{TAG}_\text{M})$;
  - $C_\text{W} = (C_{\text{W}0}, C_{\text{W}1}, C_{\text{W}2}, C_{\text{W}3}, \text{TAG}_\text{W})$;
  - $\sigma = (R_\sigma, S_\sigma, T_\sigma, W_{\sigma 1}, W_{\sigma 2})$;
- and finally declares the ciphertext $\mathcal{U} = (vk_S, C_\text{M}, C_\text{W}, \sigma)$.

Decrypt: To decrypt the ciphertext $\mathcal{U} = (u_1, u_2, u_3, u_4)$, the receiver does the following:

- obtains $\tilde{g}_1, \tilde{f}_1, \tilde{v}_1, \tilde{v}_2, \tilde{v}_3, \tilde{k}$ from u_1;
- obtains $R_\sigma, S_\sigma, T_\sigma, W_{\sigma 1}, W_{\sigma 2}$ from u_4;
- computes $h = H(u_2 \| u_3)$;
- chooses $\tilde{\text{M}} \xleftarrow{\$} G_T, \tilde{s} \xleftarrow{\$} \mathbb{Z}_q^\times, \text{TAG}_{\tilde{\text{M}}} \xleftarrow{\$} \mathbb{Z}_q^\times$;
- computes
  - $C_{\tilde{\text{M}}0} := \tilde{\text{M}} \cdot \tilde{k}^{\tilde{s}}$,
  - $C_{\tilde{\text{M}}1} := \tilde{g}_1^{\tilde{s}}$,
  - $C_{\tilde{\text{M}}2} := \tilde{f}_1^{\tilde{s}}$,
  - $C_{\tilde{\text{M}}3} := \tilde{v}_1^{\tilde{s}} \tilde{v}_2^{h\tilde{s}} \tilde{v}_3^{\tilde{s} \text{TAG}_{\tilde{\text{M}}}}$;
- checks whether the PKE+PEKS ciphertext $\mathcal{U}$ is *valid*. That is, whether

$$\tilde{\text{M}} = \frac{C_{\tilde{\text{M}}0} e(C_{\tilde{\text{M}}3}, R_\sigma)}{e(C_{\tilde{\text{M}}1}, S_\sigma^{\text{TAG}_{\tilde{\text{M}}}} T_\sigma) e(C_{\tilde{\text{M}}2}, W_{\sigma 1} W_{\sigma 2}^{\text{TAG}_{\tilde{\text{M}}}})}. \tag{1}$$

- If the above equality does not hold then outputs $\bot$.
- Otherwise it obtains $C_{\text{M}0}, C_{\text{M}1}, C_{\text{M}2}, C_{\text{M}3}, \text{TAG}_\text{M}$ from u_2;
- computes $\text{V} = J(u_1)$;
- sets $i_\text{V} = H(0\|\text{V})$;
- computes a corresponding decryption key

$$SK_{i_\text{V}} = (R_\text{V}, S_\text{V}, T_\text{V}, W_{\text{V}1}, W_{\text{V}2});$$

where

- $r \xleftarrow{\$} \mathbb{Z}_q^\times$,
- $R_{\mathrm{v}} = g_2^r$,
- $S_{\mathrm{v}} = f_2^r$,
- $T_{\mathrm{v}} = g_2^{u+r(d+i_{\mathrm{v}}e)}$,
- $W_{\mathrm{v}1} = g_2^{-p-r(l+i_{\mathrm{v}}m)}$, and
- $W_{\mathrm{v}2} = g_2^{-rn}$;

• finally, it outputs

$$\mathrm{M} \leftarrow \frac{C_{\mathrm{M}0}\,e(C_{\mathrm{M}3}, R_{\mathrm{v}})}{e(C_{\mathrm{M}1}, S_{\mathrm{v}}^{\mathrm{TAG_M}} T_{\mathrm{v}})\,e(C_{\mathrm{M}2}, W_{\mathrm{v}1} W_{\mathrm{v}2}^{\mathrm{TAG_M}})}. \tag{2}$$

Tokengen: To generate a token t_{w} for the keyword w to give to the server, the receiver chooses $r \xleftarrow{\$} \mathbb{Z}_q^\times$, computes

• $i_{\mathrm{w}} = H(1\|\mathrm{w})$,
• $R_{\mathrm{w}} = g_2^r$,
• $S_{\mathrm{w}} = f_2^r$,
• $T_{\mathrm{w}} = g_2^{u+r(d+i_{\mathrm{w}}e)}$,
• $W_{\mathrm{w}1} = g_2^{-p-r(l+i_{\mathrm{w}}m)}$, and
• $W_{\mathrm{w}2} = g_2^{-rn}$,

and outputs the token:

$$t_{\mathrm{w}} = (R_{\mathrm{w}}, S_{\mathrm{w}}, T_{\mathrm{w}}, W_{\mathrm{w}1}, W_{\mathrm{w}2}). \tag{3}$$

Test: To test whether the ciphertext $\mathcal{U} = (u_1, u_2, u_3, u_4)$ includes the keyword w or not using the token t_{w}, the server does the following:

• obtains $\tilde{g}_1, \tilde{f}_1, \tilde{v}_1, \tilde{v}_2, \tilde{v}_3, \tilde{k}$ from u_1;
• obtains $R_\sigma, S_\sigma, T_\sigma, W_{\sigma 1}, W_{\sigma 2}$ from u_4;
• computes $h = H(u_2 \| u_3)$;
• chooses $\tilde{\mathrm{M}} \xleftarrow{\$} G_T, \tilde{s} \xleftarrow{\$} \mathbb{Z}_q^\times, \mathrm{TAG}_{\tilde{\mathrm{M}}} \xleftarrow{\$} \mathbb{Z}_q^\times$;
• computes
  - $C_{\tilde{\mathrm{M}}0} := \tilde{\mathrm{M}} \cdot \tilde{k}^{\tilde{s}}$,
  - $C_{\tilde{\mathrm{M}}1} := \tilde{g}_1^{\tilde{s}}$,
  - $C_{\tilde{\mathrm{M}}2} := \tilde{f}_1^{\tilde{s}}$,
  - $C_{\tilde{\mathrm{M}}3} := \tilde{v}_1^{\tilde{s}} \tilde{v}_2^{h\tilde{s}} \tilde{v}_3^{\tilde{s}\mathrm{TAG}_{\tilde{\mathrm{M}}}}$;
• checks whether the PKE+PEKS ciphertext $\mathcal{U}$ is *valid*. That is, whether

$$\tilde{\mathrm{M}} = \frac{C_{\tilde{\mathrm{M}}0}\,e(C_{\tilde{\mathrm{M}}3}, R_\sigma)}{e(C_{\tilde{\mathrm{M}}1}, S_\sigma^{\mathrm{TAG}_{\tilde{\mathrm{M}}}} T_\sigma)\,e(C_{\tilde{\mathrm{M}}2}, W_{\sigma 1} W_{\sigma 2}^{\mathrm{TAG}_{\tilde{\mathrm{M}}}})}. \tag{4}$$

• If the above equality does not hold then outputs 0.
• Otherwise it obtains $C_{\mathrm{w}0}, C_{\mathrm{w}1}, C_{\mathrm{w}2}, C_{\mathrm{w}3}, \mathrm{TAG}_{\mathrm{w}}$ from u_3 and checks if

$$J(u_1) = \frac{C_{\mathrm{w}0}\,e(C_{\mathrm{w}3}, R_{\mathrm{w}})}{e(C_{\mathrm{w}1}, S_{\mathrm{w}}^{\mathrm{TAG_w}} T_{\mathrm{w}})\,e(C_{\mathrm{w}2}, W_{\mathrm{w}1} W_{\mathrm{w}2}^{\mathrm{TAG_w}})}. \tag{5}$$

• If yes then outputs 1, else outputs 0.

Remark 2. Note that to maintain a "uniformity" we have used the Naor transform of the IBE of [JR13] as a signature. We could have used the signature scheme of [JR13] for a little more efficiency of our proposed PKE+PEKS. Again, to maintain "uniformity" and comparability with the previous schemes, in the *Decrypt* and *Test* algorithms, we have done a generic Naor transform verification of the ciphertext validity; we can improve the efficiency by making it more direct. Finally, in the *Decrypt* algorithm, the receiver can use its secret key sk_R to directly decrypt the ciphertext instead of generating the "secret key" corresponding to i_V to increase efficiency.

4.1   Correctness of the Proposed Scheme

Theorem 1. *The proposed scheme is correct.*

Proof. With the terms in the expressions below defined as in the algorithms *Setup, KeyGen, Encrypt, Decrypt, TokenGen,* and *Test* defined in the proposed scheme in Sect. 4, we note that for a correctly generated ciphertext $\mathcal{U} = (u_1, u_2, u_3, u_4)$,

- $u_1 = vk_S = (\tilde{g}_1, \tilde{f}_1, \tilde{v}_1, \tilde{v}_2, \tilde{v}_3, \tilde{k})$;
- $u_2 = C_M = (C_{M0} := M \cdot k^x, C_{M1} := g_1^x, C_{M2} := f_1^x, C_{M3} := v_1^x v_2^{x i_V} v_3^{x \mathrm{TAG_M}}, \mathrm{TAG_M})$;
- $u_3 = C_W = (C_{W0} := V \cdot k^y, C_{W1} := g_1^y, C_{W2} := f_1^y, C_{W3} := v_1^y v_2^{y i_W} v_3^{y \mathrm{TAG_W}}, \mathrm{TAG_W})$;
  and
- $u_4 = \sigma = (R_\sigma = \tilde{g}_2^z, S_\sigma = \tilde{f}_2^z, T_\sigma = \tilde{g}_2^{\tilde{u} + z(\tilde{d} + h\tilde{e})}, W_{\sigma 1} = \tilde{g}_2^{-\tilde{p} - z(\tilde{l} + h\tilde{m})}, W_{\sigma 2} = \tilde{g}_2^{-z\tilde{n}})$.

Thus, the three pairings in the Eq. (2) can be simplified as follows.

$$
\begin{aligned}
e(C_{M3}, R_V) &= e(v_1^x v_2^{x i_V} v_3^{x \mathrm{TAG_M}}, g_2^r) \\
&= e((g_1^{d-bl})^x (g_1^{e-bm})^{x i_V} (g_1^{c-bn})^{x \mathrm{TAG_M}}, g_2^r) \\
&= e(g_1^{(d-bl+ei_V-bmi_V+c\mathrm{TAG_M}-bn\mathrm{TAG_M})x}, g_2^r) \\
&= e(g_1, g_2)^{(d-bl+ei_V-bmi_V+c\mathrm{TAG_M}-bn\mathrm{TAG_M})xr};
\end{aligned} \tag{6}
$$

$$
\begin{aligned}
e(C_{M1}, S_V^{\mathrm{TAG_M}} T_V) &= e(g_1^x, (f_2^r)^{\mathrm{TAG_M}} g_2^{u+r(d+i_V e)}) \\
&= e(g_1^x, (g_2^c)^{r\mathrm{TAG_M}} g_2^{u+r(d+i_V e)}) \\
&= e(g_1^x, g_2^{cr\mathrm{TAG_M}+u+r(d+i_V e)}) \\
&= e(g_1, g_2)^{ux+(c\mathrm{TAG_M}+d+i_V e)xr};
\end{aligned} \tag{7}
$$

$$
\begin{aligned}
e(C_{M2}, W_{V1} W_{V2}^{\mathrm{TAG_M}}) &= e(f_1^x, g_2^{-p-r(l+i_V m)} (g_2^{-rn})^{\mathrm{TAG_M}}) \\
&= e((g_1^b)^x, g_2^{-p-r(l+i_V m)-rn\mathrm{TAG_M}}) \\
&= e((g_1, g_2)^{-bxp-bxr(l+i_V m+n\mathrm{TAG_M})};
\end{aligned} \tag{8}
$$

Hence, the decryption Eq. (2) is correct since

$$\frac{C_{\text{M0}}e(C_{\text{M3}}, R_{\text{V}})}{e(C_{\text{M1}}, S_{\text{V}}^{\text{TAG}_{\text{M}}}T_{\text{V}})e(C_{\text{M2}}, W_{\text{V1}}W_{\text{V2}}^{\text{TAG}_{\text{M}}})}$$

$$= \frac{(\text{M} \cdot k^x)(e(g_1, g_2)^{(d-bl+ei_{\text{V}}-bmi_{\text{V}}+c\text{TAG}_{\text{M}}-bn\text{TAG}_{\text{M}})xr})}{(e(g_1, g_2)^{ux+(c\text{TAG}_{\text{M}}+d+i_{\text{V}}e)xr})(e((g_1, g_2)^{-bxp-bxr(l+i_{\text{V}}m-n\text{TAG}_{\text{M}})}))}$$

$$\text{(from Equations (6), (7) and (8))}$$

$$= (\text{M} \cdot k^x)e(g_1, g_2)^{-x(u-bp)}$$

$$= (\text{M} \cdot k^x)k^{-x}$$

$$= \text{M}. \tag{9}$$

Since the terms in the Eqs. (1), (4) and (5) are generated similarly to those in the Eq. (2), the correctness of the *Test* follows similarly as that of *Decrypt*. Hence the proposed scheme is correct.

5   Security Proof

In this section, we analyse the security of our scheme. We prove that the presented scheme is secure under the SXDH assumption.

We follow the security proof of the IBE in [JR13] using the simulation technique of [Wat09] of using a sequence of games and adopting *semi-functional keys* and *semi-functional ciphertexts*. For the notion of construction of these *semi-functional*-values, [CLL+12, JR13] can be referred. The advantage of an adversary in winning the IND-PKE+PEKS-CCA game is then shown to be bounded in terms of its advantage in distinguishing between successive games.

Remark 3. For the sake of brevity and page limitation, the parts of the proof which are already available in literature, has been cited and presented here only briefly.

Theorem 2. *If the DDH assumption holds in both the groups G_1 and G_2 then there is no IND-PKE+PEKS-CCA adversary $\mathcal{A}$ for the presented integrated PKE+PEKS scheme.*

Proof: Let $\mathcal{A}$ be a t-time IND-PKE+PEKS-CCA adversary making at most q_w token queries, at most q_t test queries and at most q_d decryption queries, and with advantage ε.

Let (m_0^*, w_0^*) and (m_1^*, w_1^*) be the target message-keyword output by $\mathcal{A}$ at the end of Phase 1. Let $b \xleftarrow{\$} \{0, 1\}$, $\bar{b} = 1 - b$ and $u^* = (u_1^*, u_2^*, u_3^*, u_4^*) \leftarrow Encrypt(pk, m_b^*, w_b^*)$ be the challenge ciphertext. Let b^* be the guess output by $\mathcal{A}$ at the end of Phase 2.

We prove that if the challenger $\mathcal{C}$ chooses a random message $\tilde{m} \xleftarrow{\$} G_T$ and a random keyword $\tilde{w} \xleftarrow{\$} \{0, 1\}^*$ and gives $\tilde{u}^* = (\tilde{u}_1^*, \tilde{u}_2^*, \tilde{u}_3^*, \tilde{u}_4^*) \leftarrow$

$Encrypt(pk, \tilde{m}, \tilde{w})$ instead of $u^* = (u_1^*, u_2^*, u_3^*, u_4^*)$ to the adversary $\mathcal{A}$ as the challenge ciphertext, the view of the adversary will remain computationally indistinguishable (in view of the SXDH assumption on G) and $\mathcal{A}$ will not be any wiser and will keep playing the game without aborting.

Since $\tilde{u}^*$ is completely random and independent of the target message-keyword pairs (m_0^*, w_0^*) and (m_1^*, w_1^*) in the view of the adversary $\mathcal{A}$, the guess output b^* by $\mathcal{A}$ at the end of Phase 2 must also be completely random.

Hence the advantage $\mathbf{Adv}_{\mathcal{A}}$ of $\mathcal{A}$ in winning the IND-PKE+PEKS-CCA game is then bounded in terms of its advantage in distinguishing between successive games and hence must be negligible and the scheme must be IND-PKE+PEKS-CCA secure.

We achieve this through a sequence of games where each successive game differs from the preceding game in such a way that the two games are either statistically indistinguishable or computationally indistinguishable in view of the SXDH assumption on G defined as follows:

Game $\mathcal{G}_0$: This is the actual IND-PKE+PEKS-CCA security game as defined in Section 3.

Game $\mathcal{G}_1$: This game is similar to the previous game in all aspects except that instead of actual ciphertexts, the challenger outputs *partial semifunctional ciphertexts* as follows:

- Let $\mathcal{U} = (u_1, u_2, u_3, u_4)$ be the actual ciphertext with

$$u_2 = C_M = (C_{M0} := M \cdot k^x, C_{M1} := g_1^x, C_{M2} := f_1^x,$$
$$C_{M3} := v_1^x v_2^{xi_v} v_3^{xTAG_M}, TAG_M) \quad \text{and}$$
$$u_3 = C_W = (C_{W0} := V \cdot k^y, C_{W1} := g_1^y, C_{W2} := f_1^y,$$
$$C_{W3} := v_1^y v_2^{yi_w} v_3^{yTAG_W}, TAG_W).$$

- The challenger picks $x', y' \xleftarrow{\$} \mathbb{Z}_q$ and sets the corresponding *partial semifunctional* components as:

$$u_2' = C_M' = (C_{M0}' := C_{M0} \cdot e(g_1, g_2)^{ux'}, C_{M1}' := C_{M1} \cdot g_1^{x'}, C_{M2}' := C_{M2},$$
$$C_{M3}' := C_{M3} \cdot g_1^{(d+ei_v+cTAG_M)x'}, TAG_M)$$
$$= (C_{M0}' := M \cdot k^x \cdot e(g_1, g_2)^{ux'}, C_{M1}' := g_1^x \cdot g_1^{x'}, C_{M2}' := f_1^x,$$
$$C_{M3}' := v_1^x v_2^{xi_v} v_3^{xTAG_M} \cdot g_1^{(d+ei_v+cTAG_M)x'}, TAG_M)$$

and

$$u_3' = C_W' = (C_{W0}' := C_{W0} \cdot e(g_1, g_2)^{uy'}, C_{W1}' := C_{W1} \cdot g_1^{y'}, C_{W2}' := C_{W2},$$
$$C_{W3}' := C_{W3} \cdot g_1^{(d+ei_v+cTAG_W)y'}, TAG_W)$$
$$= (C_{W0}' := V \cdot k^y \cdot e(g_1, g_2)^{uy'}, C_{W1}' := g_1^y \cdot g_1^{y'}, C_{W2}' := f_1^y,$$
$$C_{W3}' := v_1^y v_2^{yi_w} v_3^{yTAG_W} \cdot g_1^{(d+ei_v+cTAG_M)y'}, TAG_W).$$

– Finally, the challenger outputs the (partial semifunctional) ciphertext

$$\mathcal{U}' = (u_1, u_2', u_3', u_4)$$

as the ciphertext.

In view of the DDH assumption in the group G_1, the two pairs of tuples

$$(\langle g_1, g_1^b, g_1^{xb}, g_1^x \rangle, \langle g_1, g_1^b, g_1^{xb}, g_1^{x+x'} \rangle)$$

and

$$(\langle g_1, g_1^b, g_1^{yb}, g_1^y \rangle, \langle g_1, g_1^b, g_1^{yb}, g_1^{y+y'} \rangle)$$

are indistinguishable to the adversary. Hence from the view of the adversary $\mathcal{A}$, the games $\mathcal{G}_0$ and $\mathcal{G}_1$ are computationally indistinguishable.

We note here that the advantage gap between two consecutive games can be proved by the reduction to the DDH assumption following the same proofs given in [CLL+12, JR13]. From here onwards wherever we need to show this reduction we mention it as 'indistinguishable from the view of adversary'.

Game $\mathcal{G}_2$: This game is similar to the previous game in all aspects except that instead of partial semifunctional ciphertexts, the challenger outputs *semifunctional ciphertexts* as follows:

– Let $\mathcal{U} = (u_1, u_2', u_3', u_4)$ be the partial semifunctional ciphertext with

$$u_1 = vk_S = (\tilde{g}_1, \tilde{f}_1 = \tilde{g}_1^{\tilde{b}}, \tilde{v}_1 = \tilde{g}_1^{\tilde{d}-\tilde{b}\tilde{l}}, \tilde{v}_2 = \tilde{g}_1^{\tilde{e}-\tilde{b}\tilde{m}}, \tilde{v}_3 = \tilde{g}_1^{\tilde{c}-\tilde{b}\tilde{n}},$$
$$\tilde{k} = e(\tilde{g}_1, \tilde{g}_2)^{\tilde{u}-\tilde{b}\tilde{p}} \quad \text{and}$$
$$u_4 = \sigma = (R_\sigma = \tilde{g}_2^z, S_\sigma = \tilde{f}_2^z, T_\sigma = \tilde{g}_2^{\tilde{u}+z(\tilde{d}+h\tilde{e})},$$
$$W_{\sigma 1} = \tilde{g}_2^{-\tilde{p}-z(\tilde{l}+h\tilde{m})}, W_{\sigma 2} = \tilde{g}_2^{-z\tilde{n}}).$$

– The challenger sets the corresponding *semifunctional* components as:

$$u_1' = vk_S' = (\tilde{g}_1, \tilde{f}_1 = \tilde{g}_1^{\tilde{b}}, \tilde{v}_1 = \tilde{g}_1^{-\tilde{l}}, \tilde{v}_2 = \tilde{g}_1^{-\tilde{m}}, \tilde{v}_3 = \tilde{g}_1^{-\tilde{n}},$$
$$\tilde{k} = e(\tilde{g}_1, \tilde{g}_2)^{-\tilde{p}}; \quad \text{and}$$
$$u_4' = \sigma' = (R_\sigma = \tilde{g}_2^z, S_\sigma = \tilde{f}_2^z, T_\sigma = \tilde{g}_2^{\tilde{u}+z(\tilde{d}+h\tilde{e})},$$
$$W_{\sigma 1} = \tilde{g}_2^{-\tilde{p}-\tilde{u}-z(\tilde{l}+\tilde{d}+h(\tilde{m}+\tilde{e}))/\tilde{b}}, W_{\sigma 2} = \tilde{g}_2^{-z(\tilde{n}+\tilde{c})/\tilde{b}}).$$

– Finally, the challenger outputs the (semifunctional) ciphertext

$$\mathcal{U}' = (u_1, u_2', u_3', u_4)$$

as the ciphertext.

Since $\tilde{l}, \tilde{m}, \tilde{n}, \tilde{p} \xleftarrow{\$} \mathbb{Z}_q^\times$, from the view of the adversary $\mathcal{A}$, the games $\mathcal{G}_1$ and $\mathcal{G}_2$ are statistically indistinguishable.

Game $\mathcal{G}_3$: This game is similar to the previous game in all aspects except that instead of actual tokens, the challenger outputs *partial semifunctional keys/tokens* as follows:

– Given a keyword w and the corresponding identity $i_w = H(1\|w)$, let the corresponding public key and token be:

$$pk_w = (g_1, f_1 = g_1^b, v_1 = g_1^{d-bl}, v_2 = g_1^{e-bm}, v_3 = g_1^{c-bn},$$
$$k = e(g_1, g_2)^{u-bp} \text{ and}$$
$$t_w = (R_w = g_2^z, S_w = f_2^z, T_w = g_2^{u+z(d+he)},$$
$$W_{w1} = g_2^{-p-z(l+hm)}, W_{w2} = g_2^{-zn}).$$

– The challenger sets the corresponding *partial semifunctional keys* as:

$$pk_w' = (g_1, f_1 = g_1^b, v_1 = g_1^{-l}, v_2 = g_1^{-m}, v_3 = g_1^{-n},$$
$$k = e(g_1, g_2)^{-p} \text{ and}$$
$$t_w' = (R_w = g_2^z, S_w = f_2^z, T_w = g_2^{u+z(d+he)},$$
$$W_{w1} = g_2^{-p-u-z(l+d+h(m+e))/b}, W_{w2} = g_2^{-z(n+c)/b}).$$

Since $l, m, n, p \xleftarrow{\$} \mathbb{Z}_q^\times$, from the view of the adversary $\mathcal{A}$, the games $\mathcal{G}_2$ and $\mathcal{G}_3$ are statistically indistinguishable.

Game $\mathcal{G}_4$: This is a sequence of several hybrid games, used to generate tokens on various keywords. For $j = 0$, we define the game $\mathcal{G}_{4,0}$ to be the same as $\mathcal{G}_3$. We define the j-th hybrid game $\mathcal{G}_{4,j}$ by changing the simulation of the j-th token on the keyword w_j, and outputs a *semifunctional token* instead of the actual token as follows:

– Challenger randomly picks r_j, r_j' and r_j'' and sets the token t_{w_j} for the keyword w_j as:

$$R_w = g_2^{r_j}, \quad S_w = g_2^{r_j c + r_j'}, \quad T_w = g_2^{r_j'' + r_j \cdot (d+i_{w_j} e)},$$
$$W_{w1} = g_2^{[-p'-r_j''-r_j(l'+d+i_{w_j}(m'+e))]/b}, W_{w2} = g_2^{-r_j'-r_j(n'+c)/b}.$$

Observe that u has completely vanished from the j-th and earlier token responses. In view of the DDH assumption in the group G_2, it can be seen [JR13] that the view of the adversary $\mathcal{A}$ in game $\mathcal{G}_{4,j}$ is *computationally indistinguishable* from the view of the adversary $\mathcal{A}$ in game $\mathcal{G}_{4,j-1}$.

Game $\mathcal{G}_5$: This game is just the game $\mathcal{G}_{4,q}$ where q is the total number of secret key queries. Observe that in the game $\mathcal{G}_4$, the only place where u is used is in the ciphertext components $C_{M0} = M \cdot k^x \cdot e(g_1, g_2)^{u \cdot x'}$ and $C_{w0} = V \cdot k^y \cdot e(g_1, g_2)^{u \cdot y'}$. Hence C_{M0} and C_{w0} are completely random and independent of the target message-keyword pairs (m_0^*, w_0^*) and (m_1^*, w_1^*) in the view of the adversary $\mathcal{A}$ in the game $\mathcal{G}_5$. Note that u is non-zero with high probability. Hence the SXDH assumption implies computational indistinguishability from the chosen ciphertext adversary. That is, the scheme achieves IND-PKE+PEKS-CCA security.

6   Efficiency Analysis

In this section, we provide an efficiency comparison of various parameters in existing PEKS schemes in Table 1 and the efficiency comparison of existing PKE+PEKS schemes in Table 2.

We compare various PEKS schemes with ours in the Table 1 based on the following parameters:

- #pk – number of group elements in the public parameters
- #sk – number of group elements in the master secret
- #ct – number of group elements in the ciphertext
- (a, b, c, d) denotes a elements from G_1, b elements from G_2, c elements from G_T and d elements from Z_q where $q = |G_1|$.

Table 1. Comparison of various PEKS schemes

Scheme →	[BSS06]	[ZI07]	[CZLZ14]	[BLSS15]	Our scheme
Pairing	Type 1	Type 1	Type 1	Type 3	Type 3
Security	IK-PKE-CCA IND-PEKS-CKA	IK-PKE-CCA IND-PEKS-CKA	IND-PKE+ PEKS-CCA	IND-PKE+ PEKS-CCA	IND-PKE+ PEKS-CCA
Security model	RO	STD	STD	STD	STD
Assumption	CDH	DADHE	q-ABDHE /SDH	SXDH	SXDH
#pk	$(2, -, 0, 0)$	$(3, -, 2, 0)$	$(5, -, 0, 1)$	$(8, 0, 1, 0)$	$(5, 0, 1, 0)$
#sk	$(0, -, 0, 1)$	$(0, -, 0, 5)$	$(0, -, 0, 1)$	$(0, 8, 0, 1)$	$(0, 2, 0, 7)$
#ct	$(1, -, 0, 3)^{\#}$	$(2, -, 3, 3)^{\dagger}$	$(6, -, 4, 1)$	$(12, 8, 3, 0)$	$(11, 5, 3, 2)$

1. * in [BDOP04], ciphertext contains one element from G_1 and one element of size $\log p$, for more detail please refer [BDOP04].
2. # in [BSS06], ciphertext contains one element from G_1 and three elements of maximum bitlength $\approx l$, where $l = \max(l_1, l_3, l_4)$; for more details please Refer to [BSS06].
3. † in [ZI07], ciphertext contains one MAC output and one element of the length of the message which we have included in the integer count; for more detail please refer [ZI07].
4. RO – Random Oracle, STD – Standard Model.
5. In the row "Assumption", the standard abbreviations like BDH – Bilinear Diffie-Hellman, CDH – Computational Diffie-Hellman are used. For details of assumptions please refer respective paper.

Finally, in Table 2, we compare the efficiency of the proposed integrated PKE+PEKS scheme with the existing PEKS and integrated PKE+PEKS schemes [BSS06, BLSS15, CZLZ14, ZI07] and show that our scheme is more efficient than these schemes. In each of the four phases: Encryption, Decryption, Token Gen. and Test, we compare the total number of bilinear pairings (P),

Table 2. Efficiency comparison

Operation	Scheme	P	E(Z_q)	I(Z_q)	E(G_1)	M(G_1)	E(G_2)	M(G_2)	E(G_T)	M(G_T)
Encryption	[BSS06]	1	0	0	2	0	-	-	1	0
	[ZI07]	2	0	0	2	1	-	-	6	1
	[CZLZ14]	5	0	1	7	2	-	-	5	2
	[BLSS15]	1	0	0	16	0	12	0	3	2
	Our scheme	1	0	0	15	4	6	0	3	2
Decryption	[BSS06]	0	0	0	1	0	-	-	0	0
	[ZI07]	0	0	0	0	0	-	-	2	1
	[CZLZ14]	3	0	1	3	2	-	-	0	1
	[BLSS15]	8	0	0	4	4	4	0	0	7
	Our scheme	6	0	0	5	2	9	4	1	7
Token Gen	[BSS06]	0	0	0	1	0	-	-	0	0
	[ZI07]	0	0	0	1	1	-	-	0	0
	[CZLZ14]	0	0	1	1	1	-	-	0	0
	[BLSS15]	0	0	0	0	0	4	0	0	0
	Our scheme	0	0	0	0	0	5	0	0	0
Test	[BSS06]	1	0	0	0	0	-	-	0	0
	[ZI07]	1	0	0	0	0	-	-	1	1
	[CZLZ14]	4	1	0	2	2	0	0	2	3
	[BLSS15]	8	0	0	4	4	0	0	0	7
	Our scheme	6	0	0	5	2	9	4	1	7
Overall comparison	[BSS06]	2	0	0	4	1	-	-	1	0
	[ZI07]	3	0	0	3	2	-	-	9	3
	[CZLZ14]	12	1	3	13	7	-	-	7	6
	[BLSS15]	17	0	0	24	8	20	8	3	16
	Our scheme	13	0	0	25	8	29	8	5	16

exponentiations and inverse in Z_q denoted as $E(Z_q)$ and $I(Z_q)$, exponentiations and multiplications in G_1 (resp. G_2 and G_T) denoted as $E(G_1)$ (resp. $E(G_2)$ and $E(G_T)$) and $M(G_1)$ (resp. $M(G_2)$ and $M(G_T)$). Since [BLSS15] is the only construction of PEKS other than ours with *asymmetric pairing*, that is, Type 3 pairing ($e : G_1 \times G_2 \rightarrow G_T$), for these schemes, we have considered operations in all the three different groups, that is, in G_1, G_2 and G_T, and since all the previous schemes use symmetric pairings, that is, Type 1 pairing ($e : G_1 \times G_1 \rightarrow G_T$) [GPS08], we have counted operations in groups G_1 and G_2 only for these schemes, considering $|G_1| \approx |G_2|$.

From the efficiency comparison Table 1, it is evident that the proposed integrated PKE+PEKS scheme is (computationally) more efficient than the schemes given in [BSS06, ZI07, CZLZ14, BLSS15]. Note that first two schemes [BSS06, ZI07] provide only CPA security so they are naturally a bit more efficient. The third scheme [CZLZ14] uses symmetric pairings and even though the numbers in some cells of the table show smaller number of operations, the operations are much more expensive in their case. Finally, in the fourth scheme [BLSS15] the smaller numbers in some cells are adequately compensated by the smaller number of pairings in our scheme.

7 Conclusion

We have proposed an efficient and practical integrated PKE+PEKS scheme and proved its security in the strongest security notion for PKE+PEKS schemes. The security of our scheme relies on SXDH assumption which is a much simpler and more standard hardness assumption than the ones used in most of the comparable schemes. Ours is the first fully secure integrated PKE+PEKS scheme using asymmetric pairings which enable an extremely fast implementation useful for practical applications. Finally, providing a relative analysis of parameters, assumptions, securities and efficiency, we have compared our scheme with the existing similar schemes and shown that our scheme is more efficient than those schemes.

Acknowledgements. We thank the anonymous reviewers for the constructive and helpful comments. We thank Francesco Buccafurri and Gianluca Lax for the useful discussions. We are thankful to Olivier Markowitch for the support.

References

[ABC+05] Abdalla, M., Bellare, M., Catalano, D., Kiltz, E., Kohno, T., Lange, T., Malone-Lee, J., Neven, G., Paillier, P., Shi, H.: Searchable Encryption Revisited: Consistency Properties, Relation to Anonymous IBE, and Extensions. In: Shoup, V. (ed.) CRYPTO 2005. LNCS, vol. 3621, pp. 205–222. Springer, Heidelberg (2005). https://doi.org/10.1007/11535218_13

[ABN10] Abdalla, M., Bellare, M., Neven, G.: Robust encryption. In: Micciancio, D. (ed.) TCC 2010. LNCS, vol. 5978, pp. 480–497. Springer, Heidelberg (2010). https://doi.org/10.1007/978-3-642-11799-2_28

[BDOP04] Boneh, D., Di Crescenzo, G., Ostrovsky, R., Persiano, G.: Public key encryption with keyword search. In: Cachin, C., Camenisch, J.L. (eds.) EUROCRYPT 2004. LNCS, vol. 3027, pp. 506–522. Springer, Heidelberg (2004). https://doi.org/10.1007/978-3-540-24676-3_30

[BDPR98] Bellare, M., Desai, A., Pointcheval, D., Rogaway, P.: Relations among notions of security for public-key encryption schemes. In: Krawczyk, H. (ed.) CRYPTO 1998. LNCS, vol. 1462, pp. 26–45. Springer, Heidelberg (1998). https://doi.org/10.1007/BFb0055718

[BF01] Boneh, D., Franklin, M.: Identity-based encryption from the weil pairing. In: Kilian, J. (ed.) CRYPTO 2001. LNCS, vol. 2139, pp. 213–229. Springer, Heidelberg (2001). https://doi.org/10.1007/3-540-44647-8_13

[BLSS15] Buccafurri, F., Lax, G., Sahu, R.A., Saraswat, V.: Practical and secure integrated PKE+PEKS with keyword privacy. In: SECRYPT, pp. 448–453. SciTePress (2015)

[BSS06] Baek, J., Safavi-Naini, R., Susilo, W.: On the integration of public key data encryption and public key encryption with keyword search. In: Katsikas, S.K., López, J., Backes, M., Gritzalis, S., Preneel, B. (eds.) ISC 2006. LNCS, vol. 4176, pp. 217–232. Springer, Heidelberg (2006). https://doi.org/10.1007/11836810_16

[BSS08] Baek, J., Safavi-Naini, R., Susilo, W.: Public key encryption with keyword search revisited. In: Gervasi, O., Murgante, B., Laganà, A., Taniar, D., Mun, Y., Gavrilova, M.L. (eds.) ICCSA 2008. LNCS, vol. 5072, pp. 1249–1259. Springer, Heidelberg (2008). https://doi.org/10.1007/978-3-540-69839-5_96

[BW06] Boyen, X., Waters, B.: Anonymous hierarchical identity-based encryption (without random oracles). In: Dwork, C. (ed.) CRYPTO 2006. LNCS, vol. 4117, pp. 290–307. Springer, Heidelberg (2006). https://doi.org/10.1007/11818175_17

[CLL+12] Chen, J., Lim, H.W., Ling, S., Wang, H., Wee, H.: Shorter IBE and signatures via asymmetric pairings. In: Abdalla, M., Lange, T. (eds.) Pairing 2012. LNCS, vol. 7708, pp. 122–140. Springer, Heidelberg (2013). https://doi.org/10.1007/978-3-642-36334-4_8

[CZLZ14] Chen, Y., Zhang, J., Lin, D., Zhang, Z.: Generic constructions of integrated PKE and PEKS. In: Designs, Codes and Cryptography, pp. 1–34 (2014)

[DK05] Dodis, Y., Katz, J.: Chosen-ciphertext security of multiple encryption. In: Kilian, J. (ed.) TCC 2005. LNCS, vol. 3378, pp. 188–209. Springer, Heidelberg (2005). https://doi.org/10.1007/978-3-540-30576-7_11

[DS07] Di Crescenzo, G., Saraswat, V.: Public key encryption with searchable keywords based on Jacobi symbols. In: Srinathan, K., Rangan, C.P., Yung, M. (eds.) INDOCRYPT 2007. LNCS, vol. 4859, pp. 282–296. Springer, Heidelberg (2007). https://doi.org/10.1007/978-3-540-77026-8_21

[FP07] Fuhr, T., Paillier, P.: Decryptable searchable encryption. In: Susilo, W., Liu, J.K., Mu, Y. (eds.) ProvSec 2007. LNCS, vol. 4784, pp. 228–236. Springer, Heidelberg (2007). https://doi.org/10.1007/978-3-540-75670-5_17

[GM84] Goldwasser, S., Micali, S.: Probabilistic encryption. J. Comput. Syst. Sci. **28**(2), 270–299 (1984)

[GPS08] Galbraith, S.D., Paterson, K.G., Smart, N.P.: Pairings for cryptographers. Discrete Appl. Math. **156**(16), 3113–3121 (2008). Applications of Algebra to Cryptography

[INHJ11] Ibraimi, L., Nikova, S., Hartel, P., Jonker, W.: Public-key encryption with delegated search. In: Lopez, J., Tsudik, G. (eds.) ACNS 2011. LNCS, vol. 6715, pp. 532–549. Springer, Heidelberg (2011). https://doi.org/10.1007/978-3-642-21554-4_31

[JR13] Jutla, C.S., Roy, A.: Shorter Quasi-adaptive NIZK proofs for linear subspaces. In: Sako, K., Sarkar, P. (eds.) ASIACRYPT 2013. LNCS, vol. 8269, pp. 1–20. Springer, Heidelberg (2013)

[Kur02] Kurosawa, K.: Multi-recipient public-key encryption with shortened ciphertext. In: Naccache, D., Paillier, P. (eds.) PKC 2002. LNCS, vol. 2274, pp. 48–63. Springer, Heidelberg (2002). https://doi.org/10.1007/3-540-45664-3_4

[PSST11] Paterson, K.G., Schuldt, J.C.N., Stam, M., Thomson, S.: On the joint security of encryption and signature, revisited. In: Lee, D.H., Wang, X. (eds.) ASIACRYPT 2011. LNCS, vol. 7073, pp. 161–178. Springer, Heidelberg (2011). https://doi.org/10.1007/978-3-642-25385-0_9

[SR14] Strizhov, M., Ray, I.: Multi-keyword Similarity Search over Encrypted Cloud Data. In: Cuppens-Boulahia, N., Cuppens, F., Jajodia, S., Abou El Kalam, A., Sans, T. (eds.) SEC 2014. IAICT, vol. 428, pp. 52–65. Springer, Heidelberg (2014). https://doi.org/10.1007/978-3-642-55415-5_5

[SVEG10] Shmueli, E., Vaisenberg, R., Elovici, Y., Glezer, C.: Database encryption: an overview of contemporary challenges and design considerations. ACM SIGMOD Rec. **38**(3), 29–34 (2010)

[Wat09] Waters, B.: Dual system encryption: realizing fully secure IBE and HIBE under simple assumptions. In: Halevi, S. (ed.) CRYPTO 2009. LNCS, vol. 5677, pp. 619–636. Springer, Heidelberg (2009). https://doi.org/10.1007/978-3-642-03356-8_36

[ZI07] Zhang, R., Imai, H.: Generic combination of public key encryption with keyword search and public key encryption. In: Bao, F., Ling, S., Okamoto, T., Wang, H., Xing, C. (eds.) CANS 2007. LNCS, vol. 4856, pp. 159–174. Springer, Heidelberg (2007). https://doi.org/10.1007/978-3-540-76969-9_11

Differential Fault Attack on Grain v1, ACORN v3 and Lizard

Akhilesh Siddhanti[1], Santanu Sarkar[2]([✉]), Subhamoy Maitra[3],
and Anupam Chattopadhyay[4]

[1] BITS Pilani KK Birla Goa Campus, Zuarinagar 403 726, Goa, India
akhileshsiddhanti@gmail.com
[2] Department of Mathematics, IIT Madras, Chennai 600 036, India
sarkarsantanubir@gmail.com
[3] Applied Statistics Unit, ISI Kolkata, 203 B T Road, Kolkata 700 108, India
subho@isical.ac.in
[4] School of Computer Engineering, NTU, Singapore 639 798, Singapore
anupam@ntu.edu.sg

Abstract. Differential Fault Attack (DFA) is a very well known technique to evaluate security of a stream cipher. This considers that the stream cipher can be weakened by injection of the fault. In this paper we study DFA on three ciphers, namely Grain v1, Lizard and ACORN v3. We show that Grain v1 (an eStream cipher) can be attacked with injection of only 5 faults instead of 10 that has been reported in 2012. For the first time, we have mounted the fault attack on Lizard, a very recent design and show that one requires only 5 faults to obtain the state. ACORN v3 is a third round candidate of CAESAR and there is only one hard fault attack on an earlier version of this cipher. However, the 'hard fault' model requires a lot more assumption than the generic DFA. In this paper, we mount a DFA on ACORN v3 that requires 9 faults to obtain the state. In case of Grain v1 and ACORN v3, we can obtain the secret key once the state is known. However, that is not immediate in case of Lizard. While we have used the basic framework of DFA that appears in literature quite frequently, specific tweaks have to be explored to mount the actual attacks that were not used earlier. To the best of our knowledge, these are the best known DFAs on these three ciphers.

Keywords: Differential Fault Attack · Stream cipher · Grain v1 ·
ACORN v3 · Lizard

1 Introduction

In search of stream ciphers suitable for widespread adoption, the eStream portfolio [20] was started in 2004 by EU ECRYPT network. By this date, three ciphers form the hardware profile of the portfolio, namely Grain v1 [10], Trivium [7] and MICKEY 2.0 [1]. Stream ciphers find a special application in providing securities in case of resource-constrained or low power scenarios like RFID tags or

© Springer International Publishing AG 2017
S.S. Ali et al. (Eds.): SPACE 2017, LNCS 10662, pp. 247–263, 2017.
https://doi.org/10.1007/978-3-319-71501-8_14

hearing aids, due to their very low gate requirements. A natural attention was drawn towards Grain v1 for being the 'lightest' in terms of the state size and the Boolean functions used among the three, and many lightweight stream ciphers have been hence proposed based on Grain v1. The DFA proposed in [2,18] shows that by injecting 10 or more faults during the Pseudo Random bit Generation Algorithm (PRGA), the secret key can be deduced hence compromising the security of the cipher. However, the attack can be further optimized. In this work, we claim that the fault requirement can be further brought down to just 5 using optimized techniques.

Following the estream portfolio, a new competition for authenticated ciphers called CAESAR [21] has been hosted. Enlisting fifteen different ciphers as final candidates, a cipher with unique design has emerged called ACORN v3 [22]. A lightweight stream cipher composed of 6 Linear Feedback Shift Registers (LFSRs) making a state size of 293 bits, ACORN v3 promises a 128-bit security using a 128-bit secret key and IV. Since very limited study has been done on such type of cipher constructs, we explore how the design performs against mounting of a DFA. As per our experiments, cryptanalysis is possible in this case with a requirement of 9 faults. We are aware of a fault attack on an earlier version of ACORN as in [8], but that is only in a restricted model of hard fault, which considers a fault to be permanent. Our model of DFA here is much more well accepted in literature.

Inheriting the ideas from Grain v1, another interesting lightweight stream cipher Lizard has been designed. A unique feature of Lizard [9] is that the secret key cannot be found even if the secret state is known. This ensures additional security, specifically in places where the secret state can get compromised. Till now, there has been no reported cryptanalysis on Lizard apart from a related key/IV (Initialization Vector) attack shown in [5]. We show that a successful DFA can be performed against Lizard using a minimum of 5 faults.

For all the above mentioned ciphers viz. Grain v1, Lizard and ACORN v3, we follow a similar approach as in [14] that has been used many times in earlier papers too (see references in [14]). We choose these three ciphers because of their similarities. The correct location of the fault is obtained by finding the correlation between faulty and fault-free key streams. Using the given set of faulty and fault-free key streams, equations are generated and fed into a SAT solver.

1.1 Our Contribution

While a specific mode of DFA, that we discuss in this paper, is well standardized, most of the stream cipher designers do not consider evaluating such attack on the new designs. This leaves an open space towards implementing such attacks on specific ciphers. Further, blind implementation of some standard techniques do not immediately help in mounting a successful DFA. For this the exact implementation related to a specific cipher requires certain optimization. In this paper, we have two specific modes of optimization.

- What we feed to the SAT solver for obtaining the states are some equations based on the differential key streams. For the first time we show that corresponding to a state we should consider the equations both forward and backward. Earlier we have only considered the equations while moving forward. This drastically reduces the number of faults as experienced in Grain v1 and the method succeeded for Lizard too.
- Due to the large state of ACORN v3 and the clever state update, it is not easy to obtain the solutions through the SAT solver directly. Thus we need to consider fixing some bits before exploiting the SAT solver. This indeed increases the overall complexity, but at the same time makes the DFA possible. The exhaustive search over the assumed bits can be trivially parallelized keeping the complete attack practical. However, our attack on ACORN works only when all bits of the plaintext are zero. So our fault attack on ACORN is chosen plaintext attack model, whereas our attacks on Grain and Lizard are known plaintext attack model.

1.2 Paper Organisation

The outline of DFA will be discussed in Sect. 2. In Sect. 3, we describe the process of finding the exact location of fault. In Sect. 4, we explain the procedure of finding the state variables and the recovery of secret key once the exact location of fault is known. For optimizing the SAT solver to find solutions faster, we consider key stream bits from previous rounds as well. This is the main tweak in our approach over the existing works and briefly mentioned in Sects. 4.1, 4.2, 4.3. In Sect. 5, we conclude the paper summarizing our work. The description of the ciphers is available in the Appendix.

2 Proposed Outline of DFA

Fault Attacks have always been studied in cryptanalytic literature with great interest. By inducing a fault, we mean flipping one bit ($1 \rightarrow 0$ or $0 \rightarrow 1$) for some particular state of the cipher. Such faults can be induced at the beginning of the PRGA round, hence causing a change in the key stream bits. The difference between the key stream bits can be used to deduce the internal state of the cipher. Fault attack techniques range from simple glitches (caused by perturbations in the clock or power supply), focused laser beam injection, Body Bias injection to Electromagnetic injection. The range of attacks is much wider if one considers the non-volatile memories, for which, one may use hot air gun or even software-based Rowhammer attack. Depending on the level of intrusion that is enabled by the attack setup, attacks can be classified to be non-invasive, semi-invasive and invasive.

Fault injection attacks of various forms [6] is becoming an important tool in the arsenal of modern cryptanalysts. Rapidly evolving techniques for attacks and their countermeasures [17] indicate that a proper feasibility analysis of the implementation is imperative. Although inducing a fault might seem quite complicated, there have been many works in this area. Implementations of well-known ciphers like RSA, AES and DES have already been cryptanalyzed. In fact, all the final candidates of eStream [20] hardware portfolio (namely Grain v1, MICKEY 2.0 and Trivium) have been cryptanalyzed using DFA [2–4,11–13,18]. This work aims to highlight that ACORN v3 and Lizard can also be cryptanalyzed using DFA and the existing knowledge against Grain v1 can be improved.

Let us now clearly explain the assumptions while mounting the DFA. Generally too many assumptions can make an attack impractical. Further, the number of faults injected should be low, as there is a chance of damaging the device completely. Based on the documents in cryptanalytic literature on fault attacks, we consider that the attacker:

1. can restart the cipher and re-key it as well with the original Key/IV more than once,
2. can inject the fault with certain precision of timing,
3. has the equipment/required technology for injecting the fault,
4. does not need to know the exact location during fault injection.

Next we will discuss several steps of DFA. Note that the basic methodology is the same which is basically the Differential Attack, but the Key Scheduling Algorithm (KSA) is ignored. That is, we consider that one can inject the fault during the PRGA. We will follow the basic methodology as in [14] and the references in this work which are in the same line. Our specific tweaks will be described in the process.

3   Identifying Fault Locations

The first step of the DFA requires identification of fault signatures. We consider the most common signature methods that had been used in [14] too. Consider that the certain changes in the key stream bits are achieved by injecting a fault at some random location f. By random location, we mean some LFSR (Linear Feedback Shift Register) or NFSR (Non-linear Feedback Shift Register) bit, which is a part of secret state of the cipher. Thus, by injecting a fault at location f means it might be a location in the LFSR or NFSR according to the specific description of the cipher. For example, in case of Grain v1, $f \in [0, 79]$ means injecting a fault at LFSR bit l_f, whereas $f \in [80, 159]$ underlines injecting a fault in NFSR bit $n_{(f-80)}$.

In the attack model, we consider that for some fault location f, it is possible to obtain the respective fault-free key stream z_i and faulty key stream $z_i^{(f)}$ for λ key stream bits. To form a unique pattern of the key stream sequence, we compute a signature vector $Q^{(f)}$ which we define as:

$$Q^{(f)} = (q_0^{(f)}, q_1^{(f)}, \ldots, q_{\lambda-1}^{(f)}) \tag{1}$$

where

$$q_i^{(f)} = \frac{1}{2} - Pr(z_i \neq z_i^{(f)}), \forall\, i \in [0, \lambda - 1]. \tag{2}$$

This probability is estimated by sufficient number of experiments beforehand. The sharpness of a signature is defined as follows:

$$\sigma(Q^{(f)}) = \frac{1}{\lambda} \sum_{i=0}^{\lambda-1} |q_i^{(f)}|. \tag{3}$$

Following similar convention for ACORN v3, the fault in location f simply corresponds to fault in bit S_f. The corresponding plot is presented in Fig. 1. For Lizard, the convention is fault location in S_f for first 31 bits and fault location in $B_{(f-90)}$ for next 90 bits. With $\lambda = 90, 64, 64$ respectively, we execute 2^{15} runs with random key-IV pairs to obtain the signatures $Q^{(0)}, Q^{(1)}, \ldots$ for each of Grain v1, ACORN v3 and Lizard.

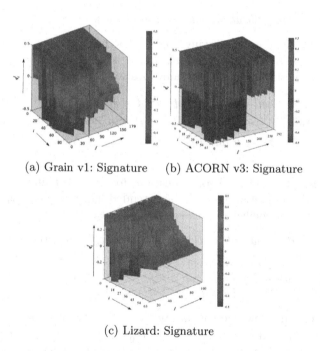

(a) Grain v1: Signature   (b) ACORN v3: Signature

(c) Lizard: Signature

Fig. 1. Signatures for Grain v1 (plot of $Q^{(f)}\, \forall f \in [0, 159]$), ACORN v3 (plot of $Q^{(f)}\, \forall f \in [0, 292]$) and Lizard (plot of $Q^{(f)}\, \forall f \in [0, 120]$) with $\lambda = 64$ for ACORN v3 and Lizard, and $\lambda = 90$ for Grain v1.

As we can see in Fig. 1, the Z-axis has been plotted from -0.5 to 0.5. The signatures are said to be strong if the curve is closer to -0.5 or 0.5 for some fault location f. In all the three cases of Grain v1, ACORN v3 and Lizard, the signatures are quite strong, in fact stronger than Plantlet [14] and Sprout [15]. Hence, the identification of the fault will be easier for these ciphers. The signatures are pre-computed during the offline phase of the attack, and they are stored for comparisons with differential key stream later. To clarify this, we require to explain a few more definitions.

Suppose we inject a fault in a random unknown location g and obtain the fault-free and faulty key streams z_i and $z_i^{(g)}$ respectively. Then we define the following:

$$\nu_i^{(g)} = \frac{1}{2} - \eta_i^{(g)} \tag{4}$$

where $\eta_i^{(g)} = z_i \oplus z_i^{(g)}$.

Definition 1. *The vector*

$$\Gamma^{(g)} = (\nu_0^{(g)}, \nu_1^{(g)}, \ldots, \nu_{\lambda-1}^{(g)})$$

is called trail of the fault at the unknown location g.

Note that there is no probability involved in this scenario, as one actually injects a fault and checks against the signatures. That is, one can compare $\Gamma^{(g)}$ for each of the $Q^{(f)}$'s, to estimate the exact fault location.

Definition 2. *We call a relation between the signature $Q^{(f)} = (q_0^{(f)}, q_1^{(f)}, \ldots, q_{\lambda-1}^{(f)})$ and a trail $\Gamma^{(g)} = (\nu_0^{(g)}, \nu_1^{(g)}, \ldots, \nu_{\lambda-1}^{(g)})$ a mismatch, if there exists at least one i, $(0 \leq i \leq \lambda - 1)$ such that $(q_i^{(f)} = \frac{1}{2}, \nu_i^{(g)} = -\frac{1}{2})$ or $(q_i^{(f)} = -\frac{1}{2}, \nu_i^{(g)} = \frac{1}{2})$ hold true.*

However, this is for excluding some locations for possible faults, but to identify the location, this definition needs to be extended. For this purpose, we incorporate the correlation coefficient between two sets of data.

Definition 3. *It is natural to use correlation coefficient $\mu(Q^{(f)}, \Gamma^{(g)})$ between the signature $Q^{(f)} = (q_0^{(f)}, q_1^{(f)}, \ldots, q_{\lambda-1}^{(f)})$ and a trail $\Gamma^{(g)} = (\nu_0^{(g)}, \nu_1^{(g)}, \ldots, \nu_{\lambda-1}^{(g)})$ for checking a match. Naturally, $-1 \leq \mu(Q^{(f)}, \Gamma^{(g)}) \leq 1$. In case of a mismatch, (as per the Definition 2), then $\mu(Q^{(f)}, \Gamma^{(g)}) = -1$.*

Let us now explain how one can locate the faults. For each known fault g, it is possible to calculate the trail $\Gamma^{(g)} = (\nu_0^{(g)}, \nu_1^{(g)}, \ldots, \nu_{\lambda-1}^{(g)})$, and hence the corresponding $\mu(Q^{(f)}, \Gamma^{(g)})$ for each of the faults f. The following quantities are noted:

1. $\max_f \mu(Q^{(f)}, \Gamma^{(g)})$,
2. $\mu(Q^{(g)}, \Gamma^{(g)})$, and
3. $\alpha(Q^{(g)}) = \#_f |\{\mu(Q^{(f)}, \Gamma^{(g)}) > \mu(Q^{(g)}, \Gamma^{(g)})\}|$.

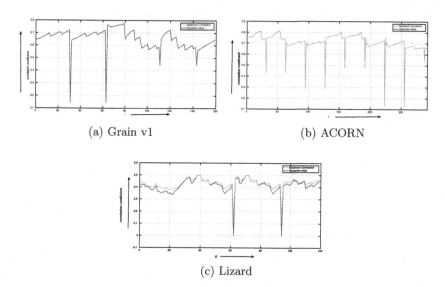

(a) Grain v1   (b) ACORN

(c) Lizard

Fig. 2. Plot of $\max_{f=0}^{100} \mu(Q^{(f)}, \Gamma^{(g)})$ (blue) and $\mu(Q^{(g)}, \Gamma^{(g)})$ (red) for all three ciphers. (Color figure online)

In the following Fig. 2, when $\mu(Q^{(g)}, \Gamma^{(g)})$ (drawn in red) is close to $\max_{f=0}^{100}$ $\mu(Q^{(f)}, \Gamma^{(g)})$ (drawn in blue), $\alpha(Q^{(g)})$ is small, it is easier to locate these faults. However, if $\mu(Q^{(g)}, \Gamma^{(g)})$ is much smaller than $\max_f \mu(Q^{(f)}, \Gamma^{(g)})$ (blue), i.e., $\alpha(Q^{(g)})$ is large, that means it is harder to locate the fault for that particular fault location f from differential key stream. In fact, the difference between the red and blue lines for ACORN v3 is so small that it is barely visible. Hence, we should expect ACORN v3 to have better expected ranks than Grain v1 and Lizard.

Given $\alpha(Q^{(g)})$, for each g, we can estimate how many attempts we should require to obtain the actual fault location. As one can see in Fig. 3, the rank of the correct set of fault locations is very low for all three ciphers, with ranks for ACORN v3 being the strongest. The ranks for ACORN v3 and Grain v1 lie between 1 and 2, hence we can get the correct set of fault locations very quickly using this technique. The ranks of correct set of fault locations for Lizard also comes very close to the other two ciphers. However ACORN v3 has the highest fault requirement (9 faults) due to its large state size, and also due to an additional complexity of 2^{20} incorporated (explained in Sect. 4) for faster solving, ACORN v3 has higher complexity ($2^{25.40}$) than Grain v1 ($2^{3.49}$) and Lizard ($2^{10.69}$).

Thus, to summarize, the exact algorithm for mounting a fault is as follows. Consider that every fault is injected at the same round t of PRGA routine.

– Inject a fault at some random fault location.
– Obtain the differential trail (for some unknown g) $\Gamma^{(g)} = (\nu_0^{(g)}, \nu_1^{(g)}, \ldots, \nu_{\lambda-1}^{(g)})$.
– For each f in $[0, 159]$ (for e.g. Grain v1), calculate $\mu(Q^{(f)}, \Gamma^{(g)})$.

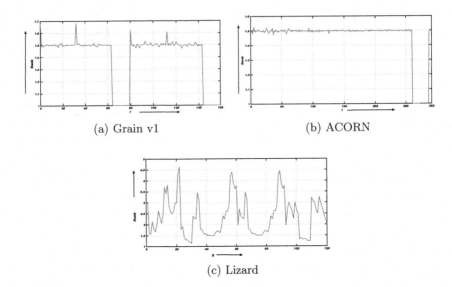

(a) Grain v1   (b) ACORN

(c) Lizard

Fig. 3. Ranks of actual fault locations in list of predicted fault locations for all the three ciphers. (lower the better).

– For the fault, prepare a ranked table T_g arranging the possible fault locations f with more priority according to $\mu(Q^{(f)}, \Gamma^{(g)})$.
– After creating tables T_g for the required number of faults, compute using SAT solvers as mentioned in Sect. 4 for each of the combinations.

In case, the correct fault set can be selected in the above algorithm, one can obtain the correct state, which will in turn discover the secret key bits. This can be confirmed as one can check and match with the existing fault free and faulty key streams at hand. To obtain the streams, the attacker needs to re-key the cipher a few times and inject the required number of faults.

3.1   Estimated Complexity to Find the Correct Set of Faults

The DFA will be more efficient when the faults are in the locations where it is easier to identify them. That is a location g such that $\alpha(Q^{(g)})$ is small will provide better result. That is, lower the $\alpha(Q^{(g)})$, lesser the the number of possible combinations of faults, and lesser the number of times one needs to run the SAT solver. It has been noted in [14] that for Plantlet, the signature of the faults are quite sharp. Interestingly, signatures of Grain v1, Lizard and ACORN v3 are sharper than Plantlet. As we will see later, for the actual attack, we require at least 5, 9 and 5 faults for Grain v1, ACORN v3 and Lizard respectively. In the following table we provide the experimental estimation of the number of attempts to get the exact fault locations for these three ciphers. Note that the data provided in Table 1 is logarithm to the base 2.

Table 1. Maximum and average number of combinations to check for all three ciphers for different number of faults. The values (except for faults) have been given in logarithm to the base 2.

Cipher	Faults reqd.	Maximum	Average
Grain v1	5	3.49	2.44
	6	4.10	2.93
	7	4.71	3.42
ACORN v3	7	4.21	3.78
	8	4.80	4.32
	9	5.40	4.86
Lizard	5	10.69	6.16
	6	12.76	7.39
	7	14.71	8.62

4   Deducing the State Variables and Secret Key

Once we obtain the differential key streams for some set of fault locations, we need to find at least one state of the cipher for some round t which in-turn can help us find the secret key. We start off by noting that for every key stream bit produced, we can formulate following three equations:

1. The output function,
2. The NFSR feedback function,
3. The LFSR feedback function.

Hence, at the beginning of the first round of PRGA, we have 160 unknown variables (80 for each LFSR and NFSR) in case of Grain v1, 293 variables in case of ACORN v3 and 121 variables in case of Lizard. With every new round of the ciphers, the complexity of the above equations increase sharply. To combat this, new variables are introduced at every step, and hence new equations are formed. Two new variables are added and three new equations are formed for every round of the ciphers. Note than in case of ACORN v3, there are 6 LFSRs hence 7 new variables are added with each cycle (6 from LFSRs and 1 from feedback) and 8 new equations are formed. We collect all these equations and feed them into a SAT solver. However, the number of equations becomes very high and hence the SAT solver cannot find a solution, hence steps specific to each cipher need to be taken.

4.1   Optimizing SAT Solver for Grain v1

Grain v1 has been constructed in such a way that the higher 16 bits of LFSR and NFSR are not used at all. Hence, we can safely discard the equations formed during the last 16 rounds of our set of equations. Next, we observe that if the fault has taken place in LFSR, the NFSR equations do not change till the fault reaches location l_0. Hence, we remove all such NFSR equations. Now, if the fault has taken place in NFSR, we need not consider any equation of LFSR because LFSR remains unaffected throughout the clocking. Since LFSR equations are linear and easier to calculate for the SAT solver, we consider injecting faults in LFSR only.

Note that Grain v1 is reversible, i.e. given one state, we can easily determine the previous state of the cipher by solving feedback equations. Considering that the fault has been injected at PRGA round t, we can form more equations by considering key stream bits of round $t-1, t-2$ and so on. Although the number of equations increase, it is added only once (not for every fault) and helps in finding a solution faster.

After performing the above optimizations, the fault requirement for Grain v1 is 5 faults with a time complexity of $2^{3.49}$.

Example 1. Consider the following set of 5 fault locations for Grain v1: $S = \{6, 16, 50, 51, 69\}$. (This set of numbers is randomly generated and not specifically chosen.) The estimated number of fault locations to check for is $2^{2.29}$. The equations are formed and fed into the SAT solver. The number of key stream bits considered is 250, with 40 reverse key stream bits considered, and the total time required by the SAT solver for the correct set of fault locations is 1756.45 s.

4.2   Optimizing SAT Solver for ACORN v3

The state size of ACORN v3 is much larger than Grain v1, Lizard, Plantlet and Sprout. Also, the number of equations added at each clock cycle is much higher than compared to the latter. Hence, we propose a different approach - we consider that some n bits for example $l_0, l_1, \ldots, l_{n-1}$ are known. Now we try to find a solution assuming these n bits are correct. Now the SAT solver is able to find a solution much faster. Note that this raises our attack complexity by 2^n, but we can try getting as small value of n as possible while still being able to find solutions faster. Our experiments show that for $n = 20$ we can deduce the state using 9 faults, whereas with $n = 40$ or $n = 60$ we can deduce the state even with 8 or 7 faults. From Table 1, we know the maximum number of combinations to be $2^{4.21}$, $2^{4.80}$, $2^{5.40}$ in case of 7, 8 and 9 faults. Considering the above optimizations, the complexity will be $2^{64.21}$ in case of 7 faults, $2^{44.80}$ and $2^{25.40}$ in case of 8 and 9 faults. However, there are some cases in which we cannot solve for the entire state with 7 or 8 faults, and hence we consider 9 faults to be minimum for a successful attack.

Since the solving time depends upon which n bits (say 20) are known, a good choice would be choosing the 15 tap locations of ACORN v3 and then further considering higher bits like $S_{292}, S_{291}, \ldots, S_{287}$ and so on. Like Grain v1 and Lizard, we can further reduce the number of faults by using key stream bits from rounds prior to injecting of the fault. We have not performed this optimization in our work for ACORN v3, but we believe that this could better our results further.

Example 2. Suppose we have the following set of 9 locations for ACORN v3, $S = \{279, 238, 10, 129, 9, 121, 271, 225, 166\}$. The number of variables considered to be known are $s_0, \ldots, s_{19}$, i.e. $n = 20$ bits. The number of combinations to check, for this set of fault locations will be $2^{4.92}$. Thus the number of times SAT solver is run will be $2^{20} \times 2^{4.92} = 2^{24.92}$. The number of key stream bits considered is 1200. For solving the correct set of fault locations, the SAT solver takes 342.43 s.

4.3   Optimizing SAT Solver for Lizard

In case of Lizard, the fault requirement is comparatively very high (more than ten) when we adopt the strategy used in case of ACORN v3 and Grain v1. However, we use some optimizations to improve our results. Firstly, we have used 90 key stream bits $z_t, z_{t+1}, z_{t+2}, \ldots, z_{t+89}$ to formulate equations, where t refers to the round in which the fault has been injected. Since Lizard is reversible without using key bits during the PRGA, we reverse the state (S_t, B_t) upto $(S_{(t-90)}, B_{(t-90)})$ and formulate equations for $z_{t-1}, z_{t-2}, \ldots, z_{t-89}$. Next, we consider that if we are able to inject faults in NFSR2 (register B) only, we can reduce the number of variables drastically, and hence obtain results faster. This is because the S register is independent of B register, and we need not include more variables for NFSR1 update equations (NFSR1 remains same post fault injection in NSFR2). Also, we note that the highest bit used in NFSR2 update function is B_{84}, hence we need not include any variables from round 85 for all faults.

As mentioned before, we can only solve for the secret state and not for the secret key in case of Lizard. However, we can obtain the secret key once the secret state is known in case of Grain v1 and ACORN v3. Solving for the state of Lizard takes a fault requirement of 5 faults with a time complexity of $2^{10.69}$.

Example 3. Considering 5 fault locations $S = \{33, 59, 10, 5, 43\}$ and combinations to check for being $2^{5.52}$, the SAT solver takes 2092.41 s to compute the states of LFSR and NFSR. The number of key stream bits considered is 90 and 40 key stream bits are taken from the previous rounds.

4.4   Summary of Comparison

Here we present the summary of DFA on the three ciphers based on our theory and experiments. According to our study, all the ciphers could be attacked using

Table 2. Results observed while obtaining state from fault attack.

Cipher	#Faults	Time complexity	Time taken by SAT solver		
			Max	Avg	Min
Grain v1	5	$2^{3.49}$	26798.64	7165.48	204.48
ACORN v3	9	$2^{25.40}$	369.56	293.75	194.80
Lizard	5	$2^{10.69}$	720.42	201.82	20.46

DFA with very few faults. The above experiments were performed on ciphers implemented in Sage-7.6 [19] along with Cryptominisat-2.9.6 as SAT solver on a laptop running Ubuntu-17.04. The hardware configuration is based on Intel (R) Core (TM) i5-4200M CPU @ 2.50 GHz and 8 GB RAM (Table 2).

5   Conclusion

Most of the popular and commercial Feedback Shift Register (FSR) based stream ciphers have come out to be vulnerable against Differential Fault Attack. In this paper, we presented successful DFA against a finalist of eStream portfolio Grain v1 (improvisation over previous DFA), a phase-3 candidate of CAESAR called ACORN v3 and a lightweight stream cipher Lizard. We explored the identification of fault locations using correlation of signatures and trail of a faulty key stream for all the three ciphers and expected number of checks required to obtain a correct state was presented. Equations were formed from faulty and fault-free key streams and fed into a SAT solver. Further cipher-specific optimizations were performed towards minimizing the number of faults as well as to speed up solving time. This is the novel contribution of this work. The analysis performed in this work can be further extended to other stream ciphers as well, and future work in this area could be promising. We are working towards optimizing our attacks on these three ciphers to succeed with even fewer faults. Further, our technique on Grain v1 can also be implemented on Grain 128 and Grain 128a. These we will include in the final version of the paper. Based on our work and the development in this domain, it is evident that FSR based ciphers in nonlinear combiner/filter generator model will generally be vulnerable against DFA. Implementors need to come up with new ways to protect against such fault attack scenarios.

Acknowledgements. The first author would like to thank Department of Science and Technology DST-FIST Level-1 Program Grant No. SR/FST/MSI-092/2013 for providing the computational facilities.

Appendix: Description of the ciphers

A1: Grain v1

Grain v1 has two registers, LFSR and NFSR of 80 bits each and we use the notation $s_i, s_{1+i}, \ldots, s_{79+i}$ and $b_i, b_{1+i}, \ldots, b_{79+i}$ for state bits of LFSR and NFSR respectively. The output function calculates the key stream bit and then the LFSR and NFSR states are updated. The output function is given by:

$$z_i = b_{i+1} \oplus b_{i+2} \oplus b_{i+4} \oplus b_{i+10} \oplus b_{i+31}$$
$$\oplus b_{i+43} \oplus b_{i+56} \oplus h(s_{i+3}, s_{i+25}, s_{i+46}, s_{i+64}, b_{i+63})$$

where $h(x_0, x_1, x_2, x_3, x_4)$ is given by:

$$h(x_0, x_1, x_2, x_3, x_4) = x_1 \oplus x_4 \oplus x_0 x_3 \oplus x_2 x_3 \oplus x_3 x_4 \oplus x_0 x_1 x_2$$
$$\oplus\, x_0 x_2 x_3 \oplus x_0 x_2 x_4 \oplus x_1 x_2 x_4 \oplus x_2 x_3 x_4.$$

The LFSR feedback bit s_{i+80} is calculated as:

$$s_{i+80} = s_{i+62} \oplus s_{i+51} \oplus s_{i+38} \oplus s_{i+23} \oplus s_{i+13} s_i$$

and the NFSR feedback bit is calculated as:

$$b_{i+80} = s_i \oplus b_{i+62} \oplus b_{i+60} \oplus b_{i+52} \oplus b_{i+45} \oplus b_{i+37}$$
$$\oplus\, b_{i+33} \oplus b_{i+28} \oplus b_{i+9} \oplus b_i \oplus b_{i+63} b_{i+60} \oplus b_{i+37} b_{i+33}$$
$$\oplus\, b_{i+15} b_{i+9} \oplus b_{i+60} b_{i+52} b_{i+45} \oplus b_{i+33} b_{i+28} b_{i+21}$$
$$\oplus\, b_{i+63} b_{i+45} b_{i+28} b_{i+9} \oplus b_{i+60} b_{i+52} b_{i+37} b_{i+33}$$
$$\oplus\, b_{i+63} b_{i+60} b_{i+52} b_{i+45} b_{i+37} \oplus b_{i+33} b_{i+28} b_{i+21} b_{i+15} b_{i+9}$$
$$\oplus\, b_{i+52} b_{i+45} b_{i+37} b_{i+33} b_{i+28} b_{i+21}$$

The cipher is initialized using the key and IV bits as per the following:

$$b_i = k_i \qquad \text{for} \quad 0 \le i \le 79,$$
$$s_i = IV_i \qquad \text{for} \quad 0 \le i \le 63$$
$$s_i = 1 \qquad \text{for} \quad 64 \le i \le 79$$

After initialization, the cipher is clocked 160 times without producing any key stream bit. In fact, the key stream bit is XOR'd with the feedback bit during the KSA. After 160 rounds, we get our first key stream bit.

A2: ACORN v3

We briefly state here the description of ACORN v3 relevant to our work, i.e. we assume the plaintext message to be a stream of 0's and are concerned only about the key stream generation process (PRGA), hence initialization of the cipher has been omitted. As stated before, ACORN v3 has 6 LFSRs concatenated to form a 293 bit state. We denote the state of the cipher by S^t and its respective bits as: $S_0^t \dots S_{292}^t$. The cipher has the following three functions:

1. **Output Function.** The output bit z_t for any state t is generated as:

$$z_t = S_{12}^t \oplus S_{154}^t \oplus maj(S_{235}^t, S_{61}^t, S_{193}^t)$$
$$\oplus\, ch(S_{230}^t, S_{111}^t, S_{66}^t), \tag{5}$$

where $maj(x, y, z) = xy \oplus xz \oplus yz$ and $ch(x, y, z) = xy \oplus (\sim x)z$.

2. **Feedback Function.** The feedback bit f_t for any state t is generated as:

$$f_t = S_0^t \oplus (\sim S_{107}^t) \oplus maj(S_{244}^t, S_{23}^t, S_{160}^t)$$
$$\oplus\, (ca_t\, \& S_{196}^t) \oplus (cb_t\, \& z_t), \tag{6}$$

where ca_t and cb_t are binary values based on the length of the message.

3. **State Update Function.** Before performing the shift, the bits $S^t_{289}, S^t_{230},$
$S^t_{193}, S^t_{154}, S^t_{107}, S^t_{61}$ are updated as follows:

$$S^t_{289} = S^t_{289} \oplus S^t_{235} \oplus S^t_{230}$$
$$S^t_{230} = S^t_{230} \oplus S^t_{196} \oplus S^t_{193}$$
$$S^t_{193} = S^t_{193} \oplus S^t_{160} \oplus S^t_{154}$$
$$S^t_{154} = S^t_{154} \oplus S^t_{111} \oplus S^t_{107}$$
$$S^t_{107} = S^t_{107} \oplus S^t_{66} \oplus S^t_{61}$$
$$S^t_{61} = S^t_{61} \oplus S^t_{23} \oplus S^t_{0}$$

And then the bits are shifted in the following manner:

$$S^{t+1}_i = S^t_{i+1} \ \forall \ i \ \in \ [0, 291]$$

with the last bit initialized with the feedback bit is

$$S^{t+1}_{292} = f_t,$$

when all bits of the pliantext are zero.

A3: Lizard

The 121-bit inner state of Lizard is divided into two NFSRs namely NFSR1 and NFSR2. At time t, the first NFSR, NFSR1 is denoted by $(S^t_0, \ldots, S^t_{30})$ and the second NFSR, NFSR2 by $(B^t_0, \ldots, B^t_{89})$. NFSR1 is of 31 bit and the update rule of this NFSR is

$$
\begin{aligned}
S^{t+1}_{30} = {} & S^t_0 \oplus S^t_2 \oplus S^t_5 \oplus S^t_6 \oplus S^t_{15} \oplus S^t_{17} \oplus S^t_{18} \oplus S^t_{20} \\
& \oplus S^t_{25} \oplus S^t_8 S^t_{18} \oplus S^t_8 S^t_{20} \oplus S^t_{12} S^t_{21} \oplus S^t_{14} S^t_{19} \\
& \oplus S^t_{17} S^t_{21} \oplus S^t_{20} S^t_{22} \oplus S^t_4 S^t_{12} S^t_{22} \oplus S^t_4 S^t_{19} S^t_{22} \\
& \oplus S^t_7 S^t_{20} S^t_{21} \oplus S^t_8 S^t_{18} S^t_{22} \oplus S^t_8 S^t_{20} S^t_{22} \oplus S^t_{12} S^t_{19} S^t_{22} \\
& \oplus S^t_{20} S^t_{21} S^t_{22} \oplus S^t_4 S^t_7 S^t_{12} S^t_{21} \oplus S^t_4 S^t_7 S^t_{19} S^t_{21} \\
& \oplus S^t_4 S^t_{12} S^t_{21} S^t_{22} \oplus S^t_4 S^t_{19} S^t_{21} S^t_{22} \oplus S^t_7 S^t_8 S^t_{18} S_{21} \\
& \oplus S^t_7 S^t_8 S^t_{20} S^t_{21} \oplus S^t_7 S^t_{12} S^t_{19} S^t_{21} \oplus S^t_8 S^t_{18} S^t_{21} S^t_{22} \\
& \oplus S^t_8 S^t_{20} S^t_{21} S^t_{22} \oplus S^t_{12} S^t_{19} S^t_{21} S^t_{22}.
\end{aligned}
\tag{7}
$$

The second register NFSR2 is of 90 bit and the update rule of this NFSR is

$$
\begin{aligned}
B^{t+1}_{89} = {} & S^t_0 \oplus B^t_0 \oplus B^t_{24} \oplus B^t_{49} \oplus B^t_{79} \oplus B^t_{84} \oplus B^t_3 B^t_{59} \\
& \oplus B^t_{10} B^t_{12} \oplus B^t_{15} B^t_{16} \oplus B^t_{25} B^t_{53} \oplus B^t_{35} B^t_{42} \\
& \oplus B^t_{55} B^t_{58} \oplus B^t_{60} B^t_{74} \oplus B^t_{20} B^t_{22} B^t_{23} \\
& \oplus B^t_{62} B^t_{68} B^t_{72} \oplus B^t_{77} B^t_{80} B^t_{81} B_{83}.
\end{aligned}
\tag{8}
$$

Output bit z_t is a function from $\{0,1\}^{53}$ to $\{0,1\}$. At time t,

$$z_t = \mathcal{L}_t \oplus \mathcal{Q}_t \oplus \mathcal{T}_t \oplus \overline{T}_t, \tag{9}$$

where

- $\mathcal{L}_t = B_7^t \oplus B_{11}^t \oplus B_{30}^t \oplus B_{40}^t \oplus B_{45}^t \oplus B_{54}^t \oplus B_{71}^t$

- $\mathcal{Q}_t = B_4^t B_{21}^t \oplus B_9^t B_{52}^t \oplus B_{18}^t B_{37}^t \oplus B_{44}^t B_{76}^t$

- $\mathcal{T}_t = B_5^t \oplus B_8^t B_{82}^t \oplus B_{34}^t B_{67}^t B_{73}^t \oplus B_2^t B_{28}^t B_{41}^t B_{65}^t \oplus B_{13}^t B_{29}^t B_{50}^t B_{64}^t B_{75}^t \oplus$
  $B_6^t B_{14}^t B_{26}^t B_{32}^t B_{47}^t B_{61}^t \oplus B_1^t B_{19}^t B_{27}^t B_{43}^t B_{57}^t B_{66}^t B_{78}^t$

- $\overline{T}_t = S_{23}^t \oplus S_3^t S_{16}^t \oplus S_9^t S_{13}^t B_{48}^t \oplus S_1^t S_{24}^t B_{38}^t B_{63}^t$

The state initialization process is divided into 4 phases.

Phase 1: Key and IV Loading. Let $K = (K_0, \ldots, K_{119})$ be the 120-bit key and $IV = (IV_0, \ldots, IV_{63})$ the 64-bit public IV. The state is initialized as follows:

$$B_j^0 = \begin{cases} K_j \oplus IV_j, & \text{for } 0 \le j \le 63 \\ K_j, & \text{for } 64 \le j \le 89 \end{cases}$$

$$S_j^0 = \begin{cases} K_{j+90}, & \text{for } 0 \le j \le 28 \\ K_{119+1}, & \text{for } j = 29 \\ 1, & \text{for } j = 30 \end{cases}$$

Phase 2: Grain-like Mixing. In this phase the output bit z_t is fed back into both NFSRs for $0 \le t \le 127$. This type of approach is used in Grain family.

Phase 3: Second Key Addition. In this phase, the 120-bit key is XORed to both NFSRs as follows:

$$B_j^{129} = B_j^{128} \oplus K_j, \text{ for } 0 \le j \le 89$$

$$S_j^{129} = \begin{cases} S_j^{128} \oplus K_{j+90}, & \text{for } 0 \le j \le 29 \\ 1, & \text{for } j = 30 \end{cases}$$

Phase 4: Final Diffusion. This phase is exactly similar to phase 2 except z_t is not fed back into the NFSRs. In this phase, one has to run both NFSRs 128 rounds. So after this phase, registers are $(S_0^{257}, \ldots, S_{30}^{257})$ and $(B_0^{257}, \ldots, B_{89}^{257})$. Now Lizard is ready to produce output key stream bits. The first keystream bit that is used for encryption is z_{257}. For $t \ge 257$, the states $(S_0^{t+1}, \ldots, S_{30}^{t+1})$ and $(B_0^{t+1}, \ldots, B_{89}^{t+1})$ and the output bit z_t are computed using Eqs. (7), (8) and (9) respectively.

References

1. Babbage, S., Dodd, M.: The stream cipher MICKEY 2.0. ECRYPT stream cipher project report. http://ecrypt.eu.org/stream/p3ciphers/mickey/mickey_p3.pdf
2. Banik, S., Maitra, S., Sarkar, S.: A differential fault attack on the grain family of stream ciphers. In: Prouff, E., Schaumont, P. (eds.) CHES 2012. LNCS, vol. 7428, pp. 122–139. Springer, Heidelberg (2012). https://doi.org/10.1007/978-3-642-33027-8_8
3. Banik, S., Maitra, S.: A differential fault attack on MICKEY 2.0. In: Bertoni, G., Coron, J.-S. (eds.) CHES 2013. LNCS, vol. 8086, pp. 215–232. Springer, Heidelberg (2013). https://doi.org/10.1007/978-3-642-40349-1_13
4. Banik, S., Maitra, S., Sarkar, S.: Improved differential fault attack on MICKEY 2.0. J. Cryptogr. Eng. 5(1), 13–29 (2015). https://doi.org/10.1007/s13389-014-0083-9
5. Banik, S., Isobe, T.: Some cryptanalytic results on Lizard. http://eprint.iacr.org/2017/346.pdf
6. Barenghi, A., Breveglieri, L., Koren, I., Naccache, D.: Fault Injection attacks on cryptographic devices: theory, practice, and countermeasures. Proc. IEEE 100(11), 3056–3076 (2012). https://doi.org/10.1109/JPROC.2012.2188769
7. De Cannire, C., Preneel, B.: TRIVIUM specifications. eSTREAM, ECRYPT Stream Cipher Project, Report
8. Dey, P., Rohit, R.S., Adhikari, A.: Full key recovery of ACORN with a single fault. J. Inf. Secur. Appl. 29(C), 57–64 (2016). https://doi.org/10.1016/j.jisa.2016.03.003. Elsevier Science Inc. New York, NY, USA
9. Hamann, M., Krause, M., Meier, W.: LIZARD - a lightweight stream cipher for power-constrained devices. IACR Trans. Symmetric Cryptol. 2017(1), 45–79 (2017). http://tosc.iacr.org/index.php/ToSC/article/view/584
10. Hell, M., Johansson, T., Meier, W.: Grain - a stream cipher for constrained environments. ECRYPT stream cipher project report 2005/001 (2005). http://www.ecrypt.eu.org/stream
11. Hojsík, M., Rudolf, B.: Differential fault analysis of Trivium. In: Nyberg, K. (ed.) FSE 2008. LNCS, vol. 5086, pp. 158–172. Springer, Heidelberg (2008). https://doi.org/10.1007/978-3-540-71039-4_10
12. Hojsík, M., Rudolf, B.: Floating fault analysis of Trivium. In: Chowdhury, D.R., Rijmen, V., Das, A. (eds.) INDOCRYPT 2008. LNCS, vol. 5365, pp. 239–250. Springer, Heidelberg (2008). https://doi.org/10.1007/978-3-540-89754-5_19
13. Hu, Y., Gao, J., Liu, Q., Zhang, Y.: Fault analysis of Trivium. Des. Codes Cryptograph. 62(3), 289–311 (2012)
14. Maitra, S., Siddhanti, A., Sarkar, S.: A dierential fault attack on plantlet. IEEE Trans. Comput. 66(10), 1804–1808 (2017). https://doi.org/10.1109/TC.2017.2700469. An earlier version is available at Cryptology ePrint Archive: Report 2017/088, 4 February 2017. http://eprint.iacr.org/2017/088
15. Maitra, S., Sarkar, S., Baksi, A., Dey, P.: Key recovery from state information of sprout: application to cryptanalysis and fault attack (2015). http://eprint.iacr.org/2015/236
16. Mikhalev, V., Armknecht, F., Müller, C.: On ciphers that continuously access the non-volatile key. In: FSE 2017. TOSC, vol. 2016, no. 2, pp. 52–79 (2016). http://tosc.iacr.org/index.php/ToSC/article/view/565/507
17. Sugawara, T., Suzuki, D., Fujii, R., Tawa, S., Hori, R., Shiozaki, M., Fujino, T.: Reversing stealthy dopant-level circuits. In: Batina, L., Robshaw, M. (eds.) CHES 2014. LNCS, vol. 8731, pp. 112–126. Springer, Heidelberg (2014). https://doi.org/10.1007/978-3-662-44709-3_7

18. Sarkar, S., Banik, S., Maitra, S.: Dierential fault attack against grain family with very few faults and minimal assumptions. IEEE Trans. Comput. **64**(6), 1647–1657 (2015)
19. Stein, W.: Sage Mathematics Software. Free Software Foundation, Inc., (2009). http://www.sagemath.org. (Open source project initiated by W. Stein and contributed by many)
20. The ECRYPT stream cipher project. eSTREAM portfolio of stream ciphers. http://www.ecrypt.eu.org/stream/
21. The project CAESAR on authenticated ciphers. http://competitions.cr.yp.to/caesar.html
22. Wu, H.: ACORN: a lightweight authenticated cipher (v3) (2016). https://competitions.cr.yp.to/round3/acornv3.pdf

Certain Observations on ACORN v3 and the Implications to TMDTO Attacks

Akhilesh Anilkumar Siddhanti[1]($\boxtimes$), Subhamoy Maitra[2], and Nishant Sinha[3]

[1] BITS Pilani, Goa Campus, Goa, India
akhileshsiddhanti@gmail.com
[2] Applied Statistics Unit, Indian Statistical Institute,
203, B. T. Road, Kolkata 700108, India
subho@isical.ac.in
[3] Department of Computer Science and Engineering,
Indian Institute of Technology Roorkee, Roorkee 247667, India
nishantsinha.iitr@gmail.com

Abstract. ACORN is a lightweight authenticated cipher which is one of the selected designs among the fifteen third round candidates. This is based on the underlying model of a stream cipher with 6 LFSRs of different lengths and three additional bits. In this paper we consider the scenario that certain amount of key stream bits and some portion of the state is known. Then we try to discover the rest of the state bits. For example, we show that the LFSR of length 47 can be recovered from 47 key stream bits and guessing the rest of the state bits. We also present the implication of such results towards mounting TMDTO attack on ACORN v3. We show that a TMDTO attack can be mounted with preprocessing complexity 2^{171} and 2^{180} (without and with the help of a SAT solver) and the maximum of online time, memory and data complexity 2^{122} and 2^{120} respectively. While our results do not refute any claim of the designer, these observations might be useful for further understanding of the cipher.

Keywords: ACORN v3 · Authenticated encryption · CAESAR · Cryptanalysis · Stream cipher

1 Introduction

A new competition CAESAR (Competition for Authenticated Encryption: Security, Applicability, and Robustness) [4] has been initiated recently with the first submission deadline in March 2014. The selected candidates of the third round are now available and ACORN v3 is one among those [10]. This is a lightweight authenticated stream cipher composed of 6 Linear Feedback Shift Registers (LFSRs) and four additional bits, making a state size of 293 bits. It promises a 128-bit security using a 128-bit secret key and IV.

Given that the present ciphers are designed with well informed efforts, refuting the designer's claim are quite challenging and sometimes even elusive. However, there are important observations discovered by the cryptanalysts that help

© Springer International Publishing AG 2017
S.S. Ali et al. (Eds.): SPACE 2017, LNCS 10662, pp. 264–280, 2017.
https://doi.org/10.1007/978-3-319-71501-8_15

in providing more robust ciphers. This is the reason ACORN has been revised twice and the current version is ACORN v3. In this paper we concentrate on this cipher and try to see how well one can obtain certain portion of the state bits of ACORN v3 given some key stream bits and the rest of the bits of the state. This is related to sampling resistance as noted in [2,3]. In particular, we observe that the LFSR of length 47 ($S_{107}, \ldots, S_{153}$) can be recovered from 47 key stream bits and knowing the rest $293 - 47 = 246$ state bits of ACORN v3. This is achieved by writing a set of several equations and feeding them to a SAT solver such as SAGE [8]. Similarly, the 60 bits ($S_0, \ldots, S_{59}$) of the LFSR having length 61 ($S_0, \ldots, S_{60}$) could be recovered from 72 key stream bits and the rest 233 state bits of the cipher. This is presented in Sect. 2. This kind of observation helps in mounting Time-Memory-Data-Trade-Off (TMDTO) attack on stream ciphers with varied parameters.

In TMDTO attack, we have four parameters, the preprocessing time P, the amount of Memory (table in secondary storage) required M, the amount of Data D (which is the key stream in case of a stream cipher) and the time T (the number of accesses to the table, i.e., the secondary storage). In case the key is of k-bits and all the parameters P, M, T, D are less than 2^k, then it can be considered as a break. It has been pointed out in [10, Sect. 3.3.2] that as the state size ($n = 293$) of ACORN v3 is more than twice the secret key size ($k = 128$), such an attack is elusive. However, there is another implication of TMDTO attack, where we allow the preprocessing time to be more than the exhaustive key search and then try to minimize the maximum of the online parameters M, T, D. In case the online parameters are less than 2^k, that attracts some interest in terms of cryptanalysis. In case of BG attack [1,5], the best situation is achieved when $P = T = M = D = 2^{\frac{n}{2}}$ and M, D can be reduced at the cost of increasing $P = T$. Thus, achieving $\max\{T, M, D\} < 2^{\frac{n}{2}}$ is not possible even when $P > 2^{\frac{n}{2}}$. Rather, we follow the idea of [2,3], where it is possible to reduce all three of the online parameters T, M, D less than $2^{\frac{n}{2}}$ at the cost of increasing the preprocessing time P over $2^{\frac{n}{2}}$. In this regard, we obtain parameters like $P = 2^{171}, M = T = D = 2^{120}$, where all the online parameters are less than the complexity of exhaustive key search 2^{128} in case of ACORN v3 [10]. This is presented in Sect. 3. Before proceeding further, let us describe the cipher first.

1.1   Description of ACORN v3

We briefly state here the description of ACORN v3 relevant to our work. We assume the plaintext message to be a stream of 0's and we concentrate only on the Pseudo Random Generation Algorithm (PRGA) that provides the key stream. We omit the Key Loading Algorithm (KLA) and the Key Scheduling Algorithm (KSA) of the cipher that are available at [10]. This is because the recovery of secret state bits during the PRGA and further the TMDTO attack can be studied irrespective of the initialization process. As stated before, ACORN v3 has 6 LFSRs and four additional bits concatenated to form the 293 bit state. The block diagram of ACORN is represented in Fig. 1 where f_t represents the feedback bit and m_t represents the message bit at t^{th} step [10]. We denote the state of the cipher by $\mathscr{S}_t$ and its respective bits as: $S_{t+0} \ldots S_{t+292}$. The cipher has the following three functions.

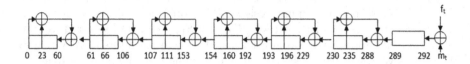

Fig. 1. The internal state of ACORN cipher.

Output Function. The output bit z_t for any state t is generated as:

$$z_t = S_{t+12} \oplus S_{t+154} \oplus maj(S_{t+235}, S_{t+61}, S_{t+193}) \\ \oplus ch(S_{t+230}, S_{t+111}, S_{t+66}) \tag{1}$$

Feedback Function. The feedback bit f_t for any state t is generated as:

$$f_t = S_{t+0} \oplus (\sim S_{t+107}) \oplus maj(S_{t+244}, S_{t+23}, S_{t+160}) \\ \oplus (ca_t \& S_{t+196}) \oplus (cb_t \& z_t) \tag{2}$$

State Update Function. Before performing the shift, the bits $S_{t+289}, S_{t+230}, S_{t+193}, S_{t+154}, S_{t+107}, S_{t+61}$ are updated as follows:

$$S_{(t+289)} = S_{(t+289)} \oplus S_{(t+235)} \oplus S_{(t+230)} \tag{3}$$
$$S_{(t+230)} = S_{(t+230)} \oplus S_{(t+196)} \oplus S_{(t+193)} \tag{4}$$
$$S_{(t+193)} = S_{(t+193)} \oplus S_{(t+160)} \oplus S_{(t+154)} \tag{5}$$
$$S_{(t+154)} = S_{(t+154)} \oplus S_{(t+111)} \oplus S_{(t+107)} \tag{6}$$
$$S_{(t+107)} = S_{(t+107)} \oplus S_{(t+66)} \oplus S_{(t+61)} \tag{7}$$
$$S_{(t+61)} = S_{(t+61)} \oplus S_{(t+23)} \oplus S_{(t+0)} \tag{8}$$

And then the next bit is initialized with the feedback bit:

$$S_{t+293} = f_t \tag{9}$$

2   Methods to Recover Certain Bits of the State

The underlying motivation of BSW sampling [2,3] is the fact that certain bits of the state can be recovered by observing the key stream sequence z^t and guessing the remaining part of the state. This reduces the search space and offers a wider range of parameters to choose from in TMDTO attack. We consider two approaches here. The first one is using the SAT solver and the other one is by discovering the equations by hand using trial and error.

2.1 Using SAT Solver

Towards this we first form a family of equations and then feeding them into a SAT solver. While forming the equations, the degree of equations formed increases rapidly, which makes it very difficult to find solutions. Hence, we have to adopt a specific approach for formulating equations by introducing new variables. This is in line of [9]. Consider some PRGA round t of ACORN v3. The equations for the same round are:

1. 1 output bit equation,
2. 1 feedback bit equation, and
3. 6 state update equations.

At the beginning of PRGA, the adversary has 293 state variables $S_0, S_1, \ldots, S_{292}$. The adversary has access to an ℓ-length key stream $z_0, z_1, \ldots z_{\ell-1}$. We will now explain how the output equation is introduced into the system of equations. The output equation as mentioned in (1) is:

$$z_t = S_{t+12} \oplus S_{t+154} \oplus maj(S_{t+235}, S_{t+61}, S_{t+193})$$
$$\oplus\ ch(S_{t+230}, S_{t+111}, S_{t+66}) \tag{10}$$

To add an equation to the SAT solver, the equations are represented in a way such that it is zero in the ring of Boolean polynomials. That is, the output equation is written as

$$z_t \oplus S_{t+12} \oplus S_{t+154} \oplus maj(S_{t+235}, S_{t+61}, S_{t+193})$$
$$\oplus\ ch(S_{t+230}, S_{t+111}, S_{t+66}) \equiv 0, \tag{11}$$

for $t = 0, 1, 2, \ldots, \ell - 1$ and added to the system. Thus we have an array of output equations as:

$$z_0 \oplus S_{12} \oplus S_{154} \oplus maj(S_{235}, S_{61}, S_{193}) \oplus ch(S_{230}, S_{111}, S_{66}) \equiv 0$$
$$z_1 \oplus S_{13} \oplus S_{155} \oplus maj(S_{236}, S_{62}, S_{194}) \oplus ch(S_{231}, S_{112}, S_{67}) \equiv 0$$

$$\vdots \quad \cdots \quad \cdots \quad \cdots \quad \cdots \quad \cdots \quad \cdots \quad \cdots \quad \cdots \quad \cdots \quad \cdots$$

$$z_{(\ell-1)} \oplus S_{(\ell-1+12)} \oplus S_{(\ell-1+154)} \oplus maj(S_{(\ell-1+235)}, S_{(\ell-1+61)}, S_{(\ell-1+193)})$$
$$\oplus\ ch(S_{(\ell-1+230)}, S_{(\ell-1+111)}, S_{(\ell-1+66)}) \equiv 0$$

Next we discuss the inclusion of feedback bit equation into the system of equations. The equation as mentioned in (2) for PRGA is:

$$f_t = S_{t+0} \oplus (\sim S_{t+107}) \oplus maj(S_{t+244}, S_{t+23}, S_{t+160}) \oplus S_{t+196} \tag{12}$$

However, the feedback bit generated is not known. Thus directly substituting the state variable S_{t+293} by feedback equations increases non-linearity. Instead, the we introduce new variables $f_0, f_1, \ldots f_{\ell-1}$ and add these equations to the SAT solver in the following manner:

$$f_0 \oplus S_0 \oplus (\sim S_{107}) \oplus maj(S_{244}, S_{23}, S_{160}) \oplus S_{196} \equiv 0$$
$$f_1 \oplus S_1 \oplus (\sim S_{108}) \oplus maj(S_{245}, S_{24}, S_{161}) \oplus S_{197} \equiv 0$$

$$\vdots \quad \cdots \quad \cdots \quad \cdots \quad \cdots \quad \cdots \quad \cdots \quad \cdots \quad \cdots$$

$$\vdots \quad \cdots \quad \cdots \quad \cdots \quad \cdots \quad \cdots \quad \cdots \quad \cdots \quad \cdots$$

$$f_{(\ell-1)} \oplus S_{(\ell-1)} \oplus (\sim S_{(\ell-1+107)})$$
$$\oplus maj(S_{(\ell-1+244)}, S_{(\ell-1+23)}, S_{(\ell-1+160)}) \oplus S_{(\ell-1+196)} \equiv 0$$

By now, 2ℓ new equations and ℓ new variables have been introduced into the system. The variables $S_{t+289}, S_{t+230}, S_{t+193}, S_{t+154}, S_{t+107}, S_{t+61}$ are updated in Step 3 as mentioned earlier. For this, we introduce 6ℓ new variables $a_1^0, a_2^0, a_3^0,$ $a_4^0, a_5^0, a_6^0, \ldots, a_1^{\ell-1}, a_2^{\ell-1}, a_3^{\ell-1}, a_4^{\ell-1}, a_5^{\ell-1}, a_6^{\ell-1}$ and add the following equations to the system (for $t = 0, 1, \ldots, \ell - 1$):

$$a_1^t \oplus S_{(t+289)} \oplus S_{(t+235)} \oplus S_{(t+230)} \equiv 0$$
$$a_2^t \oplus S_{(t+230)} \oplus S_{(t+196)} \oplus S_{(t+193)} \equiv 0$$
$$a_3^t \oplus S_{(t+193)} \oplus S_{(t+160)} \oplus S_{(t+154)} \equiv 0$$
$$a_4^t \oplus S_{(t+154)} \oplus S_{(t+111)} \oplus S_{(t+107)} \equiv 0$$
$$a_5^t \oplus S_{(t+107)} \oplus S_{(t+66)} \oplus S_{(t+61)} \equiv 0$$
$$a_6^t \oplus S_{(t+61)} \oplus S_{(t+23)} \oplus S_{(t+0)} \equiv 0$$

Since new variables have been introduced, new equations need to be introduced to maintain consistency of the system. That is, the following equations are added to the system:

$$a_1^t \oplus S_{(t+288)} \equiv 0$$
$$a_2^t \oplus S_{(t+229)} \equiv 0$$
$$a_3^t \oplus S_{(t+192)} \equiv 0$$
$$a_4^t \oplus S_{(t+153)} \equiv 0$$
$$a_5^t \oplus S_{(t+106)} \equiv 0$$
$$a_6^t \oplus S_{(t+60)} \equiv 0$$

for $t = 0, 1, \ldots, \ell - 1$. Finally, we substitute the feedback bit into the state variable:

$$S_{293+t} = f_t \qquad \forall t \in [0, \ell - 1].$$

Therefore, the number of variables used are $293 + \ell + 6\ell = 293 + 7\ell$ and the number of equations formulated are $\ell + \ell + 6\ell = 8\ell$ equations. All the equations are collected and fed to the SAT solver.

We set the SAT solver to find all possible solutions for the above system of equations. In this way, we are guaranteed that if the SAT solver returns only one solution, no other solution exists for the system of equations, and hence we are able to solve for the state. However, in few cases of our experiments we could not achieve that. For example, when we consider recovery of 60 bits with the help of 70 key stream bits, we sometimes obtain two solutions. The reason for the same is that the number of key stream bits is not enough and thus the SAT solver provides more solutions instead of a unique solution.

We use the SAT solver Cryptominisat-2.9.6 available with Sage-7.6 [8]. The experiments were performed on a laptop having hardware configuration Intel(R) Core(TM) i5-4200M CPU @ 2.50 GHz and 8 GB RAM running with Ubuntu-16.10. A few experimental data are provided where each row is based on 2^{15} experiments.

Table 1. Experimental results for solving the equations. The time required to run the PRGA for 293 clocks is 0.088 s on an average.

Key stream bits used	State bits recovered	Location of recovered bits	Proportion of multiple (two) solutions	Average time (sec)
47	47	$S_{107} \ldots S_{153}$	0	0.076
43	43	$S_{12} \ldots S_{54}$	0	0.067
72	60	$S_0 \ldots S_{59}$	$1/2^{10}$	0.127
60	53	$S_{107} \ldots S_{150}, S_{56}, \ldots S_{64}$	$1/2^{14}$	0.097

2.2   Formation of Equations by Observation, not Using SAT Solver

In this section, we build the system of equations used to recover 49 bits of internal state by using first 49 bits of keystream. To perform this recovery, we need to fix 10 bits of internal state with a particular pattern and guess remaining state bits. The internal state bits to be recovered are represented by set $\mathscr{R} = \mathscr{R}_1 \cup \mathscr{R}_2$, where $\mathscr{R}_1 = \{S_{(t+107)} : t = 0, \ldots, 43\}$ and $\mathscr{R}_2 = \{S_{(t+56)} : t = 0, \ldots, 4\}$. The Eq. (1) for genrating keystream can be written as:

$$z_t = S_{(t+12)} \oplus \overline{S_{(t+154)}} \oplus S_{(t+235)}\overline{S_{(t+61)}} \oplus S_{(t+235)}\overline{S_{(t+193)}} \oplus \overline{S_{(t+193)}}S_{(t+61)}$$
$$\oplus \overline{S_{(t+230)}}S_{(t+111)} \oplus \overline{S_{(t+230)}}S_{(t+66)} \oplus S_{(t+66)}.$$
$$(13)$$

Note that in the above equation, over-lined bits are feedback bits. The state bits are updated according to the following equations before generating the output bit:

$$S_{(t+289)} = S_{(t+289)} \oplus S_{(t+235)} \oplus S_{(t+230)}$$
$$S_{(t+230)} = S_{(t+230)} \oplus S_{(t+196)} \oplus S_{(t+193)}$$
$$S_{(t+193)} = S_{(t+193)} \oplus S_{(t+160)} \oplus S_{(t+154)}$$
$$S_{(t+154)} = S_{(t+154)} \oplus S_{(t+111)} \oplus S_{(t+107)} \tag{14}$$
$$S_{(t+107)} = S_{(t+107)} \oplus S_{(t+66)} \oplus S_{(t+61)}$$
$$S_{(t+61)} = S_{(t+61)} \oplus S_{(t+23)} \oplus S_{(t+0)}$$

Thus, the Eq. (13) can be written as

$$
\begin{aligned}
S_{(t+107)} = {}& z_t \oplus S_{(t+12)} \oplus S_{(t+154)} \oplus S_{(t+111)} \oplus S_{t+235}(S_{(t+61)} \oplus S_{(t+23)} \oplus S_{(t+0)}) \\
& \oplus S_{(t+235)}(S_{(t+193)} \oplus S_{(t+160)} \oplus S_{(t+154)}) \\
& \oplus (S_{(t+193)} \oplus S_{(t+160)} \oplus S_{(t+154)})(S_{(t+61)} \oplus S_{(t+23)} \oplus S_{(t+0)}) \\
& \oplus (S_{(t+230)} \oplus S_{(t+196)} \oplus S_{(t+193)})S_{(t+111)} \\
& \oplus (S_{(t+230)} \oplus S_{(t+196)} \oplus S_{(t+193)})S_{(t+66)} \oplus S_{(t+66)},
\end{aligned}
\tag{15}
$$

which makes the recovery simpler, because all the bits on the RHS of the equation are state bits (and not feedback bits) for $t = 0, \ldots, 32$. However when we place $t = 33, \ldots, 48$ in Eq. (15), feedback bits are also involved and need to be calculated.

Now we use Eq. (15) to recover internal state bits of set $\mathscr{R}_1$. The recovery of state bits is done in a certain order. For example, if we attempt to recover S_{107} by placing $t = 0$ in Eq. (15), then S_{111} appears on the RHS of the equation and requires the knowledge of S_{111}. Thus, S_{111} is recovered before performing the recovery of S_{107}.

We define four sets $\mathscr{R}_3, \mathscr{R}_4, \mathscr{R}_5, \mathscr{R}_6$, where

$$\mathscr{R}_3 = \{S_{(t+107)} : t = 40, 36, \ldots, 0\}$$
$$\mathscr{R}_4 = \{S_{(t+107)} : t = 41, 37, \ldots, 1\}$$
$$\mathscr{R}_5 = \{S_{(t+107)} : t = 42, 38, \ldots, 2\}$$
$$\mathscr{R}_6 = \{S_{(t+107)} : t = 43, 39, \ldots, 3\}$$

and each $\mathscr{R}_i \subset \mathscr{R}_1$, for $i = 3 \ldots, 6$. The order of recovery of state bits is $\mathscr{R}_3, \mathscr{R}_4, \mathscr{R}_5, \mathscr{R}_6$ and $\mathscr{R}_2$, respectively, i.e. the state bits of $\mathscr{R}_3$ are recovered first then $\mathscr{R}_4$ and so on. For each set $\mathscr{R}_i : i = 2 \ldots, 6$, the higher index elements are recovered first. We need not fix any internal state bits for recovering $\mathscr{R}_1$. However, to recover $\mathscr{R}_2$, the internal state bits are fixed according to Table 2. Let the set $\mathscr{F}$ represent the internal state bits which are fixed according to Table 2.

Now we describe recovery of $\mathscr{R}_3$. The internal state bit S_{147} is recovered by substituting $t = 40$ in Eq. (15). From this we have

$$
\begin{aligned}
S_{147} = {}& z_{40} \oplus S_{52} \oplus \overline{S_{194}} \oplus S_{151} \oplus S_{275}(S_{101} \oplus \overline{S_{63}} \oplus S_{40}) \\
& \oplus S_{275}(\overline{S_{233}} \oplus \overline{S_{200}} \oplus \overline{S_{194}}) \oplus (\overline{S_{233}} \oplus \overline{S_{200}} \oplus \overline{S_{194}})(S_{101} \oplus \overline{S_{63}} \oplus S_{40}) \\
& \oplus (S_{270} \oplus \overline{S_{236}} \oplus \overline{S_{233}})S_{151} \oplus (S_{270} \oplus \overline{S_{236}} \oplus \overline{S_{233}})S_{106} \oplus S_{106}.
\end{aligned}
\tag{16}
$$

Table 2. State bits fixed.

Row no.	State bits and value
1	$S_{i+268} = 0 : i = 0 \dots, 4$
2	$S_{i+187} = S[i+226] \oplus S[i+193] \oplus S[i+160] \oplus S[i+154] : i = 0 \dots, 3$
3	$S_{191} = S[230] \oplus S[196] \oplus S[193] \oplus S[197] \oplus S[164] \oplus S[158]$

In Eq. (16), all the bits appearing on the RHS of the equation are guessed, except the over-lined bits. The over-lined bits are feedback bits, and not internal state bits due to Eq. (14). Thus, we need to guess more internal state bits to calculate the value of $S_{63}, S_{194}, S_{200}, S_{233}$ and S_{236} using Eq. (14). In this way, we recover S_{147}.

Now the internal state bit of S_{143} is recovered by placing $t = 36$ in Eq. (15) and we derive

$$
\begin{aligned}
S_{143} = {} & z_{36} \oplus S_{48} \oplus S_{190} \oplus S_{147} \oplus S_{271}(S_{97} \oplus S_{59} \oplus S_{36}) \\
& \oplus S_{271}(S_{229} \oplus \overline{S_{196}} \oplus S_{190}) \oplus (S_{229} \oplus \overline{S_{196}} \oplus S_{190})(S_{97} \oplus S_{59} \oplus S_{36}) \quad (17) \\
& \oplus (S_{266} \oplus \overline{S_{232}} \oplus S_{229})S_{147}(\oplus S_{266} \oplus \overline{S_{232}} \oplus S_{229})S_{102} \oplus S_{102}.
\end{aligned}
$$

Similarly, in Eq. (17), all the state bits appearing on the right side of equation need to be guessed, except S_{271}, S_{190} and the over-lined bits. The internal state bits S_{271} and S_{190} are fixed according to Table 2. The over-lined bits are calculated using Eq. (14). Thus, we need to guess more internal state bits to calculate the value of S_{196}, S_{232} and recover S_{143}.

The remaining state bits of $\mathscr{R}_3$ i.e. $S_{139}, S_{135}, \dots, S_{107}$ are recovered by substituting $t = 32, 28, \dots, 0$, respectively, in Eq. (15). While placing $t = 32, 28, \dots, 0$ in Eq. (15), the internal state bits appearing on the RHS of the equation are guessed, except state bits belonging to $\mathscr{R}$ and $\mathscr{F}$. Following the same methodology, the internal state bits of set $\mathscr{R}_4, \mathscr{R}_5$ and $\mathscr{R}_6$ are recovered.

To recover the state bits of set $\mathscr{R}_2$, all things are same as done earlier, except for Eq. (13) which is rewritten as

$$
\begin{aligned}
S_{t+12} = {} & z_t \oplus S_{(t+107)} \oplus S_{(t+154)} \oplus S_{(t+111)} \oplus S_{t+235}(S_{(t+61)} \oplus S_{(t+23)} \oplus S_{(t+0)}) \\
& \oplus S_{t+235}(S_{(t+193)} \oplus S_{(t+160)} \oplus S_{(t+154)}) \\
& \oplus (S_{(t+193)} \oplus S_{(t+160)} \oplus S_{(t+154)})(S_{(t+61)} \oplus S_{(t+23)} \oplus S_{(t+0)}) \\
& \oplus (S_{(t+230)} \oplus S_{(t+196)} \oplus S_{(t+193)})S_{t+111} \\
& \oplus (S_{(t+230)} \oplus S_{(t+196)} \oplus S_{(t+193)})S_{t+66} \oplus S_{t+66}.
\end{aligned}
$$

$$(18)$$

Thus, the internal state bits $S_{56}, \dots, S_{60}$ are recovered by using $t = 44, \dots, 48$ in Eq. (18), respectively. Another difference between recovery of $\mathscr{R}_1$ and $\mathscr{R}_2$ is that it is not necessary to recover the higher index elements first (as done before).

In this way, we recover 49 bits of $\mathscr{R}$ by fixing the 10 internal state bits of set $\mathscr{F}$ and guessing the remaining 234 state bits. However, there are nine internal state bits i.e. $S_{284}, \ldots, S_{292}$ which are not appeared in the equations used for recovery. However these bits are also considered as guessed bits during application of TMDTO attack. In the Table 3, the details of equations are given used for recovery of state bits of set $\mathscr{R}$. The over-lined state bits and underlined state bits in Table 3 are feedback bits and fixed state bits (according to Table 2), respectively.

3   Complexity of TMDTO Attack

Now we will describe the TMDTO attack in complete detail. We have a state size of $n = 293$ bits. Thus, the standard TMDTO formula [2,3] with a single table will be as follows:

- $TM^2D^2 = N^2$, where $N = 2^n$,
- $D^2 \leq T$,
- $P = \frac{N}{D}$.

During the preprocessing phase, we will prepare a table with m rows and t columns, where $mt^2 = N$ for a successful attack. The number of tables is $\frac{t}{D}$ and given a single table we have $t = D$. Each row of the table contains a chain of t elements. Consider that a specific state of $n = 293$ bits is ζ and f is the one way function. Here by one way function f, we mean that the cipher with the state ζ will be run for n times again to generate n many key stream bits. Those bits will be loaded as the new state, which is called η. That is $\eta = f(\zeta)$. We will start with a random state and then generate a row of t elements by this method. There will be m such rows. Thus, the total table size is mt. However, the complete row will not be saved. Only the starting and the final element will be saved. Thus, the storage requirement of the table will be $O(m)$, which is actually the memory parameter M.

3.1   Knowledge of 47 Bits of State from 47 Key Stream Bits

Now consider the case when we are able to recover ψ bits of the state from ψ consecutive key stream bits and the rest of the state bits. In this case, we consider a fixed pattern for the key stream bits and only when that pattern is found in the key stream, we try to search the state in the table. Thus, in this case, we consider a state size of $n - \psi$ bits and the parameters are referred as $N' = 2^{n-\psi}$, P', M', T', D'. Let us now consider the exact parameters referring to Table 1, where $\psi = 47$. Thus, $T'M'D'^2 = N'^2 = 2^{2(293-47)}$. Let us consider $D'^2 = T$. Thus, we have $T'M' = 2^{293-47} = 2^{246}$. Now, one can consider, $T' = M' = 2^{123}$ and $D' = 2^{61.5}$. However, as we have discussed that during the online phase, we can only mount the attack when a specific ψ-bit pattern comes, we have $D = 2^{\psi}D'$. Thus, finally, we will have the parameters $T = T' = 2^{123}$, $M = M' = 2^{123}$, $D = 2^{\psi}D' = 2^{47} \cdot 2^{61.5} = 2^{108.5}$, $P = P' = \frac{N'}{D'} = 2^{184.5}$. This provides the maximum of online parameters as 2^{123}, which is less than the exhaustive secret key search of complexity 2^{128}. However, as expected, the pre-processing time is much larger than the exhaustive key search.

Table 3. Recovery of 49 bits of the internal state after fixing 10 bits

Steps	Equations used for recovery	Guessed bits
0	$S_{147} = z_{40} \oplus S_{52} \oplus \overline{S_{194}} \oplus S_{151} \oplus S_{275}(S_{101} \oplus \overline{S_{63}} \oplus S_{40})$ $\oplus\ S_{275}(\overline{S_{233}} \oplus \overline{S_{200}} \oplus \overline{S_{194}}) \oplus (\overline{S_{233}} \oplus \overline{S_{200}} \oplus \overline{S_{194}})$ $(S_{101} \oplus \overline{S_{63}} \oplus S_{40}) \oplus (\underline{S_{270}} \oplus \overline{S_{236}} \oplus \overline{S_{233}})S_{151}$ $\oplus\ (\underline{S_{270}} \oplus \overline{S_{236}} \oplus \overline{S_{233}})S_{106} \oplus S_{106}$	$S_{52}, S_{101}, S_{63}, S_{25}, S_2,$ $S_{40}, S_{275}, S_{233}, S_{199},$ $S_{196}, S_{200}, S_{167}, S_{161},$ $S_{194}, S_{155}, S_{236}, S_{202},$ S_{151}, S_{106}
1	$S_{143} = z_{36} \oplus S_{48} \oplus \overline{S_{190}} \oplus S_{147} \oplus \underline{S_{271}}(S_{97} \oplus S_{59} \oplus S_{36})$ $\oplus\ \underline{S_{271}}(S_{229} \oplus \overline{S_{196}} \oplus \underline{S_{190}}) \oplus (S_{229} \oplus \overline{S_{196}} \oplus \underline{S_{190}})$ $(S_{97} \oplus S_{59} \oplus S_{36}) \oplus (S_{266} \oplus \overline{S_{232}} \oplus S_{229})S_{147}$ $\oplus\ (S_{266} \oplus \overline{S_{232}} \oplus S_{229})S_{102} \oplus S_{102}$	$S_{48}, S_{97}, S_{36}, S_{229},$ $S_{163}, S_{157}, S_{266}, S_{232},$ $S_{198}, S_{195}, S_{102}$
2	$S_{139} = z_{32} \oplus S_{44} \oplus S_{186} \oplus S_{143} \oplus S_{267}(S_{93} \oplus S_{55} \oplus S_{32})$ $\oplus\ S_{267}(S_{225} \oplus S_{192} \oplus S_{186}) \oplus (S_{225} \oplus S_{192} \oplus S_{186})$ $(S_{93} \oplus S_{55} \oplus S_{32}) \oplus (S_{262} \oplus S_{228} \oplus S_{225})S_{143}$ $\oplus\ (S_{262} \oplus S_{228} \oplus S_{225})S_{98} \oplus S_{98}$	$S_{44}, S_{93}, S_{55}, S_{32},$ $S_{267}, S_{225}, S_{192}, S_{186}$ S_{262}, S_{228}, S_{98}
3	$S_{135} = z_{28} \oplus S_{40} \oplus S_{182} \oplus S_{139} \oplus S_{263}(S_{89} \oplus S_{51} \oplus S_{28})$ $\oplus\ S_{263}(S_{221} \oplus \underline{S_{188}} \oplus S_{182}) \oplus (S_{221} \oplus \underline{S_{188}} \oplus S_{182})$ $(S_{89} \oplus S_{51} \oplus S_{28}) \oplus (S_{258} \oplus S_{224} \oplus S_{221})S_{139}$ $\oplus\ (S_{258} \oplus S_{224} \oplus S_{221})S_{94} \oplus S_{94}$	$S_{89}, S_{51}, S_{28}, S_{263},$ $S_{221}, S_{182}, S_{258}, S_{224},$ S_{94}
4	$S_{131} = z_{24} \oplus S_{36} \oplus S_{178} \oplus S_{135} \oplus S_{259}(S_{85} \oplus S_{47} \oplus S_{24})$ $\oplus\ S_{259}(S_{217} \oplus S_{184} \oplus S_{178}) \oplus (S_{217} \oplus S_{184} \oplus S_{178})$ $(S_{85} \oplus S_{47} \oplus S_{24}) \oplus (S_{254} \oplus S_{220} \oplus S_{217})S_{135}$ $\oplus\ (S_{254} \oplus S_{220} \oplus S_{217})S_{90} \oplus S_{90}$	$S_{85}, S_{47}, S_{24}, S_{259},$ $S_{217}, S_{184}, S_{178}, S_{254},$ S_{220}, S_{90}
5	$S_{127} = z_{20} \oplus S_{32} \oplus S_{174} \oplus S_{131} \oplus S_{255}(S_{81} \oplus S_{43} \oplus S_{20})$ $\oplus\ S_{255}(S_{213} \oplus S_{180} \oplus S_{174}) \oplus (S_{213} \oplus S_{180} \oplus S_{174})$ $(S_{81} \oplus S_{43} \oplus S_{20}) \oplus (S_{250} \oplus S_{216} \oplus S_{213})S_{131}$ $\oplus\ (S_{250} \oplus S_{216} \oplus S_{213})S_{86} \oplus S_{86}$	$S_{81}, S_{43}, S_{20}, S_{255},$ $S_{213}, S_{180}, S_{174},$ S_{250}, S_{216}, S_{86}
6	$S_{123} = z_{16} \oplus S_{28} \oplus S_{170} \oplus S_{127} \oplus S_{251}(S_{77} \oplus S_{39} \oplus S_{16})$ $\oplus\ S_{251}(S_{209} \oplus S_{176} \oplus S_{170}) \oplus (S_{209} \oplus S_{176} \oplus S_{170})$ $(S_{77} \oplus S_{39} \oplus S_{16}) \oplus (S_{246} \oplus S_{212} \oplus S_{209})S_{127}$ $\oplus\ (S_{246} \oplus S_{212} \oplus S_{209})S_{82} \oplus S_{82}$	$S_{77}, S_{39}, S_{16}, S_{251},$ $S_{209}, S_{176}, S_{170}, S_{246},$ S_{212}, S_{82}
7	$S_{119} = z_{12} \oplus S_{24} \oplus S_{166} \oplus S_{123} \oplus S_{247}(S_{73} \oplus S_{35} \oplus S_{12})$ $\oplus\ S_{247}(S_{205} \oplus S_{172} \oplus S_{166}) \oplus (S_{205} \oplus S_{172} \oplus S_{166})$ $(S_{73} \oplus S_{35} \oplus S_{12}) \oplus (S_{242} \oplus S_{208} \oplus S_{205})S_{123}$ $\oplus\ (S_{242} \oplus S_{208} \oplus S_{205})S_{78} \oplus S_{78}$	$S_{73}, S_{35}, S_{12}, S_{247},$ $S_{205}, S_{172}, S_{166}, S_{242},$ S_{208}, S_{78}
8	$S_{115} = z_8 \oplus S_{20} \oplus S_{162} \oplus S_{119} \oplus S_{243}(S_{69} \oplus S_{31} \oplus S_8)$ $\oplus\ S_{243}(S_{201} \oplus S_{168} \oplus S_{162}) \oplus (S_{201} \oplus S_{168} \oplus S_{162})$ $(S_{69} \oplus S_{31} \oplus S_8) \oplus (S_{238} \oplus S_{204} \oplus S_{201})S_{119}$ $\oplus\ (S_{238} \oplus S_{204} \oplus S_{201})S_{74} \oplus S_{74}$	$S_{69}, S_{31}, S_8, S_{243},$ $S_{201}, S_{168}, S_{162}, S_{238},$ S_{204}, S_{74}
9	$S_{111} = z_4 \oplus S_{16} \oplus S_{158} \oplus S_{115} \oplus S_{239}(S_{65} \oplus S_{27} \oplus S_4)$ $\oplus\ S_{239}(S_{197} \oplus S_{164} \oplus S_{158}) \oplus (S_{197} \oplus S_{164} \oplus S_{158})$ $(S_{65} \oplus S_{27} \oplus S_4) \oplus (S_{234} \oplus S_{200} \oplus S_{197})S_{115}$ $\oplus\ (S_{234} \oplus S_{200} \oplus S_{197})S_{70} \oplus S_{70}$	$S_{65}, S_{27}, S_4, S_{239},$ $S_{197}, S_{164}, S_{158}, S_{234},$ S_{70}

(continued)

Table 1. (*continued*)

Steps	Equations used for recovery	Guessed bits
10	$S_{107} = z_0 \oplus S_{12} \oplus S_{154} \oplus S_{111} \oplus S_{235}(S_{61} \oplus S_{23} \oplus S_0)$ $\oplus\, S_{235}(S_{193} \oplus S_{160} \oplus S_{154}) \oplus (S_{193} \oplus S_{160} \oplus S_{154})$ $(S_{61} \oplus S_{23} \oplus S_0) \oplus (S_{230} \oplus S_{196} \oplus S_{193})S_{111}$ $\oplus\, (S_{230} \oplus S_{196} \oplus S_{193})S_{66} \oplus S_{66}$	$S_{61}, S_{23}, S_0, S_{235},$ $S_{193}, S_{160}, S_{154}, S_{230},$ S_{66}
11	$S_{148} = z_{41} \oplus S_{53} \oplus \overline{S_{195}} \oplus S_{152} \oplus S_{276}(S_{102} \oplus \overline{S_{64}} \oplus S_{41})$ $\oplus\, S_{276}(\overline{S_{234}} \oplus \overline{S_{201}} \oplus \overline{S_{195}}) \oplus (\overline{S_{234}} \oplus \overline{S_{201}} \oplus \overline{S_{195}})$ $(S_{102} \oplus \overline{S_{64}} \oplus S_{41}) \oplus (\underline{S_{271}} \oplus \overline{S_{237}} \oplus \overline{S_{234}})S_{152}$ $\oplus\, (\underline{S_{271}} \oplus \overline{S_{237}} \oplus \overline{S_{234}})\overline{S_{107}} \oplus \overline{S_{107}}$	$S_{53}, S_{64}, S_{26}, S_3,$ $S_{41}, S_{276}, S_{156}, S_{237},$ S_{203}, S_{152}
12	$S_{144} = z_{37} \oplus S_{49} \oplus \underline{S_{191}} \oplus S_{148} \oplus \underline{S_{272}}(S_{98} \oplus S_{60} \oplus S_{37})$ $\oplus\, \underline{S_{272}}(\overline{S_{230}} \oplus \overline{S_{197}} \oplus \underline{S_{191}}) \oplus (\overline{S_{230}} \oplus \overline{S_{197}} \oplus \underline{S_{191}})$ $(S_{98} \oplus S_{60} \oplus S_{37}) \oplus (S_{267} \oplus \overline{S_{233}} \oplus \overline{S_{230}})S_{148}$ $\oplus\, (S_{267} \oplus \overline{S_{233}} \oplus \overline{S_{230}})S_{103} \oplus S_{103}$	S_{49}, S_{37}, S_{103}
13	$S_{140} = z_{33} \oplus S_{45} \oplus \underline{S_{187}} \oplus S_{144} \oplus \underline{S_{268}}(S_{94} \oplus S_{56} \oplus S_{33})$ $\oplus\, \underline{S_{268}}(S_{226} \oplus \overline{S_{193}} \oplus \underline{S_{187}}) \oplus (S_{226} \oplus \overline{S_{193}} \oplus \underline{S_{187}})$ $(S_{94} \oplus S_{56} \oplus S_{33}) \oplus (S_{263} \oplus S_{229} \oplus S_{226})S_{144}$ $\oplus\, (S_{263} \oplus S_{229} \oplus S_{226})S_{99} \oplus S_{99}$	$S_{45}, S_{94}, S_{33},$ S_{226}, S_{99}
14	$S_{136} = z_{29} \oplus S_{41} \oplus S_{183} \oplus S_{140} \oplus S_{264}(S_{90} \oplus S_{52} \oplus S_{29})$ $\oplus\, S_{264}(S_{222} \oplus \underline{S_{189}} \oplus S_{183}) \oplus (S_{222} \oplus \underline{S_{189}} \oplus S_{183})$ $(S_{90} \oplus S_{52} \oplus S_{29}) \oplus (S_{259} \oplus S_{225} \oplus S_{222})S_{140}$ $\oplus\, (S_{259} \oplus S_{225} \oplus S_{222})S_{95} \oplus S_{95}$	$S_{29}, S_{264}, S_{222},$ S_{183}, S_{95}
15	$S_{132} = z_{25} \oplus S_{37} \oplus S_{179} \oplus S_{136} \oplus S_{260}(S_{86} \oplus S_{48} \oplus S_{25})$ $\oplus\, S_{260}(S_{218} \oplus S_{185} \oplus S_{179}) \oplus (S_{218} \oplus S_{185} \oplus S_{179})$ $(S_{86} \oplus S_{48} \oplus S_{25}) \oplus (S_{255} \oplus S_{221} \oplus S_{218})S_{136}$ $\oplus\, (S_{255} \oplus S_{221} \oplus S_{218})S_{91} \oplus S_{91}$	$S_{260}, S_{218}, S_{185},$ S_{179}, S_{91}
16	$S_{128} = z_{21} \oplus S_{33} \oplus S_{175} \oplus S_{132} \oplus S_{256}(S_{82} \oplus S_{44} \oplus S_{21})$ $\oplus\, S_{256}(S_{214} \oplus S_{181} \oplus S_{175}) \oplus (S_{214} \oplus S_{181} \oplus S_{175})$ $(S_{82} \oplus S_{44} \oplus S_{21}) \oplus (S_{251} \oplus S_{217} \oplus S_{214})S_{132}$ $\oplus\, (S_{251} \oplus S_{217} \oplus S_{214})S_{87} \oplus S_{87}$	$S_{21}, S_{256}, S_{214},$ S_{181}, S_{175}, S_{87}
17	$S_{124} = z_{17} \oplus S_{29} \oplus S_{171} \oplus S_{128} \oplus S_{252}(S_{78} \oplus S_{40} \oplus S_{17})$ $\oplus\, S_{252}(S_{210} \oplus S_{177} \oplus S_{171}) \oplus (S_{210} \oplus S_{177} \oplus S_{171})$ $(S_{78} \oplus S_{40} \oplus S_{17}) \oplus (S_{247} \oplus S_{213} \oplus S_{210})S_{128}$ $\oplus\, (S_{247} \oplus S_{213} \oplus S_{210})S_{83} \oplus S_{83}$	$S_{17}, S_{252}, S_{210},$ S_{177}, S_{171}, S_{83}
18	$S_{120} = z_{13} \oplus S_{25} \oplus S_{167} \oplus S_{124} \oplus S_{248}(S_{74} \oplus S_{36} \oplus S_{13})$ $\oplus\, S_{248}(S_{206} \oplus S_{173} \oplus S_{167}) \oplus (S_{206} \oplus S_{173} \oplus S_{167})$ $(S_{74} \oplus S_{36} \oplus S_{13}) \oplus (S_{243} \oplus S_{209} \oplus S_{206})S_{124}$ $\oplus\, (S_{243} \oplus S_{209} \oplus S_{206})S_{79} \oplus S_{79}$	$S_{13}, S_{248}, S_{206},$ S_{173}, S_{79}
19	$S_{116} = z_9 \oplus S_{21} \oplus S_{163} \oplus S_{120} \oplus S_{244}(S_{70} \oplus S_{32} \oplus S_9)$ $\oplus\, S_{244}(S_{202} \oplus S_{169} \oplus S_{163}) \oplus (S_{202} \oplus S_{169} \oplus S_{163})$ $(S_{70} \oplus S_{32} \oplus S_9) \oplus (S_{239} \oplus S_{205} \oplus S_{202})S_{120}$ $\oplus\, (S_{239} \oplus S_{205} \oplus S_{202})S_{75} \oplus S_{75}$	$S_9, S_{244}, S_{169}, S_{75}$

(*continued*)

Table 1. (*continued*)

Steps	Equations used for recovery	Guessed bits
20	$S_{112} = z_5 \oplus S_{17} \oplus S_{159} \oplus S_{116} \oplus S_{240}(S_{66} \oplus S_{28} \oplus S_5)$ $\oplus S_{240}(S_{198} \oplus S_{165} \oplus S_{159}) \oplus (S_{198} \oplus S_{165} \oplus S_{159})$ $(S_{66} \oplus S_{28} \oplus S_5) \oplus (S_{235} \oplus S_{201} \oplus S_{198})S_{116}$ $\oplus (S_{235} \oplus S_{201} \oplus S_{198})S_{71} \oplus S_{71}$	$S_5, S_{240}, S_{165},$ S_{159}, S_{71}
21	$S_{108} = z_1 \oplus S_{13} \oplus S_{155} \oplus S_{112} \oplus S_{236}(S_{62} \oplus S_{24} \oplus S_1)$ $\oplus S_{236}(S_{194} \oplus S_{161} \oplus S_{155}) \oplus (S_{194} \oplus S_{161} \oplus S_{155})$ $(S_{62} \oplus S_{24} \oplus S_1) \oplus (S_{231} \oplus S_{197} \oplus S_{194})S_{112}$ $\oplus (S_{231} \oplus S_{197} \oplus S_{194})S_{67} \oplus S_{67}$	$S_{62}, S_1, S_{231}, S_{67}$
22	$S_{149} = z_{42} \oplus S_{54} \oplus \overline{S_{196}} \oplus S_{153} \oplus S_{277}(S_{103} \oplus \overline{S_{65}} \oplus S_{42})$ $\oplus S_{277}(\overline{S_{235}} \oplus \overline{S_{202}} \oplus \overline{S_{196}}) \oplus (\overline{S_{235}} \oplus \overline{S_{202}} \oplus \overline{S_{196}})$ $(S_{103} \oplus \overline{S_{65}} \oplus S_{42}) \oplus (\underline{S_{272}} \oplus \overline{S_{238}} \oplus \overline{S_{235}})S_{153}$ $\oplus (\underline{S_{272}} \oplus \overline{S_{238}} \oplus \overline{S_{235}})\overline{S_{108}} \oplus \overline{S_{108}}$	$S_{54}, S_{42}, S_{277}, S_{153}$
23	$S_{145} = z_{38} \oplus S_{50} \oplus \overline{S_{192}} \oplus S_{149} \oplus S_{273}(S_{99} \oplus \overline{S_{61}} \oplus S_{38})$ $\oplus S_{273}(\overline{S_{231}} \oplus \overline{S_{198}} \oplus S_{192}) \oplus (\overline{S_{231}} \oplus \overline{S_{198}} \oplus S_{192})$ $(S_{99} \oplus \overline{S_{61}} \oplus S_{38}) \oplus (\underline{S_{268}} \oplus \overline{S_{234}} \oplus \overline{S_{231}})S_{149}$ $\oplus (\underline{S_{268}} \oplus \overline{S_{234}} \oplus \overline{S_{231}})S_{104} \oplus S_{104}$	$S_{50}, S_{38}, S_{273}, S_{104}$
24	$S_{141} = z_{34} \oplus S_{46} \oplus \underline{S_{188}} \oplus S_{145} \oplus \underline{S_{269}}(S_{95} \oplus S_{57} \oplus S_{34})$ $\oplus \underline{S_{269}}(S_{227} \oplus \overline{S_{194}} \oplus \underline{S_{188}}) \oplus (S_{227} \oplus \overline{S_{194}} \oplus \underline{S_{188}})$ $(S_{95} \oplus S_{57} \oplus S_{34}) \oplus (S_{264} \oplus \overline{S_{230}} \oplus S_{227})S_{145}$ $\oplus (S_{264} \oplus \overline{S_{230}} \oplus S_{227})S_{100} \oplus S_{100}$	S_{46}, S_{34}, S_{227} S_{100}
25	$S_{137} = z_{30} \oplus S_{42} \oplus S_{184} \oplus S_{141} \oplus S_{265}(S_{91} \oplus S_{53} \oplus S_{30})$ $\oplus S_{265}(S_{223} \oplus \underline{S_{190}} \oplus S_{184}) \oplus (S_{223} \oplus \underline{S_{190}} \oplus S_{184})$ $(S_{91} \oplus S_{53} \oplus S_{30}) \oplus (S_{260} \oplus S_{226} \oplus S_{223})S_{141}$ $\oplus (S_{260} \oplus S_{226} \oplus S_{223})S_{96} \oplus S_{96}$	$S_{30}, S_{265}, S_{223}, S_{96}$
26	$S_{133} = z_{26} \oplus S_{38} \oplus S_{180} \oplus S_{137} \oplus S_{261}(S_{87} \oplus S_{49} \oplus S_{26})$ $\oplus S_{261}(S_{219} \oplus S_{186} \oplus S_{180}) \oplus (S_{219} \oplus S_{186} \oplus S_{180})$ $(S_{87} \oplus S_{49} \oplus S_{26}) \oplus (S_{256} \oplus S_{222} \oplus S_{219})S_{137}$ $\oplus (S_{256} \oplus S_{222} \oplus S_{219})S_{92} \oplus S_{92}$	S_{261}, S_{219}, S_{92}
27	$S_{129} = z_{22} \oplus S_{34} \oplus S_{176} \oplus S_{133} \oplus S_{257}(S_{83} \oplus S_{45} \oplus S_{22})$ $\oplus S_{257}(S_{215} \oplus S_{182} \oplus S_{176}) \oplus (S_{215} \oplus S_{182} \oplus S_{176})$ $(S_{83} \oplus S_{45} \oplus S_{22}) \oplus (S_{252} \oplus S_{218} \oplus S_{215})S_{133}$ $\oplus (S_{252} \oplus S_{218} \oplus S_{215})S_{88} \oplus S_{88}$	$S_{22}, S_{257}, S_{215}, S_{88}$
28	$S_{125} = z_{18} \oplus S_{30} \oplus S_{172} \oplus S_{129} \oplus S_{253}(S_{79} \oplus S_{41} \oplus S_{18})$ $\oplus S_{253}(S_{211} \oplus S_{178} \oplus S_{172}) \oplus (S_{211} \oplus S_{178} \oplus S_{172})$ $(S_{79} \oplus S_{41} \oplus S_{18}) \oplus (S_{248} \oplus S_{214} \oplus S_{211})S_{129}$ $\oplus (S_{248} \oplus S_{214} \oplus S_{211})S_{84} \oplus S_{84}$	$S_{18}, S_{253}, S_{211}, S_{84}$
29	$S_{121} = z_{14} \oplus S_{26} \oplus S_{168} \oplus S_{125} \oplus S_{249}(S_{75} \oplus S_{37} \oplus S_{14})$ $\oplus S_{249}(S_{207} \oplus S_{174} \oplus S_{168}) \oplus (S_{207} \oplus S_{174} \oplus S_{168})$ $(S_{75} \oplus S_{37} \oplus S_{14}) \oplus (S_{244} \oplus S_{210} \oplus S_{207})S_{125}$ $\oplus (S_{244} \oplus S_{210} \oplus S_{207})S_{80} \oplus S_{80}$	$S_{14}, S_{249}, S_{207}, S_{80}$

(*continued*)

Table 1. (*continued*)

Steps	Equations used for recovery	Guessed bits
30	$S_{117} = z_{10} \oplus S_{22} \oplus S_{164} \oplus S_{121} \oplus S_{245}(S_{71} \oplus S_{33} \oplus S_{10})$ $\oplus\, S_{245}(S_{203} \oplus S_{170} \oplus S_{164}) \oplus (S_{203} \oplus S_{170} \oplus S_{164})$ $(S_{71} \oplus S_{33} \oplus S_{10}) \oplus (S_{240} \oplus S_{206} \oplus S_{203})S_{121}$ $\oplus\, (S_{240} \oplus S_{206} \oplus S_{203})S_{76} \oplus S_{76}$	S_{10}, S_{245}, S_{76}
31	$S_{113} = z_6 \oplus S_{18} \oplus S_{160} \oplus S_{117} \oplus S_{241}(S_{67} \oplus S_{29} \oplus S_6)$ $\oplus\, S_{241}(S_{199} \oplus S_{166} \oplus S_{160}) \oplus (S_{199} \oplus S_{166} \oplus S_{160})$ $(S_{67} \oplus S_{29} \oplus S_6) \oplus (S_{236} \oplus S_{202} \oplus S_{199})S_{117}$ $\oplus\, (S_{236} \oplus S_{202} \oplus S_{199})S_{72} \oplus S_{72}$	S_6, S_{241}, S_{72}
32	$S_{109} = z_2 \oplus S_{14} \oplus S_{156} \oplus S_{113} \oplus S_{237}(S_{63} \oplus S_{25} \oplus S_2)$ $\oplus\, S_{237}(S_{195} \oplus S_{162} \oplus S_{156}) \oplus (S_{195} \oplus S_{162} \oplus S_{156})$ $(S_{63} \oplus S_{25} \oplus S_2) \oplus (S_{232} \oplus S_{198} \oplus S_{195})S_{113}$ $\oplus\, (S_{232} \oplus S_{198} \oplus S_{195})S_{68} \oplus S_{68}$	S_{68}
33	$S_{150} = z_{43} \oplus S_{55} \oplus \overline{S_{197}} \oplus \overline{S_{154}} \oplus S_{278}(S_{104} \oplus \overline{S_{66}} \oplus S_{43})$ $\oplus\, S_{278}(\overline{S_{236}} \oplus \overline{S_{203}} \oplus \overline{S_{197}}) \oplus (\overline{S_{236}} \oplus \overline{S_{203}} \oplus \overline{S_{197}})$ $(S_{104} \oplus \overline{S_{66}} \oplus S_{43}) \oplus (S_{273} \oplus \overline{S_{239}} \oplus \overline{S_{236}})\overline{S_{154}}$ $\oplus\, (S_{273} \oplus \overline{S_{239}} \oplus \overline{S_{236}})\overline{S_{109}} \oplus \overline{S_{109}}$	S_{278}
34	$S_{146} = z_{39} \oplus S_{51} \oplus \overline{S_{193}} \oplus S_{150} \oplus S_{274}(S_{100} \oplus \overline{S_{62}} \oplus S_{39})$ $\oplus\, S_{274}(\overline{S_{232}} \oplus \overline{S_{199}} \oplus \overline{S_{193}}) \oplus (\overline{S_{232}} \oplus \overline{S_{199}} \oplus \overline{S_{193}})$ $(S_{100} \oplus \overline{S_{62}} \oplus S_{39}) \oplus (\underline{S_{269}} \oplus \overline{S_{235}} \oplus \overline{S_{232}})S_{150}$ $\oplus\, (\underline{S_{269}} \oplus \overline{S_{235}} \oplus \overline{S_{232}})S_{105} \oplus S_{105}$	S_{274}, S_{105}
35	$S_{142} = z_{35} \oplus S_{47} \oplus \underline{S_{189}} \oplus S_{146} \oplus \underline{S_{270}}(S_{96} \oplus S_{58} \oplus S_{35})$ $\oplus\, \underline{S_{270}}(S_{228} \oplus \overline{S_{195}} \oplus \underline{S_{189}}) \oplus (S_{228} \oplus \overline{S_{195}} \oplus \underline{S_{189}})$ $(S_{96} \oplus S_{58} \oplus S_{35}) \oplus (S_{265} \oplus \overline{S_{231}} \oplus S_{228})S_{146}$ $\oplus\, (S_{265} \oplus \overline{S_{231}} \oplus S_{228})S_{101} \oplus S_{101}$	–
36	$S_{138} = z_{31} \oplus S_{43} \oplus S_{185} \oplus S_{142} \oplus S_{266}(S_{92} \oplus S_{54} \oplus S_{31})$ $\oplus\, S_{266}(S_{224} \oplus \underline{S_{191}} \oplus S_{185}) \oplus (S_{224} \oplus \underline{S_{191}} \oplus S_{185})$ $(S_{92} \oplus S_{54} \oplus S_{31}) \oplus (S_{261} \oplus S_{227} \oplus S_{224})S_{142}$ $\oplus\, (S_{261} \oplus S_{227} \oplus S_{224})S_{97} \oplus S_{97}$	–
37	$S_{134} = z_{27} \oplus S_{39} \oplus S_{181} \oplus S_{138} \oplus S_{262}(S_{88} \oplus S_{50} \oplus S_{27})$ $\oplus\, S_{262}(S_{220} \oplus \underline{S_{187}} \oplus S_{181}) \oplus (S_{220} \oplus \underline{S_{187}} \oplus S_{181})$ $(S_{88} \oplus S_{50} \oplus S_{27}) \oplus (S_{257} \oplus S_{223} \oplus S_{220})S_{138}$ $\oplus\, (S_{257} \oplus S_{223} \oplus S_{220})S_{93} \oplus S_{93}$	–
38	$S_{130} = z_{23} \oplus S_{35} \oplus S_{177} \oplus S_{134} \oplus S_{258}(S_{84} \oplus S_{46} \oplus S_{23})$ $\oplus\, S_{258}(S_{216} \oplus S_{183} \oplus S_{177}) \oplus (S_{216} \oplus S_{183} \oplus S_{177})$ $(S_{84} \oplus S_{46} \oplus S_{23}) \oplus (S_{253} \oplus S_{219} \oplus S_{216})S_{134}$ $\oplus\, (S_{253} \oplus S_{219} \oplus S_{216})S_{89} \oplus S_{89}$	–

(*continued*)

Table 1. (*continued*)

Steps	Equations used for recovery	Guessed bits
39	$S_{126} = z_{19} \oplus S_{31} \oplus S_{173} \oplus S_{130} \oplus S_{254}(S_{80} \oplus S_{42} \oplus S_{19})$ $\oplus S_{254}(S_{212} \oplus S_{179} \oplus S_{173}) \oplus (S_{212} \oplus S_{179} \oplus S_{173})$ $(S_{80} \oplus S_{42} \oplus S_{19}) \oplus (S_{249} \oplus S_{215} \oplus S_{212})S_{130}$ $\oplus (S_{249} \oplus S_{215} \oplus S_{212})S_{85} \oplus S_{85}$	S_{19}
40	$S_{122} = z_{15} \oplus S_{27} \oplus S_{169} \oplus S_{126} \oplus S_{250}(S_{76} \oplus S_{38} \oplus S_{15})$ $\oplus S_{250}(S_{208} \oplus S_{175} \oplus S_{169}) \oplus (S_{208} \oplus S_{175} \oplus S_{169})$ $(S_{76} \oplus S_{38} \oplus S_{15}) \oplus (S_{245} \oplus S_{211} \oplus S_{208})S_{126}$ $\oplus (S_{245} \oplus S_{211} \oplus S_{208})S_{81} \oplus S_{81}$	S_{15}
41	$S_{118} = z_{11} \oplus S_{23} \oplus S_{165} \oplus S_{122} \oplus S_{246}(S_{72} \oplus S_{34} \oplus S_{11})$ $\oplus S_{246}(S_{204} \oplus S_{171} \oplus S_{165}) \oplus (S_{204} \oplus S_{171} \oplus S_{165})$ $(S_{72} \oplus S_{34} \oplus S_{11}) \oplus (S_{241} \oplus S_{207} \oplus S_{204})S_{122}$ $\oplus (S_{241} \oplus S_{207} \oplus S_{204})S_{77} \oplus S_{77}$	S_{11}
42	$S_{114} = z_7 \oplus S_{19} \oplus S_{161} \oplus S_{118} \oplus S_{242}(S_{68} \oplus S_{30} \oplus S_7)$ $\oplus S_{242}(S_{200} \oplus S_{167} \oplus S_{161}) \oplus (S_{200} \oplus S_{167} \oplus S_{161})$ $(S_{68} \oplus S_{30} \oplus S_7) \oplus (S_{237} \oplus S_{203} \oplus S_{200})S_{118}$ $\oplus (S_{237} \oplus S_{203} \oplus S_{200})S_{73} \oplus S_{73}$	–
43	$S_{110} = z_3 \oplus S_{15} \oplus S_{157} \oplus S_{114} \oplus S_{238}(S_{64} \oplus S_{26} \oplus S_3)$ $\oplus S_{238}(S_{196} \oplus S_{163} \oplus S_{157}) \oplus (S_{196} \oplus S_{163} \oplus S_{157})$ $(S_{64} \oplus S_{26} \oplus S_3) \oplus (S_{233} \oplus S_{199} \oplus S_{196})S_{114}$ $\oplus (S_{233} \oplus S_{199} \oplus S_{196})S_{69} \oplus S_{69}$	–
44	$S_{56} = z_{44} \oplus S_{151} \oplus \overline{S_{198}} \oplus S_{155} \oplus S_{279}(S_{105} \oplus \overline{S_{67}} \oplus S_{44})$ $\oplus S_{279}(\overline{S_{237}} \oplus \overline{S_{204}} \oplus \overline{S_{198}}) \oplus (\overline{S_{237}} \oplus \overline{S_{204}} \oplus \overline{S_{198}})$ $(S_{105} \oplus \overline{S_{67}} \oplus S_{44}) \oplus (S_{274} \oplus \overline{S_{240}} \oplus \overline{S_{237}})S_{155}$ $\oplus (S_{274} \oplus \overline{S_{240}} \oplus \overline{S_{237}})\overline{S_{110}} \oplus \overline{S_{110}}$	S_{279}
45	$S_{57} = z_{45} \oplus S_{152} \oplus \overline{S_{199}} \oplus S_{156} \oplus S_{280}(S_{106} \oplus \overline{S_{68}} \oplus S_{45})$ $\oplus S_{280}(\overline{S_{238}} \oplus \overline{S_{205}} \oplus \overline{S_{199}}) \oplus (\overline{S_{238}} \oplus \overline{S_{205}} \oplus \overline{S_{199}})$ $(S_{106} \oplus \overline{S_{68}} \oplus S_{45}) \oplus (S_{275} \oplus \overline{S_{241}} \oplus \overline{S_{238}})\overline{S_{156}}$ $\oplus (S_{275} \oplus \overline{S_{241}} \oplus \overline{S_{238}})\overline{S_{111}} \oplus \overline{S_{111}}$	S_{280}
46	$S_{58} = z_{46} \oplus S_{153} \oplus \overline{S_{200}} \oplus S_{157} \oplus S_{281}(S_{107} \oplus \overline{S_{69}} \oplus S_{46})$ $\oplus S_{281}(\overline{S_{239}} \oplus \overline{S_{206}} \oplus \overline{S_{200}}) \oplus (\overline{S_{239}} \oplus \overline{S_{206}} \oplus \overline{S_{200}})$ $(\overline{S_{107}} \oplus \overline{S_{69}} \oplus S_{46}) \oplus (S_{276} \oplus \overline{S_{242}} \oplus \overline{S_{239}})\overline{S_{157}}$ $\oplus (S_{276} \oplus \overline{S_{242}} \oplus \overline{S_{239}})\overline{S_{112}} \oplus \overline{S_{112}}$	S_{281}
47	$S_{59} = z_{47} \oplus \overline{S_{154}} \oplus \overline{S_{201}} \oplus \overline{S_{158}} \oplus S_{282}(S_{108} \oplus \overline{S_{70}} \oplus S_{47})$ $\oplus S_{282}(\overline{S_{240}} \oplus \overline{S_{207}} \oplus \overline{S_{201}}) \oplus (\overline{S_{240}} \oplus \overline{S_{207}} \oplus \overline{S_{201}})$ $(\overline{S_{108}} \oplus \overline{S_{70}} \oplus S_{47}) \oplus (S_{277} \oplus \overline{S_{243}} \oplus \overline{S_{240}})\overline{S_{158}}$ $\oplus (S_{277} \oplus \overline{S_{243}} \oplus \overline{S_{240}})\overline{S_{113}} \oplus \overline{S_{113}}$	S_{282}
48	$S_{60} = z_{48} \oplus \overline{S_{155}} \oplus \overline{S_{202}} \oplus \overline{S_{159}} \oplus S_{283}(S_{109} \oplus \overline{S_{71}} \oplus S_{48})$ $\oplus S_{283}(\overline{S_{241}} \oplus \overline{S_{208}} \oplus \overline{S_{202}}) \oplus (\overline{S_{241}} \oplus \overline{S_{208}} \oplus \overline{S_{202}})$ $(\overline{S_{109}} \oplus \overline{S_{71}} \oplus S_{48}) \oplus (S_{278} \oplus \overline{S_{244}} \oplus \overline{S_{241}})\overline{S_{159}}$ $\oplus (S_{278} \oplus \overline{S_{244}} \oplus \overline{S_{241}})\overline{S_{114}} \oplus \overline{S_{114}}$	S_{283}

At this point, we like to explain about certain 'unit' cost related to exact complexity. Such unit cost may involve several computations related to the cipher operations. In a most generic way, given a k-bit secret key, the exhaustive attack asks for a complexity of 2^k units, where each unit may require several CPU clocks. While mounting the TMDTO attack the same situation is valid. Thus, in our technique, we also consider all the operations as unit cost. However, we will point out a few cases when our calculations are most costly and that should be taken care of in the complexity analysis. For example, simply generating a 293-bit key stream (that will become the state η) of ACORN v3 from a state ζ requires 0.088 s in our computing facility. However, to recover the 47 bits of the state from 47 bits of key stream and the remaining state bits requires a time of 0.076 s, which is almost as same as the time taken to generate ζ. Thus, no additional complexity is required for solving. Hence for this scenario our parameters are as follows. We can take $T' = 2^{122}, M' = 2^{124}$ and $D' = 2^{61}$. Then, $T = T' \cdot 2^0 = 2^{122}$, $M = M' = 2^{124}$, $D = 2^\psi \cdot D' = 2^{47} \cdot 2^{61} = 2^{108}$, $P = P' = \frac{N'}{D'} = 2^{185}$.

3.2 Knowledge of 53 Bits of State from 60 Key Stream Bits

We follow a similar procedure as mentioned in Sect. 3.1. However, when the SAT solver is populated with equations and is set to find all possible solutions for 53 state bits using only 53 key stream bits, the SAT solver fails to find a unique solution. Instead, we get multiple solutions, where each solution provides the same 53-bit key stream pattern. To combat this problem, we involve a new idea. Instead of searching for a 53-bit pattern (say 53 continuous 0's), we search for a 240-bit pattern where the first 53-bit sequence and the last 7-bit sequence are fixed (say to 0's). This is based on the fact that the key stream sequence generated by all solutions are different. The SAT solver identifies the difference between the sequence of last 7 bits and removes all additional solutions. However, this gives us an additional Data complexity of 2^7. Considering this constraint into the SAT solver in a similar fashion, (as explained in Sect. 2.1), we get the data mentioned in Table 1. However, in very few cases, two solutions sets are possible which generate the same keystream. Since the proportion is very small and our success probability is $\frac{2^{14}-1}{2^{14}}$, the time complexity should be multiplied by $T' = T' \times \frac{2^{14}}{2^{14}-1} \approx T' \times 1 = T'$. However, we still attempt to deal with this edge case scenario of two solutions. The idea is to simply discard the second solution during the offline phase and continue with the first solution set. The matrix stopping rule ensures the entire search space is covered with negligible collision. During the online phase, the adversary can access few more key stream bits following the fixed pattern in the key stream and hence conclude with the final solution. Our experiments show that 7 more key stream bits, i.e. 67 key stream bits in total are enough to find a unique solution.

Similar to Sect. 3.1 the time taken for solving equations is of the same order of generating ζ, hence $T = T'$.

- $T = T' = 2^{120}$ is the total time complexity of the attack,

- $M = M' = 2^{120}$ is the amount of memory required,
- $D = D' \times 2^{60} = 2^{120}$ where $D' = 2^{60}$, since the adversary must succeed in finding a 60-bit pattern,
- $P = \frac{N'}{D'} = 2^{180}$ is the preprocessing time for formulating tables.

3.3   Knowledge of 49 Bits of State from 49 Key Stream Bits and Fixing 10 State Bits

Here we consider the third approach which is similar to what has been recently considered in [7] for a TMDTO attack against Lizard [6]. We consider that ψ state bits can be recovered from ψ many key stream bits and rest of the state bits, but τ many state bits has to be fixed to a specific pattern. This follows the idea mentioned in Sect. 2.2. In this case we go back to single preprocessing table. We will consider $\psi = 49$ here, with $\tau = 10$. That is from ψ bits of key stream and the remaining $(n-\psi)$ state bits (out of which τ are fixed to a specific pattern), we will be able to solve for the ψ bits of the state. The initial table preparation goes as follows. We start with a $(n-\psi-\tau)$ bit random pattern and then take a specific pattern for ψ. Also the fixed pattern of ϕ is known. Now, using the equations as described in Sect. 2.2, we solve for the rest ψ bits of the state. This gives the complete state. Then we run the PRGA for $n-\tau$ times. The initial ψ bits will be as fixed. The remaining $(n - \psi - \tau)$ pseudorandom bits will be considered as the part of the next state bits. Thus, we have $T'M' = 2^{n-\psi-\tau} = 2^{293-49-10} = 2^{234}$. Let us take $T' = 2^{112}$ and $M' = 2^{122}$, which also gives, $D' = \sqrt{T'} = 2^{56}$. Thus, we will now have the following parameters.

- $D = D' \cdot 2^{\psi+\tau} = 2^{56+49+10} = 2^{115}$, as the specific pattern ψ should come towards consulting the table, and also for a good success rate to have the specific τ bit pattern in the state we need to try 2^{τ} many times,
- $M = M' = 2^{122}$,
- $T = T' \cdot 2^{\tau} = 2^{112+10} = 2^{122}$, as we only consult the preprocessing table when the specific ψ bit pattern appears in the key stream, but we need to try 2^{τ} times as we have that more data and here the solution time can be estimated from the operations in the equations and that can subsumed in the PRGA effort,
- $P = P' = \frac{N'}{D'} = 2^{234-56} = 2^{178}$.

A similar online parameter in this respect can be obtained considering the equation $5\psi+2\tau = n$. Here, $\psi = 49$, by fixing $\tau = 10$. However, we can easily increase τ to 24 to satisfy the equation $5\psi + 2\tau = 5 \cdot 49 + 2 \cdot 24 = 293 = n$. That is we will fix 24 state bits to a specific pattern. In this case the online complexity becomes $T = M = D = 2^{\frac{n-\psi}{2}} = 2^{\frac{293-49}{2}} = 2^{122}$. However, the preprocessing becomes less, which is $P = 2^{\frac{n+\psi}{2}} = 2^{\frac{293+49}{2}} = 2^{171}$.

4   Conclusion

In this paper we have studied how certain portion of the state of ACORN v3 can be obtained from key stream and guessing or fixing the remaining state bits. We attempt that problem by generating a set of equations and feeding that to SAT solver. At the same time, we try to consider the structure of the equations and solve a set of equations without using the SAT solver. Several examples with different parameters are presented. Based on those parameters, we note different time-memory-data trade-off for attacking ACORN v3. Indeed it is possible to mount the attack where the online complexity is less than the exhaustive key search. The pre-processing effort is higher than exhaustive search but it can be reduced further by increasing the amount of data or by recovering more internal sate bits. While our observations do not refute any security claim of the cipher, the study adds certain insight towards the cryptanalysis and may lead to further research in this area.

Acknowledgements. The first author would like to thank Department of Science and Technology DST-FIST Level-1 Program Grant No. SR/FST/MSI-092/2013 for providing the computational facilities.

References

1. Babbage, S.: A space/time tradeoff in exhaustive search attacks on stream ciphers. In: European Convention on Security and Detection. IEEE Conference Publication, no. 408, May 1995
2. Biryukov, A., Shamir, A., Wagner, D.: Real time cryptanalysis of A5/1 on a PC. In: Goos, G., Hartmanis, J., van Leeuwen, J., Schneier, B. (eds.) FSE 2000. LNCS, vol. 1978, pp. 1–18. Springer, Heidelberg (2001). https://doi.org/10.1007/3-540-44706-7_1
3. Biryukov, A., Shamir, A.: Cryptanalytic time/memory/data tradeoffs for stream ciphers. In: Okamoto, T. (ed.) ASIACRYPT 2000. LNCS, vol. 1976, pp. 1–13. Springer, Heidelberg (2000). https://doi.org/10.1007/3-540-44448-3_1
4. CAESAR. http://competitions.cr.yp.to/caesar.html
5. Golić, J.D.: Cryptanalysis of alleged A5 stream cipher. In: Fumy, W. (ed.) EURO-CRYPT 1997. LNCS, vol. 1233, pp. 239–255. Springer, Heidelberg (1997). https://doi.org/10.1007/3-540-69053-0_17
6. Hamann, M., Krause, M., Meier, W.: LIZARD - a lightweight stream cipher for power-constrained devices. In: FSE 2017. http://eprint.iacr.org/2016/926, http://tosc.iacr.org/index.php/ToSC/article/view/584
7. Maitra, S., Sinha, N., Siddhanti, A., Anand, R., Gangopadhyay, S.: A TMDTO attack against lizard (2017). http://eprint.iacr.org/2017/647
8. SAGE Mathematics Software. Free Software Foundation Inc. (2009). http://www.sagemath.org. (Open source project initiated by W. Stein and contributed by many)
9. Sarkar, S., Banik, S., Maitra, S.: Differential fault attack against grain family with very few faults and minimal assumptions. IEEE Trans. Comput. **64**(6), 1647–1657 (2015)
10. Wu, H.: ACORN: a lightweight authenticated cipher (v3). https://competitions.cr.yp.to/round3/acornv3.pdf

Efficient Implementation of Private License Plate Matching Protocols

Harshul Vaishnav[(⊠)], Smriti Sharma, and Anish Mathuria

Dhirubhai Ambani Institute of Information and Communication Technology,
Gandhinagar 382007, Gujarat, India
va.hv.02@gmail.com

Abstract. License plate matching is an important facilitator for new-age services like toll billing, calculation of road taxes and law enforcement that demand both effectiveness and efficiency. The license plate itself might not be of much importance but the information linked to it may reveal a lot about the owner. Therefore, in order to maintain the privacy of information and to ensure security of the ways in which the information is used, the search/match operations are performed in the encrypted domain. We practically analyze the performance of three existing protocols for private license plate matching based on Paillier's additively homomorphic technique. We explore various performance improvement techniques for Paillier encryption and decryption to speedup the overall matching process. In addition, we attempt to parallelise the entire procedure by separately running encryption-decryption in a multi-threaded manner, thereby speeding up the process. Finally, we perform comparative analysis of experimental results of the four implementation techniques (along with parallelisation).

Keywords: Secure license plate matching · Paillier's encryption · Performance analysis · Encryption-decryption · Parallelisation

1 Introduction

A license plate of a car can serve as an identity of its owner. Nowadays, such plate-numbers are linked to all kinds of credential proofs that a person holds including the sensitive bank account information. Carrying out plate-related transactions openly might lead to loss of privacy. In such settings it is best to keep the data encrypted and perform operations on the ciphertext in order to ensure the privacy of the data.

For a real life example, consider a police agency (**A**) trying to track the whereabouts of a suspected criminal vehicle, and an entity holding car park information about the visitors to the parking. The latter entity could be a large organization or a terminal for public transit like the Airport Authority (**B**). The airport authority should have only enough information about the license plate in order to perform the matching and the police agency just needs to know if there is a match of the license plate number. In other words, the privacy requirements are as follows:

© Springer International Publishing AG 2017
S.S. Ali et al. (Eds.): SPACE 2017, LNCS 10662, pp. 281–294, 2017.
https://doi.org/10.1007/978-3-319-71501-8_16

– The airport authority should not come to know about the actual number on the license plate.
– The police agency should not have any information about the database of license plates owned by the airport authority.

Homomorphic encryption is a cryptographic tool that enables computations over encrypted data, for example Paillier's scheme [2]. It maintains the original form of the input implying that (some of) the same operations that can be applied on plain domain can also be applied on cipher domain. After performing operations on the ciphertexts, the resulting value is identical to what is obtained when the operation is performed on the plaintexts and the answer is encrypted.

Homomorphic encryption has applications in varied privacy enhancing domains one of which is presented in Erkin et al. ([9]). This work describes a technique for face-recognition via Eigenface recognition systems working on encrypted images. A highly optimised cryptographic protocol is used for comparison of Paillier encrypted values.

In this paper we investigate secure protcols for private matching of license plates proposed by Sunil et al. in [1]. They perform character recognition first and then proceed with match functions on encrypted data. We focus on the integer matching process and explore different performance improvement techniques of Paillier. This means that we work on an integer that is a representation of an already identified and integer-converted number plate value. We have a list of integers which act as a database of number plates. The main aim of our work is to be able to perform this matching in a secure and efficient manner (in terms of run-times).

The rest of the paper is organised as follows. Section 2 reviews the previous protocols that utilize homomorphic encryption for private license plate matching. In Sect. 3 we propose a modification to strengthen the protocols against a malicious insider attack. A detailed analysis of the original encryption scheme and the optimised schemes are covered in Sect. 4. Section 5 explains the choice of parameters used in the experiments. Section 6 explains how we parallelise the implementation to make the matching process faster and compares the results obtained for different encryption bit-lengths, encryption schemes and multithreading. Section 7 concludes the paper.

2   Existing Protocols

Sunil et al. [1] proposed secure protocols for private matching of license plates for three different scenarios using two different cryptographic tools, namely additively homomorphic encryption and Gentry's fully homomorphic encryption [5]. We focus on the additively homomorphic encryption as it suffices for integer matching and is more efficient than fully homomorphic encryption. Gentry's scheme supports multiple operations without errors but integer matching doesn't require fully homomorphic property. The additive homomorphic encryption employed by the protocols is Paillier's scheme. This scheme is a probabilistic public-key cryptosystem. The encryption scheme is randomised, that is, encryptions of the same plaintext will result in different ciphertexts. The paper by Paillier [2] describes three variants of Paillier's cryptosystem and [1] employs the first one of them.

In the plaintext domain, matching of license plate numbers can simply be done by subtracting the integer representations of the test plate and the plates in the database. This operation is done in the cipher domain using Paillier's additively homomorphic scheme. This scheme has the property that $[[m_1 + m_2]]$ is equal to $c_1 c_2$ in the cipher domain where, $c_1 = [[m_1]]$ and $c_2 = [[m_2]]$. So, in order to compute $c_1 - c_2$, we multiply c_1 with the inverse of c_2. The matching process can roughly be stated as follows:

- Generate public and private keys.
- Encrypt the test license plate (to be matched) as well as the plates in the database using the public key.
- Perform the matching in encrypted domain by multiplying the encrypted test value with the inverse of the encrypted database plate.
- Decrypt the difference values using the private key. If any decryption result is equal to zero, then there is a match.

Table 1 lists the notations used throughout the paper.

Table 1. Notations

A	Entity holding the test license plate
B	Entity holding the database of license plates
T	Trusted third party
pk	Public key
sk	Private key
$[[var]]$	var encrypted using pk of a Paillier's cryptosystem
y_i	Database entries in plaintext
d_i	Database containing difference values
$\hat{d}_i$	Database with randomised differences

Table 2 lists the salient features of the three scenarios.

Table 2. Salient features of the three scenarios

	Holder of private key	Matching performed at	Database exchanges
Scenario 1	**A**	**B**	1
Scenario 2	**B**	**A**	2
Scenario 3	**T**	**B**	1

Here, **A** is the requesting entity (police agency), **B** is the number plates'
database holder (airport authority) and **T** is a third party trusted by both **A**,
and **B**. We briefly review these scenarios below.

2.1 Scenario 1

In this scenario, **A** generates the keys pk and sk and the matching process is performed at **B**. Table 3 gives step by step execution of this scenario. **B** encrypts its
database with the public key generated by **A**. **A** provides **B** with the encrypted
test plate. It then performs the matching by multiplying the encrypted test plate
with the inverse of encrypted database license plates. The resulting values are
then multiplied with a random number. Note that if there is a 'zero' within the
results, it remains zero after the multiplication. The sequence of values is sent
back to **A**. As **A** is the sole possessor of the private key, only **A** can decrypt the
results to find whether there is a match; **B** does not learn the outcome.

Table 3. Protocol 1.

Entity A	Entity B
Generate pk, sk	
Encrypt test plate:- $[[x]]$	
$\xrightarrow{\;[[x]],pk\;}$	
	Encrypt database using pk :- $[[y_i]]$
	Compute $[[d_i]] = [[x]][[y_i]]^{-1}$
	Generate a random number R
	$[[\hat{d}_i]] = [[d_i]]^R$
$\xleftarrow{\;[[\hat{d}_i]]\;}$	
Decrypt $[[\hat{d}_i]]$ to $\hat{d}_i$ using sk.	
Check if any $\hat{d}_i = 0$	

2.2 Scenario 2

In this scenario, **B** generates both the keys and therefore has a pre-encrypted
database (Table 4). The public key, along with the encrypted database, is sent to
A. Then **A** performs the matching, randomises the order and sends the results
back to **B**. **B** decrypts the results and tells **A** whether there is a match. Thus,
both the entities come to know about the final result. As before, the data generated after subtraction is multiplied by a random number so that **B** does not
come to know about the test plate number that **A** possessed. As the database
is pre-encrypted, even if an attacker steals the database, he will not be able to
access the number plates stored at **B**. However, Protocol 2 is more expensive in
communication than Protocol 1 as it requires two database exchanges.

Table 4. Protocol 2.

Entity A	Entity B
	Generate pk, sk and encrypt database $[[y_i]]$
	$\xleftarrow{pk,[[y_i]]}$
Encrypt test plate using pk :- $[[x]]$	
Compute $[[d_i]] = [[x]][[y_i]]^{-1}$	
Generate a random number R	
$[[\hat{d}_i]] = [[d_i]]^R$	
$\xrightarrow{[[d_i]]^R}$	
	Decrypt $[[\hat{d}_i]]$ to $\hat{d}_i$ using sk.
	Check if any $\hat{d}_i = 0$:
$\xleftarrow{result}$	

2.3 Scenario 3

In this scenario, **T** generates the keys pk and sk and sends the pk to **A** and **B** (Table 5). **A** encrypts its test plate and sends it to **B** which has its encrypted database ready for the match. **B** performs the calculation and sends the result database to **T** who checks whether there is a match (as only **T** can decrypt using sk). The final result becomes known to both **A** and **T**. This technique pre-encrypts the original database and requires communicating the big database only once (from **B** to **T**). However, having a third party trusted by both **A** and **B** is a very strong requirement, as it violates the assumption of distrustful parties.

Table 5. Protocol 3.

Entity A	Entity B	T
		Generate pk, sk
		$\xleftarrow{pk,\ to\ A\ and\ B}$
Encrypt test plate using pk:- $[[x]]$	Encrypt database using pk:- $[[y_i]]$	
$\xrightarrow{[[x]]}$		
	Compute $[[d_i]]=[[x]][[y_i]]^{-1}$	
	Generate a random number R	
	$[[\hat{d}_i]] = [[d_i]]^R$	
	$\xrightarrow{[[\hat{d}_i]]}$	
		Decrypt $[[\hat{d}_i]]$ to $\hat{d}_i$ using sk.
		Check if any $\hat{d}_i = 0$:

3   Countering Malicious Adversaries

There are two different types of adversaries that could attack the privacy goals of the protocol: passive (also called semi-honest) and malicious. A passive adversary is one that does not deviate from the protocol. A malicious adversary is allowed to deviate from the protocol. Protocols 1–3 assume a passive adversary. We construct an attack to show how a malicious adversary can breach privacy and suggest a simple modification that resists this attack.

In the previous protocols, a single random number is used to blind the difference database. We show that the use of a single random number makes protocol 1 unsafe against malicious adversaries. Table 6 shows how a malicious **A** can breach the privacy of **B**'s database.

Table 6. Insider attack by **A**

Entity A	Entity B
Holds the keys pk, sk. Also holds some y_1 and y_2	Holds database of size n: y_1, y_2, y_3, ..., y_n
Encrypts fake test-plate using pk :- $[[y_1+y_2]]$	
$\xrightarrow{\quad pk,\ [[y_1+y_2]]\quad}$	
	Computes $[[d_i]]=[[y_1 + y_2]][[y_i]]^{-1}$
	Generates a random R
	$[[\hat{d}_i]] = [[d_i]]^R$
$\xleftarrow{\quad [[\hat{d}_i]]^R \quad}$	
Decrypt $[[\hat{d}_i]]$ to $\hat{d}_i = R[(y_1+y_2)-y_i]$ using sk.	
Divide $\hat{d}_i$ by y_1 and get t_1	
Divide $\hat{d}_i$ by y_2 and get t_2	
Look for and find a common R in t_1 and t_2	
Divide $\hat{d}_i$ by R to obtain the whole database	

Suppose **A** already knows two of the plate numbers y_1 and y_2 that it matched with **B**'s database previously. Next **A** sends a new test plate $y_1 + y_2$, to **B**. This would look like a regular test plate to **B** and it would perform the calculations, sending back the difference database randomized by a single random number **R**. **A** then decrypts the difference values. As y_1 and y_2 would each be subtracted once during the computation, we would have both the instances y_1R and y_2R in the difference database. From this, **A** can obtain **R** by dividing the database once each with y_1 and y_2. Once **R** is found, the whole database at **B**'s side can be calculated by **A**.

A fix for this attack is to use a distinct random number for blinding every entry in the difference database. We make use of this technique in our experiments.

For scenario 2, **B** cannot come to know about **A**'s license plate as **B** receives the difference database only and all it would find is a decrypted zero on a match. For scenario 3, a trusted third party handles the decryption procedure. Hence, the security of both **A** and **B** is maintained as long as **T** remains honest.

4   Performance Improvements

This section reviews two schemes of Paillier and their optimised versions.

4.1   Scheme 1

Key Generation
Choose two large primes, p and q, and let $n = pq$. Then $\lambda(pq) = \text{lcm}(p-1, q-1)$, where λ denotes the Carmichael function.

Choose $g \in Z_{n^2}^*$ such that n and $L(g^\lambda \bmod n^2)$ are co-prime, where

$$L : Z_{n^2}^* \rightarrow Z_n \tag{1}$$

$$L(u) \mapsto \frac{u-1}{n} \tag{2}$$

Public key is (n, g) and Private key is (p, q).

Encryption
This procedure involves the following steps to come up with the ciphertext.

Choose a message $m \in Z_n$.

Choose a random $r \in Z_n^*$.

Output ciphertext in Z_n^2:

$$c = g^m r^n \bmod n^2 \tag{3}$$

Decryption
Decryption requires the ciphertext c and sk pair (p, q).

The message is retrieved by the following calculation:

$$m = \frac{L(c^\lambda \bmod n^2)}{L(g^\lambda \bmod n^2)} \bmod n \tag{4}$$

Though this particular scheme is able to give results as fast as key generation time of 0.4 s and encryption time of about 5 μs (C++ implementation, stated in [1]), better schemes exist. One allows us to reduce the decryption times thereby reducing the overall execution time. Another helps in speeding up the encryption process through pre-computation of some exponents for a parameter ([3]). We have experimented with these schemes and compared their performance against the original scheme used in [1].

4.2   Scheme 3

Scheme 3 of Paillier's cryptosystem allows for a faster decryption by changing the domain of work from $Z_{n^2}^*$ to a subset generated by $< g >$ of order αn, where α is a factor of λ. This in turn facilitates in taking exponentiation to the power α instead of λ, thereby decreasing the decryption time considerably. Equation (4) now becomes:

$$m = \frac{L(c^\alpha \ mod \ n^2)}{L(g^\alpha \ mod \ n^2)} \ mod \ n \qquad (5)$$

Also, the ciphertext is modified to the form:

$$c = g^m (g^n)^r \ mod \ n^2 \qquad (6)$$

The original scheme of Paillier sets the condition of $r < n$ but it suffices to have an $r < \alpha$. Two kinds of attacks are presented by Jost et al. ([3]) which give insight into the way that α should be calculated.

In scheme 3, g must be of order αn. The problem of solving for α, given (n, g) as public is similar to the discrete logarithm problem as $(g^n)^\alpha = 1 \ mod \ n^2$. If α is small enough then baby-step giant-step can be used to obtain α, as suggested by Paillier [2].

4.3   Optimised Scheme 3

Jost et al. [3] propose a method to optimise scheme 3. The factor g^n is responsible for bringing randomisation to encryption. This involves taking an (bitlength of r) exponent of the noise factor which provides a scope for optimisation. Since the multiplication of two random numbers gives a new random number, it is sufficient to pre-compute *some* random powers of g^n. Instead of choosing an explicit r, it is chosen implicitly when $(g^n)^r$ is calculated on the fly by multiplying the previously computed powers of (g^n). This reduces encryption time as multiplication is less costlier than exponentiation. For pre-computing these values, we require space for storing the random powers of (g^n). This presents us with a kind of trade off between the number of pre-computed values and the number of multiplications required during actual computation of the ciphertext.

4.4   Optimised Scheme 1

We have extended the idea of optimisation of Scheme 3 to Scheme 1. The encryption operation of Scheme 1 involves multiplication with a random value for noise generation. This also involves taking an (bitlength of n) exponent of the noise factor (random number r). As in Scheme 3, it is sufficient to pre-compute *some* random powers of r and generate new random powers from that when required. So instead of choosing an explicit power n for r, it is chosen implicitly when r^n is calculated by multiplying the previously computed powers of r. Another optimisation is to pre-compute the denominator of Eq. (4). Through our experiments, we found that this greatly reduces decryption time as denominator calculation takes as much as 45% of the decryption time.

5   Experiment Setup

We implement protocol as per scenario 2 (Sect. 2.2) using the Paillier schemes and their optimisations (Sects. 4.1 through 4.4) in C++ and compare the time performance based on factors like security level - identified by the bit-length of n and database size. We choose this scenario as it is safer to keep the database pre-encrypted.

5.1   Test Database

In our case, the numerals (0 through 9) are mapped to themselves and the alphabets are mapped to the integers 10–35. Hence for a 10 character license plate, we require integers of 60 bits to identify it (5.1.2 [4]). For other types of plates, we could apply a similar scheme, with more or less number of integers in the final representation. For a typical Indian license plate, one would require an integer of 60 bits for representing the license plate apart from other country-specific features.

A set of data files containing different number of 64-bit integers representing hypothetical license plate numbers are constructed and the test plate is checked against these databases for a match. There are various parameters to be determined, based on the type of scheme adopted. The choice of these parameters is briefly discussed below.

5.2   Parameters

- n denotes the size of the plain- and cipher-domains. As the security of Paillier cryptosystem is based on integer factoring, we consider three different bit-lengths: 1024, 2048 and 4096.
- p and q are the prime factors of n, hence their bit-lengths are half of that of n.
- λ is the least common multiple of the primes p and q, hence its bit-length is the same as that of n.
- α is a factor of λ and speeds up decryption since we decrypt over α, a smaller number, instead of λ, of bit-length same as that of n.
- A small value of g is recommended for performance reasons. We choose $g = 2$ for scheme 1. For scheme 3, g is computed such that the order of g is αn.
- r is the random number responsible for noise generation in the cipher. The bit-length of r is 80 where we multiply 5 random values to get a new random power.

6   Implementation and Results

Encryption of plaintexts and decryption of ciphertexts are independent of each other, so to minimize the execution time we use parallelization for both encryption and decryption of the database. Parallelization is done in C++, using threads by making use of OpenMP API. We consider the following options for parallelization:

Single thread. All participants (**A** and **B**) have only one thread for their respective process of encryption or decryption. This in fact means that there is no parallelisation at all.

One side threaded. One participant runs two or more threads while other participant runs only one thread.

Both side threaded. All participants have the number of threads specified for each domain. All experiments are done by running multiple threads on both sides as that gives the most optimal performance.

In the single thread case, both **A** and **B** have a single thread or flow of execution that processes the database entries one after the other. For example, a single thread on **A**'s side in Scenario 2 would simply take out entries one-by-one from the encrypted database received from **B**. It would then perform the matching in encrypted domain. Hence this is a sequential process.

In the multiple thread case, there are differences in code segments of the threads corresponding to **A** and **B**. In thread of **A**, we make use of flags as many in number as the number of threads. Each flag takes care of whether a match is found within the entries of the difference database assigned to that particular thread. The assignment of entries is static which means that each thread knows what set of entries it has to work on, a priori. The workload is almost the same for each thread: each one has to find the decryption of a fixed size difference value that would probably take the same amount of time for every entry. When all the threads are joined, their respective flags are checked for a '1'. If anyone of them returns 1, it is an indication of a match being found.

In thread of **B**, the parallelised part includes the overall database-encryption and calculation of difference of the encrypted values. For this purpose, separate difference lists are maintained per thread in which each one stores its own difference results. Before sending these off, the lists are combined into a consolidated one containing all difference values.

6.1   Comparison of Run-Times

We have implemented Protocol 2 in C++ using GMP and OpenMP library. The machine used is Intel i7-4750HQ with a clock speed of 2 GHz, having 4 cores and 8 GB RAM. Given below are a set of tables for encryptions per second for the four schemes (Scheme 1 and Scheme 3 of Paillier, Optimised Scheme 1 and Optimised Scheme 3). These times are experimentally measured for three separate bit-lengths of n for all the schemes and presented in Table 7.

We provide some details regarding implementation of the schemes. In schemes optimised 1 and 3, we pre-compute r^n and g^{nr} for 2^{16} distinct values of r and store them in an array. During the noise generation part of encryption in these respective schemes, 5 random powers are taken and multiplied together resulting into a new noise factor for every encryption.

Table 8 shows the number of modular multiplications required to perform one encryption and one decryption for the four Paillier schemes. r is a random

Table 7. Encryptions per second

Scheme	Bitlength		
	1024 bits	2048 bits	4096 bits
Scheme 1	769	91	15
Scheme 1 Opt	11112	1923	787
Scheme 3	393	68	14
Scheme 3 Opt	6250	1920	714

Table 8. Comparison of arithmetic operations for one encryption and one decryption.

Scheme	Operations	
	Encryption	Decryption
Scheme 1	$n + m + 1$	$2(\lambda + 2) + 1$
Scheme 1 Opt	$5 + m + 1$	$\lambda + 2 + 2$
Scheme 3	$nr + m + 1$	$2(\alpha + 2) + 1$
Scheme 3 Opt	$5 + m + 1$	$\alpha + 2 + 2$

number of length 80 bits. The difference in encryption per second for schemes -
1 optimised and 3 optimised is because of the computational size, i.e. for the
former, we need to compute r^n. Since r is a 80-bit number, the result is of order
$2^{2^{7+n_b}}$, where n_b is the number of bits of n. Similarly for the latter, we need to
compute g^{rn} and as g is $n_b - \alpha_b$ bit number, where α_b is the number of bits of
α, the result of computation is of order $2^{2^{g_b + n_b + r_b}}$. So, the 5 multiplications in
this scheme are larger and takes more computation time than scheme 1 opt.

In scheme 1 optimised, g is equal to 2 while in scheme 3 optimised, g is of
higher value (λ / α).

From Table 7 we see that optimised schemes are able to achieve higher
throughput in terms of number of encryptions per second as compared to non-
optimised schemes. Also, optimised scheme 1 outperforms others because encryption procedure is made faster due to pre-computation.

The run time for a specific run includes the encryption time for the test plate,
the time for matching and the time for decryption of the result database.

The next set of tables (Tables 9, 10 and 11) contain the execution times for a
database of size 2500 and Scenario 2, thread-number wise to give a comparative
study across the schemes.

The optimised scheme 3 is the fastest in terms of execution times. For 4096
bits, it has an execution-time of 10.8 s vs. 231.6 s of the original scheme (4
threads). The factor with which it beats the original scheme 1 keeps on increasing as we increase the bit-length. Another observation is comparable run times
of Scheme 3 and Optimised Scheme 3 for 1024 bits. This is because the database
containing plates, against which the test plate is matched, is already encrypted
and not included in the run-time. This way, the only difference in the two schemes

Table 9. Run times for a single thread

Scheme	Bitlength		
	1024 bits	2048 bits	4096 bits
Scheme 1	15.15 s	95.01 s	543.28 s
Scheme 1 Opt	7.88 s	48.62 s	274.69 s
Scheme 3	3.05 s	13.47 s	43.16 s
Scheme 3 Opt	1.88 s	7.84 s	24.89 s

Table 10. Run times for 4 threads

Scheme	Bitlength		
	1024 bits	2048 bits	4096 bits
Scheme 1	7.19 s	44.22 s	231.57 s
Scheme 1 Opt	4.48 s	22.77 s	117.53 s
Scheme 3	1.84 s	6.57 s	18.65 s
Scheme 3 Opt	1.05 s	3.81 s	10.78 s

Table 11. Run times for 6 threads

Scheme	Bitlength		
	1024 bits	2048 bits	4096 bits
Scheme 1	7.51 s	40.14 s	232.61 s
Scheme 1 Opt	4.20 s	21.13 s	118.16 s
Scheme 3	1.74 s	6.09 s	18.83 s
Scheme 3 Opt	1.04 s	3.61 s	10.82 s

in scenario 2 is the time required for decryption and matching which shows considerable difference only when the bit length increased from 1024 bits here.

We plot the graphs of run time vs. database sizes for the four schemes for a single thread each for bit-length of 2048 and 4096 bits.

From the Figs. 1 and 2, a trend of increasing run time for increasing size of databases is seen. This is explainable as run time is directly proportional to the number of entries in the database.

There is a large variation in the run times for the 4 schemes in each case. Sunil et al. ([1]) discussed results for n = 1024 but it is seen here that even for bigger n - sizes, the schemes achieve considerable speedup. This shows us that the optimised scheme 3 [3] in fact gives a huge improvement over the other schemes and is a good candidate for employing in practical scenarios.

There is a tradeoff in optimised scheme 3 between the number of powers precomputed and run-time. This translates to the more common memory space vs. time trade off that we generally face for huge computations. In short, the size of the array storing random powers of g^n should be large enough for catering to the encryption needs of the entire plaintext domain.

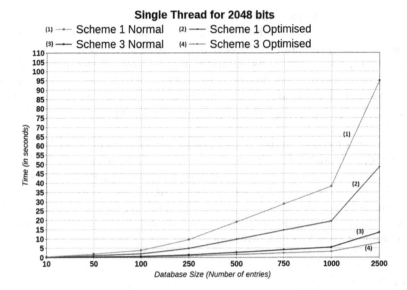

Fig. 1. Run time comparison for n = 2048, single thread.

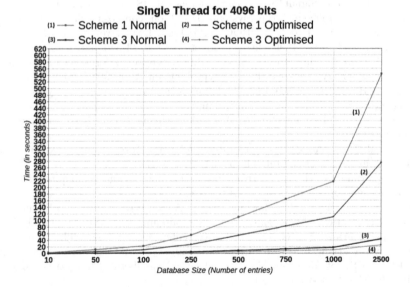

Fig. 2. Run time comparison for n = 4096, single thread.

7   Conclusions and Future Work

Based on the study and implementation of the additively homomorphic secure license plate matching technique, we conclude that the optimised scheme 3 gives a considerable speedup over the original technique and is the most optimal for application in the practical scenario. By the introduction of threads, the overall process, due to its inherent property of mutual independence within each phase (encryption and decryption), the results get even better i.e. the run times decrease even further. As an alternative to Paillier's scheme, ElGamal's additively homomorphic encryption scheme [6,8] can also be used. Simultaneous multi-exponentiation algorithms like the 2^k-ary and 2^k-ary matrix methods explained in [10] can be applied for optimising multi-exponentiation in commutative groups.

We have not factored in the communication costs in our analysis. The method for reducing the communication cost proposed in [1] can be used to do the same. Based on additive homomorphism of Paillier's scheme, a parallel homomorphic encryption (PHE) scheme proposed by Min et al. [7] can be used for plaintexts having larger bitlengths. In our implementation having 64 bits long license plate numbers, we could not achieve a significant speedup through PHE because of a more dominant parallelisation overhead.

References

1. Sunil, A.B., Erkiny, Z., Veugenyz, T.: Secure matching of Dutch car license plates. In: 24th European Signal Processing Conference (EUSIPCO), pp. 2116–2120 (2016)
2. Paillier, P.: Public-key cryptosystems based on composite degree residuosity classes. In: Stern, J. (ed.) EUROCRYPT 1999. LNCS, vol. 1592, pp. 223–238. Springer, Heidelberg (1999). https://doi.org/10.1007/3-540-48910-X_16
3. Jost, C., Lam, H., Maximov, A., Smeets, B.: Encryption performance improvements of the Paillier cryptosystem. IACR Cryptol. ePrint Arch. **2015**, 864 (2015)
4. Sunil, A.B.: Secure License Plate Matching using Homomorphic Encryption. Masters thesis, Vrije Universiteit Amsterdam (2015)
5. Gentry, C.: A fully homomorphic encryption scheme. Ph.D. thesis, Stanford University (2009)
6. ElGamal, T.: A public-key cryptosystem and a signature scheme based on discrete logarithms. IEEE Trans. Inf. Theory **31**(4), 469–472 (1985)
7. Min, Z., Yang, G., Shi, J.: A privacy-preserving parallel and homomorphic encryption scheme. Open Phys. **15**, 135–142 (2017)
8. Cramer, R., Gennaro, R., Schoenmakers, B.: A secure and optimally efficient multi-authority election scheme. Eur. Trans. Telecommun. **8**(5), 481–490 (1997)
9. Erkin, Z., Franz, M., Guajardo, J., Katzenbeisser, S., Lagendijk, I., Toft, T.: Privacy-preserving face recognition. In: Goldberg, I., Atallah, M.J. (eds.) PETS 2009. LNCS, vol. 5672, pp. 235–253. Springer, Heidelberg (2009). https://doi.org/10.1007/978-3-642-03168-7_14
10. Jakobsen, T.P., Makkes, M.X., Nielsen, J.D.: Efficient implementation of the Orlandi protocol. In: Zhou, J., Yung, M. (eds.) ACNS 2010. LNCS, vol. 6123, pp. 255–272. Springer, Heidelberg (2010). https://doi.org/10.1007/978-3-642-13708-2_16

Author Index

Printed in the United States
By Bookmasters